Economic Opening Up and Growth in Russia

Springer
Berlin
Heidelberg
New York
Hong Kong
London
Milan
Paris
Tokyo

Evgeny Gavrilenkov
Paul J. J. Welfens
Ralf Wiegert
Editors

Economic Opening Up and Growth in Russia

Finance, Trade, Market Institutions, and Energy

With 61 Figures
and 70 Tables

Springer

Professor Dr. Evgeny Gavrilenkov
Troika Dialog
4 Romanov pereulok
Moscow 125009
Russia
Evgeny_Gavrilenkov@troika.ru

Professor Dr. Paul J. J. Welfens
Jean-Monnet-Professor for
European Economic Integration
President of EIIW at
the University of Wuppertal
Gaußstr. 20
42119 Wuppertal
Germany
welfens@uni-wuppertal.de
http://www.euroeiiw.de
and
http://www.progressinfo.net

Dr. Ralf Wiegert
European Institute for International
Economic Relations (EIIW)
Potsdam University
August-Bebel-Str. 89
14482 Potsdam
Germany
wiegert@rz.uni-potsdam.de

ISBN 3-540-20459-8 Springer-Verlag Berlin Heidelberg New York

Cataloging-in-Publication Data applied for
A catalog record for this book is available from the Library of Congress.
Bibliographic information published by Die Deutsche Bibliothek
Die Deutsche Bibliothek lists this publication in the Deutsche Nationalbibliografie; detailed bibliographic data is available in the Internet at <http://dnb.ddb.de>.

Springer-Verlag is a part of Springer Science+Business Media

springeronline.com

Hardcover-Design: Erich Kirchner, Heidelberg

SPIN 10969786 43/3130/DK-5 4 3 2 1 0 – Printed on acid-free paper

Table of Contents

Introduction

After nearly a decade of economic decline, Russia has achieved remarkable economic growth under President Putin. High oil prices, restructuring and political stability are obviously factors, which have contributed to overcoming the transformation recession as well as the crisis of 1998. The negative growth rate of 5 % in 1998 was offset by a growth rate of 5.6 % in 1999 and the strong boost of 10 % in 2000. With 5 % in 2001, 4.3 % in 2002 and an expected 6-7 % in 2003 and 2004, Russia has become a dynamic transition country whose growth is strongly influenced by its natural resources sector. Given the technology and modernization gap (vis-à-vis OECD countries) in this sector at the beginning of transition, there should be considerable opportunities for high growth provided Western foreign direct investment flows can be attracted. If such a development can be achieved there will be, however, the problem of a rising export concentration on natural resources – mainly oil and gas. Such dependency will in turn bring about a higher volatility of the Ruble exchange rate, which will strongly be influenced by changes in world market prices in oil and gas. Strong export growth and indeed a positive current balance could be characteristic for the new Russia in its opening up process. Under President Putin, Russia's integration into the world economy has made strong progress; moreover, as there is a large budget surplus the revenue effects from import tariffs have become less important, reinforcing prospects for a sustained integration of the new Russia into the world economy. As regards membership in international organizations, the envisaged WTO membership – and full member status in the OECD – is a final landmark still to be achieved.

With the pains of transitional recession almost over, reform focus has shifted towards identifying factors for sustained economic growth and requirements for deepening the integration of Russia within the world economy. This integration, with foreign direct investment accelerating and trade increasing, will be a long-term process temporarily undermined by the trade diversion effects of EU eastern enlargement. The trade structure – in particular with respect to exports – is more concentrated on raw materials and especially oil and gas than ever. One reason for this slow integration might be attributed to the fact that negotiations for WTO membership are slow and face considerable criticism within Russia's powerful industrial lobby. WTO membership for Russia would certainly stimulate FDI inflows into Russia industry outside the so far dominant oil and gas sector.

In 2002, Russia was granted market economy status by the G-7 countries. Another sign of the international recognition of Russia's strategic political role is that from 2005 onwards, Russia will be a fully fledged G-8 member country. Much will depend here not only on the relations between Russia and the EU, but also on Russian relations with the US. It is not yet clear whether Russia has an international strategy as a dynamic market economy with major interests both in Europe and Asia.

With external integration far from complete, a mirror development is occurring within Russia itself. The country appears to be highly disintegrated from an economic point of view. There are high interregional price differences, though only part of this can be attributed to transport prices. Moreover, there are high persisting interregional differences in per-capita-incomes, with Moscow and St. Petersburg plus several resource-rich regions taking the lead over many rather poor regions. Various barriers for trade and migration contribute to such an unequal development and the distribution of economic welfare. Official intra-Russian barriers to migration have been established most visibly in Moscow where the regulated housing market and restrictive permissions for outsiders to move to Moscow help to maintain large interregional income gaps. To the extent that such gaps could go along with political and social instability within Russia in the future, it is unclear if Russia's integration into the world economy is sustainable. At the same time it is clear that restrictions for foreign investors will have to be lifted in the future if the integration process is to be completed. Opening up banking markets and insurance markets for foreign investors is economically desirable and indispensable for WTO membership in the long run. However, the main Russian financial centers are, of course, Moscow and St. Petersburg; thus full opening up for FDI will further aggravate interregional economic imbalances.

This volume looks into some key topics and issues of Russia's integration and modernization. The contributions in this book shed light on growth requirements for Russia, such as the role of financial markets and further liberalization efforts in this field and institution building with respect to mechanisms underlying a market economy. A special focus is on the crucial oil and gas sector in the Russian economy as well as Russian WTO membership, which seems to be essential for both further restructuring of Russia's economy and a strenghtening of its economic ties with the rest of the world.

The contribution of Paul J.J. Welfens and Albrecht Kauffmann takes on the issue of how to achieve sustained economic growth and which factors are essential for long-term output dynamics. Based on standard theory and new growth theory, they look at key factors for growth dynamics in transition countries and other countries empirically. The policy conclusions suggested are clear: no long-term catching-up without industrial upgrading, a modernization of the telecommunications infrastructure and macroeconomic stability. Markus Neimke narrows the focus by specifically assessing the relationship between the financial sector and economic growth by applying insights from approaches related to neoclassical and new growth theory to the transition economies in central and eastern Europe and CIS countries. He runs an empirical analysis to investigate the impact of financial sector development on total investment and factor productivity and points out the importance of building up sound and efficient financial markets. Noer Azam Achsani and Hans Gerhard Strohe look into the linkages between Russian stock exchanges and other selected stock exchanges worldwide. Even if Russian stock markets can be considered of minor importance with respect to their trading volume and market capitalisation, they establish interesting reciprocal relationships between the stock markets under investigation.

Starting with the contribution of Olga Nosova, we switch to issues relating to Russia's trade relations and its trade structure. While she gives detailed accounting of Russia's trade patterns, Christian von Hirschhausen takes a deeper look into the role of the Russian Gas Industry with respect to its impact on the economy as a whole and on the country's future export performance. With the focus also on a particular industry, Gert Ziener provides a comprehensive assessment of another core part of Russia's economy, namely the oil industry. Ziener outlines the main problems as regards restructuring and modernisation of production and transport facilities as well as the interference of state authorities within the oil industry, and he explains the linkages between the oil industry and the development of the fiscal budget.

With the contribution of Ralf Wiegert, the focus shifts back to the growth issue, yet with a different perspective. Examining the incomplete institutional setting for a market economy, high and pervasive corruption, large subsidies and hence low competition, he concludes that the basic requirements for sustained economic growth from an institutional perspective are still not in place in Russia. Persisting capital flight and low investment-output ratios indicate that there are severe problems in Russia for enterprises to restructure or to take root and expand their business. Evgeny Gavrilenkov gives a detailed assessment of Russia's macroeconomic development and points out the main reasons for the upswing of the economy after 1998 and the following consolidation of public budgets as well as the necessities for future economic growth and catching up, namely an increasing investment-output ratio. He therefore links the Russian economy with developments in the US and in South-East Asian economies.

Turning once again to the issue of integrating Russia into the world economy, Grigori Feiguine and Tatjana Sedash provide an overview of selected problems of a ever-deeper integration of the country's financial sector within foreign financial markets and call for some decisive action on the field of banking reform. Ruslan Grinberg and Ognian Hishow then discuss Russia's negotiations for future WTO membership. Whereas Grinberg argues mostly from the Russian perspective with his focus primarily on politico-economic problems, Hishow takes into account Russia's concerns as well as the interests of its economic partners from the European Union. The volume closes with a look at Russia's regions and in particular St. Petersburg and its surrounding environment, providing insight into the economic circumstances for business development there. Critical comments by Natalja von Westernhagen, Andre Jungmittag, Frank Bohn, Joachim Ahrens, Cathleen Faber, Rolf Jungnickel, Michael Vogelsang and Markus Ksoll are very much appreciated.

We hope that this book will contribute to a more intense debate on the benefits and risks of integrating Russia into the world economy and related growth perspectives. Integration into the world economy clearly has a twin regional aspect in the case of Russia: Europe and Asia – the latter being more economically dynamic than the EU, but also more subject to the potential instabilities associated with terrorist attacks as well as Muslim extremists. Russia's successful international economic integration would contribute to international stability and growth. With the anticipation of some setbacks in Russia's integration efforts, we will continue to direct attention to major economic developments in Russia and its growing interrelations with the international economic community in our research. It will also be necessary to keep a critical eye on the EU, which has expressed considerable concern toward eastern enlargement but relatively little to improving economic relations with Russia. The intellectual links between Russia and the EU-15 is apparently relatively weak.

The analytical papers are part of an ongoing international EIIW research project generously supported by the Alfried Krupp von Bohlen und Halbach-Foundation. The European Institute for International Economic Relations has relocated its headquarters to Wuppertal University as of July 2003, but EIIW research continues in both Potsdam and Wuppertal. For more information visit our websites: www.euroeiiw.de and www.progressinfo.net.

We are very grateful for the editorial assistance of Albrecht Kauffmann, Katja Markova, Mathias Peyer and Michael Agner; the latter has particularly supported the editorial work in an excellent way, which is strongly appreciated.

Moscow, Wuppertal and Potsdam, September 2003

Evgeny Gavrilenkov, Paul J.J. Welfens and Ralf Wiegert

A. Investment, Financial Markets, New Economy Dynamics and Growth in Transition Countries

Paul J.J. Welfens and Albrecht Kauffmann

1. Introduction

The transition to a market economy in the former CMEA area is more than a decade old and one can clearly distinguish a group of relatively fast growing countries – including Estonia, Poland, the Czech Republic, Hungary and Slovenia – and a majority of slowly growing economies, including Russia and the Ukraine. Initial problems of transition were natural in the sense that systemic transition to a market economy has effectively destroyed part of the existing capital stock that was no longer profitable under the new relative prices imported from world markets; and there was a transitory inflationary push as low state-administered prices were replaced by higher market equilibrium prices. Indeed, systemic transformation in eastern Europe and the former Soviet Union have brought serious transitory inflation problems and a massive transition recession; negative growth rates have continued over many years in some countries, including Russia and the Ukraine, where output growth was negative throughout the 1990s (except for Russia, which recorded slight growth in 1997). For political and economic reasons the economic performance of Russia is of particular relevance for the success of the overall transition process. If Russia would face stagnation and instability, this would undermine political and economic stability in the whole of Europe and prospects for integrating Russia into the world economy.

Russia has achieved sustained growth under president Putin, part of which must be attributed on the one hand to systemic reform and economic policy reforms – including the introduction of a low uniform income tax rate of 13 % – and on the other hand to high oil prices that stimulate the energy sector and generate high tax revenues. During the 1990s, the overall economic performance of Russia was weak by historical standards and from an international comparative perspective; compared to the Visegrad countries economic development in Russia at large was disappointing. Various explanations for slow growth in Russia and the Ukraine have been offered in the literature, including insufficient foreign direct investment, widespread corruption and high transaction costs plus inefficient financial markets (eg VON WESTERNHAGEN, 2002, WIEGERT, 2003).

With regard to the acceptance of market economy and democracy in Eastern Europe and Russia, it is quite obvious that sustained economic growth is a key requirement for the legitimacy of the new system. Sustained growth in turn mainly depends upon:

- a high investment output ratio in the private sector

- sustained adequate public investment which often raises deficit financing problems as tax receipts and tariffs receipts are rather small
- mobilizing gains from trade through a broad diversified trade network
- organizing an efficient innovation process
- stimulating the diffusion of new knowledge and innovations, respectively
- avoiding excessive exposure to negative external shocks

This list of growth-enhancing factors is not much different than a century ago. However, there are several side-constraints that have to be considered at the beginning of the 21st century:

- Structural change in industrialized countries implies that not only the manufacturing industry but also the services sector plays an important role for private investment; in Germany, the services sector has become the leading ordering sector for investment goods in the late 1990s. In eastern Europe, the first stage of post-socialist transition has been characterized by a massive reduction of the share of manufacturing industry in overall output, in a second stage the share of industry has increased in many countries.
- The issue of deficit financing problems often is associated with external imbalances or exchange rate instability which means that the IMF could become involved if there are serious and recurrent problems.
- Sustained gains from trade cannot simply be mobilized through liberalization of trade, rather the respective country must be a WTO member because it will otherwise become subject to selective protectionism in phases of an international recession, especially considering that the US is the most influential country in the WTO and the dominant influence on the international business cycle economic and political relations with the US are of special relevance. Moreover, trade in services has become more important after the creation of the WTO and the GATS, respectively. Liberalizing trade in financial services in turn is often associated with the liberalization of foreign direct investment in banking and insurance, which in turn means that countries face adjustment challenges and potential problems in politically and economically-sensitive sectors. Hence the trade liberalization issue has become a rather complex issue; moreover, trade expansion is partly linked to FDI inflows and multinational companies since about 1/3 of trade of leading OECD countries is intra-company trade of multinational companies.
- With respect to innovations – measured in terms of patent applications at the European Patent Agency – eastern European countries and Russia have shown modest performance in the early 1990s. In the late 1990s, patent applications of some transition countries have increased; this holds in particular for Hungary and the Czech Republic, which are also leading countries in terms of FDI per capita inflows. However, few transition countries have established a new efficient national innovation system.
- There is no doubt that the internet and modern telecommunications, respectively, have strongly contributed to accelerated diffusion of new knowledge. JUNGMITTAG/WELFENS (2002) have shown in empirical work – based on

time series analysis for Germany – that the use of telecommunications has contributed considerably to economic growth; and that the broader use of the internet could create several hundred thousand additional new jobs as the use of the internet accelerates diffusion of knowledge and hence can stimulate growth in the New Economy. The New Economy can be defined by an economy in which investment in information and communication technology (ICT) represent a considerable part of overall investment, in which there is a rapid expansion of digital services.

- Achieving sustained growth in transition countries in the 21st century requires the ability to cope with economic globalization in the sense that capital flows relative to GDP have strongly increased after the 1970s, with foreign direct investment accelerating in particular after 1985. Economic globalization basically means an intensified international quest for mobile capital and therefore intensified systemic competition, at the same time it means to face problems that could emerge from the potentially large volatility of short term capital flows and divergence of adjustment speeds in ever faster financial markets and relatively slow goods and factor markets – the latter problem was first discussed in the literature in the Dornbusch (1986) model.

In the following analysis we highlight the international differences in fields relevant for growth in selected eastern European countries and in Russia. We will focus in particular on the role of structural change, financial services and the New Economy, on economic growth where our main interest is in the second half of the 1990s when the transition recession had phased out in most ex-CMEA countries. Section 2 gives some basic statistics, section 3 discusses theoretical aspects of growth in transition countries and section 4 presents policy conclusions.

2. Fundamental Data on Eastern Europe and Russia

Taking into account broad macroeconomic data for transition countries in the 1990s, development can be characterized by transitorily high inflation; beginning in Poland in 1990, stabilization policies had been adopted by 1995 in all transition countries except for Turkmenistan. Depending on delays in monetary stabilization and the size of initial monetary overhang the 12-month pre-stabilization inflation rates varied widely: from 57,000 % p.a. in Georgia to a rather modest 26 % in Hungary (FISCHER/SAHAY 2001, p. 14). Moreover there was a strong transition recession in the early stages of transformation. The main exceptions were Russia and the Ukraine, which suffered from a very protracted and long-lasting output decline: While the average number of consecutive years of output decline was 3.8 in central and southeastern European countries plus the Baltic countries, the consecutive years of output decline was 6.5 years for the CIS, where Moldova, Russia, Tajikistan were negative leaders – with 7 years – together with Turmenistan and the Ukraine which had 8 and 10 years, respectively (see table A1 below). Cumulative output decline was 22.6 % on average for the countries in central and southeastern Europe plus the Baltics, but in the former CIS it was 50.5 % with the largest economy, Russia, facing a cumulative output decline of 40 %. The latter figure was slightly more than 1/3 higher than in the Great Depression in the US, compared to Germany's output development in the Great Depression, Russia's cumulated output decline was 2.5 times as high. This clearly points to enormous economic problems for Russia (and several other CIS countries) in the 1990s. At the same time there was an enormous variation in output dynamics. Among the 24 transition countries in the list only four had achieved or exceeded the output level of 1990 in 2000, namely Albania, Hungary, Poland and Slovenia.

Tab. A1: The Transition Recession

Countries	Consecutive years of output decline	Cumulative output decline (percent)	Real GDP, 2000 (1990 = 100)
CSB	3.8	22.6	106.5
Albania	3	33	110
Bulgaria	4	16	81
Croatia	4	36	87
Czech Republic	3	12	99
Estonia	5	35	85
Hungary	4	15	109
Latria	6	51	61
Litania	5	44	67
Poland	2	6	112
Romania	3	21	77
Slovak Republic	4	23	82
Slovenia	3	14	105
CIS	6.5	50.5	62.7
Armenia	4	63	67
Azerbaijan	6	60	55
Belarus	6	35	88
Georgia	5	78	29
Kazakhstan	6	41	90
Kyrgyz Republic	6	50	68
Moldova	7	63	35
Russian Federation	7	40	64
Tajikistan	7	50	48
Turkmenistan	8	48	76
Ukraine	10	59	43
Uzbekistan	6	18	95
Output decline during the Great Depression, 1930-34			
France	3	11	n.a.
Germany	3	16	n.a.
United Kingdom	2	6	n.a.
United States	4	27	n.a.

Source: World Bank country office data; World Bank (2002).

In explaining the different economic developments across countries FISCHER/SAHAY (2001) follow a similar approach as BERG et al. (1999), who emphasize that growth can be explained by the initial conditions, the degree of structural reforms – eg privatization – and macroeconomic variables. In a panel regression, FISCHER/SAHAY (2001) show in three alternative regression equations, using data up to 1998 (with starting years of transition for individual countries differing), that inflation had a significant negative impact on growth, while liberalization as measured by an index computed by DE MELO et al. (1996) had a positive impact on output growth. The small scale privatization index as measured by the EBRD also had a significant impact on output growth in one of the regression models. The fiscal variable – the deficit-GDP ratio – included in each of the three equations showed a significant negative value in only one equation; from a simple theoretical perspective a negative value could be expected since a high deficit-GDP ratio might crowd out private investment via higher real interest rates; or such deficits could reflect a rise of the relative size of government (possibly including higher subsidies for ailing industries that would impair economic efficiency), which in turn might undermine overall economic flexibility and innovation and through this output growth. However, the unclear impact of the fiscal variable is not surprising since from a broader theoretical perspective one should control for the impact of the structure of public expenditure: A rising deficit-GDP ratio that reflects a higher ratio of public investment; including the field of education and R&D subsidies, could even raise the private investment-GDP ratio and hence long-term growth.

If one assumes that a certain output decline can be compensated for in terms of higher quality of goods and greater variety of products, one might argue that countries which almost had returned to 1989 output levels by 2000 stood for a rather successful transition process: Three countries had achieved between 90 and 99 % of the 1989 output level in 2000, namely Uzbekistan, Kyrgyz Republic and the Czech Republic. Given the fact that Russia and the Ukraine as the largest economies in terms of population stood in 2000 at 64 % and 43 % of 1989 output levels, respectively, one may state that the 1990s essentially witnessed only very modest success in terms of transition in the overall ex-CMEA area. From this perspective, it is all the more important that eastern Europe achieves sustained economic growth. Given the overall economic depression in the ex-CMEA area in the 1990s, it is also clear that achieving sustained and high economic growth in Russia and the Ukraine would stimulate regional trade and overall regional output growth considerably.

Economic Growth in Transition Countries, EU-15 and Asian NICs

Long term economic growth differs across countries; however, from a neoclassical perspective one would assume that poor countries will catch up so that the hypothesis in many regression approaches on growth is that the per capita income of the respective country relative to US per capita income will enter with a negative value. With regard to transition countries, the first half of the 1990s did not show relatively high economic growth; rather negative growth rates were dominant across countries. However, the second half of the 1990s showed positive growth rates for almost all transition countries.

Fig. A1: Mean Annual Growth in Transition Countries in %

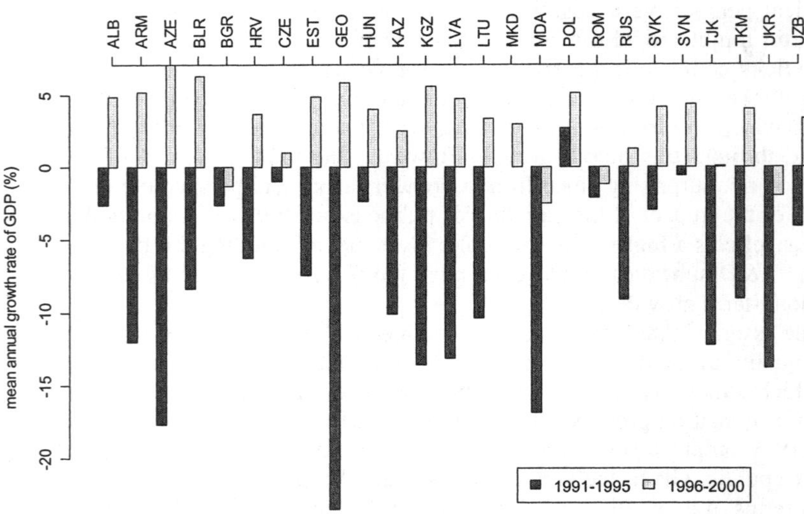

Data Source: WDI (2000), WDI (2002).

How much economic growth should one expect in transition economies whose per capita income in purchasing power parity figures is generally below that of Greece, Ireland, Spain or Portugal? With respect to these four relatively poor EU countries, one can clearly see that they all faced accelerating economic growth after EU membership, Greece obviously with a very long delay. With regard to transition countries, one should clearly expect relatively high growth in the medium term.

Structural conditions and macroeconomical policies as well as institutional shortcomings have played a crucial role for slow growth or negative growth rates in transition countries, including Russia (WELFENS/GAVRILENKOV 2001). Russia and several other CIS countries have suffered not only from a lack of capital inflows; indeed, there was considerable capital flight in the 1990s. The enormous inequality in terms of income and wealth potentially contributes to the phenomenon of capital flight.

Fig. A2: Mean Annual Growth in EU Countries

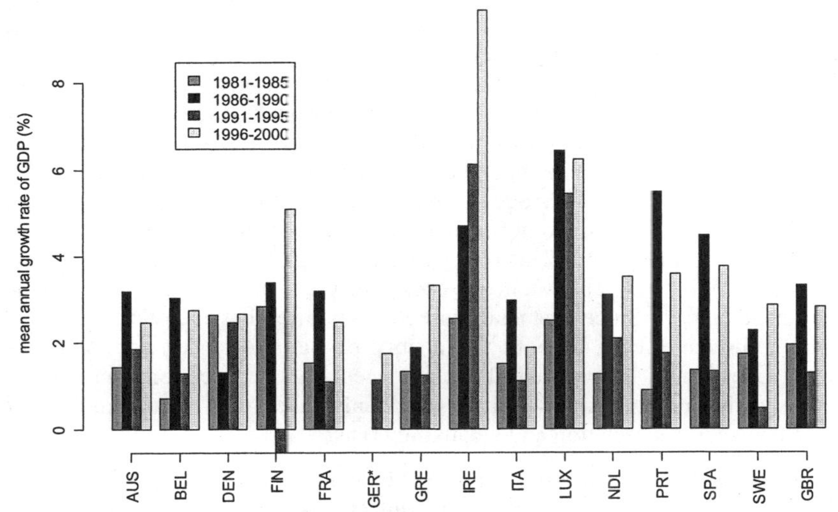

Data Source: WDI (2000), WDI (2002).

Whether this potential economic growth is really exhausted – and indeed should be fully exhausted at any point of time – is doubtful. Asian Newly Industrializing Countries (NICs) have shown high growth rates of 5–9 % over many years (except for the Phillippines), but the Asian crisis in the 1997/98 when growth rates became negative in many Asian NICs demonstrate that very dramatic swings in growth rates can occur under unfavorable circumstances and in the presence of structural domestic problems in the banking system. One may have to raise the question whether some countries would not have fared better in the long run if economic growth had been slightly more modest: government might not only have a role in nurturing economic growth in stagnating economies, it also might have a role in avoiding overheating and excessive bank lending – the latter often occurred in Asia in combination with two forms of balance sheet mismatches that led to problems later during the Asian crisis and indeed were part and parcel of the crisis sources (McKINNON 2000):

- Maturity mismatch: lending for investment projects was long term but refinancing through deposits and domestic financial market instruments was mainly short term; lack of long term domestic financing occurred because of underdeveloped domestic financial markets. While every standard textbook of finance suggests avoiding long term lending in combination with short term refinancing, this is exactly what could be observed in many Asian NICs and in many transition countries, except for Hungary, Poland, the Czech Republic and Estonia.

- Currency mismatch: banks and firms took – in an environment of de facto exchange rate pegging – foreign long term loans, mostly $-denominated, which were considered to be an ideal cheap substitute for the missing long term end of the domestic bond market. With earnings of investment projects often accruing in domestic currency, any major depreciation of the currency was bound to undermine financial stability of banks and firms. If we normalize the initial exchange rate to unity one can show that a firm's (or bank's) overall debt-capital ratio will increase by 30 % – assuming domestic debt is given – if the ratio of foreign debt to overall capital is 50 % initially and the depreciation rate of the currency is 60 %. Failure to hedge against the risk of currency depreciation – an hedging is unattractive if domestic interest rates are high and world interest rates are low while government is pegging the exchange rate de facto or formally – thus will bring about a major economic crisis once there is a large currency depreciation. Since financial market crises often have an element of regional spillover effects, as both the history of Latin America and Asia has shown, one should be worried about any medium-sized economy in eastern Europe, Asia or Latin America that is suddenly faced with a combination of strong currency depreciation and a banking crisis.

As governments in Asian NICs supported economic growth even when it was very high, there was a natural incentive for banks to take fairly large risks: Assuming that domestic firms would grow at more or less the same rate as the aggregate economy, there was every incentive to step up loans to firms and refinance these loans through borrowing abroad long term or borrowing at home short term: both strategies were bound to fail once a confidence crisis either in domestic bond markets or in the foreign exchange market occurred. Looking at Asian NICs is thus encouraging for transition countries in the sense that poor countries that adopt adequate policies and institutional reforms can indeed have high or even very high growth rates over many years. Hence one might want to follow the model of Asian NICs that adopted various growth-enhancing strategies. At the same time, transition countries might want to avoid excessive growth in the short term and strive rather to achieve a combination of high sustained growth and stable plus efficient institutions, including financial markets. What is surprising when taking a closer look at growth performance in transition countries is the enormous heterogeneity of growth rates, and this needs to be explained.

Fig. A3: Mean Annual Growth in Asian NICs, and US

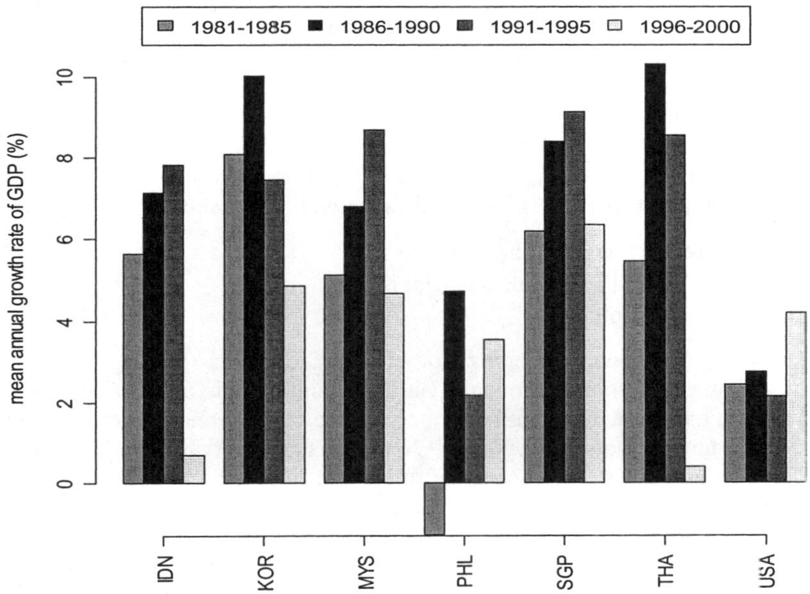

Data Source: WDI (2000), WDI (2002).

Investment Dynamics

When taking a closer look at selected macroeconomic indicators of transition countries, selected NICs and selected EU countries plus the US, we can identify certain key developments among transition countries. Relatively fast growth is experienced by countries with a high investment-GDP ratio (see table A2 in the Appendix), here defined as a range between 25 and 30 %. Countries with low investment-GDP ratios such as Bulgaria or Russia have experienced low economic growth in the 1990s. We are particularly interested in the second half of the 1990s; that is, the period after initial distortions had been overcome and the transition recession had more or less phased out.

FDI-GDP ratios (table A3) can be seen as indicators for growth expectations and for progress of integration of transition economies. During the second half of the 1990ies FDI GDP and Investment GDP ratios coincided in many country cases.

With respect to budget deficits (table A4) and inflation rates (table A5), the situation has improved in the second half of the 1990s in many transition countries.

EBRD Transition Indicators

Looking at progress in transition according to the EBRD transition indicators – defined for a range form 1 to 4+ (4+ represents OECD standard) –, we find that considerable progress across the majority of transition countries has been made in the field of trade and foreign exchange regime, except for Belarus (2-), Russia (2+), Turkmenistan (1), and Uzbekistan (1); all other countries recorded 3 and above in 2000 (see table A6a). It is noteworthy that competition policy indicators are weak across the board except for the Czech Republic and Poland. With respect to financial institutions, the EBRD has made a distinction between:

- banking reforms and interest liberalization,
- securities markets and non-bank financial institutions
- and financial regulation

With respect to financial liberalization, Hungary was the leading transition economy, followed by Poland, Slovenia, Lithuania and Estonia in 2000; leading is defined here as having achieved at least one 4 in one of the three categories and at least a 3- in the other two subcategories. We essentially find that financial regulation is fairly good across the majority of countries; in contrast, banking reforms have made insufficient progress across countries.

Taking a closer look at infrastructure, we are mainly interested in telecommunications – important for competition and price arbitrage, respectively – but also for national and international networking plus outsourcing in the business community. Here we find a broader group of leading countries (having 3 or better), namely Albania, Bosnia Herzegovina, Bulgaria, Croatia, Czech Republic, Estonia, Hungary, Latvia, Lithuania, Poland, Romania and Russia; thus 12 of 26 countries showed a fairly good record in 2000 (see table 6 b). Since Russia is the most populous country among transition countries, one can argue that modernization of telecommunications has made considerable progress in transition countries. With regard to railways, roads and water plus waste water, there is still broad need for modernization that, however, might be quite difficult if financial institutions remain underdeveloped. Indeed, financing restructuring and expansion of infrastructure is important for both growth and internationalization of the economy in eastern Europe and the CIS.

3. Growth Dynamics

3.1 Neoclassical Theory and New Growth Theory

From a theoretical perspective, the main sources of economic growth can be summarized rather easily as is shown in the following figure. We concentrate on three main pillars of economic growth, namely the impact of financial market efficiency and market stability, the role of human capital formation and the impact of innovation and diffusion. LUCAS (1990) has emphasized the role of human capital endowment in explaining international differences in capital flows: according to his view, human capital creates a positive externality that raises the productivity of skilled labor, at the same time human capital raises the productivity of physical capital. Relative abundance of human capital therefore can stimulate inflows of foreign direct investment, and the latter is part of overall capital inflows that might contribute to international economic convergence. The endowment of human capital is linked to the education system, financed mainly by governments in most countries. In leading OECD countries, between 6 and 7 % of GDP is devoted to education while many transition countries allocate only 3 to 4 % for education. Given the imperfections of human capital markets – overlooked in simple neoclassical growth models – investment in human capital must be mainly financed from domestic savings as emphasized by BARRO et al. (1995). From this perspective, domestic savings and adequate public funds for education are crucial. Relatively low domestic savings and inadequate public (and private) funding of education could explain the lack of convergence in per capita income across countries.

While innovation and hence research and development have traditionally been emphasized in the literature, the role of diffusion for economic growth has been underestimated. An efficient system of diffusion of best practices and of new products or process innovations can strongly contribute to economic growth – in particular in the age of the software industry, digital telecommunications and the internet, all of which offer opportunities to exploit network effects at rather low costs. More rapid diffusion could raise the average level of knowledge and also stimulate innovation as well as reinforce earlier innovation dynamics on the one hand; on the other hand, the era of digital services offers new options for launching demand-enhancing novel services that in turn might stimulate investment. One also may note that an economy with n+I sectors, where sector I initially faces a positive technology shock – with the innovation thereafter diffusing across sectors –, will experience transitory growth acceleration if more efficient diffusion technologies allows n sectors to adopt to the new technology at a faster rate than before.

Fig. A4: Basics of Economic Growth

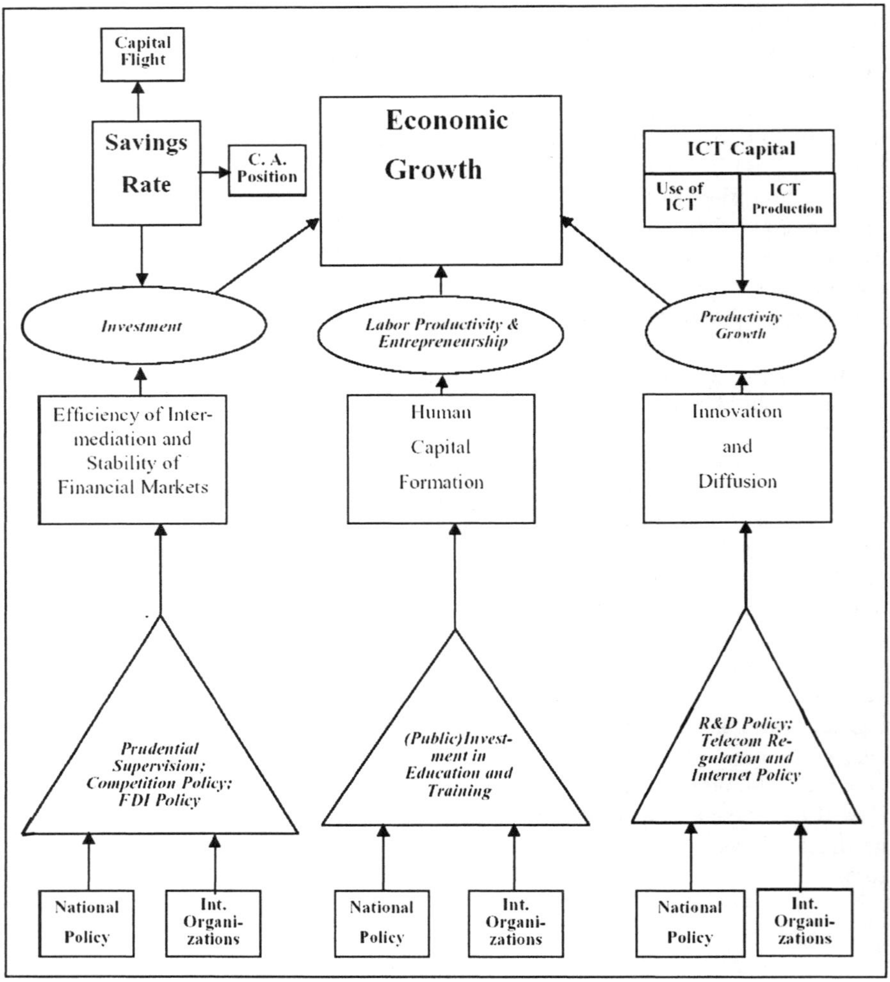

As regards financing of investment, the savings rate – corrected for capital flight and the official current account position – is crucial in a simplified perspective; a broader perspective will have to take into account the efficiency of intermediation and the stability of financial markets. With respect to the latter two aspects, reducing inflation to single digit figures is a critical requirement. This was achieved by most transition countries in the mid-1990s. Moreover, competition plus FDI inflows in banking and insurance are important ingredients for ensuring efficient financial markets, as is effective prodential supervision. In this respect, there are enormous differences across transition countries. Hungary, the Czech Republic, Estonia, Slovenia and Poland are leading countries in this group. As regards the largest country, namely Russia, competition in the financial sector has been week, FDI inflows low and prudential supervision totally inadequate in the 1990s. After the crisis of 1998, this has changed only modestly. Russia has adjusted national policy to some extent; however, Russia is not yet a WTO member country and the liberalization of financial services is there not organized within a clear framework.

Another important aspect of economic growth is human capital formation crucial for raising labor productivity and for entrepreneurship – indeed many entrepreneurs in OECD countries, especially in knowledge intensive and technology intensive fields have some form of higher education. Cohen/Soto (2001) present empirical evidence for a subgroup of 38 OECD member countries and non-member countries illustrating that human capital – adequately defined – has a significant impact on economic growth. It is noteworthy that total factor productivity in poor countries, defined as output growth net of the contribution of physical and human capital, is only about 45 % of the level of wealthy countries.

Several Visegrad countries showed relatively high public expenditures on education in the 1990s; at the same time, education spending in several other transition countries, including Russia was reduced relative to GDP. Rising private expenditures on higher education can only partly compensate for this negative development. As regards the quality of schooling, the OECD's PISA study has not only shown remarkable international differences (see table A7), it also points to the usefulness of benchmarking studies conducted by international organizations. Countries in the lower part of the ranking list will be eager to improve their relative positions by adopting adequate reforms in the medium term. There is clear empirical (cross-country) evidence that human capital formation has contributed to growth.

Since the 1980s and the 1990s, a third pillar of economic growth has become critically important in industrialized countries, namely investment in information and communication technology (ICT). A priori it is unclear whether it is mainly the production of ICT goods – that are technology intensive and knowledge intensive in terms of factor intensity – or the use of ICT goods, some of which allow the exploitation of productivity-enhancing network effects that stimulate growth. There are, however, many imperfections in digital information markets that impair prospects for a sustained new economy boom (some policy options for remedying these imperfections will be discussed in the final section). From a policy perspective, government can stimulate productivity growth not only through traditional R&D policy but also through adequate telecommunications regulation and internet policy.

From a narrow theoretical perspective, long term economic growth can be explained in basically three different supply-side approaches:

- Output growth can be explained by the product of the investment output ratio and the average marginal product of capital, where both variables have to be explained in terms of exogenous variables.
- Output development can be explained on the basis of a neoclassical growth model with exogenous technological progress, where the rate of technological

progress is equal to long term output growth; however, government policy can shift the level of the growth upwards or downwards and the level of per capita income – hence growth acceleration occurs as a transitory adjustment phenomenon. In the Solow model, steady state per capita income $y=Y/L$ (with L representing labor) is determined under the assumption of a Cobb Douglas function $Y = K^{ß}L^{(1-ß)}$ – with K standing for capital, ß for output elasticity of capital– as follows: $y = [s/(\delta+n+a)]^{ß/1-ß}$ (with s for savings rate, δ for depreciation rate, n for the growth rate of population, a for the rate of labor-augmenting technological progress). To the extent that transition brings about an increase in the depreciation rate or a fall of the savings rate, per capita output will fall.

- The new growth theory endogenizes the growth rate of technological progress in various models; e.g. productivity spillover effects from firms' investments as in ROMER (1986) or ROMER (1987) who emphasizes growth effects from product differentiation.

From a simple growth perspective it holds that output growth g_Y (g stands for growth rate and Y for real GDP) is equal to

(I) $g_Y= [I/Y]\,[Y_K]$

Growth simply is investment output ratio I/Y times the marginal product of capital Y_K. The business community and government policy plus international external variables jointly determine the investment output ratio. One may assume that the input output ratio depends on

- the real interest rate r, namely with a negative value – this in turn creates a link to the fiscal policy stance in the sense that high deficit GDP ratios could raise interest rates (unless deficits mainly reflect financing of public investment)
- the growth rate of product innovations θ, namely with a positive value: the higher the rate of product innovations, the more profitable will investment be
- the corporate tax rate τ^c, which should carry a negative value
- the expected growth rate of the population (n) which is a proxy for future demand growth
- the inflation rate whose trend value for various reasons is positively linked with inflation variability and in this perspective reflect a negative impact of inflation uncertainty (depending on the tax system also cold bracket creep)
- the sectoral composition of output (V), which can be rather capital intensive – eg the case of Russia with a high share of the capital intensive resources, reflecting its natural endowments in terms of oil and gas sites – or only modestly capital intensive (eg the case of a services-oriented economy such as Estonia or Hungary)
- the degree of political instability σ which negatively affects the investment output ratio.

(II) $I/Y = f(r, \tau^c, \theta, n, \pi, V, \sigma)$

The marginal product of capital will typically render a negative effect on capital intensity ($k=K/L$) but a positive change on human capital intensity $h=H/L$ (with

H representing the stock of human capital); note that with a Cobb Douglas production function $Y=K^{\beta}H^{\beta'}L^{(1-\beta-\beta')}$, the marginal product of capital is proportionate to the average product of capital. Moreover, we may assume that the stock of cumulated FDI inflows represents a higher level of technology, which implies thus that the ratio κ of the stock of inward FDI to national output should have a positive impact on the average marginal product of capital. In addition to this standard argument, we may assume that it positively depends on the scope of network effects (N) within or across core sectors of the economy; in a market perspective, network effects raise the demand for the respective goods or services, but in a technological perspective they facilitate the interaction of firms facing network effects so that there are implicit productivity spillover effects.

(III) $Y_K= f(K/L, N(\ldots), \kappa)$

The economy's average marginal product of capital is mainly determined by entrepreneurship, the depth of financial markets and the intensity of Schumpeterian competition in each sector and the overall economic system, respectively. Taking into account the role of information and communication technology ICT that often generates positive network effects N within an industry and across sectors, we may state the hypothesis that a high telecommunications or internet density will facilitate exploitation of network effects and also stimulate growth via other spillover effects.

Network effects can be expected to depend upon the density of the communication system and the speed of communication lines. From this perspective, investment in the telecommunications sector is particularly important.

3.2 Analyzing Growth Dynamics in a Cross Country Regression

The starting point of the empirical analysis was to take a closer look at a group of 78 countries and to decide on the basis of a cluster analysis for per capita GDP and growth in a specific period, in which two groups of countries can be distinguished (for details see Appendix 2):

- Relatively poor countries: group A; as a subgroup, A* we have the post-socialist transition countries
- industrialized market economies: group B

For the purpose of accident compensation, we took 6-year means from 1994 to 1999 for the unlagged variables of regressions. The relation to the lagged variables, which are 6-year means from 1988 to 1993, can be interpreted as causality. We specify two linear regression equations for each group (for details and regression results see Appendix 3, for data sources see Appendix 4):

$$(1) \quad g_Y = \beta_0 + \beta_1 \ln(Iq) + \beta_2 Infl + \beta_3 gTelD(-6) + \beta_4 \ln(SE.tert(-6)) + \beta_5 \ln(FDI)$$

$$(2) \quad g_Y = \beta_0 + \beta_1 \ln(Iq) + \beta_2 Infl + \beta_3 gTelD(-6) + \beta_4 \ln(SE.tert(-6)) + \beta_5 \ln(FDI) + \beta_6\, gUSPAT(+2)$$

Equation 2 takes into account the Schumpeterian innovation dynamics as proxied by the growth rate in patents granted in the US (to avoid distortionary effects we drop the US in equation 2 and 2B). The lead of two periods in the growth of utiliy patents at the US Patent and Trademark Office (USPTO) is due to the lag between development (and application, respectively) of an innovation in the innovator's home country and the year of patent grant at the USTPO.

From a theoretical perspective we expect the investment-output-ratio, the growth rate of telecommunication density, foreign direct investment, and human capital (proxied by gross tertiary school enrollment) as well as the growth rate of patents granted in the US to positively influence output growth; we expect a negative impact on the inflation rate, at least if inflation is relatively high. According to empirical studies, the investment ratios of those postcommunist transition countries that are only at the beginning of the recovery phase may have no influence on their GDP growth rate, because economic growth might be driven mainly by efficiency gains during this stage of the transition process (HAVRYLYSHYN 2001, p. 56).

The empirical findings can be summarized as follows:

As regards industrialized market economies, we find at a 10-percent-level significant coefficients – based on corrected t-results (white-estimators) – for the investment-output-ratio, the inflation rate, and foreign direct investment that FDI is a significant variable in equation 1B and 2B points to the special relevance that multinational companies have on economic growth. The coefficient for the inflation rate is positive, which, however, is not very surprising in light of the traditional assumption that low inflation rates contribute to structural change that in turn translates into economic growth. Equation 2B brings an adjusted R^2 of 0.68 and shows a significant impact on the inflation rate, the growth rate of lagged telecom density, the lagged human capital variable, foreign direct investment, and the growth rate of patents granted in the US (with a lead of two years).

In equation 1A, the group of low income countries shows a significant negative impact on the inflation rate and on lagged human capital variable. The negative role of inflation for economic growth is not surprising since these countries have faced relatively high inflation rates. As regards the human capital variable, it is well known from the literature that a significant impact is often dependent upon a very careful specification of the variable – as an example for the OECD countries, see the recent study by COHEN/SOTO (2001).

For the subgroup A* (post-socialist transition economies), equation 1A* shows only one significant parameter, namely a negative impact on the human capital variable on GDP growth. If we also take the growth of patent grants in the US for explaining the variable, the explanatory power of the model vanishes. With respect to the negative value of influence of the human capital variable in addition to the data given above, we want to point out the fact that for the period of transition the processes of economic growth (output declining and recovery) on the one hand and of human capital development (a slow but steady growth on average) on the other hand differ considerably (see fig. A5 in Appendix 3).

As regards transition countries, there is the problem of missing data for several countries. Particularly the handling of the granting of patents for inventions stemming out of the former Soviet Union – which cannot be assigned by several succeeding countries of the Soviet Union and so are simply omitted in our investigation – may lead to distortions of the influence of the GUSPAT variable in equation 2A*. Moreover, some of the initial distortions might still be relevant in transition countries to such a degree that investment decisions still are not reflecting efficient decision-making in the business community. Only after most firms have been privatized and competition policy plus external liberalization strongly influence investment decisions could one expect results in cross country regressions which are similar to normal industrialized market economies. Moreover, efficient capital markets and bond markets are obviously important for achieving efficiency-enhancing investment decisions.

3.3 Role of Financial Sector Liberalization for Economic Growth

From a theoretical perspective, poor transition countries could raise investment-GDP ratios and hence growth if there would be efficient financial intermediation and high domestic savings; or if there were sustainable current account deficits and high long term capital inflows, respectively. Therefore financial markets play a critical role in eastern Europe and Russia.

As regards the banking system and stock markets economists, have for decades underestimated the crucial role of efficient financial intermediation; GOLDSMITH (1969) and McKINNON (1973) were early to point out that efficiently channeling investment funds to profitable investment projects can contribute to growth. The more recent literature (survey LEVINE, 1997; FRANCOIS/ ESCHENBACH/SCHUKNECHT, 2002) has brought up a rich array of theoretical and empirical arguments along this line of reasoning. ROUBINI/SALA-I-MARTIN (1992) and MATTESINE (1996) find a negative link between real interest rate distortions and lending-deposit spreads and growth. DEMETRIADES/ HUSSEIN (1996) report a bi-rectional relationship between financial sector development (and depth) and growth. LEVINE/ZERVOS (1998) find evidence – based on 49 countries – on the link between stock market activities and economic growth. HARRIS (1997) in a cross-country study and ARESTIS/DEMETRIADES/ LUINTEL (2001) – focusing on five countries using time-series evidence – present weak evidence for a positive link between stock market activity and growth, yet they find a more important role for a positive link between bank lending and economic growth. BENHABIB/SPIEGEL (2000) also present evidence that financial development fosters growth through a rise of investment and total factor productivity.

FRANCOIS/ESCHENBACH/SCHUKNECHT (2002) focus both on developing countries and OECD countries, whereby the latter have a rather liberal financial services markets; moving from the average level of openness among the poorest developing countries to the average among the higher income countries is associated with an increased degree of competition in the financial services sector and in turn with growth rates that are then higher – the mechanics emphasized by the authors concern dynamic effects of market structure and competition mechanisms. The basic equilibrium equation in their model is the following equation:

$$(1) \quad Y_K = \rho + \delta + \varphi$$

Hence the marginal product of capital in equilibrium is equal to the sum of three elements: the subjective rate of time discount ρ, the rate of capital stock depreciation δ and the cost of financial intermediation φ. To the extent that international opening up of the financial sector and other policy measures reduce the cost of financial intermediation, the optimal capital stock is raised, thereby resulting in higher investment. Inherent distortions in the financial sector and in particular the lack of competition and adequate prudential supervision raise the cost of financial intermediation. Under standard theoretical assumptions the cost of intermediation can be shown to be a negative function of the intensity of competition and the number of firms in the financial sector.

A critical issue for transition countries is whether they are moving towards sustained financial liberalization. There is no doubt that all EU accession countries will have to accept liberalization as part of EU rules (Acquis Communautaire). However, as regards other transition countries, one must raise the issue whether there are impulses for long term liberalization. HARMS/MATTOO/SCHUKNECHT (2002) present a political economy model of financial trade liberalization and look into the issue of GATS commitments in the banking sector and in securities services. An underdeveloped financial sector, macroeconomic volatility, poor prudential regulation, weak representation of workers' interests, and low market penetration by foreigners are also correlated with less commitments to reduce protectionist barriers in financial markets; these findings indirectly suggest that Russia will be reluctant to liberalize financial markets and this in turn implies reduced prospects for long term economic growth. Another remarkable finding of the authors is that the potential for trading market access commitments in future trade negotiations, especially for countries with exports facing high barriers abroad, is a crucial reason to withhold market access commitments for financial services liberalization. From this perspective one may suggest that all countries of the former USSR that are not yet a WTO member country will be reluctant to undertake financial sector liberalization. Indeed, it is rational for these countries to adopt a wait-and-see attitude and postpone financial sector liberalization until they can trade such liberalization for better access to foreign goods markets.

Lessons from EU Southern Enlargement?

From the southern EU enlargement (Greece, Spain and Portugal in the 1980s) one may conclude that EU membership can help to achieve a higher ratio of FDI inflows in total gross capital inflows. Spain and Portugal raised relative FDI inflows and thus benefited from an external contribution to overall investment and technological progress. Greece recorded a slight reduction in the 1980s compared to the period 1975-80, but this probably reflected both the fact that in 1975-80 the share of FDI in total capital inflows already was rather high, namely 29.1 %, partially reflecting perhaps an anticipation effect on the side of international investors. At the same time, one must take into account that both the Spanish and the Portuguese governments adopted broad internal liberalization and privatization measures that encouraged foreign investors to strongly take advantage of the fall in the political risk premium associated with EU membership; accepting the EU's set of rules (acquis communautaire) clearly implies a tying of government's hands in the sense that the scope for discretionary and protectionist intervention is much smaller than before.

BUCH/HEINRICH/PIAZOLO (1998) argue that with the beginning of systemic transformation in Visegrad countries, the share of FDI inflows in total inflows reduced in Greece, Portugal and Spain. There was FDI diversion towards eastern Europe, but in terms of portfolio inflows, eastern European countries were and remained behind the poor EU countries in the early 1990s. They argue that domestic liberalization measures can indeed reinforce positive economic effects of EU membership. EU accession countries obviously differ in the ability of the political system to deliver broad and consistent liberalization strategies. However, one may hope that benchmarking among EU accession countries and the impact of competing for global FDI sources will induce a long term institutional convergence process that should be followed by an economic convergence process.

With respect to EU outsiders among the transition countries, one can anticipate that they will suffer from both trade diversion effects and FDI diversion effects as a consequence of EU eastern enlargement in the medium term. However, to the extent that accession countries will benefit from increasing growth rates, outsider countries will benefit from regional trade creation in the long term. As regards FDI diversion effects, the situation looks less favorable for the EU outsiders unless very bold and consistent domestic liberalization measures – carefully phased in – would strongly raise the attractiveness of the outsider countries. The problem of FDI diversion is serious because both a lower political risk premium and higher growth rates in accession countries could stimulate FDI inflows. From this perspective it is all the more important that outsider countries seriously consider options for establishing special relations with the EU other than through direct membership; moreover, prudent domestic policy reforms and decisive moves towards WTO membership – in those countries that are not yet WTO members – are crucial. WTO membership would not only give domestic firms in the export sector reassurance that exports will not be discriminated. Additionally, potential foreign investors would appreciate it if the uncertainties of exporting from certain CIS countries, e.g. Russia, would be reduced via WTO membership.

Financial Markets and the New Economy

Given the enormous expansion of ICT investment in several OECD countries and the role of stock markets in financing digital firms, one should also take a look at the New Economy. The New Economy boom in the US and some EU countries in the 1990s – when stock markets played a crucial role for established high technology firms as well as dynamic newcomers in digital services – has reinforced the interest in the links between financial market dynamics, investment and growth (BANK, 2003). While there has been some disappointment about the bursting of the apparent stock market bubble in 2001/2002, one should not overlook the fact that tangible assets in modern services are a smaller part of investment than in manufacturing industry, whereby bank financing naturally should play a rather limited role as a financing source of overall investment in the New Economy.

The internet and cheaper international telephony, stimulated by rapid technological progress and economic opening up of telecommunications markets, have contributed to increasing competition in financial services in OECD countries. One may ask which role the New Economy has for transition countries and to what extent policy makers could stimulate the internet and digital services as a basis for enhanced economic growth. Transition countries were facing high excess demand in fixed line telecommunications when broader transition policies were adopted in the early 1990s; certainly, prospective EU accession countries were rather eager to restructure and privatize the respective national operator – and competition was phased in both in national and international telecommunications. Local loop unbundling is very slow in eastern Europe, where the situation is similar to EU countries in which very limited progress exists in local telephony that is so crucial for the internet. The technological innovation of mobile telephony has helped to some extent to cut the excess demand in telecommunications, but it has not helped to stimulate internet services since mobile internet under GSM and older standards is not user-friendly. In both eastern Europe and western Europe, broader progress with mobile internet applications can only be expected with the unfolding of UMTS networks that might have a broader customer base in 2004/5. As regards internet transaction, we can generally distinguish between B-2-B transactions and B-2-C (business to customers/households) transactions. The commercial relevance of the internet in OECD countries is mostly in the B-2-B channel.

In eastern Europe data security problems could undermine the growth of digital internet transactions; particular problems are expected for the former USSR. This could impair growth directly through lack of investment in digital services that are often an input to industry so that addition industrial expansion would be impaired indirectly. Moreover, internet-based transactions have increasingly become important in financial services where they account for 5-10 % of overall transactions in western OECD countries.

Internet transactions in financial markets in Europe could become important in three ways in in the early 21st century:

- The internet generally raises market transparency and therefore stimulates competition.
- The internet could be an interesting niche for establishing a government bonds market in the short term; and market places for other bonds in the medium term. Most OECD countries have established some form of digital bonds marketplaces.
- The internet can be a platform for establishing a digital venture capital market in which experienced venture capital firms – with a proven track record – can organize the financing of innovative dynamic firms in a convenient way; this avenue has already been explored in the US and some other OECD countries. Since venture capital naturally plays a strong role for financing technology-

intensive new firms, one might anticipate only a rather limited role for digital venture capitalists in transition countries in the former CMEA area. However, Hungary, the Czech Republic and Estonia as well as some other countries with a strong emphasis on innovation and technological modernization might want to explore this avenue. In principle Russia as a large country with a considerable high technological history could also pursue digital venture capitalism. However, as trust in partners in financial markets is at a high premium after the 1998 banking and financial market crisis, one might be rather pessimistic in this field. Lack of long successful track records of venture capitalists also undermines Russian prospects for internet-based venture capitalism.

3.4 New Economy Aspects of Growth

In the second half of the 1990s information and communication technology (ICT) has contributed between 1/5 and 1/3 in economic growth in leading OECD countries. The ICT sector consists basically of the computer and software industry, data services and telecommunications; the share of ICT value-added in GDP almost doubled in the 1990s in the US – the global ICT leader – where it reached almost 10 % in 2000. ICT growth has also been considerable in Scandinavian countries, the UK, the Netherlands, Spain and Portugal, although the starting levels of the ICT share in GDP were clearly lower than in the US.

In a modern society with digital services and broad computer networks combined with much human capital, one should emphasize that a broadly-defined investment output ratio must take into account many items under the heading investment:

- Investment In equipment, including computer hardware as well as factory buildings plus inventory (="gross fixed capital formation" in the traditional sense)

- Investment in computer software that reached almost 3 % in the US in the late 1990s
- R&D expenditures that actually lead to accumulation of a stock of technology knowledge (which, of course, is subject to depreciation)
- Education expenditures, whereby expenditures on university education is of particular relevance (2.3 % of GDP in the US in the late 1990s, close to 2 % in the Scandinavian countries, 1 % of GDP or lower in most other European EU countries, less than 1 % in transition countries, except for Hungary)

As regards the link between ICT expansion and growth, there is a debate among economists as to the reasons for acceleration in growth in the US and some EU countries in the second half of the 1990s:

- Mainly to rising productivity growth in the computer producing sector (GORDON 2000);
- Both to rising productivity growth in the sector producing ICT goods and the application of ICT goods and digital services. VAN ARK (2001) has provided

empirical evidence that both ICT production and the use of ICT – often in the so-called Old Economy – raised productivity growth among many OECD countries in the 1990s. WELFENS (2002a, b) theoretically emphasized the two-pronged productivity-enhancing effect of ICT; JUNGMITTAG/WELFENS (2001) provided empirical evidence on the growth-enhancing role of the use of telecommunications and the internet for Germany. The hypothesis is that more powerful data communication networks stimulate the diffusion of new knowledge, which in turn raises growth. JUNGMITTAG/WELFENS (2001b) have also emphasized the trade-enhancing nature of modern telecommunications on the basis of gravity modelling and argue that trade creation could in turn stimulate economic growth. FREUND/WEINHOLD (2003) make a similar argument, namely that the use of the internet is trade-creating; they find that developing countries could benefit from a rising internet host density even more than industrialized countries. These authors thus suggest a "twin-growth bonus of ICT expansion".

If the Gordon hypothesis is correct, only those newly industrializing countries and transition countries that are major producers of ICT goods could hope to accelerate; countries such as Korea, Taiwan, Thailand, Malaysia and Hungary would be well positioned to benefit from a growth bonus of ICT expansion under this hypothesis; from this perspective a strong focus on ICT with respect to inward foreign direct investment would be useful to stimulate growth beyond the pure contribution of aggregate capital formation. By contrast, the twin growth bonus of ICT expansion suggests that even countries that have no large ICT producing sector can benefit from an increased use of ICT goods and services. What particularly matters here is that there is a rapid increase in fixed and mobile telecommunications density and that competition plus privatization in the telecommunications sector help to stimulate the diffusion of knowledge and hence contribute to higher output growth.

The role of ICT has gradually increased in transition economies that, however, have suffered from poor fixed network telecommunications infrastructure and pent-up demand in telephony as well as problems with restructuring and privatization of state-owned telecommunications operators. From this perspective, it is not surprising that mobile telephony in the US and the EU has largely been considered a complementary to fixed network services, a true substitute for fixed telephony in eastern Europe, the Ukraine, Russia and other countries of the former Soviet Union. Mobile telephony is in technical terms a good substitute for fixed line voice telephony, but mobile internet applications clearly have a lower quality than fixed network access – including cable TV networks – with respect to internet services. With respect to the introduction of competition into long distance and international telecommunication, EU accession countries have adopted phasing-in schedules that will make sure the EU liberalization and framework regulation regime in fixed line telephony will be adopted within a few years. Eastern European non-accession countries as well as Russia and the Ukraine face problems here since there is no external pressure to liberalize network operation and digital value-added services. As regards Russia, there will be increasing external pressure on trade liberalization in telecommunications equipment and in telecommunications services once Russia is about to become a member of the World Trade Organization. It is unclear whether Russia will be able to use a transition period until WTO membership to build up a dynamic domestic computer and telecommunications sector.

Tables A8–A12 represent selected indicators for telecommunication and internet density in selected transition countries (also with data of EU-15 countries for comparison). From table A8 we can clearly see that Hungary, Estonia, Slovenia and the Czech Republic are leading countries in eastern Europe; some of the other EU accession countries – above all the Slovak Republic in the field of fixed line density – also show relatively fast catching up in terms of telecommunications density (and also show an increasing use – in terms of minutes – of the telecommunications network). This ranking also holds for the internet host density as a proxy for the supply side of internet use (table A10). The picture is slightly different with respect to internet user density (see table A9), whereby Estonia, Lithuania, Poland and the Czech Republic are leading economies among transition countries.

As regards mobile telecommunications (see table A11), Russia's MTS (Mobilnyje Tele-Systemy, of which Deutsche Telekom AG has a 40 % share) has become the leading company among operators in transition countries in 2002; by mid-2002, they had 4.4 million subscribers, up from 3.6 million at the end of 2001. PTC (ERA GSM) and Polkomtel are No. 2 and 3 in absolute terms with 4.2 and 3.9 million subscribers in mid-2002 – up from 4.0 and 2.9 at end of 2002; Poland can thus be considered a relatively dynamic market. The Russian VimpelCom (Beeline), in which Telenor from Norway has a stake, had 3.7 million subscribers in mid-2002, up from 2.6 million at end of 2001. MegaFon is another Russia operator, in which the Swedish Telia and the Finnish Sonera each have a stake. In mid-2002, mobile telecommunication density was 7 % and in fixed line telephony 21 % in Russia. Given the low overall telecommunication density in Russia one could anticipate a rapid medium term growth, in particular in mobile telephony. By 2010, Russia's mobile telecommunication density might reach 50 %, with expansion driven by gradually increasing competition through newcomers and by falling prices. Russian telecommunication operators might indeed become international investors in the medium term as is already amply born out by Yukos' acquisition of the eastern European network of KPN Qwest in 2002. Yukos' mobile telecommunications subsidiary is thus active in Poland, Hungary, the Czech Republic, Romania and Slovakia. With regard to mobile telecommunication density, Hungary, Estonia and Slovenia are leading economies among the transition countries.

As regards computer density (table A12), eastern Europe and Russia is lagging behind western Europe, and this backwardness might continue for some time. With falling relative computer prices in world markets, the ICT modernization of eastern Europe and Russia will become easier in the long run.

Eastern Europe and the CIS countries are behind Western Europe in computer density. PC density is quite important for networking effects and productivity growth, at least if one accepts the basic hypothesis that the New Economy is associated with particular productivity growth effects that stem from the combined use of computers, modern telecommunications equipment and software.

4. Policy Implications

From a policy perspective, EU accession countries face favorable opportunities through EU membership that will not only stimulate institutional reforms but also encourage policymakers to embrace more transparency in fiscal policy – through Commission's surveillance; moreover, considerable funds will become available to some transition countries under the heading of EU structural funds. Under EU "twinship programs", EU accession countries will also enjoy support for upgrading public administrations in selected fields. These policy-related elements and full free access to EU markets should help accession countries achieve high and sustained growth. However, as the divergent experience of dynamics in Spain and Portugal in contrast to slow-growing Greece in the late 1980s and in the first half of the 1990s has shown, EU membership is no simple magic for achieving sustained high growth rates. If policymakers cannot deliver complementary domestic reforms – with adequate focus on liberalization, deregulation and competition-enhancing policies – EU membership will generate only limited benefits. Also, one should not overlook the fact that EU membership brings a rise in required regulatory and technological standards whereby the opportunities in terms of full EU market access and zero political risk for EU investors might be partly offset by stricter standards and more costly regulations in many fields.

One should not forget that even for accession countries there are considerable risks in terms of economic stability once international financial conditions become tenser in the sense that nominal and real interest rates in world markets increase or oil prices suddenly rise strongly. As the case of Mexico demonstrated in the mid-1980s, OECD membership was not the widely expected rubber stamp that would bring consistency and stability to Mexico. Indeed, Mexico faced a serious banking and confidence crisis just in the year of OECD membership. Against this background, one can only warn that financial stability will remain a crucial issue on the agenda.

For Bulgaria and Romania as well as for the Balkans countries there is at least a long term perspective for EU membership that might indeed encourage adequate long term restructuring and growth-enhancing policies. Other outsiders in the ex-CMEA area will face more problems that could undermine prospects for long term growth. Many CIS countries are likely to face serious problems in this respect.

As regards Russia, there are several specific aspects to be considered. Putin has brought political stability for Russia, and this will help the country's economic catching up process as the political risk premium in capital markets has reduced. However, there is not a firm basis for sustained high growth as long as competition policy is relatively weak in Russia and as long as the banking system and bonds markets have not been reorganized effectively. Moreover, high oil prices in 2001/2002 have reinforced the natural resources bias in Russia's economy that might face Dutch disease problems (biased structural change in favor of the natural resources sector combined with a declining share of manufacturing in overall output). There is some risk that rapidly falling oil prices in the near future could undermine stability and growth in Russia. Government indeed faces the challenge of using the petrodollar boom to carefully implement those reforms that are conducive to economic and technological modernization in all sectors of the economy.

Taking into account the decline of the Russian population in the 1990s, one may argue that the demographic factor is not supporting favorable growth prospects. However, there are other arguments that point to great opportunities for sustained growth in Russia:

- Russia has opened up toward trade and foreign investment and one should expect specialization gains from trade and higher investment-GDP ratios. It is, however, worrisome that Russia could not really attract much FDI inflows – relative to GDP – in 2001/2002. Russia's lack of FDI inflows will restrict trade expansion. This argument mainly refers to the well-known trade-expanding role of multinational companies: About 1/3 of international trade among leading OECD countries is intra-company trade; often in knowledge-intensive or technology-intensive products. From this perspective, Russia's trade intensity could still rise considerably once high FDI inflows occur over at least a decade or so.
- Russia had a serious financial market crisis in 1998 and is about to restructure banks. Given the rather imperfect restructuring process in the Russian banking market and taking into account underdevelopment of Russia's bonds market concentrated mainly around short-term maturities, one may anticipate rather inefficient intermediation that will come at a considerable cost to society. Investment-GDP ratios and hence growth rates will be lower than otherwise.
- Russia is embracing a market economy system in a period of high technological dynamics in industrialized countries. Many OECD countries, including the USA, Korea, Finland, Sweden, the UK and others have benefited strongly from the investment boom in information and communication technology. Russia as a country catching up in digital technology might benefit from being a digital latecomer. However, EU experiences have shown that only some liberalization and privatization of telecommunications will bring a wave of innovations and falling relative prices for digital services. At the same time, EU telecommunications firms have shown increased dependence on capital markets and bonds markets since firms have to finance innovation and UMTS mobile network expansion. Inadequate rules for awarding UMTS licences have undermined the financial stability of some EU telecommunications operators, which in turn has resulted in the cutting back of investment in network expansion. Russia, as well as other transition countries, could design superior auctioning rules for UMTS licenses that would ideally include secondary markets for licences whereby firms can sell licenses to competitors; a futures market for UMTS licences would also be quite useful. From this perspective, growth-enhancing ICT policies should not always simply follow EU models.

In Russia, there are substantial risks that considerable protectionism in the goods and services markets will continue in the early 21st century. Any future recession will naturally trigger various pressures in favor of external protectionism. If government seriously wants to protect some technology-dynamic sectors for a limited period of time – raising profits in the respective sector and thus strengthening accumulation of the capital necessary to finance innovations and certain investment projects – it should decide about the respective strategy in a period of non-recession. Otherwise one could anticipate that ailing old industries will be protected. If the latter strategy were adopted, this certainly would not be growth-enhancing; on the contrary. Finally, one may raise the issue that even limited sectoral protection of technology intensive or knowledge intensive sectors is bound to encourage the political demand for protectionism in all other sectors. Further research must show whether and under which circumstances the adoption of modest forms of industrial policies that were popular and successful as a transitory strategy in some Asian NICs make sense.

Appendix 1: Tables

Tab. A2 a: Gross Fixed Investment in Transition Countries as Percent of GDP, 1996-2000

	1996	1997	1998	1999	2000	mean 1996-2000
TKM	NA	38.7	45.5	46.3	39.7	42.55
BIH	41.9	41.3	37.0	20.6	NA	35.20
SVK	37.1	36.6	36.1	31.9	30.1	34.36
CZE	34.2	32.6	30.2	27.9	29.7	30.92
HUN	27.2	27.7	29.7	28.5	30.6	28.74
AZE	28.0	34.2	33.4	26.5	17.5	27.92
EST	27.8	30.9	29.4	24.6	25.8	27.70
SVN	23.5	24.2	25.6	28.4	27.8	25.90
POL	21.9	24.6	26.2	26.4	26.5	25.12
BLR	23.5	26.8	26.7	23.7	22.8	24.70
LVA	18.8	22.8	27.6	27.0	27.1	24.66
MDA	24.2	23.8	25.9	22.9	22.2	23.80
HRV	21.9	27.5	24.0	23.4	22.0	23.76
LTU	24.5	26.5	24.4	22.7	20.7	23.76
MKD	20.1	21.0	22.3	19.7	24.5	21.52
UKR	22.7	21.4	20.8	17.5	18.9	20.26
ROM	25.9	20.6	17.8	17.0	19.4	20.14
KGZ	25.2	21.7	15.4	18.0	20.0	20.06
UZB	29.2	21.7	16.8	17.5	15.1	20.06
TJK	22.3	19.7	15.4	19.1	19.9	19.28
ARM	20.0	19.1	19.1	18.4	19.2	19.16
RUS	24.6	22.8	16.1	14.7	16.6	18.96
ALB	15.5	16.0	16.0	16.8	18.6	16.58
KAZ	16.1	15.6	14.3	14.6	13.9	14.90
BGR	8.4	11.4	16.9	19.0	16.6	14.46
GEO	10.8	11.2	12.3	19.2	17.1	14.12

Source: WDI (2002), own computations.

ALB:	Albania	ARM:	Armenia	AZE:	Azerbaijan
BGR:	Bulgaria	BIH:	Bosnia and Herzegovina	BLR:	Belarus
CZE:	Czech Republic	EST:	Estonia	GEO:	Georgia
HRV:	Croatia	HUN:	Hungaria	KAZ:	Kazakhstan
KGZ:	Kyrgyz Republic	LTU:	Lithuania	LVA:	Latvia
MDA:	Moldova	MKD:	Macedonia, FYR	POL:	Poland
ROM:	Romania	RUS:	Russian Federation	SVK:	Slovak Republic
SVN:	Slovenia	TJK:	Tajikistan	TKM:	Turkmenistan
UKR:	Ukraine	UZB:	Uzbekistan		

Tab. A2 b: Gross Capital Formation in EU-15 Member Countries as Percent of GDP, 1996-2000

	1996	1997	1998	1999	2000	mean 1996-2000
PRT	23.8	25.7	26.7	27.2	28.2	26.32
AUS	23.7	24.2	24.2	24.0	NA	24.03
SPA	21.9	22.2	23.2	24.6	25.9	23.56
GER	21.6	21.6	21.8	22.2	22.7	21.98
IRE	19.6	21.5	23.4	23.3	NA	21.95
NDL	21.3	21.6	21.9	22.0	NA	21.70
GRE	19.8	20.2	21.9	22.3	NA	21.05
LUX	20.2	20.4	19.5	22.8	21.2	20.82
BEL	19.9	20.4	20.9	21.2	21.5	20.78
DEN	18.9	20.8	21.7	20.2	22.1	20.74
ITA	18.7	18.9	19.3	19.8	20.5	19.44
FRAU	18.3	17.8	19.1	19.4	20.6	19.04
FIN	16.8	18.4	19.7	19.3	19.7	18.78
GBR	16.8	17.2	18.0	17.5	17.9	17.48
SWE	15.9	15.6	16.8	17.0	17.9	16.64

Source: WDI (2002), own computations.

AUS: Austria
FIN: Finland
GER: Germany
ITA: Italy
PRT: Portugal
BEL: Belgium
FRA: France
GRE: Greece
LUX: Luxembourg
SPA: Spain
DEN: Denmark
GBR: Great Britain
IRE: Ireland
NDL: Netherlands
SWE: Sweden

Tab. A2 c: Gross Capital Formation in Selected Asian Countries and the US as Percent of GDP, 1996-2000

	1996	1997	1998	1999	2000	mean 1996-2000
SGP	36.9	38.9	32.3	32.4	31.3	34.36
MYS	41.5	43.0	26.6	22.3	26.8	32.04
KOR	37.9	34.2	21.2	26.7	28.2	29.64
THA	41.6	33.3	20.3	19.9	22.6	27.54
PHL	24.0	24.8	20.3	18.8	17.8	21.14
IDN	30.7	31.8	16.8	11.4	14.6	21.06
USA	18.6	19.5	20.4	20.7	NA	19.80

Source: WDI (2002), own computations.

IDN: Indonesia
PHL: Philippines
KOR: Republic of Korea
SGP: Singapore
MYS: Malaysia
THA: Thailand

Tab. A3 a: FDI Inflows in Transition Countries (Mill. Current US $), 1996-2000

	1996	1997	1998	1999	2000	mean 1996-2000
POL	4498.0	4908.0	6365.0	7270.0	9342.0	6476.60
RUS	2478.0	6638.0	2764.0	3309.0	2714.0	3580.60
CZE	1435.0	1286.0	3700.0	6313.0	4583.0	3463.40
HUN	2274.1	2167.0	2037.1	1976.5	1692.0	2029.30
KAZ	1136.9	1321.3	1151.0	1587.0	1250.0	1289.20
ROM	263.0	1215.0	2031.0	1041.0	1025.0	1115.00
HRV	506.0	529.6	932.0	1479.0	926.0	874.50
SVK	351.3	174.0	562.0	354.3	2052.5	698.80
AZE	627.0	1115.0	1023.0	510.3	130.0	681.10
UKR	521.0	623.0	743.0	496.0	595.0	595.60
BGR	109.0	505.0	537.0	806.1	1001.5	591.70
LTU	152.4	354.5	926.0	486.5	379.0	459.70
LVA	382.0	521.0	357.0	347.6	407.0	402.90
EST	150.2	266.2	581.0	305.2	387.0	337.90
BLR	105.0	352.0	203.0	444.0	90.0	238.80
SVN	194.0	375.2	247.9	181.2	175.5	234.80
GEO	40.0	243.0	265.3	82.0	131.0	152.30
UZB	55.0	285.0	140.0	121.0	100.0	140.20
ARM	17.6	51.9	220.8	122.0	140.0	110.50
ALB	90.1	48.0	45.0	41.0	143.0	73.40
MKD	11.0	16.0	118.0	30.1	175.6	70.10
MDA	23.6	75.7	85.9	33.5	128.0	69.30
KGZ	47.2	84.0	109.0	44.4	-2.4	56.40
TJK	16.0	4.0	30.0	21.0	24.0	19.00
BIH	NA	NA	NA	0.0	0.0	NA
TKM	108.1	107.9	130.0	NA	NA	NA

Source: WDI (2002).

Tab. A3 b: FDI Inflows in Transition Countries as Percent of GDP, 1996-2000

	1996	1997	1998	1999	2000	mean 1996-2000
AZE	19.7	28.1	23.0	11.1	2.5	16.90
EST	3.4	5.7	11.1	6.0	7.8	6.80
LVA	7.4	9.2	5.9	5.2	5.7	6.70
KAZ	5.4	6.0	5.2	9.4	6.8	6.60
CZE	2.5	2.4	6.5	11.6	9.0	6.40
ARM	1.1	3.2	11.7	6.6	7.3	6.00
BGR	1.1	5.0	4.4	6.5	8.3	5.10
MDA	1.4	3.9	5.1	2.9	9.9	4.60
GEO	1.3	6.8	7.3	2.9	4.3	4.50
LTU	1.9	3.7	8.6	4.6	3.3	4.40
HUN	5.0	4.7	4.3	4.1	3.7	4.40
HRV	2.5	2.6	4.3	7.4	4.9	4.30
POL	3.1	3.4	4.0	4.7	5.9	4.20
SVK	1.8	0.9	2.6	1.8	10.7	3.60
KGZ	2.6	4.8	6.6	3.6	-0.2	3.50
ROM	0.7	3.4	4.8	2.9	2.8	2.90
ALB	3.4	2.1	1.5	1.1	3.8	2.40
MKD	0.2	0.4	3.3	0.8	4.9	1.90
BLR	0.7	2.5	1.3	3.7	0.9	1.80
TJK	1.5	0.4	2.3	1.9	2.4	1.70
UKR	1.2	1.2	1.8	1.6	1.9	1.50
SVN	1.0	2.1	1.3	0.9	1.0	1.20
RUS	0.6	1.5	1.0	1.7	1.0	1.20
UZB	0.4	1.9	0.9	0.7	0.7	0.90
BIH	NA	NA	NA	0.0	0.0	NA
TKM	4.5	4.0	4.5	NA	NA	NA

Source: WDI (2002), own computations.

Tab. A4 a: Overall Budget Deficits in Transition Countries as Percent of GDP, 1996-2000

	1996	1997	1998	1999	2000
ALB	-12.3	-12.0	-8.5	NA	NA
AZE	-3.0	-2.2	-3.6	-2.5	NA
BLR	-1.8	-1.6	-0.9	-2.0	0.1
BGR	-15.4	2.1	2.8	1.5	0.6
HRV	-0.4	-1.3	0.6	-2.0	-4.9
CZE	0.1	-1.1	-1.6	-1.6	-3.0
EST	-0.8	2.5	-0.1	-0.2	0.2
GEO	NA	-4.5	-3.5	-4.4	-3.2
HUN	-2.6	-2.3	-6.5	-3.7	-3.6
KAZ	NA	-3.6	-4.1	-3.9	-0.6
KGZ	-5.4	-5.4	-3.0	-2.4	-2.2
LVA	-1.7	0.8	0.2	-3.8	-2.7
LTU	-3.6	-1.9	-0.4	-7.0	-1.3
MDA	-5.7	-7.6	-3.2	-3.4	-1.3
POL	-2.0	-1.8	-1.0	-0.8	0.3
ROM	-4.0	-3.9	-3.0	-1.7	NA
RUS	NA	NA	-5.2	-0.5	3.9
SVK	-1.4	-4.1	-4.2	-3.3	-3.2
SVN	0.0	-1.4	-0.8	-0.7	-1.3
TJK	NA	NA	-2.5	-0.8	-0.2
UKR	NA	NA	NA	-2.1	-0.6

Source: WDI (2002).

Tab. A4 b: Budget Balance in Selected Transition Countries (% of GDP)

	1995	1996	1997	1998	1999	2000
Belarus	-2.8	-2.0	-2.1	-1.5	-2.9	NA
Bulgaria	NA	-10.9	-39.0	-193.3	-1.2	NA
Croatia	-0.7	-0.1	-0.9	0.9	-1.8	-3.9
Czech Republ	NA	0.9	-1.9	6.6	-1.6	NA
Estonia	0.7	-0.3	2.9	0.0	-4.2	-0.1
Hungary	-2.4	-1.9	-4.0	-5.4	-2.9	-2.8
Latvia	-3.1	-1.4	1.2	0.3	-3.4	-2.8
Lithuania	-1.8	-2.5	-1.0	-1.3	-4.3	-1.0
Poland	-2.0	-2.0	-1.5	-1.2	-0.3	1.2
Romania	-4.1	-4.9	-3.6	-2.8	-2.6	NA
Russia	-5.2	-7.9	-7.0	-5.0	-1.7	-
Slovakia	NA	-4.4	-5.7	-2.6	-1.8	-3.1
Slovenia	NA	0.6	-1.1	-1.1	-0.8	-2.0
Ukraine	7.9	4.6	7.1	2.1	-1.4	NA

Note: aggregate across countries weighted using GDP in PPS.

Source: SITE (2002).

Tab. A5 a: Inflation Rates in Transition Countries, 1991-2000

	1991	1992	1993	1994	1995	1996	1997	1998	1999	2000
ALB	35.5	248.0	114.9	37.1	9.8	14.6	30.8	25.0	2.5	-1.2
ARM	79.3	568.3	1391.3	4107.3	161.2	19.6	17.7	10.7	0.1	-1.3
AZE	82.8	1350.9	560.6	1428.6	545.7	26.4	9.2	-1.0	2.2	12.4
BLR	104.0	1072.2	1064.1	1967.3	650.4	53.7	71.6	76.6	316.8	185
BIH	NA	NA	NA	NA	NA	-17.1	8.6	9.0	3.2	4.6
BGR	226.6	59.6	51.1	72.7	62.8	121.0	949.1	22.2	3.1	5.6
HRV	99.3	594.9	1466.8	111.8	5.3	3.6	7.4	8.4	4.1	6.5
CZE	36.2	12.4	21.0	13.4	10.2	8.8	8.0	10.7	3.1	0.9
EST	132.6	873.6	80.3	39.7	31.7	24.0	10.9	8.9	3.9	5.3
GEO	60.2	1205.1	18032.5	9349.2	162.7	42.2	9.1	5.6	9.2	3.3
HUN	35.7	21.5	21.3	19.5	26.7	21.2	18.5	12.6	8.4	7.5
KAZ	87.5	1611.4	1249.7	1546.7	160.9	38.9	16.1	5.7	13.3	17.4
KGZ	137.9	846.3	763.3	180.8	42.0	35.3	19.3	9.1	37.6	27.2
LVA	156.2	975.9	71.5	38.3	16.0	16.5	6.6	5.5	7.4	4.1
LTU	227.9	943.0	306.2	61.6	38.0	25.1	13.2	6.7	3.2	2.1
MKD	NA	NA	NA	134.0	13.9	2.9	4.0	1.4	2.7	7.7
MDA	142.8	945.0	860.5	278.1	38.7	27.9	12.6	9.4	39.8	27.3
POL	55.3	38.5	30.6	28.4	27.9	18.8	14.0	11.8	6.7	7.1
ROM	195.0	199.9	227.3	139.0	35.3	45.3	147.2	54.2	47.8	44.1
RUS	128.6	1490.0	888.1	307.3	163.1	44.2	14.5	16.3	65.0	40.5
SVK	34.6	11.4	15.3	13.7	9.7	4.5	6.6	5.1	6.6	6.5
SVN	NA	208.0	37.1	22.6	15.2	11.1	8.8	7.8	6.6	5.7
TJK	56.9	630.5	922.7	236.2	285.0	430.6	65.2	87.8	26.5	24.0
TKM	103.0	1941.5	1736.9	1022.1	705.7	1174.3	61.6	17.7	5.0	13.3
UKR	96.2	1766.2	3334.6	953.5	415.5	66.2	18.1	12.1	27.4	23.2
UZB	90.7	712.1	1078.9	1238.6	370.9	81.6	70.5	39.0	44	47.1

Source: WDI (2000), WDI (2002).

Tab. A5 b: Standard Deviations of Inflation Rates of Transition Countries, Percent, 1991-95 and 1996-2000

	1991-95	1996-2000
ALB	97.2	13.8
ARM	1673.6	9.7
AZE	577.7	10.7
BLR	683.0	111.2
BIH	NA	10.8
BGR	74.2	410.3
HRV	610.3	2.1
CZE	10.6	4.1
EST	361.1	8.0
GEO	7875.0	16.0
HUN	6.6	6.1
KAZ	749.7	12.4
KGZ	379.4	11.8
LVA	408.4	4.9
LTU	368.4	9.5
MKD	84.9	2.4
MDA	420.3	12.4
POL	11.5	5.0
ROM	76.4	44.6
RUS	586.0	21.1
SVK	10.1	1.0
SVN	92.0	2.1
TJK	346.6	171.9
TKM	753.2	514.7
UKR	1295.0	21.4
UZB	477.8	18.6

Source: WDI (2000), WDI (2002), own computations.

Tab. A5 c: Inflation Rates of EU-15, Percent, 1991-2000

	1991	1992	1993	1994	1995	1996	1997	1998	1999	2000
AUS	3.7	4.3	2.8	2.8	2.3	1.3	1.2	0.7	0.9	1.1
BEL	3.1	3.7	4.0	2.3	1.5	1.2	1.3	1.6	1.0	1.2
DEN	2.5	2.2	0.5	1.4	1.7	2.5	2.2	1.9	3.0	3.7
FIN	2.5	0.7	2.4	1.3	2.4	-0.2	2.1	3.0	0.5	2.9
FRA	3.3	2.1	2.5	1.5	1.6	1.4	1.3	0.9	0.5	0.9
GER	NA	5.6	4.0	2.4	2.2	1.0	0.8	1.1	0.9	-0.4
GRE	19.8	14.8	14.5	11.2	9.8	7.4	6.8	5.2	2.9	3.5
IRE	1.7	2.4	4.5	1.2	0.5	2.3	4.4	5.8	3.8	4.2
ITA	7.7	4.7	4.4	3.5	5.1	5.3	2.4	2.7	1.6	2.2
LUX	2.3	2.6	0.6	4.7	0.3	1.7	3.3	1.5	2.2	4.1
NDL	2.7	2.3	1.9	2.3	1.8	1.2	2.0	1.9	1.3	3.5
PRT	12.2	10.0	6.7	6.3	5.1	3.0	3.7	3.8	3.3	3.2
SPA	7.1	6.9	4.3	4.0	4.8	3.5	2.2	2.3	2.9	3.5
SWE	7.6	1.0	2.6	2.5	3.7	1.4	1.7	0.9	0.5	0.8
GBR	6.6	4.6	3.2	1.6	2.4	3.3	2.9	3.0	2.3	1.8

Source: WDI (2000), WDI (2002).

Tab. A5 d: Standard Deviations of Inflation Rates of EU-15 Countries, Percent, 1991-1995 and 1996-2000

	1991-95	1996-2000
AUS	0.8	0.2
BEL	1.0	0.2
DEN	0.8	0.7
FIN	0.8	1.4
FRA	0.7	0.4
GER	1.6	0.6
GRE	3.9	2.0
IRE	1.5	1.3
ITA	1.6	1.4
LUX	1.8	1.1
NDL	0.3	0.9
PRT	2.9	0.3
SPA	1.5	0.6
SWE	2.5	0.5
GBR	1.9	0.6

Source: WDI (2000), WDI (2002), own computations.

Tab. A6 a: Progress in Transition for Selected Transition Countries 2000*

	Markets and Trade			Financial Institutions		
Countries	Price liberalization	Trade & foreign exchange system	Competition policy	Banking reform & interest rate liberalization	Securities markets & non-bank financial institutions	Financial Regulation
Albania	3	4+	2-	2+	2-	2-
Armenia	3	4	1	2+	2	2+
Azerbaijan	3	3+	2	2	2-	2
Belarus	2-	2-	2	1	2	2+
Bosnia Herzegovina	3	3	1	2+	1	1
Bulgaria	3	4+	2+	3	2	3-
Croatia	3	4+	2+	3+	2+	3
Czech Repl.	3	4+	3	3+	3	3+
Estonia	3	4+	3-	4-	3	3+
FYR Macedonia	3	4	2	3	2-	2+
Georgia	3+	4+	2	2+	2-	3-
Hungary	3+	4+	3	4	4-	4
Kazakhstan	3	3+	2	2+	2+	3
Kyrgyzstan	3	4	2	2+	2	3
Latvia	3	4+	2+	3	2+	3
Lithuania	3	4	3-	3	3	4-
Moldova	3+	4	2	2+	2	2
Poland	3+	4+	3	3+	4-	4
Romania	3	4	2+	3-	2	3+
Russia	3	2+	2+	2-	2-	3
Slovak Repl.	3	4+	3	3	2+	3
Slovenia	3+	4+	3-	3+	3-	4
Tajikistan	3	3+	2-	1	1	2
Turkmenistan	2	1	1	1	1	n.a.
Ukraine	3	3	2+	2	2	3-
Uzbekistan	2	1	2	2-	2	2

*Range of Indicators: 1 (no or only minimal reform) to 4+ (OECD standard).

Source: EBRD (2000): Transition Report, London.

Tab. A6 b: Progress in Transition for Selected Transition Countries 2000*

	Infrastructure				
Countries	Telecom-munications	Electric power	Railways	Roads	Water and waste water
Albania	3+	2+	2	2	1+
Armenia	2+	3+	2	2+	2
Azerbaijan	1+	2	2+	1+	2
Belarus	2	1	1	2	1
Bosnia Herze-govina	3+	2	2	n.a.	1
Bulgaria	3	3+	3	2+	3
Croatia	3+	2+	2+	2+	3+
Czech Republic	4	2	2+	2+	4
Estonia	4	4	4	n.a.	4
FYR Macedonia	2	2+	4	n.a.	1+
Georgia	2+	3+	3	2	n.a.
Hungary	4	4	3+	3+	4
Kazakhstan	2+	3	2+	2	1+
Kyrgyzstan	2+	2+	1+	1	1
Latvia	3	3	3+	2+	3
Lithuania	3+	3	2+	2+	3+
Moldova	2+	3+	2	2	2
Poland	4	3	4	3+	4
Romania	3	3	4	3	3
Russia	3	2	2+	2	2+
Slovak Republic	2+	2	2+	2+	n.a.
Slovenia	2+	3	3+	3	4
Tajikistan	1+	1	1	n.a.	n.a.
Turkmenistan	1	1	1+	1	1
Ukraine	2+	3	2	2	1+
Uzbekistan	2	1	2+	1	1

*Range of Indicators: 1 (no or only minimal reform) to 4+ (OECD standard).

Source: EBRD (2000): Transition Report, London.

Tab. A7: Ranking of Countries in PISA Study (2002)

Reading Literacy

	Countries	Mean performance on the combined reading literacy scale: Mean	S.E.	Range of possible rank order positions: Upper	Lower
Countries statistically significantly above the OECD average	Finland	546	(2.6)	1	1
	Canada	534	(1.6)	2	4
	New Zealand	529	(2.8)	2	8
	Australia	528	(3.5)	2	9
	Ireland	527	(3.2)	3	9
	Korea	525	(2.4)	4	9
	United Kingdom	523	(2.6)	5	9
	Japan	522	(5.2)	3	10
	Sweden	516	(2.2)	9	11
	Austria	507	(2.4)	11	16
	Belgium	507	(3.6)	11	16
	Iceland	507	(1.5)	11	15
Countries not statistically different from the OECD average	Norway	505	(2.8)	11	16
	France	505	(2.7)	11	16
	United States	504	(7.0)	10	20
	Denmark	497	(2.4)	16	19
	Switzerland	494	(4.2)	16	21
Countries statistically significantly below the OECD average	Spain	493	(2.7)	17	21
	Czech Republic	492	(2.4)	17	21
	Italy	487	(2.9)	19	24
	Germany	484	(2.5)	21	25
	Liechtenstein[2]	483	(4.1)	20	26
	Hungary	480	(4.0)	21	26
	Poland	479	(4.5)	21	27
	Greece	474	(5.0)	23	28
	Portugal	470	(4.5)	24	28
	Russian Fed.[2]	462	(4.2)	27	29
	Latvia[2]	458	(5.3)	27	29
	Luxembourg	441	(1.6)	30	30
	Mexico	422	(3.3)	31	31
	Brazil[2]	396	(3.1)	32	32
	Netherlands[1]	-	-	2	14

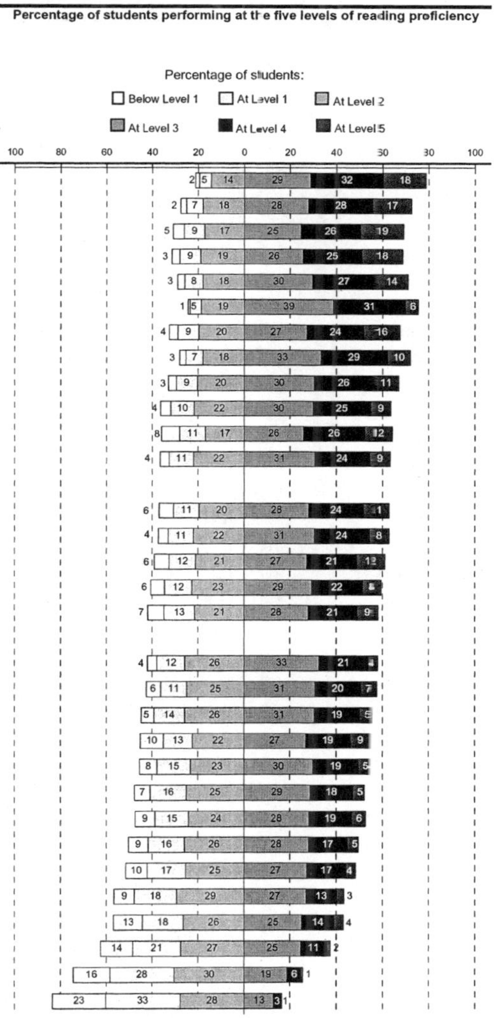

1. Response rate is too low to ensure comparability (see Annex A3).
2. Non-OECD country

Tab. A7: (continued)

Mathematical Literacy

	Countries	Mean performance on the mathematical literacy scale		Range of possible rank order positions	
		Mean	S.E.	Upper	Lower
Countries statistically signficantly above the OECD average	Japan	557	(5.5)	1	3
	Korea	547	(2.8)	2	3
	New Zealand	537	(3.1)	4	8
	Finland	536	(2.1)	4	7
	Australia	533	(3.5)	4	9
	Canada	533	(1.4)	5	8
	Switzerland	529	(4.4)	4	10
	United Kingdom	529	(2.5)	6	10
	Belgium	520	(3.9)	9	15
	France	517	(2.7)	10	15
	Austria	515	(2.5)	10	16
	Denmark	514	(2.4)	10	16
	Iceland	514	(2.3)	11	16
	Liechtenstein[2]	514	(7.0)	9	18
	Sweden	510	(2.5)	13	17
Countries not statistically different from	Ireland	503	(2.7)	16	19
	Norway	499	(2.8)	17	20
	Czech Republic	498	(2.8)	17	20
	United States	493	(7.6)	16	23
Countries statistically significantly below the OECD average	Germany	490	(2.5)	20	22
	Hungary	488	(4.0)	20	23
	Russian Fed.[2]	478	(5.5)	21	25
	Spain	476	(3.1)	23	25
	Poland	470	(5.5)	23	26
	Latvia[2]	463	(4.5)	25	28
	Italy	457	(2.9)	26	28
	Portugal	454	(4.1)	26	29
	Greece	447	(5.6)	27	30
	Luxembourg	446	(2.0)	29	30
	Mexico	387	(3.4)	31	31
	Brazil[2]	334	(3.7)	32	32
	Netherlands[1]	-	-	1	4

Scientific Literacy

	Countries	Mean performance on the scientific literacy scale		Range of possible rank order positions	
		Mean	S.E.	Upper	Lower
Countries statistically signficantly above the OECD average	Korea	552	(2.7)	1	2
	Japan	550	(5.5)	1	2
	Finland	538	(2.5)	3	4
	United Kingdom	532	(2.7)	3	7
	Canada	529	(1.6)	4	8
	New Zealand	528	(2.4)	4	8
	Australia	528	(3.5)	4	8
	Austria	519	(2.5)	8	10
	Ireland	513	(3.2)	9	12
	Sweden	512	(2.5)	9	13
	Czech Republic	511	(2.4)	10	13
Countries not statistically different from the OECD average	France	500	(3.2)	13	18
	Norway	500	(2.7)	13	18
	United States	499	(7.3)	11	21
	Hungary	496	(4.2)	13	21
	Iceland	496	(2.2)	14	20
	Belgium	496	(4.3)	13	21
	Switzerland	496	(4.4)	13	21
Countries statistically significantly below the OECD average	Spain	491	(3.0)	16	22
	Germany	487	(2.4)	19	23
	Poland	483	(5.1)	19	25
	Denmark	481	(2.8)	21	25
	Italy	478	(3.1)	22	25
	Liechtenstein[2]	476	(7.1)	20	26
	Greece	461	(4.9)	25	29
	Russian Fed.[2]	460	(4.7)	26	29
	Latvia[2]	460	(5.6)	25	29
	Portugal	459	(4.0)	26	29
	Luxembourg	443	(2.3)	30	30
	Mexico	422	(3.2)	31	31
	Brazil[2]	375	(3.3)	32	32
	Netherlands[1]	-	-	3	14

1. Response rate is too low to ensure comparability (see Annex A3).
2. Non-OECD country

Source: OECD PISA Study.

Tab. A8: Telecommunication Indicators for Eastern Europe

a) Total number of lines per 100 inh. – Evolution 1996-2000

	1996	1997	1998	1999	2000
Albania	1.5	2.4	3.5	4.5	5.2
Bosnia	8.1	9.3	22.3	26.0	24.8
Bulgaria	32.2	33.0	35.1	38.9	44.3
Czech Rep	29.3	36.9	45.8	57.1	77.6
Estonia	34.9	43.7	53.9	64.1	2.0
Hungary	30.6	37.4	44.0	51.7	60.8
Latvia	30.6	33.2	37.3	42.6	46.9
Lithuania	28.4	35.8	39.0	39.4	43.0
Poland	17.5	21.8	26.7	36.9	44.5
Macedonia	38.9	39.7	40.4	42.2	45.6
Romania	14.2	16.4	19	23.5	32.3
Slovenia	35.6	41.0	48.7	76.1	104.7
Slovakia	23.7	29.6	37.3	47.9	52.9
CEEC Average	20.1	23.9	28.5	35.9	45.0

b) number of mobile lines per 100 inh. – Evolution 1996-2000

	1996	1997	1998	1999	2000
Albania	0.1	0.1	0.1	0.3	0.9
Bosnia	0	0.2	0.5	1.4	2.6
Bulgaria	0.4	0.7	1.6	4	8.2
Czech Rep.	2	5.1	9.4	19.2	38.9
Estonia	4.8	10.5	17.4	26.8	41.1
Hungary	4.6	7	10.6	16.1	29.8
Latvia	1.1	3.1	6.9	11.9	15.9
Lithuania	1.7	7.5	8.9	8.1	10.8
Macedonia	0.5	1.3	2	3.5	8.3
Poland	0.6	2.1	5	10.6	15.5
Romania	0.2	1.1	2.9	6	12.5
Slovenia	2.1	4.6	9.8	33.3	57.3
Slovakia	0.5	3.7	8.7	17	21.5
CEEC Average	1.1	2.6	5	9.8	17

Source: ESIS II Report: Information Society Indicators in the CEEC countries.

Tab. A9 a: Share of Internet Users as Percent of Population in Transition Countries, 1996-2000

	1996	1997	1998	1999	2000
ALB	0.03	0.04	0.06	0.07	0.10
ARM	0.08	0.09	0.11	0.79	1.31
AZE	0.01	0.03	0.04	0.10	0.15
BLR	0.03	0.05	0.07	0.50	1.80
BIH	0.01	0.05	0.13	0.18	0.50
BGR	0.72	1.20	1.82	2.86	5.27
HRV	0.88	1.80	3.41	4.57	5.71
CZE	1.94	2.91	3.89	6.81	9.73
EST	3.45	5.61	10.67	14.42	28.6
GEO	0.04	0.06	0.09	0.4	0.46
HUN	0.97	1.95	3.91	5.87	14.5
KAZ	0.03	0.07	0.13	0.47	0.67
KGZ	NA	NA	0.07	0.21	1.05
LVA	0.8	2.03	3.27	4.36	6.32
LTU	0.28	0.98	1.97	2.92	6.42
MKD	0.08	0.5	0.99	1.49	2.46
MDA	0	0.03	0.26	0.58	1.23
POL	1.29	2.07	4.09	5.43	7.24
ROM	0.22	0.44	2.22	2.67	3.57
RUS	0.27	0.48	0.82	1.03	2.13
SVK	1.86	3.53	9.28	11.12	12.03
SVN	5.02	7.55	10.09	12.59	15.09
TJK	NA	NA	NA	0.03	0.05
TKM	NA	NA	NA	0.04	0.12
UKR	0.10	0.20	0.30	0.40	0.61
UZB	0	0.01	0.02	0.03	0.48

Source: WDI (2002).

Tab. A9 b: Share of Internet Users as Percent of Population in EU-15 Countries and US, 1997-2000

	1996	1997	1998	1999	2000
AUS	3.10	4.46	8.79	15.45	25.89
BEL	2.95	4.91	7.84	11.73	22.69
DEN	5.70	11.35	18.86	28.20	36.54
FIN	16.78	19.46	25.44	32.27	37.22
FRA	2.59	4.29	6.34	9.16	14.43
GER	3.05	6.7	9.87	17.54	29.21
GRE	1.43	1.91	3.33	7.12	9.47
IRE	2.20	4.09	8.08	18.10	20.66
ITA	1.02	2.26	4.51	14.22	22.88
LUX	5.53	7.12	11.72	17.36	22.81
NDL	5.8	6.41	10.19	18.98	24.50
PRT	2.32	2.71	5.02	10.01	24.98
SPA	1.34	2.80	4.40	7.18	13.65
SWE	9.05	23.73	33.45	41.39	45.64
GBR	4.08	7.30	13.50	21.01	30.13
USA	11.19	14.73	21.83	26.63	33.87

Source: WDI (2002).

Tab. A10 a: Internet Hosts per 10000 Inhabitants in Transition Countries, 1994-98

	1994	1995	1996	1997	1998
ALB	0	0.109	0.242	0.324	0.228
ARM	0	0.460	0.466	0.877	1.228
AZE	0.012	0.021	0.039	0.103	0.292
BLR	0.001	0.016	0.249	0.439	0.621
BIH	0	0	0.102	0.159	0.924
BGR	0.161	1.256	3.971	6.635	7.437
HRV	2.246	5.271	10.309	14.782	13.59
CZE	10.059	21.156	39.599	47.655	63.791
EST	7.698	24.111	54.323	45.035	130.702
GEO	0	0.105	0.391	0.549	1.161
HUN	6.652	15.437	29.275	33.302	73.153
KAZ	0.004	0.116	0.507	0.721	0.896
KGZ	0	0	NA	0.233	0.387
LVA	2.057	5.25	23.204	20.996	33.136
LTU	0.341	1.233	4.664	7.451	23.619
MKD	0	0.458	0.975	2.148	2.025
MDA	0	0.012	0.014	0.39	NA
POL	2.793	5.982	13.686	11.225	25.552
ROM	0.23	0.767	3.457	2.659	6.087
RUS	0.441	1.481	3.932	5.506	8.878
SVK	2.648	5.610	14.857	20.357	26.255
SVN	8.18	28.216	69.347	85.878	91.241
TJK	0	0	0	NA	0.093
TKM	0	0	NA	0.004	0.627
UKR	0.102	0.467	1.287	2.074	2.639
UZB	0	0.015	0.053	0.065	0.082

Source: WDI (2000).

Tab. A10 b: Internet Host per 10000 Inhabitants in EU-15 Countries and the US, 1994-98

	1994	1995	1996	1997	1998
AUS	34.0	66.3	110.2	108.3	163.7
BEL	17.2	30.2	64.0	84.6	150.7
DEN	35.4	96.7	202.8	259.3	359.0
FIN	134.1	422.3	613.0	653.6	996.6
FRAU	14.4	26.0	40.6	49.8	73.2
GER	24.4	58.1	84.5	106.7	140.7
GRE	3.4	7.4	16.0	18.8	38.1
IRE	15.4	37.3	74.1	90.2	121.0
ITA	5.0	13.2	25.8	36.8	55.7
LUX	12.5	45.9	84.7	91.4	144.0
NDL	55.9	111.1	174.3	218.9	327.9
PRT	5.1	11.9	23.6	18.2	45.3
SPA	7.0	13.1	28.8	31.0	61.8
SWE	84.3	164	268.9	321.5	430.0
GBR	38.7	75.0	122.3	148.8	0.0
USA	122.1	230.4	381.3	441.8	975.0

Source: WDI (2000).

Tab. A11: Leading Supplier Mobile Telecommunication Operating in Eastern Europe and Russia

GSM Standard Name	Country	Subscribers in Million		Change (percent of Subscribers at 12/31/01)
		12/31/2001	07/31/2002	
MTS	Russia	3.6	4.4	22.2
PTC (ERA GSM)	Poland	4.0	4.2	5.0
Polkomtel	Poland	2.9	3.9	34.5
Vimpel-Com (Beeline)	Russia	2.6	3.7	42.3
Euro Tel	Czech Rep.	3.2	3.6	12.5
Centertel (Idea)	Poland	2.8	3.6	28.6
RadioMobil (T-mobile)	Czech Rep.	3.0	3.1	3.3
Westel Mobile	Hungary	2.8	3.0	7.1
Pannon	Hungary	2.1	2.3	9.5
MobiFon	Romania	2.0	2.3	15.0
Megafon	Russia	1.1	2.0	81.8

Source: Handelsblatt, 09/10/2002.

Tab. A12: PC Density (Personal Computers per 1000 inhabitants)

..	1996	1997	1998	1999	2000
ALB	1.4	2.7	4.0	5.2	6.4
ARM	NA	2.4	4.2	5.7	7.1
BGR	19.1	21.7	24.0	26.6	43.9
HRV	33.4	44.6	55.8	67.0	80.7
CZE	67.9	82.5	97.3	107.2	122.0
EST	68.1	96.0	113.8	135.2	152.9
HUN	44.1	58.0	64.8	74.7	85.3
LVA	20.0	40.3	61.0	82.0	140.3
LTU	27.0	33.7	54.0	59.5	64.9
MDA	2.5	3.9	6.4	8.0	14.5
POL	31.1	38.8	49.1	62.0	68.9
ROM	15.5	17.7	21.4	26.8	31.9
RUS	23.7	29.9	34.6	37.4	42.9
SVK	46.5	69.6	87.2	109.3	136.9
SVN	125.9	188.9	210.7	251.4	275.9
UKR	10.0	11.8	14.0	15.8	17.6
IDN	6.6	7.9	8.2	9.1	9.9
KOR	131.7	150.7	168.8	181.8	237.9
MYS	41.6	46.1	59.8	68.7	103.1
PHL	11.6	13.4	15.1	16.9	19.3
SGP	263.0	331.8	375.1	436.6	483.1
THA	17.2	20.4	21.9	23.0	24.3
AUS	173.7	210.6	233.4	256.8	276.5
BEL	216.6	245.4	286.0	315.2	344.5
DEN	304.7	360.2	377.4	414.0	431.5
FIN	272.8	310.9	348.8	360.1	396.1
FRA	162.0	193.8	232.2	267.5	304.3
GER	208.5	238.9	279.1	297.0	336.0
GRE	35.3	44.7	51.9	60.2	70.5
IRE	209.6	240.4	272.6	315.1	359.1
ITA	92.4	113.3	132.5	157.0	179.8
LUX	370.5	377.6	384.4	390.2	453.2
NDL	231.3	281.1	323.6	359.3	394.1
PRT	67.4	74.3	81.2	93.0	299.3
SPA	78.9	96.6	109.2	119.4	142.9
SWE	294.0	339.1	395.3	451.4	506.7
GBR	216.0	238.9	268.4	302.5	337.8
USA	363.9	406.9	458.8	517.1	585.2

Source: WDI (2002).

Appendix 2: Countries Included in Cross-Country-Regressions

For the cross-country regression in subsection 3.2, we chose countries based on their status as post-socialist transition countries or advanced economies or a certain level of economic development. Further factors for the inclusion of a country were that it has not been heavily involved in war or civil war, and the independence of their economies of export in only one basic commodity.

ALB	Albania	ARG	Argentina	ARM	Armenia
AUS	Australia	AUT	Austria	AZE	Azerbaijan
BLR	Belarus	BEL	Belgium	(BIH	Bosnia/Herzegovina)*
BRA	Brazil	BGR	Bulgaria	CAN	Canada
CHL	Chile	CHN	China	COL	Colombia
CRI	Costa Rica	HRV	Croatia	CYP	Cyprus
CZE	Czech Republic	DNK	Denmark	ECU	Ecuador
EGY	Egypt, Arab Rep.	SLV	El Salvador	EST	Estonia
FIN	Finland	FRA	France	GEO	Georgia
DEU	Germany	GRC	Greece	HKG	Hong Kong, China
HUN	Hungary	ISL	Iceland	IND	India
IDN	Indonesia	IRL	Ireland	ISR	Israel
ITA	Italy	JPN	Japan	KAZ	Kazakhstan
KEN	Kenya	KOR	Korea, Rep.	KGZ	Kyrgyz Republic
LVA	Latvia	LBN	Lebanon	LTU	Lithuania
LUX	Luxembourg	MKD	Macedonia, FYR	MYS	Malaysia
MEX	Mexico	MDA	Moldova	MNG	Mongolia
MAR	Morocco	NLD	Netherlands	NZL	New Zealand
NOR	Norway	PAK	Pakistan	PER	Peru
PHL	Philippines	POL	Poland	PRT	Portugal
ROM	Romania	RUS	Russian Federation	SGP	Singapore
SVK	Slovak Republic	SVN	Slovenia	ZAF	South Africa
ESP	Spain	SWE	Sweden	CHE	Switzerland
TJK	Tajikistan	THA	Thailand	TUN	Tunisia
TUR	Turkey	TKM	Turkmenistan	UKR	Ukraine
GBR	United Kingdom	USA	United States	UZB	Uzbekistan
VNM	Vietnam				

* removed

The cross-section regressions over all countries have hardly come to significant results. This is not surprising in light of the different stages of economic development within the whole sample. To get homogeneous groups with respect to economic development and growth, we made a cluster analysis (partitioning method), resulting in two subgroups *A* and *B*:

Group *A*: Countries with low GDP per capita (and high or low economic growth):

"ALB" "ARG" "ARM" "AZE" "BLR" "BRA" "BGR" "CHL" "CHN" "COL" "CRI" "HRV" "CYP" "CZE" "ECU" "EGY" "SLV" "EST" "GEO" "GRC" "HUN" "IND" "IDN" "KAZ" "KEN" "KOR" "KGZ" "LVA" "LBN" "LTU" "MKD"

"MYS" "MEX" "MDA" "MNG" "MAR" "PAK" "PER" "PHL" "POL" "PRT" "ROM" "RUS" "SVK" "SVN" "ZAF" "TJK" "THA" "TUN" "TUR" "TKM" "UKR" "UZB" "VNM" (54 countries)

Group *B*: Countries with high GDP per capita (and high or low economic growth):

"AUS" "AUT" "BEL" "CAN" "DNK" "FIN" "FRA" "DEU" "HKG" "ISL" "IRL" "ISR" "ITA" "JPN" "LUX" "NLD" "NZL" "NOR" "SGP" "ESP" "SWE" "CHE" "GBR" "USA" (24 countries)

We can characterize the first group as countries with low GDP per capita, and the second group as advanced economies with high GDP per capita. The dispersion of GDP per capita is compared with the dispersion of growth rates so much higher, that the resulting groups only depend on the GDP per capita vector.

Among the countries in group *A* we find the post-socialist transition countries:

"ALB" "ARM" "AZE" "BLR" "BGR" "HRV" "CZE" "EST" "GEO" "HUN" "KAZ" "KGZ" "LVA" "LTU" "MKD" "MDA" "MNG" "POL" "ROM" "RUS" "SVK" "SVN" "TJK" "TKM" "UKR" "UZB" "VNM" (27 countries)
This group we will name group *A**.

Appendix 3: Regression Results

for i = group containing n_i countries, j = last year of six-period-mean = 1999

Note: All variables are 6-year-means from (j-5) until j; for j=1999: from 1994 until 1999.

If time series data are not complete available, the variables can be *(m+1)*-year-means ($0 \leq m \leq 4$) from (j-m) until j; this refers particularly to the SE.tert[i,j-6] variable.

Signif. codes: `***' 0.01, `**' 0.05, `*' 0.1

Equation 1:

$$g_Y[i,j] = \beta_0 + \beta_1 \ln(Iq[i,j]) + \beta_2 Infl[i,j] + \beta_3 gTelD[i,j-6] + \beta_4 \ln(SE.tert[i,j-6]) + \beta_5 \ln(FDI[i,j])$$

Equation 2:

$$g_Y[i,j] = \beta_0 + \beta_1 \ln(Iq[i,j]) + \beta_2 Infl[i,j] + \beta_3 gTelD[i,j-6] + \beta_4 \ln(SE.tert[i,j-6]) + \beta_5 \ln(FDI[i,j]) + \beta_6 gUSPAT[i,j+2]$$

Tab. A13: Regression Results for Equation 1 and 2

	Group	All		Group A		Group B		Group A*	
		Eq. 1		Eq. 1A		Eq. 1B		Eq. 1A*	
k	Variable	β_k	t-value[1]	β_k	t-value[1]	β_k	t-value[1]	β_k	t-value[1]
0	1	2.886	0.790	3.422	0.730	-10.370	-1.643	11.841	1.506
1	ln(Iq)	0.581	0.493	0.626	0.412	2.659	1.831*	-1.116	-0.481
2	Infl	-0.030	-3.071***	-0.027	-2.668***	0.230	2.297**	-0.021	-1.515
3	$gTelD_{-6}$	0.052	0.998	0.052	0.932	0.558	1.681	-0.035	-0.307
4	$ln(SE.tert_{-6})$	-0.583	-1.692*	-0.869	-1.857*	0.793	0.983	-1.895	-1.951*
5	ln(FDI)	0.568	2.352**	0.428	1.171	0.911	3.809***	0.635	0.802
	n_{is}	74		52		21		25	
	multiple R^2	0.3421		0.3662		0.5971		0.388	
	adjusted R^2	0.2945		0.2988		0.4712		0.235	
		Eq. 2		Eq. 2A		Eq. 2B		Eq. 2A*	
0	1	1.295	0.315	1.451	0.270	-7.402	-1.629	8.990	1.131
1	ln(Iq)	1.082	0.808	1.232	0.680	0.185	0.117	0.236	0.078
2	Infl	-0.026	-1.776*	-0.023	-1.524	0.126	2.017*	-0.018	-0.748
3	$gTelD_{-6}$	0.042	0.798	0.037	0.625	0.653	2.419**	-0.054	-0.445
4	$ln(SE.tert_{-6})$	-0.579	-1.682*	-0.798	-1.721*	1.668	2.720**	-2.148	-1.637
5	ln(FDI)	0.557	2.478**	0.382	1.106	0.586	2.265**	0.227	0.262
6	$gUSPAT_{+2}$	0.006	0.970	0.005	0.739	0.126	2.889**	0.014	0.620
	n_i	68		47		20		20	
	multiple R^2	0.2886		0.301		0.7756		0.3573	
	adjusted R^2	0.2198		0.1987		0.6794		0.08179	

[1)] t-values are heteroskedasticity consistent (White-) estimators.

Eq. 1: all countries without GRC, HKG, LUX, SVN, TKM
Eq. 1A: group A without GRC, SVN, TKM
Eq. 1B: group B without HKG, LUX
Eq. 1A*: transition countries without SVN, TKM

Eq. 2: all countries without GRC, HKG, LUX, MKD, MDA, MNG, SVN, TJK, TKM, USA
Eq. 2A: group A without GRC, MKD, MDA, MNG, SVN, TJK, TKM
Eq. 2B: group B without HKG, LUX, USA
Eq. 2A*: transition countries without MKD, MDA, MNG, SVN, TJK, TKM

Note: The only reason for the exclusion of a country is the lack of data for this country in one or more variables.

Tab. A14: Means and Standard Deviations of Regression Variables

		Eq. 1	Eq. 1A	Eq. 1B	Eq. 1A*	Eq. 2	Eq 2A	Eq. 2B	Eq. 2A*
g_Y	mean	3.05	2.93	3.33	2.21	3.24	3.21	3.30	2.70
	sd	2.53	2.80	1.77	3.40	2.33	2.55	1.81	3.17
Iq	mean	22.77	23.29	21.56	22.83	22.73	23 20	21.67	22.55
	sd	5.08	5.46	3.94	4.94	5.19	5 61	4.01	5.18
Infl	mean	19.04	26.34	2.11	41.54	17.44	24 29	2.12	39.85
	sd	32.58	36.70	1.88	45.71	29.73	33.62	1.92	42.99
$gTelD_{-6}$	mean	6.32	7.93	2.66	5.84	6.55	8.32	2.69	6.31
	sd	5.61	6.00	1.40	4.81	5.73	6.09	1.42	5.12
$SE.tert_{-6}$	mean	27.72	21.02	43.26	24.91	27.35	21.01	41.54	25.64
	sd	16.62	11.81	15.90	11.99	15.82	12.09	14.03	12.49
FDI	mean	2.79	2.67	3.05	3.11	2.87	2.76	3.12	3.39
	sd	2.13	1.89	2.63	2.02	2.18	1.94	2.67	2.08
$gUSPAT_{+2}$	mean	--	--	--	--	19.66	22.98	12.24	21.92
	sd	--	--	--	--	30.86	36.37	8.01	31.40

Fig. A5: Means of Human Capital Variable and GDP Growth of Transition Countries

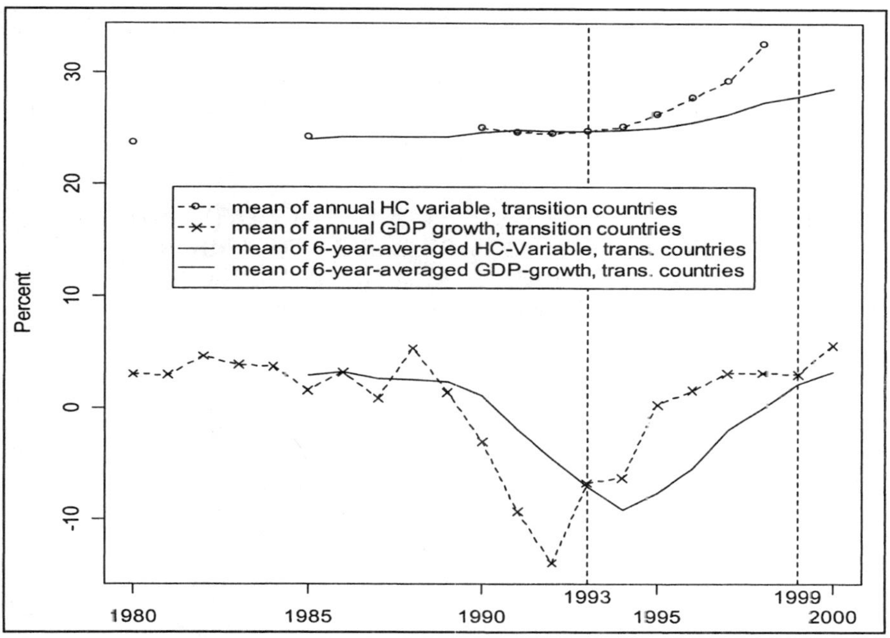

Appendix 4: List of Variables in Regressions and Data Sources

The following Data are from the World Development Indicators Database CDROM (WDI 2002):

gY	Annual GDP Growth	NY.GDP.MKTP.KD.ZG
Iq	Gross Domestic Investment as Percent of GDP	NE.GDI.TOTL.ZS
Infl	Inflation (GDP Deflator, annual %)	NY.GDP.DEFL.KD.ZG
GTelD	Annual Growth of Telephone Mainlines Density calculated from Telephone Mainlines per 1000 people	IT.MLT.MAIN.P3
SE.tert	School Enrollment (% gross), tertiary	SE.TER.ENRR
FDI	Foreign direct investment, net inflows (% of GDP)	BX.KLT.DINV.DT.GD.ZS

The Variable gUSPAT is calculated as:

$$depUSPAT_{j,P} = \sum_{i=1}^{P} \frac{P-i+1}{P} USPAT_{j-i+1}$$

(USPAT depreciated over P years, P=6)

$$depUSPATd_{j,6} = 10^6 * \frac{depUSPAT_{j,6}}{POP_j}$$

(USPAT density)

$$gUSPATd_j = 100 * \frac{depUSPATd_{j,6} - depUSPATd_{j-1,6}}{depUSPATd_{j-1,6}}$$

with

USPAT: data from PATENT COUNTS BY COUNTRY/STATE AND YEAR, UTILITY PATENTS, JANUARY 1, 1963 -- DECEMBER 31, 2001, February 2001, U.S. PATENT AND TRADEMARK OFFICE;

POP: data from WDI 2002: Population, total (SP.POP.TOTL).

References

ARESTIS, P., DEMETRIADES, P.O., LUINTEL, K.B. (2001): The Role of Financial Development in Growth and Investment. Journal of Money, Credit and Banking 33: 16-41.

BANK, M. (2003): Internet Dynamics and Expansion of European Financial Markets: Issues from a Behavioral Finance Perspective. In: BARFIELD, C.E., Heiduk, G., WELFENS, P.J.J. (eds): Internet, Economic Growth and Globalization. Springer, Berlin Heidelberg, pp. 199–248.

BARRO, R.J., MANKIW, N.G., SALA-I-MARTIN, X. (1995): Capital Mobility in the Neoclassical Models of Growth, American Economic Review 85: 103–115.

BENHABIB, J., SPIEGEL, M.M. (2000): The Role of Financial Development in Growth and Investment, Journal of Economic Growth 5: 341–360.

BERG, A., BORENSZTEIN, E., SAHAY, R., ZETTELMEYER, J. (1999): The Evolution of Output in Transition Economies, IMF Working Paper 99/73, Washington DC.

BUCH, C.M., HEINRICH, R.P., PIAZOLO, D. (1998): Southern enlargement of the European Union and capital account liberalization: lessons for Central and Eastern Europe, Kieler Arbeitspapiere 871, Institut für Weltwirtschaft, Kiel.

COHEN, D., SOTO, M. (2001): Growth and Human Capital: Good Data, Good Results, Technical Papers No 179, OECD Development Centre OECD, Paris.

DE MELO, M., DENZIER, C., GELB, A. (1996): From Plan to Market: Patterns of Transition, World Bank Economic Review 10: 379–424.

DEMETRIADES, P.O., HUSSEIN, K.A. (1996): Does Financial Development Cause Economic Growth? Time-Series Evidence from Sixteen Countries, Journal of Development Economics 51: 387–411.

DORNBUSCH (1976): Expectations and Exchange Rate Dynamics, Journal of Political Economy 84: 1161–1176.

EBRD (2000): Transition Report 2000, London.

FISCHER, S., SAHAY, R. (2001): The Transition Economies after Ten Years, In: ORLOWSKI, L.T. (ed): Transition and Growth in Post-Communist Countries, Edward Elgar, Cheltenham, pp. 3–47.

FRANCOIS, J.F., ESCHENBACH, F., SCHUKNECHT, L. (2002): Trade in Financial Services, Financial Sector Competition and Economic Growth, European Central Bank, Frankfurt, mimeo.

FREUND, C.L., WEINHOLD, D. (2003): The Internet and Evolving Patterns of International Trade, in: BARFIELD, C.E., HEIDUK, G., WELFENS, P.J.J. (eds): Internet, Economic Growth and Globalization, Springer, Berlin Heidelberg, pp. 85–104.

GAVRILENKOV, E., WELFENS, P.J.J. (2000): Restructuring, Stabilizing and Modernizing the New Russia, Springer, Heidelberg.

GOLDSMITH, R.W. (1969): Financial Structure and Development, Yale University Press, New Haven.

HARMS, P., MATTOO, A., SCHUKNECHT, L. (2002): Explaining Liberalisation Commitments in Financial Services Trade, European Central Bank, Frankfurt, mimeo.

HARRIS, R.D.F. (1997): Stock Markets and Development: A Re-assessment, European Economic Review 41: 139–146.

HAVRYLYSHYN, O. (2001): Recovery and Growth in Transition: A Decade of Evidence, in: IMF Staff Papers 48, Special Issue, pp. 53–87.

JUNGMITTAG, A., WELFENS, P.J.J. (2002): Telecommunications, Innovation and the Long-term Production Function: Theoretical Aspects and a Cointegration Analysis for West Germany 1960–1990, in: AUDRETSCH, D.B., WELFENS, P.J.J.: The New Economy and Economic Growth in Europe and the US, Springer, Berlin Heidelberg, pp. 99–128.

JUNGMITTAG, A., WELFENS, P.J.J. (2001a): Effects of an Internet Flat Rate on Growth and Employment in Germany, EIIW Discussion Paper 81: Potsdam University.

JUNGMITTAG, A., WELFENS P.J.J. (2001b): Liberalization of EU Telecommunications and Trade: Theory, Gravity Equation Analysis and Policy Implications, EIIW Discussion Paper 87: Potsdam University.

JUNGMITTAG, A., WELFENS, P.J.J. (2002): Telecommunications, Innovation and the Long-term Production Function: Theoretical Aspects and a Cointegration Analysis for West Germany 1960-1990, in: AUDRETSCH, D.B., WELFENS, P.J.J. (eds): The New Economy and Economic Growth in Europe and the US, Springer, Heidelberg, pp. 99–128.

JUNGMITTAG, A., WELFENS, P.J.J.: Auswirkungen einer Internet Flatrate auf Wachstum und Beschäftigung in Deutschland, EIIW Discussion Paper No 75: Potsdam University.

JUNGMITTAG, A., WELFENS, P.J.J.: Liberalization of EU Telecommunications and Trade: Theory, Gravity Equation Analysis and Policy Implications, EIIW Discussion Paper No 87: Potsdam University.

LEVINE, R. (1997): Financial Development and Economic Growth: Views and Agenda. Journal of Economic Literature 35: 688–726.

LEVINE, R., ZERVOS, S., (1998): Stock Markets, Banks and Economic Growth. American Economic Review 88: 537–558.

LUCAS, R. (1990): Why Doesn't Capital Flow from Rich to Poor Countries, American Economic Review 80: 92–96.

MATTESINI, F. (1996): Interest Rate Spreads and Endogenous Growth, Economic Notes 25: 111–129.

McKINNON, R.I. (1973): Money and Capital in Economic Development, Brookings, Washington DC.

McKINNON, R.I. (2000): After the Crisis, the East Asian Dollar Standard Resurrected, in: STIGLITZ, J.E., YUSUF, S. (eds): Rethinking the East Asian Miracle, Oxford University Press, Owford, pp. 197–246.

ROUBINI, N., SALA-I-MARTIN, X. (1992): Financial Repression and Economic Growth, in: Journal of Development Economics 39: 5–30.

SITE (2002): Key Economic Indicators presents macroeconomic indicators for fourteen transition economies of Central and Eastern Europe, Stockholm Institute of Transition Economies and Eastern Europe Economies, http://www.hhs.se/site/oldsite/kei/kei.htm.

VAN ARK, B. (2001): The Renewal of the Old Economy: An International Comparative Perspective, STI Working Papers 2001/5, OECD, Paris, mimeo.

VON WESTERNHAGEN, N. (2002): Systemic Transformation, Trade and Economic Growth, Springer, Heidelberg.

WDI (2000): World Development Indicators 2000, World Bank.

WDI (2002): World Development Indicators 2002, World Bank.

WELFENS, P.J.J. (2002a): Information&Communication Technology and Growth: Some Neglected Dynamic Aspects in Open Digital Economies, in: AUDRETSCH, D.B., WELFENS, P.J.J. (eds): The New Economy and Economic Growth in Europe and the US, Springer, Heidelberg, pp. 29-52.

WELFENS, P.J.J. (2002b): Interneteconomics.net. Springer, Heidelberg.

WELFENS, P.J.J., YARROW, G. (eds) (1997): Telecommunications and Energy in Systemic Transformation, Springer, Heidelberg.

WIEGERT, R. (2003): Transformationskrise, Wachstumserfordernisse und Wettbewerbsblockade in Rußland, Springer, Heidelberg, forthcoming.

Comments on: Investment, Financial Markets, New Economy Dynamics and Growth in Transition Countries*

Natalja v. Westernhagen

The paper considers the issues of transition, economic growth and the role of the new economy in economic growth for transition countries with a special focus on Russia. The authors are particularly interested in the developments which took place in the second half of the 1990s. Considering the success of transition countries in transition, the authors distinguish between more advanced transition economies such as Estonia, Poland, the Czech Republic, Hungary and Slovenia and less advanced countries such as Russia and Ukraine in which the economic growth decline was deeper and the recovery more prolonged. For political, geopolitical and economic reasons, the success of Russia in market reforms is especially important for its neighboring transition countries and Europe as a whole.

Since 2000, Russia and Ukraine have been experiencing positive economic growth. Sustaining this growth in the future will be the main challenge for these countries. In the introduction, the authors point to a number of growth-enhancing factors taking into account a high investment output ratio, the deficit financing problems, gains from trade liberalization and trade diversification, innovation and the process of knowledge diffusion through internet and telecommunications as well as reduction in the vulnerability to the external shocks. These ideas are further developed in the paper and represent the main issues for discussion.

Section 2 presents a comparison analysis of macroeconomic data for transition countries. The transition countries are compared in the paper with Asian NICs and EU-15 countries. Between 1991 and 1995, the majority of transition economies on average experienced negative growth rates and between 1996 and 2000 positive moderate growth rates. How much economic growth can one expect in transition economies in the future, taking into account growth experiences of the relatively poor EU countries such as Greece, Ireland, Spain and Portugal as well as the experience of the Asian NICs? What factors bolster economic growth and what should transition economies avoid in order to ward off financial crises?

The authors confront these questions with their data. Much of the recovery in transition countries depended on initial conditions. Inflation specifically had a significant negative impact on growth at the beginning of transition. Also a high deficit-GDP ratio could negatively influence private investment. The evidence from the data additionally shows that that there is a strong link between investment-GDP ratio and growth rate. Those countries which experienced fast growth rates also had high investment-GDP ratios. Countries which received much FDI considerably induced their capital formation. The authors also analyse a number of

* This comment represents the personal opinions of its author and does not necessarily reflect the views of the Deutsche Bundesbank.

EBRD transition indicators to rank the progress of particular countries in transition.

While looking at financial crisis in Asian NICs, one can derive many parallels in the paper with the Russian crisis as well. A number of empirical works by scholars such as VAN RIJCKEGHEN/ WEDER (2001), KAMINSKY/LIZONDO/ REINHART (1998), and BERG/PATILLO (1996) investigate the determinants and leading indicators of currency crises. Current account/GDP ratio, budget balance/GDP ratio, M2/Reserves, growth of credit to private sector, real exchange rate appreciation and trade linkages are indicators which play a significant role in identifying currency crisis. Currency crisis can potentially cause regional spillover effects. Analyzing Mexican, Asian and Russian crises, VAN RIJCKEGHEN/ WEDER (2001) find the evidence of spillover effects through banking centers to emerging markets.

Growth dynamics are covered by section 3 taking into account the main factors which influence economic growth from the perspective of neoclassical and new growth theory, the role of financial sector liberalization for economic growth and the link between New Economy and economic growth. The theoretical part of the paper which is described in section 3.1 focuses in particular on the three pillars of economic growth. The three pillars are: efficiency of intermediation and stability of financial markets; human capital formation; and innovation and diffusion, especially the impact of telecommunications and the internet. A bright strand of theoretical literature is discussed in the paper on these issues in the framework of neoclassical and new growth theory.

The authors also deliver regression analysis in section 3.2 which link inflation rate, the impact of the investment-output ratio, foreign direct investment, the growth rate of telecommunication density, school enrollment and the growth rate of patents granted in the US on growth in order to prove theoretical issues. The regressions were run for both industrialized and transition economies. The findings, however, differ in regard to industrialized market economies and transition countries. In respect of transition economies there is the problem of missing data which could influence the results but also the problem of the specification could play a role since only the parameter of human capital shows significance but has an unexpected negative impact on growth. In section 3.3 the authors consider a number of studies which point to a positive link between financial sector development and economic growth.

Section 3.4 deals more precisely with the impact of New Economy on economic growth. Thus, considering investment in information and communication technologies raises the question of whether production of technology and knowledge-intensive ICT goods or the use if ICT goods providing for diffusion of knowledge through network effects and reducing information costs will more successfully contribute to economic growth? What is then the relative importance of investment in information and communication technology for transition countries?

BAYOUMI/HAAKER (2002), who investigate welfare benefits from the expansion of the ICT sector, point to the fact that the production of ICT goods and their use goods are highly differentiated across countries. While ICT production is concentrated on emerging countries of Asia, goods are used mostly by industrial countries. The main finding of BAYOUMI/HAAKER is that the relative prices of ICT goods benefit those countries which use ICT goods more than those which produce ICT goods. But there is no consensus among economists in this issue. More empirical research is needed to answer this question for transition economies. Moreover, the authors do present a rather optimistic view as far as the impact of the New Economy on economic growth is concerned and do not take into account some recent negative developments in the ICT sector such as strong decline in the ICT equity prices since 2000 and the fact that important enterprises of the sector face difficulties.

The paper concludes with policy implications. The authors point specifically to the considerable benefits for EU accession countries from EU membership. With respect to Russia, the authors identify insufficient competition policy, weak banking system and bonds markets, the dependence of Russia on oil prices and the natural resource bias which could further reduce manufacturing and the decline in the population of Russia as the main obstacles for sustained Russian economic growth. On the other hand, political stability within Russia in recent years, the increase in trade liberalization and inflows of foreign direct investment, as well as the potential for knowledge diffusion through information and telecommunication technologies are considered promising factors for positive economic growth for Russia in the future.

References

KAMINSKY, G., LIZONDO, S., REINHARD, C. M. (1998): Leading Indicators of Currency Crisis, IMF Staff Papers, Vol. 45, No. 1 (March 1998).

BERG, A., PATILLO, C. (1999): Are Currency Crises Predictable? A test, IMF Staff Papers, Vol. 46, No. 2.

VAN RIJCKEGHEM, C., WEDER, B. (2000): Spillovers Through Banking Centers: A Panel Data Analysis, IMF Working Papers, No. 00/88.

BAYOUMI, T., HAAKER, M. (2002): It's Not What You Make, It's How You Use IT: Measuring the Welfare Benefits on the IT Revolution Across Countries, IMF Working Paper, No. 02/117.

B. Growth Dynamics in Transition Economies: The Role of Financial Development

Markus Neimke

1. Introduction

Since the collapse of the communist system in 1989, the countries in Central and Eastern Europe (CEE) as well as the former Soviet Union experienced drastic macroeconomic changes. Figure 1 illustrates the growth rates of real GDP per capita for individual country groups from 1989 until 2000. The graphic shows similar *u-shaped growth dynamics* of each group. At the beginning of transition, all economies underwent a decline in their growth rates that was pronounced but different in intensity. The countries were able, each after a different time span, to overcome the reduction and to achieve positive growth.

Fig. B1: Growth Rates of GDP per Capita (%)

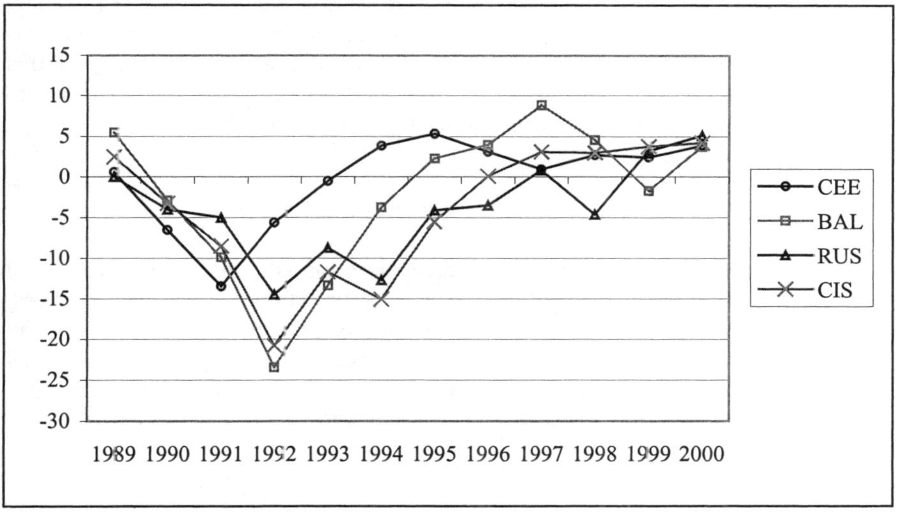

Source: Own presentation, EBRD (1999, 2001).

CEE as well as the Baltic States recovered more quickly than the other transition countries, while it took Russia and the other economies in the Commonwealth of Independent States (CIS) longer to achieve positive growth again. After a renewed decline in 1997/98, all country groups seem to have embarked on a positive course that even seems to point to a convergence of growth rates of per capita income.

Over the past few years, a number of studies have tried to explain the characteristic growth pattern of the transition economies.[1] They have identified complementing determinants belonging to the real and to the monetary sector. This paper focuses primarily on the question to what degree and through which transmission channels a functional and efficient financial sector contributes to the situation shown in Fig. B1, because the financial sector plays a crucial role, e.g. thanks to its function of channelling savings into investment projects.[2] And these investments are themselves relevant for the replacement of the capital stock "inherited" from communist times that has meanwhile become widely obsolete. Consequently, if an efficient financial sector is able to stimulate investments, it can contribute to increasing the standard of living in the transition economies.

2. Financial Development and Economic Growth

This section outlines selective links between financial market development and the real economic sector. In particular, it shows which supplementing transmission channels of the financial sector can be identified. The different approaches to finding causal combinations between financial development of an economy and its per-capita growth rate were motivated by two factors: the upcoming of the "new growth theory" and the detection of empirical phenomena such as the identification of specific convergence processes in the world economy. The aim of this section is not to review the extensive literature on the finance-growth nexus, but to give some intuitive indications on the basis of a simple growth model.

2.1 Transmission Channels of the Financial Sector

In growth theory the evolution of the financial sector as a whole represents only one determinant of country-specific differences in growth processes. Nevertheless, the financial sector appears to have special importance in two ways. First, the financial sector has the function to *canalise savings into investment*.[3] Second, it is possible to interpret the degree to which the financial sector is developed as a measure of something like *broad macroeconomic efficiency*. Thus financial devel-

---

1 See for example BARBONE and ZALDUENO (1997); BLANCHARD (1997); DE MELO et al. (1997, 2001); CHRISTOFFERSEN and DOYLE (2000); BERG et al. (1999); FALCETTI et al. (2002); FISCHER and SAHAY (2000); HAVRYLYSHYN (2001); CAMPOS (2002); FIDRMUC. (2000); MERLEVEDE (2002).

2 The analyses follows NEIMKE ET AL. (2002) and BECKMANN ET AL. (2002).

3 This view is based on the work of MCKINNON (1973) and SHAW (1973). One of the first analyses of the finance-growth nexus is GOLDSMITH (1969).

opment influences total factor productivity and the long-run growth rate.[4] These two characterisations of the financial sector as a determinant of economic growth already reflect the competing approaches of *neoclassical* and *endogenous growth theory*. In neoclassical growth theory, only increases in the level of macroeconomic efficiency are responsible for a permanent growth of per capita income, which is attained by presuming an exogenous productivity growth rate. Consequently, an increase, for example, of the savings rate induces a growth effect that is only *transitory*. Endogenous growth models, by contrast, permit also the possibility of a *permanent* stimulation of the per capita income growth rate. However, the endogenous growth approaches are often not able to explain the convergence dynamics that can be discovered empirically and constitute a special characterisation of neoclassical models.

With the following analysis of the connection between financial development and economic growth we did not attempt to discriminate between neoclassical and endogenous models.[5] The purpose of this section is rather to discuss the different *transmission channels*, identified in both neoclassical *and* endogenous growth models. These characteristics will also be implemented in a simple *integrated growth-model* in the next section.

The degree of financial development can be measured in terms of different components, namely the *size*, the *structure* and the *efficiency* of the financial sector.[6] Indicators that measure the size of the financial sector basically include information about the "depth" of financial intermediation needed to facilitate economic activity and to reduce transaction costs. With the help of structural indicators information about the allocation of resources and the relevance of an economy's different financial institutions can be obtained, e.g. the impact of private and state-owned banks. Using efficiency indicators the level of transaction cost, the extent of information asymmetries and in particular the competition environment can be recorded.

The financial sector affects both driving forces of growth, *factor accumulation* and *efficiency of allocation*. Literature has identified different channels making up the link between the financial sector and economic growth:

- Supply of credits for investment

A developed, competitive financial sector ensures relatively small deviations between lending and deposit interest rates, which in turn enlarges that part of macroeconomic savings that can be transformed into credits for investment projects of the non-banking sector.[7] According to the analysis of MCKINNON (1973) and SHAW (1973), a functioning financial sector ensures high private *saving rates* due to an attractive interest rate. High private savings facilitate investment activi-

---

4 See KING/LEVINE (1993 a, b); LEVINE (1998); RAJAN/ZINGALES (1998).

5 For an extensive summary of this discussion see LEVINE (1997).

6 See KING/LEVINE (1992) for this classification.

7 See PAGANO (1993); BERTHÉLEMY/VAROUDAKIS (1996 a, b); ATJE/JOVANOVIC (1993); KING/LEVINE (1993 b); BENCIVENGA/SMITH (1991).

ties of private firms and enable an economy to grow at a fast speed. This saving rate effect is intensified when the growth dynamics are also driven by human capital accumulation. Hence, the financial sector can raise the formation of human capital through the provision of credit to private households that use such financial means for private education investments.[8]

- Provision of information

In economic theory the task of the financial sector should be, among other things, to channel savings into the most profitable investment projects. A developed financial sector facilitates this if banks and insurance companies monitor investment projects and provide information about potentially innovative enterprises to their customers.[9]

- Insurance of risks

Since more profitable investment projects are usually associated with higher risks, improving the possibilities to ensure against these risks can significantly increase investments financed by given savings.[10] This insurance function is more important the more economic growth is driven by technological innovations that are linked to high sunk costs.[11] Through *spillover-effects* R&D drives the technological knowledge stock of an economy which in turn increases total factor productivity.

To summarise, following economic theory the growth rate is basically driven by factor accumulation and improvements in macroeconomic efficiency, i.e. growth of total factor productivity. A functioning financial sector is in part responsible for the accumulation of input factors as well as for the efficiency with which the input factors can be used. The degree of the financial sector's development can be measured in terms of its size, structure and efficiency.

2.2 A Simple Endogenous Growth Model with Financial Intermediation

Endogenous growth models opposed to traditional neoclassical approaches have the advantage of giving a convincing explanation for the direct influence financial development has on an economy's long-run growth rate. A major disadvantage of endogenous growth models is that they frequently imply parameter dependencies. This results in an immediate "jump" of economies on their equilibrium growth path which is incompatible with the empirical regularity of income convergence that takes a long time. In the model briefly outlined below the transmission channels of a functioning financial services sector can be merged to a theoretically

---

8 See DE GREGORIO (1996) and JAPPELLI and PAGANO (1994).

9 See GREENWOOD/JOVANOVIC (1990); HOLMSTRÖM/TIROLE (1997).

10 See OBSTFELD (1994).

11 See SAINT-PAUL (1992).

consistent approach. Furthermore, the model seems to be capable of analysing the impact of increasing financial market development. The chosen approach is based on a production technology that allows for representative characteristics of both endogenous and neoclassical growth models. First, it includes the empirically observed phenomenon of convergence within specific groups of countries (conditional convergence), derivable from neoclassical models. Second, it implements main characteristics of endogenous growth models with a long-term positive growth rate that are independent of exogenous technological processes. Under the assumptions of the model it is shown that the convergence behaviour as well as the equilibrium growth rate can be directly influenced by the development of the financial market.

The underlying macroeconomic production function Y exhibits constant returns to scale and transitional declining marginal products of capital and labour in F(K,L):

$$(2.1) \qquad Y = AK + F(K, L) .$$

Y stands for macroeconomic output, K for capital stock and L for the labour force of the representative economy. A describes the level of technology or, in a more wider definition, macroeconomic efficiency.[12] In per capita terms (2.1) can be written as:

$$(2.2) \qquad y = Ak + f(k) ,$$

with k standing for capital intensity K/L.

Although decreasing marginal products are assumed for the neoclassical part of the macroeconomic production function - f(k) in (2.2) - the endogenous part Ak guarantees a long-run constancy of the marginal product of capital so that a permanently positive growth rate is generated.

Capital intensity k evolves depending on investment activity I, population growth rate n and depreciation of the existing capital stock δK according to:

$$(2.3) \qquad \frac{\dot{k}}{k} := \hat{k} = \frac{\dot{K}}{K} - n = \frac{I - \delta K}{K} - n = \frac{I}{K} - (\delta + n) .$$

Following PAGANO (1993), the financial sector determines which part of savings is channelled into investment, i.e. into accumulation of the economy's capital stock.[13] Only a fraction λ of overall savings is available for investment activity:

$$(2.4) \qquad \lambda S = \lambda s Y = I \text{ ,with } 0 < \lambda < 1 .$$

The other fraction of savings (1-λ) "vanishes" in the financial sector. According to PAGANO (1993) the financial component in the growth model can be de-

---

12 This kind of production function is based on JONES/MANUELLI (1990). Time indices are suppressed.

13 PAGANO (1993).

scribed, for example, by the spread between lending and deposit interest rates. Therefore, a reduction in this spread, e.g. due to an increase in competition pressure, leads to a rising fraction of savings being channelled into investment. For the evolution of capital intensity this means:

$$\hat{k} = \frac{\lambda sY}{K} - (\delta + n) = \lambda s(A + f(k)/k) - (\delta + n). \tag{2.5}$$

Modification of (2.5) results in a fundamental equation for the capital intensity:

$$\hat{k} = \underbrace{[\lambda sA - (n + \delta)]}_{\text{long-term component}} + \underbrace{\lambda s \frac{f(k)}{k}}_{\text{convergence component}}. \tag{2.6}$$

By means of equation (2.6) a positive dependence of the growth rate on capital intensity can be identified when looking at both the long-term component and the convergence component. The influence of the convergence component decreases in time with increasing capital accumulation due to the decrease in the marginal product of capital. Countries that are already at an advanced stage of development show smaller growth rates than countries whose capital intensity falls relatively far below their equilibrium value.[14] In the long-run (i.e.$\rightarrow\infty$)$\hat{k}$ approaches a permanently positive and exogenous value which is determined by the difference between λsA and $(\delta+n)$. Hence, as conditions for positive growth rate in the long-run the validity of $\lambda sA>(\delta+n)$ must be guaranteed.

In the steady state all considered variables grow at the same rate. Accordingly, the dependence on a convergence component $\hat{y}^t(\lambda)$ and a long-run component $\hat{y}^*(\lambda)$ is also valid for the growth rate of per-capita income:

$$\hat{y} = \underbrace{[\lambda sA - (n + \delta)]}_{\text{long-run component } \hat{y}^*(\lambda)} + \underbrace{\lambda s \frac{f(k)}{k}}_{\text{convergence component } \hat{y}^t(\lambda)}. \tag{2.7}$$

According to (2.7) financial markets influence both the long-term component of the evolution of per-capita income growth and the transitional component. The level of λ is crucial determined by the level of development of the financial services sector. A shift in parameter λ following enhanced financial market development, e.g. because increased competition reduces the interest rate spread, causes a rise in the equilibrium growth rate due to a higher growth rate of total factor productivity. This effect is similar to the efficiency function of the financial sector described above. Moreover, a catching-up process can be identified that results in a higher transitional growth rate on the way to a new steady state. This second

[14] In the context of the convergence discussion it is clear that this means conditional convergence. As a consequence the considered countries that show income convergence exhibit similar characteristics of the other relevant growth determinants.

effect is induced by the accumulation function of the financial sector which stimulates investment into the macroeconomic capital stock. However, the extent of this catching-up effect depends on the stage of economic development a country is experiencing at the respective moment. This means that only a conditional convergence effect can be generated.

Figure B2 represents this way of formulating the finance-growth nexus graphically. Obviously, a shift in the degree of the financial sector's development resulting in an increase in the part of savings that are transformed into investment ($\lambda_1 > \lambda_2$) leads to a higher growth rate. The shift in development can be measured in terms of an increase in the financial sector's size or efficiency, or a change in its structure. Hence, financial market development induces a short-run acceleration of the growth rate of per capita income. Furthermore, the long-term growth rate can be raised as well. The first effect can be called the "short-run growth bonus", the second one the "long-run growth bonus" of financial market development.

Fig. B2: Financial Development Bonus

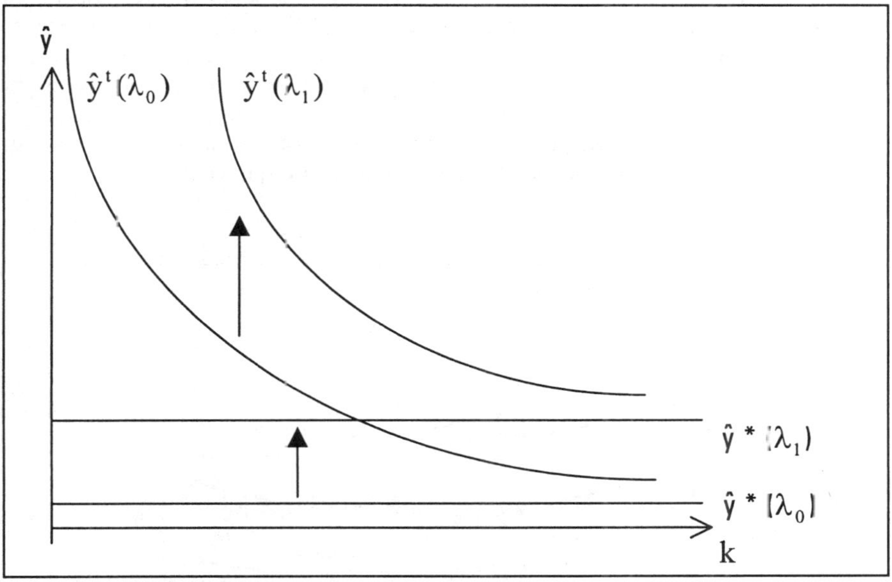

Source: Own presentation.

Financial market development enhances an economy's growth possibilities through the channels mentioned above: higher supply of credits for investment, better provision of information and more efficient insurance of risks. For example, when financial market development is connected with an increase in competition, it leads to lower profitability and overhead expenses (personal and other non-interest expenses) for banks, and this enhances economic growth by promoting banking efficiency. Besides this, enhanced competition in connection with external economies of scale forces domestic institutions to apply more modern human skills and technology. Furthermore, the presence of foreign financial companies stimulates the development of the underlying legal framework as banking supervision and enhances a country's access to international capital.

To summarise, in this section long-term and transitional links between financial markets and economic growth are identified from a macroeconomic perspective in a very simple approach. Using an integrated growth model that highlights both neoclassical and endogenous growth characteristics therefore constitutes an extension of the analysis of PAGANO (1993). This is an important aspect because, based on the convergence component, the entire macroeconomic effect that is generated by a shift in the degree of the financial sector's development results in a greater total growth bonus.

3. Financial Development in the Transition Economies

Before the start of transition from plan to market a functional financial sector to allocate private savings to investment projects in CEE and in the former Soviet Union did not exist. This task was carried out exclusively by state-controlled institutions. Consequently, in order to provide companies with the necessary credit volume at the beginning of the transition process, the economies first needed to establish a functioning financial sector.[15] With the above-mentioned classification, we can analyse the progress achieved based on different indicators.

Fig. B3: M3/GDP (%)

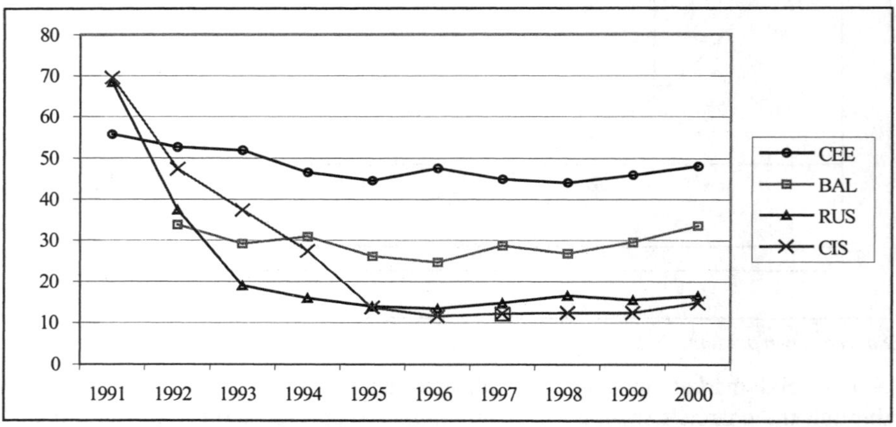

Source: Own presentation, EBRD (1999, 2001).

Size of the financial sector: The *amount of money M3*, as an indicator of the "depth" of the financial sector, has remained largely unchanged in CEE and in the

[15] For an overview, see HERMES/LENSINK (2000).

Baltic countries since the beginning of transition (Fig. B3). Only Bulgaria and the Czech Republic have recorded, since 1989, a significant decline in their degree of monetarisation. Russia as well as the other former Soviet Republics, however, has experienced a drastic decline in domestic money to under 20 % of their GDP. If one assumes that the provision of money is important for growth because it facilitates economic activity and reduces transaction costs, e.g. in comparison to barter, we can certify that especially the countries in CEE have a more favourable position than the remaining transition economies.

In terms of their *stock market capitalisation* the countries of CEE are also in a better position (Fig. B4).

Fig. B4: Stock Market Capitalisation/GDP (%)

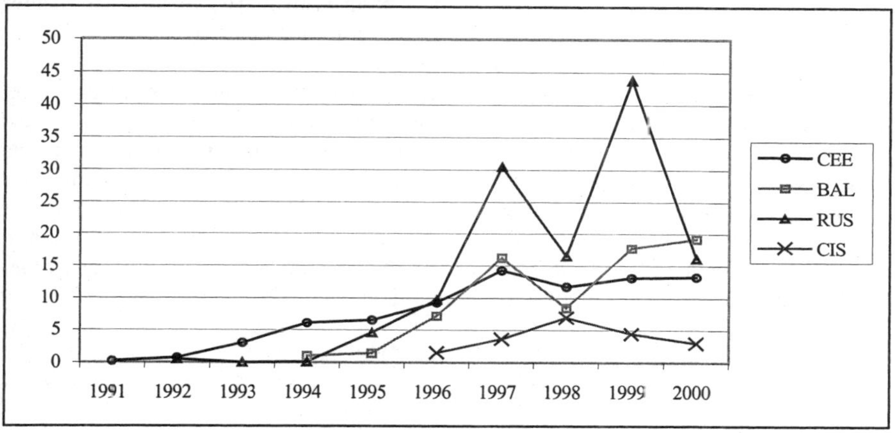

Source: Own presentation, EBRD (1999, 2001).

Fig. B5: Number of Domestic Banks (per 1 Mio. Residents)

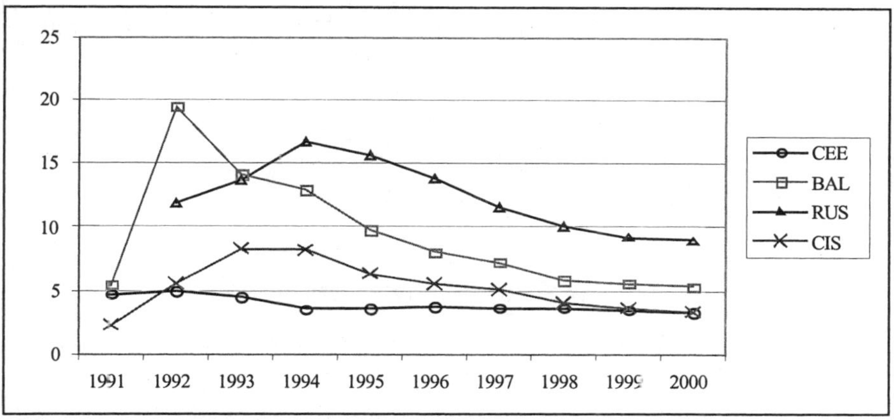

Source: Own presentation, EBRD (1999, 2001).

Particularly Estonia, Hungary, and the Czech Republic show a clear upward trend. Nevertheless, the relative value of all public corporations listed on the stock exchange (as a proportion of GDP), determined to be at 20 %, still remains considerably below the relevant quotients of Western industrialised economies. Because the stock market is of relevance in financing enterprises, further efforts especially to attract foreign investors can be very important. This holds true even more so for the CIS.

Finally, after a rise in the beginning due to privatisation, nearly all transition economies have experienced a significant decline in the *number of domestic banks* (Fig. B5). In Bulgaria, for example, the number of banks has decreased from 79 in 1992 to 35 in 2000. In Georgia this decline is even more pronounced (from 263 in 1994 to 30 in 2000). In the same time span in Russia the number of banks has nearly halved to 1311 in 2000. This development is primarily a result of stricter regulations for banking oversight as well as of numerous bank crises.

Structure of the financial sector: *Loans granted to private companies* are crucial in financing investment projects which, in turn, have a positive influence on long-term income dynamics. This structural factor has widely decreased, in part considerably as Fig. B6 reveals, in the transition economies (with some exceptions like Estonia, Latvia and the Slovak Republic). This has been caused, among other aspects, by more severe equity capital requirements. Even the relevant values of CEE are below those of the Western neighbours where the proportion of loans to private companies and GDP is often more than 100 %. Again, the former Soviet Republics have a greater potential for adjustment.

Fig. B6: Domestic Credit to the Private Sector/GDP (%)

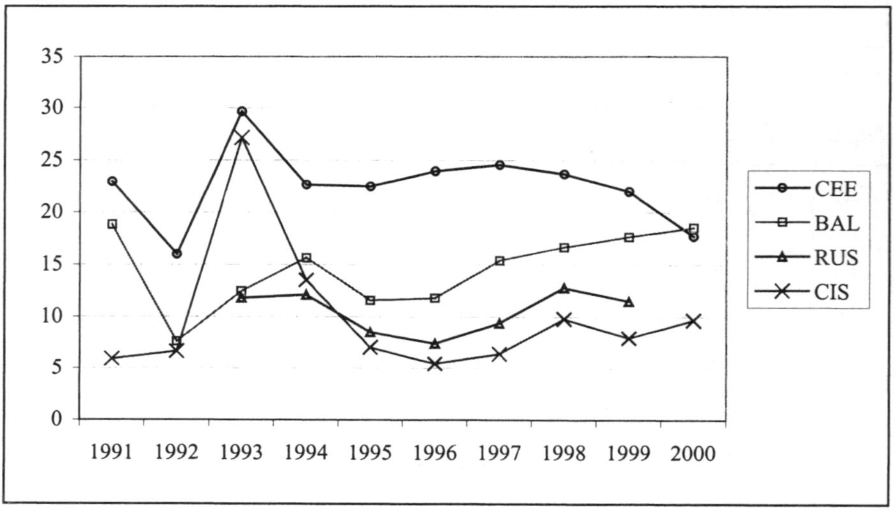

Source: Own presentation, EBRD (1999, 2001).

When taking a closer look at the efforts that the transition economies are undertaking to privatise their enterprises, it is not surprising that the *influence of state-*

owned banks is also declining substantially (Fig. B7). This development should be considered positive because one would expect banks with private owners to guarantee a more efficient allocation of existing funds for investment projects and thus to stimulate economic growth.

Fig. B7: Assets Share of State-Owned Banks (%)

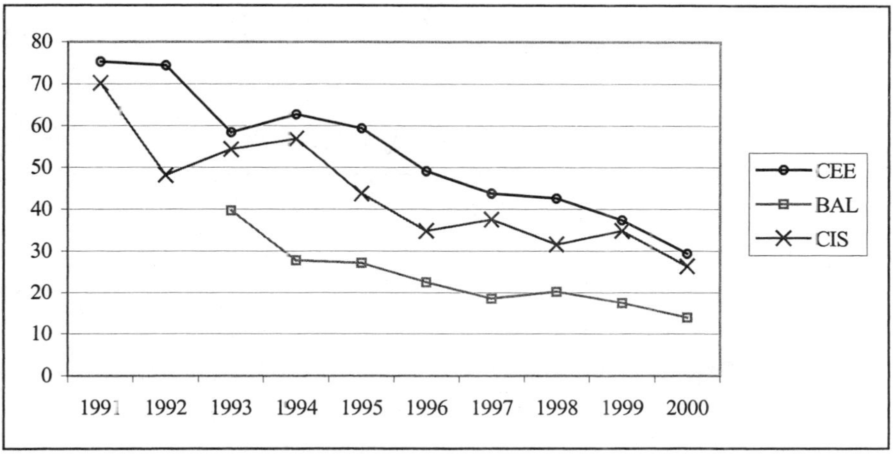

Source: Own presentation, EBRD (1999, 2001).

The biggest success has been recorded in Hungary, where the share of state-owned banks among total bank assets has been reduced from over 80 % to below 10 %, and in Kyrgyzstan (from 100 % to under 25 %) in the last 10 years. Some economies of the former Soviet Union, such as Uzbekistan (78 % in 2000), but also Western states, such as Albania (65 % in 2000) and the Slovak Republic (50 % in 2000), still have a great need for ongoing privatisation.

Efficiency of the financial sector: The relatively high interest rates for loans at the beginning of transition and the concurrent low deposit interest rates characterised a situation of insufficient competition in the banking sector. This implied a poor efficiency of the financial markets. The losses that went along with this inefficiency could be linked to the fact that the volume of financing for investment activities lagged behind the volume that would be possible if based on all existing savings.

As expected, the *spreads* were relatively high (Fig. B8). We observe, however, a considerable decline in interest rate spreads as transformation is progressing, which is mainly a result of intensified competition in the domestic banking sector, driven by privatisation and cross-border capital flows. Meanwhile, almost all transition economies have reached interest rate spreads that are comparable to those in Western industrialised nations. But some economies still need to reverse the continually high spreads, for instance Romania (20 % in 2000) and Albania (16 % in 2000). These are also the economies that still have a high degree of state control of their banking sector and a low intensity of competition.

Fig. B8: Spread between Lending and Deposit Interest Rates

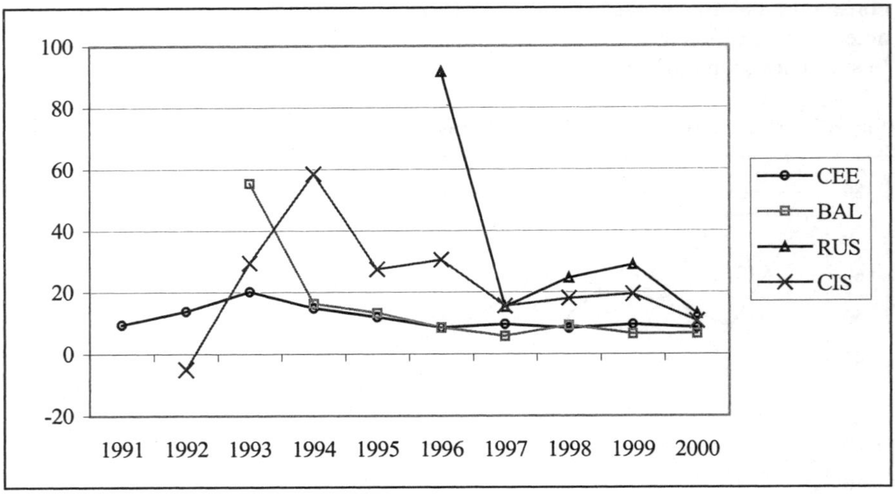

Source: Own presentation, EBRD (1999, 2001).

Fig. B9: Foreign Bank Share (%)

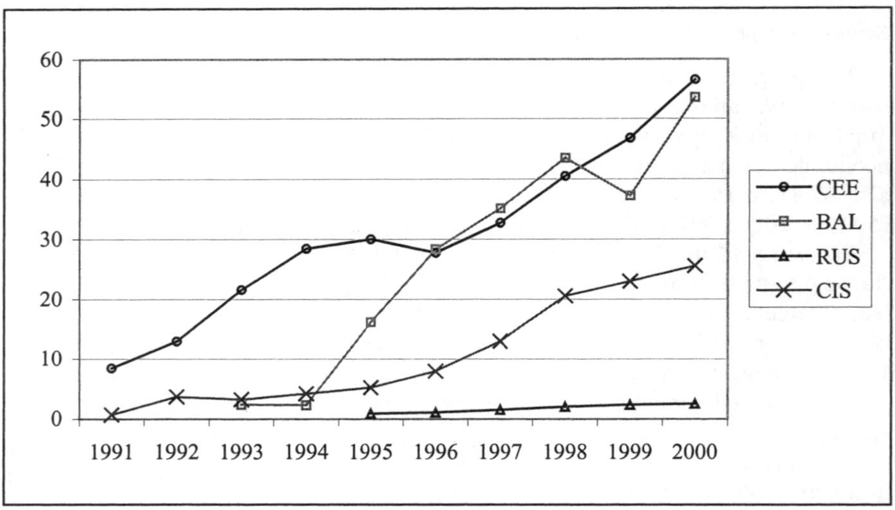

Source: Own presentation, EBRD (1999, 2001).

Moreover, we have seen the *share of foreign banks* rise significantly in all transition economies (Fig. B9). Usually, it is argued that facilitating the entry of foreign financial firms into the local market intensifies competition, improves efficiency and quality of the financial infrastructure, forces domestic institutions to apply more modern human skills and technology, stimulates the development of the underlying legal framework, for example, banking supervision, increases the number of available products, and enhances a country's access to international capital. As such, foreign firms can be seen as an important catalyst for the sort of financial development that promotes growth. It is important to mention that Hungary, with a share of foreign banks of almost 80 %, is one of the economies that were able to reduce state control by privatising significantly. That is to say, former state-owned banks in Hungary are now mostly owned by foreigners. Albania, on the other hand, has a 92 % share of foreign banks, but the share of state-controlled banks among the domestic bank assets is still at a very high degree.

In spite of isolated positive developments in the transition economies, the need for reforms continues to be important, most notably in the former Soviet Republics. Partly insufficient bank capitalisation, inefficient bank and stock exchange supervision as well as the non-compliance with international standards in banking law or minority protection in shareholder rights can be listed as factors that impede the growth processes.

4. Estimation Results

With the help of the simple endogenous growth model in section 2, it has been shown that financial development undoubtedly enhances economic growth. In the last section the theoretical considerations have been supplemented with a descriptive analysis of different indicators measuring financial development in the transition countries of Eastern Europe and the former Soviet Union. In this chapter, the theoretical perception will be combined with empirical evidence. For these purposes it is necessary to employ some econometric analysis. First, this enables us to quantify the direction of possible growth effects. Second, insights into the importance of different transmission channels can be identified, i.e. the relevance of the mentioned influence of financial development for capital accumulation and total factor productivity growth.

The theoretical model stresses the role of capital accumulation as one engine of growth. Actually, detailed empirical studies reveal that substantial investment is of special importance in the transition economies. Only the economies that are able to create a positive investment climate to advance the exchange of the inherited and obsolete capital stock are expected ultimately to achieve high growth paths. An analysis of the investment time series confirms these results. First, before the beginning of transition, CEE and the former Soviet Union were characterised by higher investment quotas than those of Western industrialised nations. But these investments were mostly controlled by state authorities and predetermined by principles of a planned economy. Decisions were frequently not based on the most productive use of the investment but rather on politically-motivated goals toward the development of certain economic sectors or the strengthening of the national military forces.

The collapse of the system necessarily went hand in hand with a *decline in investment* in all countries, which was particularly pronounced in the initial transition phase as Fig. B10 reveals. Second, we have to acknowledge that the transition economies suffered from completely *outdated capital stocks,* which did not fulfil modern production requirements. Therefore, international competitiveness was not given, making sizeable investment necessary to replace the existing capital goods. Despite these similar patterns, the situation is not the same in all economies under study. While we see a relatively quick recovery in CEE and in the Baltics, the investment quotas are falling especially in the former Soviet Republics. Consequently, the long-term growth perspectives there are not very favourable.

Fig. B10: Gross Fixed Capital Formation (% of GDP)

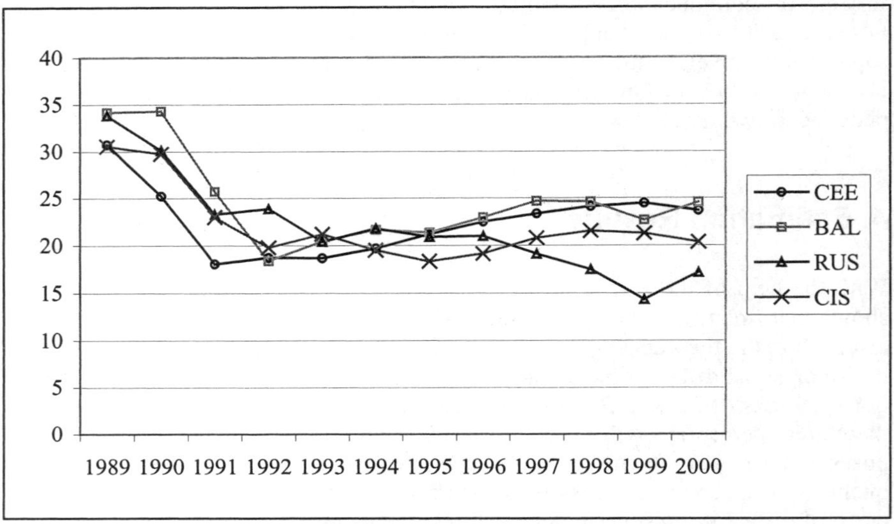

Source: Own presentation, EBRD (1999, 2001), WORLD BANK (2002).

Beside the investment rate, in correspondence with growth models, other determinants have to be considered. First, human capital (HC) is expected to have a positive growth impact. Second, the existing capital intensity is reduced each period due to depreciation (DEPR), including primarily population growth. Third, the neoclassical growth model implies a (conditional) convergence effect, i.e. economies that are far away from their steady-state are expected to grow faster than more advanced countries. Consequently, it must be controlled for the income level at the beginning of the period (STARTBIP). Fourth, when capital accumulation comes to an end and the steady-stare is reached, technological progress (TREND) acts as the engine of economic growth in the long run.

Tab. B1: Estimation Results Traditional Determinants of Economic Growth

	Reg1	Reg2	Reg3	Reg4
C	0.14	-0.58***	-	-0.58***
	(0.56)	(-2.86)		(-3.62)
LOG(STARTGDP)	-0.05*	0.07***	0.10**	0.07***
	(-1.96)	(3.68)	(2.25)	(4.13)
LOG(INV)	0.04	0.04**	0.06*	0.04**
	(0.75)	(2.20)	(1.84)	(2.12)
LOG(HC)	0.55*	-0.18	-0.47	-0.17
	(1.94)	(-0.86)	(-1.05)	(-0.93)
LOG(DEFR)	-0.16	0.02	0.03	0.02
	(-1.28)	(0.44)	(0.47)	(0.43)
TREND	-	0.02***	0.02***	0.02***
		(7.02)	(7.18)	(6.19)
R^2 (corr.)	0.23	0.22	0.23	0.22
Observation	25	208	208	208
Method	cross-section (OLS)	common constant (OLS)	fixed effects (OLS)	random effects (GLS)

The regression results depend on different estimations of a traditional growth equation with GDP per capita growth rate on the LHS. t-values are below the coefficients. *,** and *** refer to different significance values of 10 %, 5 % and 1 % respectively.

Source: Own calculations.

Following the different regression results of Tab. B1, only the investment rate (and the common time trend) shows the expected positive sign using cross-section (*Reg1*) and panel data techniques (*Reg2-Reg4*). Moreover, the coefficient differs significantly from zero in the last three approaches. As a consequence, realising the important role that investment plays in the dynamics of growth, we are faced in the context of this paper with the question of whether the outlined monetary developments have had lasting influence on investment mentioned in the growth model in section 2. Another interesting question, based on the theoretical reflections, is whether we can identify an additional "bonus growth" thanks to an increase in total factor productivity. The estimation of different equations tries to examine this topic in the following.

To identify the impact of the investment transmission channel the relevant indicators measuring size, structure and efficiency of the financial markets in the transition countries are employed with simultaneous consideration of some control variables (Tab. B2). These are at first initial conditions at the beginning of the transformation process (INITIAL), e.g. composition of GDP, years of communism, proximity to western markets etc. It is expected that extensive distortions exert a negative influence on capital accumulation, in particular in the early years.[16] Second, the inflation rate (INFL) measures the degree of uncertainty, so a

[16] Initial conditions are condensed using principle component analysis. The resulting variable is negatively defined, so a positive sign signals extensive distortions. See DE MELO et al. (2001) and FALCETTI et al. (2002).

negative influence on the investment activity is expected. Finally, with the aggregated reform indicator of the EBRD (RI and RI(-1)), actual and lagged measures for price, trade and exchange rate liberalisation – for privatisation of state-owned enterprises and so on – are included. A positive sign is expected for this variable.

Tab. B2: Financial Development and Investment

	Reg5	Reg6	Reg7	Reg8	Reg9	Reg10	Reg11
C	-1.50***	-1.95***	-1.42***	-1.16***	-1.51***	-1.87***	-1.63***
	(-8.18)	(-5.71)	(-9.42)	(-4.88)	(-8.66)	(-9.84)	(-5.60)
INFL	-0.02	-0.00	-0.05***	-0.05**	-0.08***	0.05**	-0.04
	(-0.95)	(-0.08)	(-2.93)	(-2.23)	(-3.58)	(2.04)	(-1.53)
INITIAL	0.01	-0.03*	-0.05***	-0.01	-0.05**	-0.02	-0.05***
	(0.43)	(-1.98)	(-3.36)	(-0.44)	(-3.58)	(1.22)	(-2.95)
RI	-0.90*	0.74	-0.78	-0.44	-0.67	-1.71***	-0.78
	(-1.65)	(1.17)	(-1.61)	(-0.75)	(-1.03)	(3.26)	(-1.20)
RI(-1)	1.06**	-0.06	0.31	0.28	0.35	1.93***	0.66
	(2.37)	(-0.10)	(0.71)	(0.55)	(0.60)	(4.36)	(1.10)
M3	0.18***						
	(3.54)						
STOCKS		0.04**					
		(2.25)					
BANKS			0.01				
			(0.50)				
CREDIT				0.20***			
				(4.82)			
STATE					-0.02		
					(-0.65)		
SPREAD						-0.11***	
						(-3.38)	
FBS							-0.02
							(-0.52)
R^2 (corr.)	0.13	0.24	0.11	0.24	0.17	0.17	0.11
Observations	198	105	197	150	146	165	159
Sample	91-00	91-00	90-00	90-00	90-00	91-00	91-00

The dependent variable in all (pooled) OLS regressions is the investment rate. This variable as well as the inflation rate and the indicators of financial development are employed in natural logarithms. t-values are below the coefficients. *,** and *** refer to different significance values of 10 %, 5 % and 1 % respectively

Source: Own calculations.

Following the regression results of Tab B2, the control variables largely show the expected signs. Obviously, high inflation constitutes a disadvantage to stimulate investment which in turn is connected with low growth rates. The same applies to initial conditions. Lower distortions at the beginning of the transformation process are connected with higher investment activity to replace the obsolete capital stock. Admittedly, not all of the coefficients differ from zero in a significant way. For reforms only in *Reg5* and *Reg10* a significant impact is identified. It has to be mentioned that actual reforms reduce investment activity, but that this reduction is more than compensated by reforms in the last period.

The regression analysis enables us to uncover how different elements of financial market development contribute to investment activity. Obviously, the development of the financial sector is responsible for divergent investment activities in the 25 transition economies under study. With respect to the variables of interest – the indicators of financial development – Tab. B2 reveals that the size, the structure as well as the efficiency of the financial markets influence the investment activity in Eastern Europe and the countries of the former Soviet Union significantly. In particular, the amount of money (M3) has a stimulating effect as well as the stock market capitalisation (STOCKS). From this we can derive the significance of the financial sector's "depth" for investment and thus overall economic growth. The number of domestic banks (BANKS) plays a positive but insignificant role. With respect to the structure, we can determine a significantly positive influence of the credit volume granted to the private sector (CREDIT). This is not surprising if we assume that privatised or newly-founded companies have a substantial need for financing and will use the funds granted to them immediately to build up the necessary capital stock. A large share of state-owned banks (STATE), however, together with an inefficient allocation of existing savings, has a negative (but insignificant) impact on investment. In terms of efficiency, a developed financial sector ensures a relatively small variation between lending rate and deposit rate, which is expressed in a small interest spread (SPREAD). This implies minor losses in the allocation of existing savings for investment projects. The share of foreign banks (FBS) cannot be said to have a significant competitive effect in stimulating investment.

In the next step the impact of the total factor productivity channel in Eastern Europe and the economies of the former Soviet Union, also mentioned in the theoretical descriptions, is tested empirically. To estimate the extent to which financial development influences total factor productivity growth, it is necessary to revert to former results: following growth theory the constants generated in table 1 represent the growth of total factor productivity, often termed as *Solow residual.* Here these country-specific residuals are defined as dependent variables explained by different indicators of financial development.[17] Because we have only one observation for each country, merely a cross-country analysis can be adopted.[18] The relevant control variables are considered as averages over time, with the distinctiveness that CRI is an indicator that includes *accumulated* previous reforms.

Admittedly, the results of the different cross-section OLS estimations in Tab. B3 are not overwhelming. None of the coefficients of the control variables differ significantly from zero. Moreover, the explanatory power of the approaches to explain total factor productivity growth is very low in all seven regressions. The presence of foreign banks now even turns out to have a significant negative effect on the utilisation of other production factors. On the one hand, this can be explained by pointing to the foreign banks' strict requirements concerning accounting, share of equity capital, etc. On the other hand due to data limitations, the

---

[17] The decision to employ the country specific random effects of *Reg4* rests on the result of a Durbin-Wu-Hausman-test, which says that the underlying model is more efficient than a fixed effect model. See for the relevant test procedure GREENE (2000), p. 576f.

[18] For this approach see OLSON ET AL. (2000).

presence of foreign banks can only be measured in terms of their pure number and not, e.g. in terms of their asset share. Anyhow, the analysis reveals that a rise in the number of domestic banks and in the volume of lending to private companies is connected with a "growth bonus" in form of increased total factor productivity. For all other elements of financial development, however, obviously only the transmission channel of investment is remarkable. All in all, we observe the change in factor productivity as another channel to transmit financial development to the economic growth rate of per-capita income in transition economies.

Tab. B3: Financial Development and Total Factor Productivity Growth

	Reg12	Reg13	Reg14	Reg15	Reg16	Reg17	Reg18
C	-0.001	0.005	-0.005	0.120**	-0.001	-0.001	-0.005
	(-0.140)	(0.860)	(-0.990)	(2.340)	(-0.150)	(-0.260)	(-1.070)
INFL	0.001	0.000	0.001	0.001	0.001	0.001	0.000
	(1.110)	(0.600)	(0.860)	(1.580)	(0.760)	(0.570)	(0.510)
INITIAL	0.000	-0.000	0.000	0.001	0.000	0.000	0.000
	(0.620)	(-0.640)	(0.410)	(1.450)	(0.500)	(0.690)	(0.290)
CRI	0.000	-0.001	0.000	-0.001	0.000	0.000	0.000
	(0.240)	(-0.930)	(0.001)	(-1.070)	(-0.070)	(0.320)	(0.350)
M3	0.001						
	(0.320)						
STOCKS		0.000					
		(0.180)					
BANKS			0.001**				
			(2.130)				
CREDIT				0.004***			
				(3.810)			
STATE					-0.001		
					(-0.950)		
SPREAD						0.000	
						(0.640)	
FBS							-0.002**
							(-2.290)
R^2 (corr.)	0.040	-0.110	0.220	0.480	0.080	0.050	0.240
Observations	25	20	25	24	25	25	25

The dependent variable of all OLS regressions is the country-specific random effect of Reg4 which corresponds to total factor productivity growth. The inflation rate and the indicators of financial development are all employed in natural logarithms. t-values are below the coefficients. *,** and *** refer to different significance values of 10 %, 5 % and 1 % respectively.

Source: Own calculations.

5. Conclusions

Theoretical explanations on the basis of neoclassical and endogenous approaches as well as empirical results point to financial markets having significant effects on investment and the development of factor productivity as the foundation for long-term positive growth. This is particularly true for Central and Eastern Europe as well as the former Soviet Union, economies that are suffering, on the one hand, from sharp declines in their growth rates and have inherited widely obsolete capital stocks on the other hand.

In accordance with existing studies, we can depict the financial sector of the transition economies with the help of appropriate macroeconomic indicators. These indicators are divided into the categories size, structure, and efficiency. By doing so, we can gain far-reaching new insights into the transition process, for instance great progress among the CEE countries in approaching Western financial market, and by this increasing investment and growth significantly. At the same time, however, the republics of the former Soviet Union continue to require reforms and changes in their economic policy that facilitates financial development. All in all, the continuous establishment of functional and efficient financial markets plays an important role in guiding the transition economies into the direction of higher growth paths and better standards of living.

References

ATJE, R. and JOVANOVIC, B. (1993): Stock Markets and Development, European Economic Review, Vol. 37, 632-640.

BARBONE, L., ZALDUENO, J. (1997): EU Accession and Economic Growth: The Challenge for Central and Eastern European Countries, Working Paper, No. 1721, World Bank: Washington D.C.

BECKMANN, R., EPPENDORFER, C., KÖSTERS, W., NEIMKE, M. (2000): A Single European Market for Financial Services: Integration Trends and Growth Effects, in LANG, F. P. and OHR, R., eds., Integration, Währung und Wachstum - Dimensionen internationaler Wirtschaftsbeziehungen, Berlin.

BENCIVENGA, V. R., SMITH, B. D. (1991): Financial Intermediation and Endogenous Growth, Review of Economic Studies, Vol. 58, 195-209.

BERG, A., BORENSZTEIN, E., SAHAY, R., ZETTELMEYER, J. (1999): The Evolution of Output in Transition Economies: Explaining the Differences, Working Paper, No. 73/99, International Monetary Fund: Washington D.C.

BERTHÉLEMY, J. C., VAROUDAKIS, A. (1996a): Economic Growth, Convergence Clubs, and the Role of Financial Development, Oxford Economic Papers, Vol. 48, 300-328.

BERTHÉLEMY, J. C., VAROUDAKIS, A. (1996b): Models of Financial Development and Growth. A Survey of Recent Literature, in HERMES, N. and LENSINK, R., eds., Financial Development and Economic Growth, London, 7-43.

BLANCHARD, O. (1997): The Economics of Post-Communist Transition, Oxford.

CAMPOS, N. F. (2002): Growth in Transition: What We Know, What We Don't and What We Should, Discussion Paper, No. 3246, Centre for Economic Policy Research: London.

CHRISTOFFERSEN, P., DOYLE, P. (2000): From Inflation to Growth: Eight Years of Transition, The Economics of Transition, Vol. 8 (2), 421-451.

DE GREGORIO, J. (1996): Borrowing Constraints, Human Capital Accumulation, and Growth, Journal of Monetary Economics, Vol. 37, 49-71.

DE MELO, M., DENIZER, C., GELB, A. (1997): From Plan to Market: Patterns of Transition, in BLEJER, M. I. and SKREB, M., eds., Macroeconomic Stabilization in Transition Economies, Cambridge, 17-72.

DE MELO, M., DENIZER, C., GELB, A., TENEV, S. (2001): Circumstances and Choice: the Role of Initial Conditions and Policies in Transition Economies, The World Bank Economic Review, Vol. 15 (1), 1-31.

EBRD (1999): Transition Report 1999, European Bank for Reconstruction and Development: London.

EBRD (2001): Transition Report 2001, European Bank for Reconstruction and Development: London.

FALCETTI, E., RAISER, M., SANFEY, P. (2002): Defying the Odds: Initial Conditions, Reforms, and Growth in the First Decade of Transition, Journal of Comparative Economics, Vol. 30 (2), 229-250.

FIDRMUC, J. (2000): Economic Reform, Democracy and Growth During Post-Communist Transition, Discussion Paper 2759, Centre for Economic Policy Research: London.

FISCHER, S., SAHAY, R. (2000): The Transition Economies after Ten Years, Working Paper, No. 30/00, International Monetary Fund: Washington D.C.

GOLDSMITH, R. W. (1969): Financial Structure and Development, New Haven.
GREENE, W. H. (2000): Econometric Analysis, Upper Saddle River, New Jersey.
GREENWOOD, J., JOVANOVIC, B. (1990): Financial Development, Growth, and the Distribution of Income, Journal of Political Economy, Vol. 98, 1076-1107.
HAVRYLYSHYN, O. (2001): Recovery and Growth in Transition: A Decade of Evidence, IMF Staff Papers, No. 48, 53-87.
HERMES, N., LENSINK, R. (2000): Financial System Development in Transition Economies, Journal of Banking and Finance, Vol. 24, 507-524.
HOLMSTRÖM, B., TIROLE, J. (1997): Financial Intermediation, Loanable Funds, and the Real Sector, Quarterly Journal of Economics, Vol. 112, 663-691.
JAPPELLI, T., PAGANO, M. (1994): Saving, Growth, and Liquidity Constraints, Quarterly Journal of Economics, Vol. 109, 83-109.
JONES, L. E., MANUELLI, R. E. (1990): A Convex Model of Equilibrium Growth: Theory and Policy Implications, Journal of Political Economy, Vol. 98 (5), 1008-1038.
KING, R.G., LEVINE, R. (1992): Financial Indicators and Growth in a Cross Section of Countries, Working Paper, No. 819, World Bank: Washington D.C.
KING, R.G., LEVINE, R. (1993a): Finance and Growth. Schumpeter Might Be Right, Quarterly Journal of Economics, Vol. 108, 717-738.
KING, R.G., LEVINE, R. (1993b): Finance, Entrepreneurship and Growth. Theory and Evidence, Journal of Monetary Economics, Vol. 32, 513-542.
LEVINE, R. (1997): Financial Development and Economic Growth: Views and Agenda, Journal of Economic Literature, Vol. 35, 688-726.
LEVINE, R. (1998): The Legal Environment, Banks, and Long-Run Economic Growth, Journal of Money, Credit, and Banking, Vol. 30, 597-620.
MCKINNON, R. I. (1973): Money and Capital in Economic Development, Washington D.C.
MERLEVEDE, B. (2002): Stabilisation, Reform, Initial Conditions and Output Paths in Transition Economies, in CHAREMZA, W. W., ed., East European Transition and EU Enlargement: A Quantitative Approach, 179-198.
NEIMKE, M., EPPENDORFER, C., BECKMANN, R. (2002): Deepening European Financial Integration - Theoretical Considerations and Empirical Evaluation of Growth and Employment Benefits, Discussion Paper 42, Institute for European Economy: Bochum.
OBSTFELD, M. (1994): Risk Taking, Global Diversification and Growth, American Economic Review, Vol. 84(5), 1310-1329.
OLSON, M., SARNA, N., SWAMY, A. (2000): Governance and Growth: A Simple Hypothesis Explaining Cross-Country Differences in Productivity Growth, Public Choice, Vol. 102, 34-364.
PAGANO, M. (1993): Financial Markets and Growth. An Overview, European Economic Review, Vol. 37, 613-622.
RAJAN, R. G., ZINGALES, L. (1998): Financial Dependence and Growth, American Economic Review, Vol. 88, 559-586.
SAINT-PAUL, G. (1992): Technological Choice, Financial Markets and Economic Development, European Economic Review, Vol. 36, 763-781.
SHAW, E. S. (1973): Financial Deepening in Economic Development, New York.
WORLD BANK (2002): World Development Indicators, Washington D.C.

Comments on: Growth Dynamics in Transition Countries: The Role of Financial Development

Andre Jungmittag

The paper of Markus Neimke seeks to identify the relative contributions of the monetary developments to the explanation of income dynamics in transition countries beyond the former Iron Curtain. Like the transformation process in these countries itself, the paper has two aspects. On that one hand, it first provides a short but informative survey of the different transmission channels through which the financial sector affects total economic growth. The reader also receives a comprehensive impression of different financial indicators that should capture the development of the financial sectors in the transition countries. These indicators are carefully interpreted in a descriptive analysis.

On the other hand, Neimke ties in an econometric analysis to assess the impact of financial indicator variables on economic growth in the transition countries. Clearly, due to data availability and the reliability of econometric analyses in transition countries is always a walk on the edge between desirability and feasibility, however, the author falls into some traps that can be bypassed.

The econometric analysis in the paper is divided into two parts. In the first part, a empirically feasible form of the augmented neoclassical Solow model is estimated, on the one hand, for a cross-section dataset, and, on the other hand, for a panel dataset of 25 transition countries. Based on theoretical reasoning that the financial sector can affect economic growth in such a framework via investment and total factor productivity, both are explained with different models in the second part using financial indicator variables as well as other explanatory variables.

Neimke estimated the empirically-feasible counterpart of the theoretical Solow model for the cross-section as well as for the panel dataset by means of OLS and the latter also by means of GLS (random effects model). However, these kind of models always contain a lagged endogenous variable, namely the initial per capita (or per worker) income (labeled as BASISBIP in the paper of Neimke). In a cross-section framework, the OLS estimator can actually be used, but in a panel data framework the problem with the estimation of such models occurs with the lagged dependent variable and the country specific effects correlated; this correlation persists even in large samples (cf. Lee/Longmire/Mátyás et al., 1998).[1] Therefore, the usual estimators used for panel data models (OLS, FGLS, Between) are biased here and inconsistent, and the Within estimator is only consistent when both N and $T \rightarrow \infty$, which is surely not given for the countries and time span under consideration. From several simulation studies, it is well-known that the omission of country-specific effects (pooled OLS) induces an upward bias in the estimate of β in a

---

[1] There are also some unsolved estimation problems with regard to the cross-section regressions, e.g. the treatment of country-specific effects and the issue of endogeneity (cf. CASELLI/ESQUIVEL/LEFORT, 1996).

dynamic model $y_{it} = \beta y_{i,t-1} + \mathbf{X}_{it}\gamma + \eta_i + \varepsilon_{it}$, with translates into a downward bias in the estimate of the convergence coefficient β-1. On the other hand, the Within estimator introduces a downward bias in the estimate of β, whose size depends on the value of the true β and T, if $N \rightarrow \infty$ (Nickell, 1981). Based on the calculated asymptotic values of $\hat{\beta}$ for different β and T (e.g. for β=0.9 and T10) in the works of Nickell (1981) and Breitung (1992), the asymptotic value of $\hat{\beta}$ is 0.657. In the literature, some instrument variable estimators are suggested whose usefulness, however, is limited to the context of growth regression, because they are only consistent if $N \rightarrow \infty$ (e.g. Anderson/Hsiao, 1982; Arellano, 1988, Arellano/Bond, 1991).[2] Furthermore, Blundell/Bond (1998) show that estimators relying on lagged levels as instruments for current differences are likely to perform poorly when the variables are close to a random walk (which is rather likely for GDP per capita). Alternatively, they suggest estimating a system combining two sets of equations, one set of differenced equations and another set of level equations. This system GMM estimator is more efficient than the differenced GMM estimator, provided that certain restrictions are valid.[3]

In view of the use of biased and inconsistent estimators, Neimke's conclusion that the investment ratio is an important determinant of economic growth in the transition countries seems to be doubtful, because already in his estimations this variable is only moderately significant. This does not mean that investment actually has no impact, but we cannot draw any conclusion from the presented results. Furthermore, no evidence is presented that total factor productivities differ between the transition countries. Based on the OLS and RE estimates, average log-level of TFP is -0.58+0.02t, but the adjusted R^2 is the same for both estimates, and for the FE estimate it is only slightly higher. Also, no statistics are presented that show the significance of fixed country effects.

In the next step, Neimke considers the impact of the development of financial markets on investment. In this regression he used a variable "initial condition", which is the first factor calculated by a principal components analysis based on eight "initial condition" variables. Neimke justifies this because high multicollinearity can be expected for these variables and notices that this first factor already explains 50 % of the total variance of all initial conditions. Indeed, this way of reducing variables is proposed in some textbooks to remedy multicollinearity. In this approach, attributed to Kendall (1957), correlated explanatory variables are replaced by a smaller number of artificial but orthogonal variables. The estimates of the regression coefficients of the orthogonal components can be used to calculate estimates of the parameters in the original model. Farrar/Glauber (1967) argued that the usefulness of this approach is only given if the artificial variables can be "directly identified with meaningful economic phenomena." In other cases, more information and not a reduction of available information is needed to solve the multicollinearity problem.

---

2 A survey can be found in BALTAGI (1995).

3 Applications of the system GMM estimator to growth regressions can be found e.g. in AMABLE (2000) and HOEFFLER (2000).

However, even if the artificial variable has a natural interpretation – as is the case here – the problem occurs that this procedure introduces a bias into the estimation if not all extracted factors, which explain the total variance of the original variables, are included in the regression. To sketch this problem, let us suppose the model to be estimated is:

(1) $$\mathbf{y} = \mathbf{X}\beta + \varepsilon,$$

where **y** is a Tx1 vector of observations on the dependent variable, **X** is a TxK matrix of observations of the independent variables, β is the Kx1 vector of the parameters to be estimated, and ε is a Tx1 vector of the error terms. We assume that **X** is of rank K but that multicollinearity exists, i.e., that the variables of **X** are not orthogonal.[4] Furthermore, $\mathbf{P}=(\mathbf{p}_1,\ldots,\mathbf{p}_K)$ is an orthogonal matrix of eigenvectors of **X'X**, thus

(2) $$\mathbf{y} = \mathbf{X}\beta + \varepsilon = (\mathbf{XP})(\mathbf{P}'\beta) + \varepsilon = \mathbf{Z}\theta + \varepsilon,$$

where $\mathbf{Z} = \mathbf{XP}$ is the matrix of principal components:

(3) $$\mathbf{z}_\mathrm{i} = \mathbf{X}\mathbf{p}_\mathrm{i} = \mathbf{x}_1 p_{1i} + \mathbf{x}_2 p_{2i} + \ldots + \mathbf{x}_\mathrm{K} p_{Ki}$$

and

(4) $$\mathbf{Z}'\mathbf{Z} = \Lambda = \mathrm{diag}(\lambda_1,\ldots,\lambda_K),$$

where λ_i, i=1,…,K are the eigenvalues of **X'X**. Applying OLS to the principal components model yields

(5) $$\hat{\theta} = (\mathbf{Z}'\mathbf{Z})^{-1}\mathbf{Z}'\mathbf{y} = \Lambda^{-1}\mathbf{Z}'\mathbf{y} \text{ and } \mathrm{var}(\hat{\theta}_i) = \sigma^2/\lambda_i.$$

It follows immediately that the estimates of the original parameters β are

(6) $$\hat{\beta} = \mathbf{P}\hat{\theta} \text{ with } \mathrm{cov}(\hat{\beta}) = \sigma^2\mathbf{P}\Lambda^{-1}\mathbf{P} = \sigma^2\sum_{i=1}^{K}\lambda_i^{-1}\mathbf{p}_\mathrm{i}'\mathbf{p}_\mathrm{i}$$

and for the estimate $\hat{\beta}_j$ of an individual coefficient β_j :

(7) $$\mathrm{var}(\hat{\beta}_j) = \sigma^2\sum_{i=1}^{k}\frac{p_{ij}^2}{\lambda_i}.$$

Now, let $\hat{\beta}^*_j(h)$ be the principal component estimator of β_j obtained by the deletion of the component h. Then **var**($\hat{\beta}_j$) will exceed **var**($\hat{\beta}^*_j(h)$) by the positive amount $\sigma^2 p_{hj}^2/\lambda_h$. Thus, the component estimator has a smaller variance than $\hat{\beta}_j$, and

[4] The following arguments draw heavily on MCCALLUM (1970). See also CHENG/IGLARSH (1976).

it will have a smaller mean square error (MSE) for some values of β_j On the one hand, however, it is not clear how many and which components should be deleted. The MSE criterion does not imply a necessity in deleting either the components with the smallest variances or those with the smallest *t*-values. On the other hand, the deletion of some components leads to biased estimates and the magnitude of the bias depends on the true coefficients. Thus, the MSE criterion is not operational in practice.[5] The MSE is:

(8) $$\sigma^2 \sum_{i \neq h} \frac{p_{ik}^2}{\lambda_i} + \left[\hat{\beta}_j^*(h) - \beta_j \right]^2$$

and the magnitude of the bias $E(\hat{\beta}_j^*(h))-\beta_j$ depends in general on the true values of all K regression coefficients. This can be seen if $E(\hat{\beta}) = \beta = \mathbf{P}\theta$ and $E(\hat{\beta}) = \mathbf{P}^*\theta = \mathbf{P}^*\mathbf{P}'\beta = \mathbf{P\theta}$ are compared. The bias of the vector $\hat{\beta}^*$ is then $(\mathbf{P}^*\text{-}\mathbf{P})\theta$ and for $\hat{\beta}_j^*(h)$:

(9) $$\sum_{i \neq h} p_{ij}\theta_i - \sum_{i=1}^{K} p_{ij}\theta_i = -p_{hj}\theta_h = -p_{hj}\sum_{i=1}^{K} p_{hi}\beta_i,$$

e.g. a linear combination of the true parameters and the coefficients determined by the eigenvectors of the regressor matrix. Therefore, $\hat{\beta}_j^*(h)$ will sometimes have smaller, and sometimes larger, MSE than $E(\hat{\beta}_j)$, and it is impossible to always select the better of the two estimators. However for two regressors, it can be shown that the principal component estimator will tend to outperform the LS estimator, the higher is the regressor correlation, on the one hand, and on the other, the smaller is the number of observations.

It would be very helpful if Neimke would have discussed and evaluated this trade-off before applying the principal components regression. In the case where the principal component captures 50% of the total variance, the bias might be rather considerable. Even if he is not interested in the estimation of the original coefficients of the "initial conditions" variables, there are further implications. Omitting a large part of the "initial conditions" might lead to an omitted variables problem, thereby hampering conclusions with regard to the other variables in his model (cf. Harvey, 1994). Assume that the true model is:

(10) $$y_t = \alpha + \beta x_t + \gamma q_t,$$

where in our case q_t captures the initial conditions not included in the principal component, and it is wrongly assumed that γ=0. Then the estimate of β in general will be biased, because if $\tilde{\beta}$ is the estimate of a regression of y_t on x_t:

---

[5] CHENG/IGLARSH (1976) propose an alternative criterion by comparing the probabilities that the estimates lie in an interval of radius *r* around the true coefficient, with *r* being determined by the researcher himself.

(11) $$E(\tilde{\beta}) = \beta + \gamma \frac{\sigma_{qx}}{\sigma_x^2},$$

where σ_{qx} is the covariance of q_t and χ_t, and σ^2_x is the variance of χ_t. Thus no valid conclusions with regard to the other variables are possible if q_t and χ_t are not orthogonal. However, it is rather likely that the other variables are to a certain extent correlated with the "initial conditions".[6]

The arguments just presented also hold for the TFP regressions. Additionally, the question is whether TFP differences are actually statistically significant, something that cannot be seen from Table 1. Furthermore, the author maintains that the random effects capture TFP of the individual countries. However, they only capture "potential" differences, because the estimate of log(TFP) is -0.58 + 0.02t + *RE*, but this would only change the intercept of the TFP regression.

To conclude, the paper of Neimke offers some new ideas to investigate the links between the development of financial markets and growth in transition countries, which could stimulate the discussion and carefully further empirical research. If that happens, Neimke's paper will have achieved its aim.

---

[6] For a discussion of this argument with regard to Barro's growth regressions, cf. BERNARD/ DURLAUF (1996).

References

AMABLE, B. (2000): International specialisation and growth, in: Structural Change and Economic Dynamics 11, 413-431.

ANDERSON, T.W., HSIAO, C. (1982): Formulation and estimation of dynamic models using panel data, in: Journal of Econometrics 18, 47-82.

ARELLANO, M. (1988): A note on the Anderson-Hsiao estimator for panel data, Institute of Economics, Oxford University.

ARELLANO, M., BOND, S. (1991): Some tests of specification for panel data: Monte-Carlo evidence and an application to employment equations, in: Review of Economic Studies 58, 227-298.

BALTAGI, B.H. (1995): Econometric analysis of panel data, Chichester et al.

BERNARD, A.B., DURLAUF, S.N. (1996): Interpreting tests of the convergence hypothesis, in: Journal of Applied Econometrics 71, 161-173.

BLUNDELL, R., BOND, S. (1998): Initial conditions and moment restrictions in dynamic panel data models, in: Journal of Econometrics 87, 115-143.

BREITUNG, J. (1992): Dynamische Modelle für die Paneldatenanalyse, Frankfurt/M.

CASELLI, F., ESQUIVEL, G., LEFORT, F. (1996): Reopening the convergence debate: a new look at cross-country growth empirics, in: Journal of Economic Growth 1, 363-389.

CHENG, D.C., IGLARSH, H.J. (1976): Principal component estimators in regression analysis, in: Review of Economic and Statistics 58, 229-234.

FARRAR, D.E., GLAUBER, R.R. (1967): Multicollinearity in regression analysis: the problem revisited, in: Review of Economic and Statistics 49, 92-107.

HARVEY, A.C. (1994): Ökonometrische Analyse von Zeitreihen, München/Wien.

HOEFFLER, A.E. (2000): The augmented Solow model and the African growth debate, CID (Center for International Development at Harvard University) Working Paper No. 36.

KENDALL, M.G. (1957): A course in multivariate analysis, London.

LEE, M., LONGMIRE, R., MATYAS, L. et al. (1998): Growth convergence: some panel data evidence, in Applied Economics 30, 907-912.

MCCALLUM, B.T. (1970): Artificial orthogonalization in regression analysis, in: Review of Economics and Statistics 52, 110-113.

NICKELL (1981): Biases in dynamic models with fixed effects, in: Econometrica 49, 1417-1426.

C. Dynamic Causal Links between the Russian Stock Exchange and Selected International Stock Markets

Noer Azam Achsani and Hans Gerhard Strohe

1. Introduction

This paper analyses the causal relationships and dynamic links between the Russian stock exchange with other Central and East European as well as some important international commercial centres between August 1994 to February 2001. We use the data of the corresponding stock market indices.

Stock markets linkages between national capital markets have been studied since the early 90s, i.e. after the stock market crash of October 1987 on Wall Street. The reason why shocks in one market should affect other markets is explained for example by JANAKIRAMANAN and LAMBA (1998) as follows:

- *Dominant economic power*: during the early part of the 20th century when Britain was the world economic power, actions taken by the Bank of England reverberated immediately around the world. In the post-World War period, the US became the most influential economy, since most of the international trading has been dominated by US dollars.
- *Common investor groups*: Geographically close countries normally have a similar group of investors in their markets. Therefore, these markets influence each other.
- *Multiple stock listing*: When a stock is dually listed in two markets, shocks in one market can be transmitted to the other market. For example GJERDE and SAETTEM (1995) find that Switzerland is influenced by most other European markets because a large of portion of stocks traded on the Swiss market are multi-listed in other European markets.

Other possible reasons as explained by ARSHANAPALLI and DOUKAS (1993) are "the relaxation of controls on capital movements and foreign exchange transactions, and improvements in computer and communication technology that have lowered the cost of cross-border information flows and financial transactions".

The previous studies concerning this issue have mainly focused on the US and other developed markets in the western countries. The main results of the previous studies are (ROLL, 1988; ARSHANAPALLI/DOUKAS, 1993; GJERDE/SAETTEM, 1995; EUN/SHIM, 1989):

- The international markets are becoming increasingly integrated, especially after the global shock in October 1987.
- The US is dominant and influences the other stock markets while the other markets have little, if any, influence on the US market.
- The European stock markets are also integrated with each other. The US market influences all of these, but none of these markets significantly affect the US.

Linkages among emerging stock markets have been comparatively less explored, and therefore there is a need for more research in this area. ELYASIANI *et al.* (1998) studied the interdependence and dynamic linkage between the stock market of Sri Lanka and its major trading partners. The results showed that there was no significant interdependence between the stock markets of Sri Lanka with that in the US and other Asian markets. The study of JANAKIRAMANAN and LAMBA (1998) using the data of 1988-1996 showed that Pacific-Basin stock markets are integrated with each other, except Indonesia, and the US market influences all of these markets. ACHSANI and STROHE (2002) analysed the interdependence between the stock exchanges of the region Pacific Basin and showed that all markets were integrated with each other, except China. After the Asian financial crisis 1997, the markets were more greatly integrated.

In this paper, the dynamic links of the stock exchanges of Central and Eastern Europe is empirically explored.

For this purpose we analyse the daily rate of return of the stock market indices of Russia, Slovenia, the Czech Republic, Slovakia, Poland as well as international stock exchanges of the US, Australia, Japan, Hong Kong, Great Britain and Germany, from August 1994 to February 2001. Particular interest is dedicated to the influence of the Russian Financial Crisis in 1998. In WELFENS et al. (2000), there are many examples for the disastrous effect of this crisis on the Russian economy and the living situation of the Russian population.

In Section 2, we explain the theoretical framework and the tools of the analysis. It is based mainly on a decomposition of forecasting error variances from a multivariate vector autoregressive (VAR) model, thereby establishing the structure of interactions among these stock markets. Besides, we will also apply correlation and Granger causality analysis. In Section 3, we define the variables and the data and present the descriptive statistics as first results.

In section 4, the final results are presented. Vector autoregressive (VAR) models will be estimated with the aim to examine the dynamic interactions among stock markets. Empirical structural regularities among the corresponding indices are analysed by the variance decomposition approach. In this way, we try to explore the question: how does a national exchange react to shocks in other markets in a worldwide system? We also utilize the impulse response function, addressing the question of how rapidly events in a single market are transmitted to others.

2. Framework of the Analysis

The multivariate vector autoregressive (VAR) method is a useful alternative to the conventional structural modelling procedure. The VAR analysis works with unrestricted reduced forms of econometric models, treating all variables as potentially endogenous (GJERDE/SAETTEM, 1999). The main focus is on causal relations among macroeconomic variables - such as oil prices, real activity, inflation, money supply and also industrial production index - and asset returns. The VAR technique is also a useful approach to investigate the degree of international linkages among interest rates and stock markets (GJERDE/SAETTEM, 1995; ARSHANAPALLI/DOUKAS, 1993; EUN/SHIM, 1989; JANAKIRAMAN/LAMBA, 1995).

A VAR(p) model can be described as follows :

(2.1) $$y_t = a + \Phi_1 y_{t-1} + \Phi_2 y_{t-2} + \ldots + \Phi_p y_{t-p} + \varepsilon_t$$

where y_t is an $m\times 1$ vector of jointly dependent variables, a is a $m\times 1$ vector of constant terms, Φ_i is an $m\times 1$ vector of coefficients and ε_t is an $m\times 1$ vector of white noise errors independently and normally distributed with zero mean. The method requires the time series analysed to be stationary. We employ the unit root test based on the augmented Dickey-Fuller test procedure (ADF) to do this. The order of VAR, p, can be selected using Akaike Information Criterion (AIC) or Schwarz Bayes Criterion (SBC).

One of the key questions that can be addressed with VAR is how useful some variables are for forecasting others, which is answered by the notion of Granger causality. In this paper we deal not only with bivariate but also with block Granger causality.

The bivariate granger causality test was proposed by GRANGER (1969) and popularised by SIMS (1972). The question investigated in this test is whether a lagged variable y can help forecast a variable x. If it cannot, than we say that y does not Granger-cause x. Here we assume a particular autoregressive lag length p and estimate the autoregressive distributed lag model (ARDL (p))

(2.2) $$\begin{aligned} x_t &= c_t + \alpha_1 x_{t-1} + \alpha_2 x_{t-2} + \ldots + \alpha_p x_{t-p} + \beta_1 y_{t-1} + \beta_2 y_{t-2} \\ &+ \ldots + \beta_p y_{t-p} + u_t \end{aligned}$$

by ordinary least square (OLS) method. Than an F-test of the null hypothesis

(2.3) $$H_o : \ \beta_1 = \beta_2 = \ldots = \beta_p = 0$$

versus the alternative $H_1 : \ \beta_i \neq 0$ for at least one i is conducted.

In order to implement a test variable the sum of square residuals from (2.2), $RSS_1 = \sum_{\forall t} \hat{u}_t^{\,2}$ is calculated and compared with the sum of squared residuals of univariate autoregression for x_t, $RSS_0 = \sum_{\forall t} \hat{e}_t^{\,2}$, where

(2.4) $$x_t = c_0 + \gamma_1 x_{t-1} + \gamma_2 x_{t-2} + \ldots + \gamma_p x_{t-p} + e_t$$

is also estimated by OLS. If

(2.5) $$S = \frac{(RSS_0 - RSS_1)/p}{RSS_1/(T-2p-1)}$$

is higher than the 5 % critical value for an F(*p*, *T-2p*-1) distribution the null hypothesis that *y* does not Granger-cause *x is rejected.* That means, if *S* is sufficiently large, we conclude that *y* does Granger-cause *x*. For more details see e.g. HAMILTON (1994).

Block Granger causality means that lagged values of a sub*set* of variables (say y_{2t}) of the vector y_t are important in predicting *another subset* of variables (say y_{1t}). More formally, let $y_t = (y'_{it}, y'_{2t})'$, where y_{1t} and y_{2t} are $m_1 \times 1$ and $m_2 \times 1$ subsets of y_t and $m = m_1 + m_2$. Consider now the following block decomposition of a VAR:

(2.6) $$y_{1t} = a_{10} + \sum_{i=1}^{p} \Phi_{i,11} y_{1,t-i} + \sum_{i=1}^{p} \Phi_{i,12} y_{2,t-i} + u_{1t}$$

(2.7) $$y_{2t} = a_{20} + \sum_{i=1}^{p} \Phi_{i,21} y_{1,t-i} + \sum_{i=1}^{p} \Phi_{i,22} y_{2,t-i} + u_{1t}$$

The null hypothesis that the subset y_{2t} does not Granger-cause y_{1t} is defined by $H_0 : \Phi_{12} = 0$, where $\Phi_{12} = (\Phi_{1,12}, \Phi_{2,12}, \ldots, \Phi_{p,12})$. The alternative H_1 means that at least one coefficient $\Phi_{i,12}$ differs from 0. The log-likelihood ratio statistic of this test is:

(2.8) $$LR_G = 2(\log|\tilde{\Sigma}_R| - \log|\tilde{\Sigma}|)$$

where $\tilde{\Sigma}$ is the maximum likelihood estimator of the covariance matrix Σ of the error term u for the full system, and $\tilde{\Sigma}_R$ is the maximum likelihood estimator of Σ when the restrictions $\Phi_{12} = 0$ are imposed. The statistic LR_G asymptotically follows a χ^2 distribution with $m_1 m_2 p$ degrees of freedom. For more information, see for example PESARAN and PESARAN (1997).

Furthermore, using the VAR method makes it possible to analyse the dynamic responses to shocks in the system. Using impulse response analysis, it is possible to analyse the effect of a unit shock in a variable to the changes in other variables in the successive future period. To analyse the dynamics of the system, the VAR model in equation (2.1) can be transformed into its infinite moving average (MA) representation as follows:

$$(2.9) \qquad y_t = \sum_{k=0}^{\infty} M_k \varepsilon_{t-k}$$

The component $[M_k]_{i,j}$ of the matrix M_k represents the response of the *i*-th market to a shock in the *j*-th variable, if the elements of the error vector ε_t are orthogonal. If they are correlated, the error term can be transformed by a suitable triangular matrix Q:

$$\varepsilon = Q^{-1} v \text{ with } QQ' = \Sigma$$

so that the then orthogonalized innovations v can be incorporated in the above MA model

$$(2.10) \qquad y_t = \sum_{k=0}^{\infty} P_k v_{t-k}$$

where $P_k = M_k Q$ (for details see EUN and SHIM, 1989). The component $[P_k]_{i,j}$ of the matrix P_k is the impulse response of the *i*-th variable in the period *k* to a shock in the *j*-th variable. Usually, this latter shock is given in terms of a standard error.

The VAR also provides the possibility of the decomposition of forecast error variance of one individual variable corresponding to each of all variables:

$$(2.11) \qquad \Theta_{ij,K} = \frac{\sum_{k=0}^{K} [M_k Q]_{ij}}{\sum_{k=0}^{K} [M_k \Sigma M_k']_{ij}}$$

where the square brackets refer to the indicated component of the corresponding matrix. $\Theta_{ij,K}$ gives the proportion of the contribution of the variable *j* to the whole *K*-step forecast error variance of a variable *i*. This way the shares of each variable at the variance of another variable can be interpreted as the relative importance of each variable in generating the variation in that individual variable.

3. Variables and Data

We analyse the most important general indices of the Central-Eastern European emerging stock exchanges i.e. Russia (Moscow Times = RU), Slovenia (SB120 = SN), Czech Republic (PX50 = CZ), Slovakia (SAX = SK), and Poland (WIG = PL) and of some important international markets: Australia (All Ordinaries Index = AU), Japan (Nikkei 225 = JP), Hong Kong (Han Seng = HK), Germany (DAX = DE), United Kingdom (FTSE 100 = UK), and the US (S&P 500 = US).

For each index, we have obtained the daily values in local currency terms for the period from August 1994 until February 2001. The data were compiled from the Capital Market Advisory Board of Indonesia (BAPEPAM) and Yahoo Finance. In order to get stationary time series, these indices were converted into the daily rate of return using the formula:

$$R_{j,t} = \ln(I_{j,t} / I_{j,t-1}).$$

where $I_{j,t}$ is value of index *j* on day *t* and $I_{j,t-1}$ is its value on day *t-1*. This is a good approximation for the daily increase rate $(I_{j,t} - I_{j,t-1}) / I_{j,t-1}$ of the index.

4. Empirical Results

4.1 Results of Descriptive and Correlation Analysis

Table C1 presents the main descriptive indicators of daily returns $R_{j,t}$. Before the Russian financial crisis in 1998, the stock exchanges of Russia, the Czech Republic, Slovakia, Poland, Japan and Hong Kong had negative average rates of returns. The stock exchange of the Czech Republic had the index with the smallest rate. In contrast Germany, the US, Australia, Slovenia and the United Kingdom had positive average rates.

After the Russian financial crisis, the Russian stock exchange has had the highest rate of return followed by Hong Kong. Almost all of the other indices have negative average returns, except Japan and Slovakia.

Table C2 presents the contemporary linear correlation coefficients between the rates of return of the indices under consideration. Concerning the result of a previous study (ACHSANI/STROHE (2002)), where we had found higher correlations between Pacific-Basin stock market data and lagged American data, here we also measure not only the interdependences between European/Asian indices with the US index of the *same* day, but those with the US index from the *previous* day (US(-1)) too.

The Russian index is significantly correlated with the indices of the stock markets of Australia, Hong Kong, Poland, United Kingdom and Germany. We also find high correlation with the US before the crisis, but not after the crisis.

The co-variability of the rates of Germany and the UK with those of the USA in the same day is stronger than that with the US data of the previous day (US(-1)), because Frankfurt and London are strong enough to influence New York later the day to a certain degree. But as for the other countries, their correlations with US(-1) are stronger than those with US in the same day. This more reasonable for minor exchanges because the New York exchange usually opens much later than the others and can realise its influence as late as the next day.

The stock market indices of Australia, Hong Kong, Poland, UK and Germany show tight interdependencies with the other international stock exchange indices. After the Russian financial crisis, however, their correlation with the US and Japanese indices have substantially decreased compared to those before the crisis. In contrast, the correlations with other stock market indices have increased. Before the Russian crisis, the US and Japanese indices were correlated with those of all other stock markets. However, we could not find the same relation after the crisis.

Tab. C1: Descriptive Statistics of Daily Market Returns in Local Currency Terms: August 1994 - February 2001

Panel A. Total Period

Variable(s)	US	AU	JP	HK	RU	SN
Maximum	1.0546	.060666	2.6323	.17247	.23747	.07994
Minimum	-1.0400	-.074487	-2.6287	-.14735	-.26245	-.09852
Mean	.6397E-3	.2721E-3	-.2385E-3	.3010E-3	.3755E-3	.133E-3
Std. Dev.	.037454	.0081433	.091342	.018903	.036684	.01357
Coef of Var.	58.5488	29.9324	382.9447	62.7923	97.7007	101.453

Variable(s)	CZ	SK	PL	UK	DE
Maximum	.41098	.095738	.078933	.043451	.058937
Minimum	-.054600	-.11484	-.10286	-.039334	-.064497
Mean	-.3505E-3	-.5183E-3	.2808E-3	.4023E-3	.6599E-3
Std. Dev.	.014994	.013923	.019443	.0098363	.013066
Coef of Var.	42.7721	26.8650	69.2508	24.4509	19.7994

Tab. C1: (continued)

Panel B. Before Russian Financial Crisis

Variable(s)	US	AU	JP	HK	RU	SN
Maximum	.049887	.060666	.076553	.17247	.21874	.07994
Minimum	-.071127	-.074487	-.057627	-.14735	-.26245	-.09852
Mean	.6887E-3	.1544E-3	-.3422E-3	-.2986E-3	-.3721E-3	.118E-3
Std. Dev.	.0086972	.0080956	.013394	.018946	.033808	.01631
Coef of Var.	12.6291	52.4395	39.1406	63.4480	90.8597	137.445

Variable(s)	CZ	SK	PL	UK	DE
Maximum	.41098	.095738	.078093	.032570	.043214
Minimum	-.054600	-.093690	-.10286	-.034173	-.060987
Mean	-.6483E-3	-.6082E-3	-.5956E-5	.4646E-3	.7395E-3
Std. Dev.	.015509	.012416	.020168	.0080384	.011104
Coef of Var.	23.9221	20.4147	3386.0	17.3026	14.837

Panel C. After Russian Financial Crisis

Variable(s)	US	AU	JP	HK	RU	SN
Maximum	1.0546	.025705	2.6323	.086101	.23747	.03222
Minimum	-1.0400	-.058527	-2.6287	-.089390	-.25794	-.02608
Mean	.5582E-3	.4681E-3	-.6582E-4	.0012998	.0016206	.159E-3
Std. Dev.	.060141	.0082247	.14820	.018805	.041026	.006940
Coef of Var.	107.7478	17.5720	2251.5	14.4674	25.3151	43.643

Variable(s)	CZ	SK	PL	UK	DE
Maximum	.14310	.046542	.078933	.043451	.058937
Minimum	-.047977	-.11484	-.084678	-.039334	-.064497
Mean	.1454E-3	-.3685E-3	.7583E-3	.2985E-3	.5273E-3
Std. Dev.	.014091	.016134	.018176	.012266	.015811
Coef of Var.	96.9024	43.7827	23.9690	41.0859	29.9846

Tab. C2: The Correlation Coefficients between Rates of Returns of the Stock Exchange Indices, August 1994 to February 2001

	US(-1)	US	AU	JP	HK	RU	SN	CZ	SK	PL	UK	DE
Total period												
US(-1)	1,00	-0,45	0,16	0,01	0,13	0,06	0,02	0,05	0,02	0,13	0,09	0,09
US		1,00	0,03	-0,01	0,03	0,05	0,00	0,06	-0,04	0,02	0,10	0,10
AU			1,00	0,04	0,50	0,23	0,04	0,08	0,03	0,34	0,31	0,32
JP				1,00	0,02	0,02	0,00	0,01	0,00	-0,03	0,04	0,04
HK					1,00	0,29	0,04	0,09	0,04	0,32	0,37	0,37
RU						1,00	0,06	0,17	0,04	0,19	0,30	0,31
SN							1,00	0,01	-0,01	0,04	0,04	0,04
CZ								1,00	0,00	0,14	0,19	0,19
SK									1,00	0,01	0,01	0,02
PL										1,00	0,23	0,24
UK											1,00	0,67
DE												1,00
Before the crisis												
US(-1)	1,00	0,03	0,56	0,28	0,39	0,22	0,04	0,07	0,02	0,29	0,32	0,41
US		1,00	0,11	0,07	0,17	0,11	0,00	0,03	0,01	0,08	0,40	0,32
AU			1,00	0,33	0,51	0,28	0,04	0,05	0,03	0,27	0,32	0,41
JP				1,00	0,32	0,12	-0,02	0,00	0,02	0,17	0,24	0,25
HK					1,00	0,36	0,03	0,05	0,05	0,25	0,36	0,41
RU						1,00	0,06	0,10	0,05	0,20	0,27	0,28
SN							1,00	-0,01	0,00	-0,01	0,05	0,02
CZ								1,00	0,00	0,09	0,12	0,08
SK									1,00	0,03	0,02	0,01
PL										1,00	0,18	0,19
UK											1,00	0,62
DE												1,00

Tab. C2: (continued)

After the crisis												
US(-1)	1,00	-0,46	0,13	0,01	0,13	0,05	0,03	0,07	0,02	0,15	0,07	0,05
US		1,00	0,02	-0,01	0,02	0,05	0,01	0,09	-0,06	0,01	0,06	0,08
AU			1,00	0,01	0,49	0,16	0,06	0,14	0,02	0,47	0,31	0,23
JP				1,00	-0,02	0,02	0,00	0,01	0,00	-0,08	0,03	0,02
HK					1,00	0,21	0,10	0,17	0,02	0,44	0,40	0,36
RU						1,00	0,05	0,26	-0,01	0,17	0,33	0,35
SN							1,00	0,08	-0,02	0,24	0,05	0,12
CZ								1,00	0,01	0,23	0,29	0,35
SK									1,00	0,00	0,00	0,03
PL										1,00	0,31	0,33
UK											1,00	0,70
DE												1,00

Note: Entries with bold fonts are statistically significant at least at 5-percent level.

4.2 Results of Granger-Causality and VAR Analysis

4.2.1 The VAR Model

The VAR model assumes the time series data to be stationary. In order to check this assumption, the augmented Dicky-Fuller (ADF) test up to 12 lags is applied. The tests for all series of returns cannot reject the stationarity of the variables. Akaike Information Criterion (AIC) and Schwarz Bayesian Criterion (SBC) select order 3 and 1 for the VAR model, respectively, due to the maximum value. Here we prefer to choose the VAR(1) model in order to keep the model simple. We use the US data from the previous days, because of its stronger correlation with the Russian and other Central-East European stock markets data.

The coefficients of the VAR model are presented in Appendix 1-3. The significant ones show that the Russian index is statistically influenced by its own previous value and also by the previous values of the indices of Hong Kong, the UK and Poland. On the other hand, the Russian index significantly influences that of Poland.

Among the Central-East European stock markets, the index of Poland is the most broadly dependent one. Beside its own previous value, it is significantly influenced by the data of Australia, Hong Kong, Russia, the UK, and Germany, as well as the previous values of the US index.

4.2.2 Granger Causality

Tables C3 and C4 present the important results of the bivariate and block Granger causality analysis. From the bivariate Granger causality test, we learn that the USA, Australia, Japan, Hong Kong, the UK and Germany are the most important markets in the system. They influence the future data of Russia and almost all other markets except for Slovenia and Slovakia. After the Russian currency crisis, the US stock market has not influenced the other markets more strongly than in the period before the crisis.

The Russian stock market is the most dominant market among the Central-Eastern European stock markets. It influences the stock exchanges of the Czech Republic, Slovakia, and Poland as well as the stock exchanges in other regions. On the other hand, the Russian market is strongly influenced by the past data of Poland, Hong Kong and Australia. The relative importance of the Russian stock market tends to increase following the Russian crisis.

The United Kingdom and Germany each show the strongest block Granger causality towards the block of all other countries in the system during all three time periods. On the other hand, the stock markets of the USA, Australia, Japan, Hong Kong, Russia and the Czech Republic are important for all others at least in one of the two time periods. According to block Granger causality, Russia shows an interesting phenomenon: While there is not any significant causality towards the block of all other countries during each partial period, there is a noticeable impact if we take the data of the whole period. We can therefore conclude that this causality is not very stable.

Tab. C3: Bivariate-Granger-Causality Test to Find the Importance a Index in the First Row in Predicting the Indices in the First Column

F-value	US	AU	JP	HK	RU	SN	CZ	SK	PL	UK	DE
Total period											
US		20,17	0,34	17,29	9,14	0,11	5,41	1,85	9,24	48,11	44,56
AU	0,04		1,18	3,61	3,41	0,61	0,44	1,00	0,66	86,83	62,01
JP	0,01	0,34		0,13	7,02	0,08	5,46	0,13	0,95	13,16	6,72
HK	0,73	0,92	2,73		1,05	1,36	0,04	1,10	0,35	54,31	16,20
RU	1,94	5,73	0,23	8,76		0,76	0,42	0,45	7,20	2,38	0,60
SN	0,21	0,23	0,15	0,11	1,50		0,67	0,23	0,43	1,15	1,96
CZ	3,68	1,18	31,44	3,06	6,67	3,62		1,03	0,42	3,95	2,86
SK	0,32	0,57	0,00	1,26	1,04	0,31	0,19		1,54	1,51	0,66
PL	2,89	3,47	3,24	0,10	11,94	0,69	6,12	1,39		31,89	27,90
UK	2,44	5,17	2,10	2,24	3,50	1,01	2,17	0,19	0,48		0,40
DE	0,91	2,96	0,63	1,67	2,98	1,14	1,26	0,38	0,05	9,10	

Tab. C3: (continued)

Before the crisis											
US		8,85	3,21	18,26	6,56	2,05	0,31	0,04	3,23	115,37	75,07
AU	5,62		0,03	1,54	0,33	0,36	0,15	0,24	0,17	48,81	17,83
JP	2,57	0,86		0,55	0,35	1,46	1,29	3,11	0,18	24,94	13,24
HK	3,34	1,38	0,61		0,29	0,98	0,13	0,84	0,71	33,62	4,23
RU	4,93	4,60	4,10	11,88		0,65	0,04	2,29	3,51	0,73	1,08
SN	3,50	0,36	1,1	0,10	0,63		0,32	0,94	0,09	0,71	1,59
CZ	0,33	4,03	5,02	2,92	6,23	2,25		0,77	0,44	3,17	2,63
SK	2,14	1,9	0,96	4,34	5,67	0,56	0,26		3,33	0,57	2,53
PL	3,05	4,57	0,45	0,00	3,73	0,77	2,25	1,89		15,9	9,14
UK	5,05	4,34	6,71	2,80	1,56	0,90	1,01	0,60	1,10		0,20
DE	5,09	3,19	3,38	2,18	0,48	0,77	0,01	0,96	0,35	12,14	
After the crisis											
US		5,62	0,09	5,31	3,58	0,43	4,61	1,57	4,43	13,09	12,27
AU	0,12		1,16	4,82	3,88	0,66	0,52	1,17	0,85	42,12	48,25
JP	0,01	0,03		2,47	6,16	0,37	5,99	0,02	0,46	5,93	2,43
HK	0,73	0,03	2,47		3,59	0,53	0,11	0,94	0,99	22,38	12,75
RU	1,04	1,89	0,3	2,15		0,35	1,3	0,28	4,28	1,56	0,65
SN	0,06	2,04	0,97	0,52	2,4		3,60	0,92	2,02	1,69	1,91
CZ	5,55	1,25	36,62	2,08	1,36	1,79		0,36	2,33	1,93	0,63
SK	0,1	2,87	0,01	0,88	1,78	0,08	0,01		0,82	0,87	2,49
PL	2,17	3,90	3,40	0,05	10,70	0,16	6,57	0,04		21,92	27,13
UK	1,1	2,01	0,95	0,28	1,79	2,69	2,82	0,12	0,18	1,68	0,18
DE	0,31	0,49	0,26	0,44	3,96	2,39	3,20	0,02	0,98	1,95	

Note: Entries with bold fonts are statistically significant at least at 5-percent level.

Tab. C4: Block-Granger-Causality-Test of the Importance of an Index in the First Column in Predicting all Indices in the System

Market	χ^2 value		
	All period	Before the crisis	After the crisis
US	15,49	37,75	12,75
AU	19,00	14,82	14,58
JP	63,78	17,28	78,23
HK	20,07	29,39	4,00
RU	17,06	13,41	10,14
SN	4,58	10,00	12,81
CZ	15,15	4,10	26,68
SK	9,44	11,98	5,04
PL	11,66	10,81	16,57
UK	106,4	133,95	24,75
DE	40,52	34,64	41,81

Note: Entries with bold fonts are statistically significant at least at 5 % level.

4.2.3 Decomposition of Forecasting Error Variance

When measured by the decomposition of the forecasting error variance of the other indices, the US index cannot significantly explain their behaviour in the whole period of study. But before the Russian crisis, it explained 3 to 11.5 % of the forecasting error variance of the indices of Australia, Hong Kong, Poland, UK and Germany. However, we could not find the same result in the period after the crisis.

As an indicator of growing integration among the markets, the influence of all foreign markets on a specific national index generally increased after the Russian crisis, for example for SN, CZ, PL, UK and DE. On the other hand, influence of foreign indices on the US decreased from 53 % before the crisis to 7 % of the whole forecast error variance after the crisis and on JP from 28 % before the crisis to 6 % after the crisis, suggesting that the latter exchanges have become more independent.

The results also show that the Russian stock market is the most dominant market among Central-Eastern European markets. Especially after the crisis, the Russian market has played an important role. The variation of its index can explain 3 to 6 % of the forecasting error variance of the other markets. Not surprisingly, the indices of Slovenia and Slovakia play almost no role in explaining the behaviour of other markets.

The strongest foreign contribution to the variability of the Russian index comes from Germany, the UK and Hong Kong with about 6 % of the forecasting error variance. In total, about 30 % of its forecast error variance can be explained through foreign market indices. In Germany, foreign indices contribute about

50 % of the DAX forecast error variance. The FTSE index of the UK is the most independent index – with only 24 % –, followed by Hong Kong, Australian and Russian indices. For an exception, the foreign indices play only a very small role in predicting error variance in the US index. More than 90 % of the forecast error variance in the US index depends on its own previous values, and the foreign indices can explain only about 8 % (see Fig. C1–C3).

Fig. C1: Decomposition of Forecasting Error Variance for the Russian Index, Aug 1994 - Feb 2001

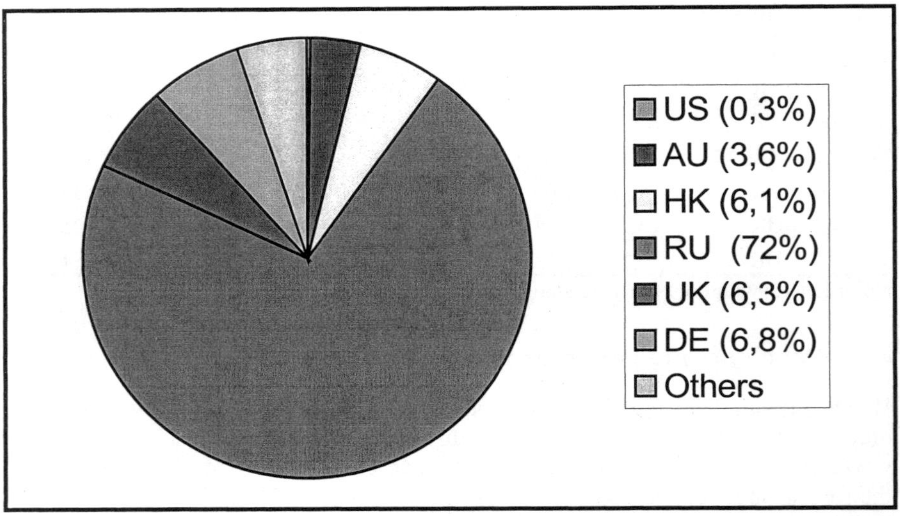

Fig. C2: Decomposition of Forecasting Error Variance for the US Index, Aug 1994 - Feb 2001

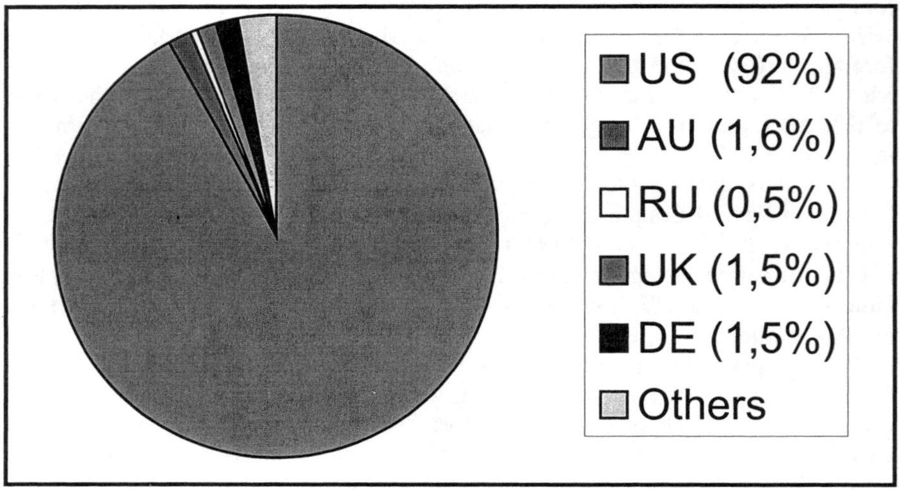

Fig. C3: Decomposition of Forecasting Error Variance for the German Index, Aug 1994 - Feb 2001

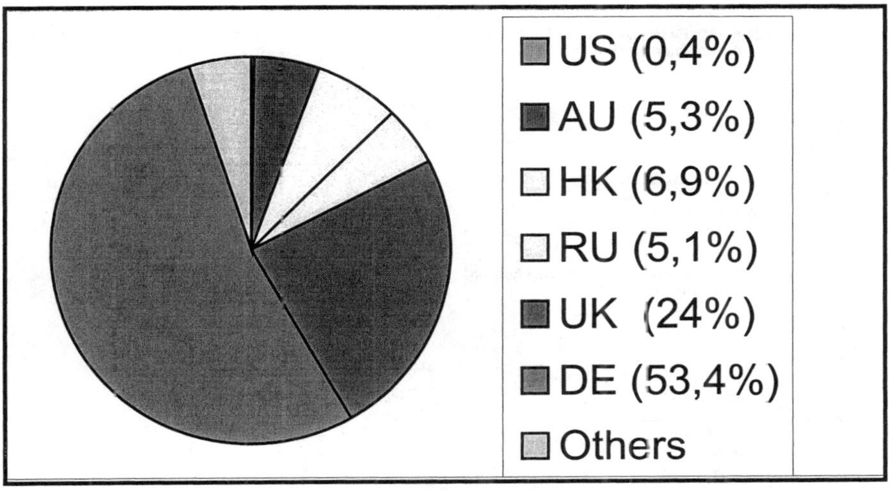

The complete results of the decomposition of forecasting error variances for all indices can be seen in Appendix 4A-4C.

4.2.4 Impulse Response Analysis

Figures C4 and C5 present selected results of the impulse response analysis related to Russian stock exchange. The complete results can not be presented here. They are available from the authors upon request.

The results show that shocks in the US stock exchange would be transmitted to the stock markets of Australia, Hong Kong, the Czech Republic, the UK and Germany in the same day. They are also transmitted to the other markets, but without such a remarkable response.

Shocks in international stock markets are rapidly transmitted during the same day to Russia as presented in Figure C4. The Russian index responds mostly to the shocks from Germany, the UK, Hong Kong and Australia. Shocks in other markets will also be transmitted to Russia, but without such a remarkable response. On the other hand, shocks in the Russian stock market are also rapidly responded to by the other markets considered in this study, especially by Hong Kong, Germany, Poland, the UK, Czech Republic and also the USA.

Fig. C4: Response of the Russian Stock Market to One Standard Error Shocks in other Stock Markets

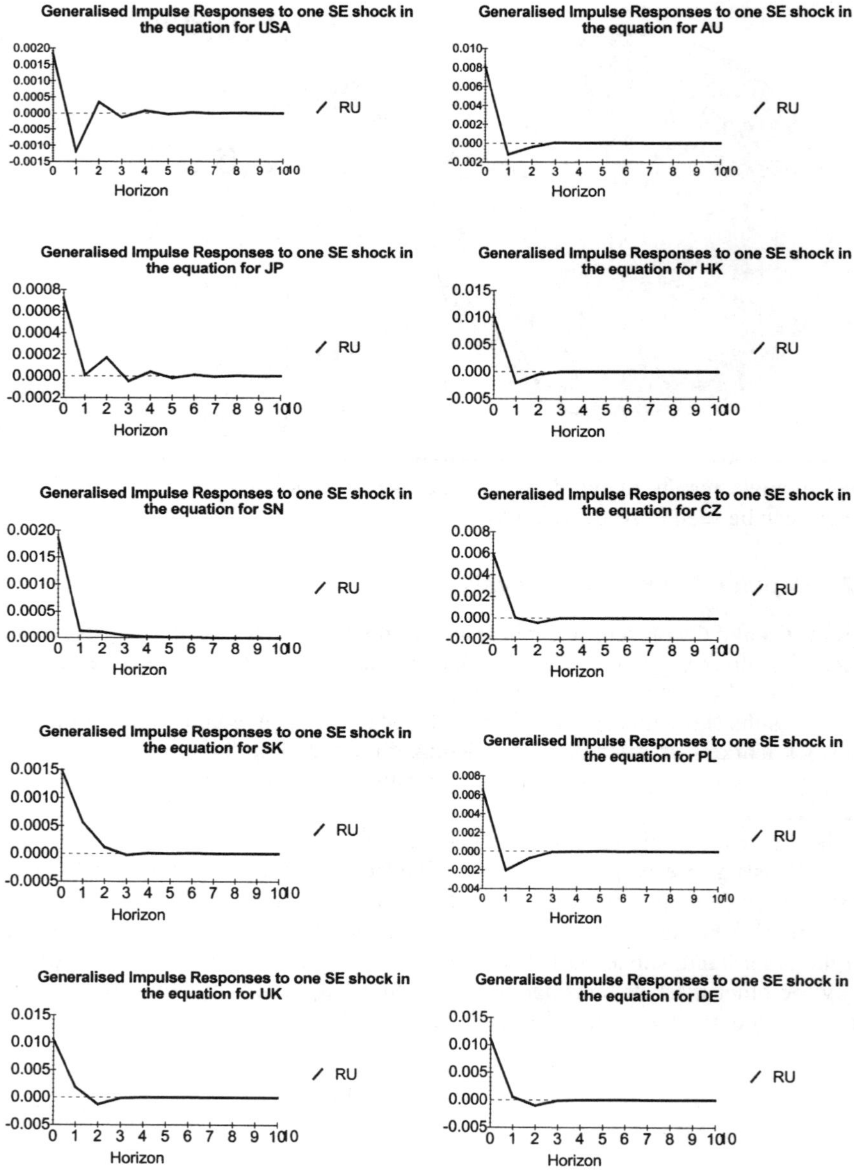

Fig. C5: Response of the Selected International Stock Markets to One Standard Error Shocks in the Russian Stock Market

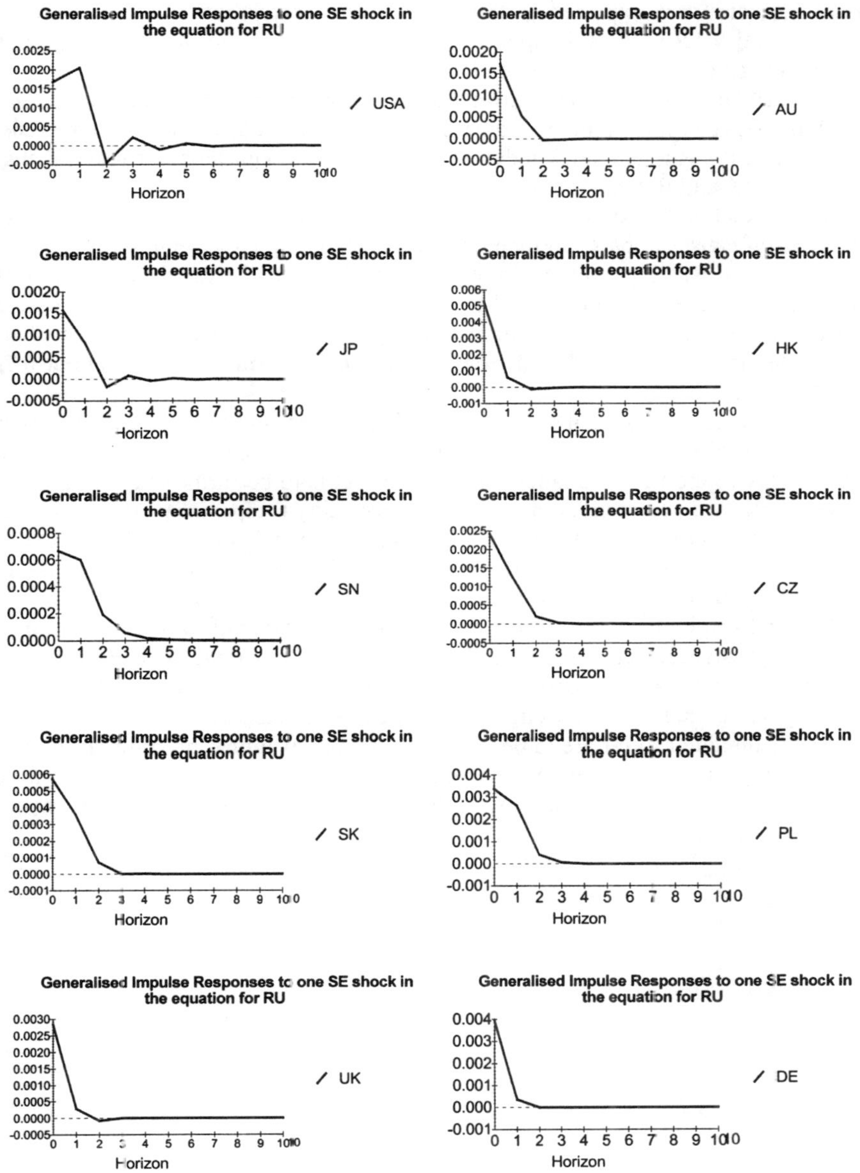

5. Conclusions

Causal relationships between Central-Eastern European markets with six international markets were explored in this paper using correlation analysis, Granger causality and VAR models. Despite responding to different questions, all methods used in this study generally give qualitatively similar results.

The correlation analysis has shown that there are remarkable mutual linear relationships between most indices. Some of them decreased after the Russian crisis. Particularly, the Russian stock index is closely related with those of Hong Kong, Germany, UK and Poland.

More specifically, Russia is causally influenced by Poland and Hong Kong. Russia itself causes impact in Poland, the US, Japan, and the Czech Republic. The dominance of Russian market among Central-Eastern European exchanges is confirmed by the decomposition of their forecasting error variance: The Russian index can "explain" 3 – 6 % of the variability of Central-Eastern European indices, while Germany, the UK and Hong Kong provide explanations of about 6 % each for Russia.

Furthermore, shocks in the Russian market are transmitted not only to other Central-Eastern European countries but also to Germany, the UK, Hong Kong and with a delay to the US. The latter surprising effect is to be further explored as the above-mentioned corresponding Granger causality, especially the question whether this is a direct impact of the Russian index or rather a secondary effect of close connection with third markets. On the other hand, the Russian market responds sensitively to shocks from Germany, the UK and Hong Kong.

Different results for most indicators were found when analysing data before or after the Russian currency crisis in 1998. Therefore it would be worthwhile to more closely examine the importance of this crisis for the structure of the international dynamic causal relationships between stock exchanges. In the near future, the results obtained so far are to be completed by the examination of the influence of singular political and economical events on the relationships between the stock markets under consideration and by the investigation of the more detailed mechanism of causal dependencies.

Appendix 1

Tab. C5: The Augmented Dickey-Fuller Unit Root Tests for Stationarity of the Daily Market Return Series, Aug 1994 - Feb 2001

Test	US	AU	JP	HK	RU	SN	CZ	SK	PL	UK	DE
DF	-70,92	-43,70	-75,76	-43,39	-40,52	-33,19	-40,17	-45,40	-35,26	-42,00	-42,91
ADF (1)	-49,22	-32,18	-53,18	-32,24	-28,67	-30,00	-29,08	-32,61	-27,96	-32,81	-31,61
ADF (2)	-38,56	-25,49	-42,84	-23,69	-23,38	-23,79	-23,74	-26,20	-22,73	-28,10	-26,10
ADF (3)	-32,83	-22,94	-36,63	-21,93	-20,72	-21,36	-20,96	-22,37	-19,97	-23,60	-21,45
ADF (4)	-28,46	-20,52	-31,86	-20,27	-18,77	-18,69	-19,29	-19,14	-18,54	-21,22	-19,69
ADF (5)	-25,38	-19,26	-28,61	-18,61	-16,64	-17,01	-18,09	-17,77	-17,63	-20,20	-18,81
ADF (6)	-22,90	-18,22	-26,08	-17,53	-15,29	-14,70	-16,67	-16,22	-16,50	-18,81	-18,11
ADF (7)	-21,21	-17,05	-23,98	-16,32	-14,67	-13,70	-15,54	-14,88	-15,37	-17,24	-16,41
ADF (8)	-19,56	-15,97	-22,33	-14,99	-13,91	-12,71	-14,40	-14,08	-13,68	-15,87	-15,68
ADF (9)	-17,92	-15,17	-20,66	-13,77	-12,58	-11,72	-12,88	-13,46	-12,55	-15,16	-14,15
ADF (10)	-16,64	-14,31	-19,36	-13,03	-11,64	-11,71	-11,85	-13,01	-11,85	-13,78	-13,61
ADF (11)	-15,87	-13,35	-18,27	-12,24	-10,97	-12,02	-10,88	-12,43	-11,40	-13,17	-13,21
ADF (12)	-15,21	-12,23	-17,22	-11,29	-10,25	-11,64	-10,38	-11,64	-10,34	-12,35	-12,82

Note: 95 % critical value for the augmented Dickey-Fuller statistic = -3.4147.

Appendix 2

Tab. C6: Test Statistics and Choice Criteria for Selecting the Order of the VAR Model

Order	AIC	SBC
6	49256,8	47254,5
5	49293,4	47619,9
4	49312,1	47619,9
3	49313,1	48297,0
2	49222,1	48534,7
1	49033,8	48534,7
0	48360,3	48330,5

Note: AIC = Akaike Information Criterion SBC = Schwarz Bayes Criterion.

Appendix 3

Tab. C7: Coefficients of the Unrestricted VAR(1) Model

Regressor	Dependent Variables										
	US	AU	JP	HK	RU	SN	CZ	SK	PL	UK	DE
US(-1)	-0,47	-0,01	-0,01	-0,01	-0,03	0,00	-0,03	0,01	-0,03	-0,01	-0,01
AU(-1)	0,18	-0,06	-0,15	-0,11	-0,08	-0,05	0,02	-0,01	-0,18	-0,10	-0,10
JP(-1)	-0,01	0,00	-0,50	-0,01	0,00	0,00	0,03	0,00	-0,01	-0,01	0,00
HK(-1)	0,04	-0,02	0,09	-0,04	-0,17	-0,01	0,02	0,01	-0,08	-0,01	-0,03
RU(-1)	0,02	0,00	0,00	-0,01	0,13	0,01	0,02	0,01	0,04	0,01	0,01
SN(-1)	0,00	-0,01	-0,07	-0,03	0,00	0,28	0,02	-0,01	-0,05	0,00	0,00
CZ(-1)	0,11	-0,02	-0,02	-0,05	-0,04	0,00	0,09	0,00	0,02	-0,03	-0,01
SK(-1)	-0,09	0,00	-0,05	-0,05	0,03	0,00	0,01	-0,04	0,05	-0,01	-0,01
PL(-1)	0,04	-0,01	0,09	-0,02	-0,12	0,01	0,00	0,02	0,13	0,00	0,01
UK(-1)	0,24	0,22	0,32	0,57	0,33	0,03	0,06	0,02	0,28	0,08	0,20
DE(-1)	0,17	0,09	0,11	-0,02	-0,07	0,04	0,01	0,00	0,17	0,02	-0,05
INPT	0,00	0,00	0,00	0,00	0,00	0,00	0,00	0,00	0,00	0,00	0,00

Note: Entries with bold fonts are statistically significant at least at 5-percent level.

Appendix 4A

Tab. C8: Generalized Decomposition of Forecast Error Variances of Daily Market Returns for all Stock Market Indices, August 1994 - February 2001 (in percent)

i\j	day k	US	AU	JP	HK	RU	SN	CZ	SK	PL	UK	DE	All
US	1	92,12	1,60	0,00	1,23	0,47	0,06	0,54	0,19	0,70	1,52	1,55	7,88
	5	92,05	1,59	0,01	1,24	0,48	0,06	0,61	0,23	0,70	1,49	1,55	7,95
	10	92,05	1,59	0,01	1,24	0,48	0,06	0,61	0,23	0,70	1,49	1,55	7,95
AU	1	1,11	57,23	0,06	12,28	3,12	0,06	0,31	0,03	4,97	11,00	9,82	42,77
	5	1,11	57,19	0,07	12,28	3,12	0,06	0,33	0,03	4,97	11,01	9,83	42,81
	10	1,11	57,19	0,07	12,28	3,12	0,06	0,33	0,03	4,97	11,01	9,84	42,81
JP	1	0,00	0,02	97,79	0,26	0,04	0,00	0,89	0,01	0,61	0,22	0,16	2,21
	5	0,00	0,03	97,68	0,31	0,04	0,00	0,87	0,01	0,66	0,23	0,17	2,32
	10	0,00	0,03	97,68	0,31	0,04	0,00	0,87	0,01	0,66	0,23	0,17	2,32
HK	1	0,81	12,07	0,22	57,13	4,77	0,11	0,48	0,13	4,78	11,05	8,44	42,87
	5	0,81	12,08	0,24	57,05	4,77	0,12	0,50	0,13	4,78	11,07	8,45	42,95
	10	0,81	12,08	0,24	57,05	4,77	0,12	0,50	0,13	4,78	11,07	8,45	42,95
RU	1	0,26	3,63	0,03	6,14	72,14	0,19	1,94	0,13	2,57	6,25	6,72	27,86
	5	0,27	3,63	0,03	6,14	71,97	0,19	1,95	0,13	2,60	6,33	6,76	28,03
	10	0,27	3,63	0,03	6,14	71,97	0,19	1,95	0,13	2,60	6,33	6,76	28,03
SN	1	0,01	0,10	0,00	0,16	0,43	98,44	0,01	0,01	0,11	0,35	0,37	1,56
	5	0,01	0,10	0,00	0,16	0,45	98,41	0,01	0,01	0,11	0,35	0,38	1,59
	10	0,01	0,10	0,00	0,16	0,45	98,41	0,01	0,01	0,11	0,35	0,38	1,59
CZ	1	0,27	0,52	2,82	0,90	2,84	0,05	83,68	0,01	1,33	3,91	3,67	16,32
	5	0,32	0,52	3,19	0,90	2,84	0,05	83,24	0,01	1,33	3,92	3,66	16,76
	10	0,32	0,52	3,20	0,90	2,84	0,05	83,24	0,01	1,33	3,92	3,66	16,76
SK	1	0,06	0,06	0,00	0,14	0,23	0,01	0,01	99,17	0,14	0,08	0,11	0,83
	5	0,06	0,06	0,00	0,14	0,23	0,01	0,01	99,15	0,14	0,08	0,12	0,85
	10	0,06	0,06	0,00	0,14	0,23	0,01	0,01	99,15	0,14	0,08	0,12	0,85
PL	1	0,60	5,80	0,28	5,73	3,53	0,08	1,51	0,08	68,95	6,79	6,65	31,05
	5	0,61	5,82	0,28	5,73	3,56	0,09	1,51	0,09	68,89	6,79	6,64	31,11
	10	0,61	5,82	0,28	5,73	3,56	0,09	1,51	0,09	68,89	6,79	6,64	31,11
UK	1	0,38	5,08	0,12	7,14	4,61	0,09	2,25	0,01	2,64	53,93	23,75	46,07
	5	0,40	5,08	0,13	7,14	4,60	0,09	2,26	0,01	2,70	53,86	23,74	46,14
	10	0,40	5,08	0,13	7,14	4,60	0,09	2,26	0,01	2,70	53,86	23,74	46,14

Tab. C8: (continued)

DE	1	0,36	5,31	0,06	6,88	5,05	0,07	2,10	0,03	2,78	23,93	53,43	46,57
	5	0,37	5,32	0,06	6,88	5,05	0,07	2,10	0,03	2,78	23,95	53,40	46,60
	10	0,37	5,32	0,06	6,88	5,05	0,07	2,10	0,03	2,78	23,95	53,40	46,60

Note: a) Entries in each cell are the percentage of the forecast error variance of the index *i* in the first column explained by the index *j* in the first row; b) Entries in 'All' column indicate the total percentage of the forecast error variance of the index in the first column explained by all foreign indices.

See also for Tab. C9 and Tab. C10.

Appendix 4B

Tab. C9: Generalized Decomposition of Forecast Error Variances of Daily Market Returns for all Stock Market Indices before the Russian Currency Crisis, August 1994 – August 1998 (in percent)

i\j	day k	US	AU	JP	HK	RU	SN	CZ	SK	PL	UK	DE	All
US	1	46,49	11,56	2,02	6,81	3,19	0,11	0,13	0,00	2,97	13,58	13,12	53,51
	5	46,35	11,60	2,15	6,84	3,19	0,13	0,13	0,01	2,96	13,55	13,10	53,65
	10	46,35	11,60	2,15	6,84	3,19	0,13	0,13	0,01	2,96	13,55	13,10	53,65
AU	1	11,46	49,04	3,99	10,47	3,96	0,03	0,05	0,06	2,46	9,25	9,22	50,96
	5	11,44	48,95	4,05	10,48	3,95	0,05	0,05	0,06	2,46	9,27	9,23	51,05
	10	11,44	48,95	4,05	10,48	3,95	0,05	0,05	0,06	2,46	9,27	9,23	51,05
JP	1	2,91	5,86	71,21	5,53	0,91	0,25	0,20	0,45	1,37	6,10	5,22	28,79
	5	2,91	5,86	71,20	5,53	0,91	0,25	0,20	0,45	1,37	6,10	5,22	28,80
	10	2,91	5,86	71,20	5,53	0,91	0,25	0,20	0,45	1,37	6,10	5,22	28,80
HK	1	6,02	11,10	4,10	52,04	7,00	0,05	0,11	0,17	2,78	9,03	7,62	47,96
	5	6,01	11,10	4,12	51,94	6,99	0,06	0,11	0,17	2,78	9,08	7,64	48,06
	10	6,01	11,10	4,12	51,94	6,99	0,06	0,11	0,17	2,78	9,08	7,64	48,06
RU	1	3,67	5,26	1,06	9,23	67,12	0,24	0,69	0,53	2,75	4,55	4,88	32,88
	5	3,66	5,25	1,07	9,23	67,01	0,24	0,69	0,54	2,76	4,66	4,90	32,99
	10	3,66	5,25	1,07	9,23	67,01	0,24	0,69	0,54	2,76	4,66	4,90	32,99
SN	1	0,22	0,05	0,30	0,06	0,48	98,22	0,05	0,02	0,02	0,33	0,26	1,78
	5	0,22	0,06	0,36	0,08	0,49	98,11	0,05	0,02	0,02	0,33	0,26	1,89
	10	0,22	0,06	0,36	0,08	0,49	98,11	0,05	0,02	0,02	0,33	0,26	1,89
CZ	1	0,14	0,79	0,53	0,75	1,95	0,09	92,14	0,01	0,61	1,86	1,12	7,86
	5	0,15	0,79	0,54	0,76	1,97	0,11	92,05	0,01	0,61	1,88	1,12	7,95
	10	0,15	0,79	0,54	0,76	1,97	0,11	92,05	0,01	0,61	1,88	1,12	7,95
SK	1	0,02	0,17	0,04	0,25	0,82	0,01	0,01	97,98	0,56	0,03	0,10	2,02
	5	0,02	0,18	0,05	0,25	0,83	0,02	0,02	97,87	0,57	0,06	0,13	2,13
	10	0,02	0,18	0,05	0,25	0,83	0,02	0,02	97,87	0,57	0,06	0,13	2,13
PL	1	3,95	3,76	1,49	3,94	3,68	0,06	0,68	0,23	72,94	5,14	4,12	27,06
	5	3,94	3,76	1,50	3,93	3,73	0,06	0,70	0,24	72,87	5,16	4,12	27,13
	10	3,85	3,67	1,47	3,85	3,65	0,05	0,68	0,23	73,48	5,04	4,03	26,52
UK	1	5,00	4,89	2,70	6,15	3,71	0,14	0,71	0,07	1,44	54,40	20,80	45,60
	5	5,00	4,89	2,71	6,15	3,70	0,16	0,71	0,07	1,44	54,36	20,80	45,64
	10	5,03	4,31	2,73	6,19	3,72	0,16	0,72	0,07	1,45	54,70	20,93	45,30
DE	1	7,95	7,55	2,86	6,97	3,68	0,05	0,34	0,01	1,48	19,71	49,38	50,62
	5	7,94	7,54	2,87	6,96	3,68	0,07	0,34	0,01	1,48	19,77	49,33	50,67
	10	7,94	7,54	2,87	6,96	3,68	0,07	0,34	0,01	1,48	19,77	49,33	50,67

Appendix 4C

Tab. C10: Generalized Decomposition of Forecast Error Variances of Daily Market Returns for all Stock Market Indices after the Russian Currency Crisis, September 1998 - February 2001 (in percent)

i\j	day k	US	AU	JP	HK	RU	SN	CZ	SK	PL	UK	DE	All
US	1	92,53	1,34	0,01	1,20	0,45	0,04	1,33	0,45	0,93	0,79	0,93	7,47
	5	92,37	1,31	0,10	1,16	0,45	0,06	1,43	0,54	0,91	0,76	0,92	7,63
	10	92,29	1,32	0,11	1,17	0,46	0,06	1,44	0,54	0,92	0,76	0,93	7,71
AU	1	0,92	53,54	0,31	11,01	1,94	0,46	1,20	0,01	8,77	11,38	10,46	46,46
	5	0,91	53,22	0,32	11,00	1,93	0,60	1,31	0,01	8,74	11,40	10,56	46,78
	10	0,91	53,22	0,32	11,00	1,93	0,60	1,31	0,01	8,74	11,40	10,56	46,78
JP	1	0,00	0,11	93,55	1,02	0,03	0,01	2,83	0,00	2,23	0,13	0,08	6,45
	5	0,00	0,12	93,38	1,10	0,03	0,01	2,79	0,00	2,34	0,15	0,09	6,62
	10	0,00	0,12	93,38	1,10	0,03	0,01	2,79	0,00	2,34	0,15	0,09	6,62
HK	1	0,78	10,29	0,90	52,99	2,66	0,69	1,85	0,10	8,77	12,41	8,57	47,01
	5	0,78	10,29	0,92	52,84	2,65	0,76	1,91	0,10	8,77	12,40	8,58	47,16
	10	0,78	10,29	0,92	52,84	2,65	0,76	1,91	0,10	8,77	12,40	8,58	47,16
RU	1	0,22	1,65	0,02	2,78	70,55	0,24	5,47	0,04	2,32	7,73	8,97	29,45
	5	0,25	1,65	0,03	2,78	70,27	0,24	5,53	0,04	2,33	7,80	9,07	29,73
	10	0,25	1,65	0,03	2,78	70,27	0,24	5,53	0,04	2,33	7,80	9,07	29,73
SN	1	0,03	0,55	0,07	1,45	0,85	86,89	1,33	0,07	5,60	0,89	2,28	13,11
	5	0,03	0,55	0,08	1,47	0,91	86,55	1,40	0,07	5,61	0,97	2,36	13,45
	10	0,03	0,55	0,08	1,47	0,91	86,55	1,40	0,07	5,61	0,97	2,36	13,45
CZ	1	0,67	1,40	6,54	2,17	4,94	0,26	64,49	0,02	3,21	7,29	9,00	35,51
	5	0,75	1,39	7,37	2,16	4,89	0,26	63,82	0,02	3,22	7,21	8,90	36,18
	10	0,75	1,39	7,37	2,16	4,89	0,26	63,82	0,02	3,22	7,21	8,90	36,18
SK	1	0,14	0,02	0,03	0,07	0,12	0,07	0,01	98,69	0,07	0,19	0,60	1,31
	5	0,14	0,02	0,00	0,07	0,12	0,07	0,01	98,69	0,07	0,19	0,61	1,31
	10	0,14	0,02	0,00	0,07	0,12	0,07	0,01	98,69	0,07	0,19	0,61	1,31
PL	1	0,82	8,56	1,01	8,48	3,37	3,06	3,54	0,03	52,49	8,59	10,06	47,51
	5	0,83	8,57	1,04	8,50	3,35	3,08	3,55	0,03	52,29	8,62	10,14	47,71
	10	0,83	8,57	1,04	8,50	3,35	3,08	3,55	0,03	52,29	8,62	10,14	47,71
UK	1	0,29	4,82	0,20	7,93	5,07	0,64	5,54	0,01	4,73	47,53	23,25	52,47
	5	0,34	4,80	0,20	7,93	5,06	0,65	5,58	0,01	4,73	47,43	23,26	52,57
	10	0,33	4,80	0,20	7,92	5,05	0,65	5,57	0,01	4,72	47,35	23,40	52,65
DE	1	0,11	2,55	0,04	5,65	6,36	1,05	6,66	0,05	4,91	23,93	48,69	51,31
	5	0,16	2,53	0,04	5,60	6,30	1,06	6,59	0,05	4,87	23,67	48,15	51,85
	10	0,12	2,56	0,04	5,66	6,36	1,07	6,66	0,05	4,92	23,92	48,65	51,35

References

ACHSANI, N. A, STROHE, H. G. (2002): Dynamische Zusammenhänge zwischen den Börsen der Region Pazifisches Beckens vor und nach der Asiatischen Krise 1997. Statistische Diskussionsbeiträge Nr. 18, Wirtschafts- und Sozialwissenschaftliche Fakultät der Universität Potsdam.

ARSHANAPALLI, B., DOUKAS, J. (1993): International stock market linkages: Evidence from the pre- and post-October 1987 period. J. of Banking and Finance, 17, 193-208.

ELYASIANI, E., PERERA, P., PURI, T.N. (1998): Interdependence and dynamic linkage between stock markets of Sri Lanka and its trading partners. J. of Multinational Financial Management 8, 89-101.

EUN, S.C., SHIM, S. (1989): International Transmission of Stock Market Movements. J. of Financial and Quantitative Analysis, 24, 241-256.

GJERDE, O., SAETTERM, F. (1999): Causal relations among stock markets returns and macroeconomic variables in small, open economy. J. of International Financial Markets, Institutions and Money 9, 61-74.

GJERDE, O., SAETTEM, F. (1995): Linkages among European and world stock markets. The European J. of Finance, 1, 165-179.

HAMILTON, J.D. (1994): Time Series Analysis. Princeton University Press.

JANAKIRAMAN, S., LAMBA, A.S. (1998): An empirical examination of linkages between Pacific-Basin stock markets. J. of International Financial Markets, Institutions and Money 8, 155-174.

PESARAN, M. H., PESARAN, B. (1997): Working with Microfit 4.0: Interactive Econometric Analysis. Oxford University Press.

ROLL, R. (1998): The international crash of October 1987. Financial Analyst J. 44, 19-35.

WELFENS, P.J.J., GAVRILENKOV, Y. (Eds.) (2000): Restructuring, Stabilizing and Modernizing the New Russia, Springer-Verlag.

YAHOO FINANCE, http://finance.yahoo.com/.

Comments on: Dynamic Causal Links between the Russian Stock Exchange and Selected International Stock Markets

Frank Bohn

Achsani and Strohe analyse dynamic effects of both the Russian stock market on other stock markets and of other stock markets on the Russian stock market. They employ four different methods. The first one uses correlation analysis to measure the co-variability of two stock markets. The other three are based on a vector auto-regressive model (VAR). The second method draws on Granger causality to test if other stock markets help explain the development of the Russian stock market for instance. The third method employs impulse response functions to measure how, for instance, the Russian stock market responds over time to a shock in another stock market. Method number four uses forecast error decomposition to measure how much of the variation in, for instance, the Russian stock market can be explained by the variation in other stock markets.

Achsani and Strohe apply an established methodology (based, inter alia, on SIMS, 1980; EUN/SHIM, 1989) to the Russian stock market and obtain some interesting results. Suggestions for making both aim and analysis more transparent and for improving the presentation of results were made to the authors separately and are not repeated here. However, a few comments and critical remarks on each methodological step may be appropriate before looking at one of the key results and related questions in some more detail.

To obtain stationary time series data, the authors use "first differences" in terms of the percentage change of the present day stock price index over the previous day stock price index:

$$Daily.rate.of.return = \ln\left(\frac{stock.index_t}{stock.index_{t-1}}\right) \approx \frac{stock.index_t}{stock.index_{t-1}} - 1 \quad .$$

Calculating correlation coefficients is a useful measure for the co-variability of two stock markets. Results reported in table 2 are presumably based on univariate regressions between two stock markets in turn, but this is not clear from the paper. It should also be made clear which criterion is used for determining a "strong influence" between two stock markets. The authors include correlation coefficients for the lagged US stock market index. This makes sense, because the US stock market is the last one in the day and can, therefore, affect some of the other markets only on the following day. But should we not – by the same argument – include lagged European indices, too, when thinking about their link with the Asian markets. The role of shifted trading hours of stock markets in never discussed in the paper.

The rest of the analysis is based on a VAR model. Bivariate and block Granger causality tests are reported in tables 6 and 7, but in table 7, it is not clear which sets of indices (all?) are predicted by which sets of indices (Russia's?). The forecast error decomposition is reported in table 8, but the methodology could be clarified by defining the forecast error variance and discussing the alternative significance levels used. The impulse response analysis is correct but suffers from the presentation of results in table 9. If we want to understand the dynamics, it is not sufficient to report impulse responses after 1, 5 and 10 days (especially when the response is zero or close to zero after 5 days in most cases). A graphical illustration of ("continuous") impulse responses of the entire time period after the shock – as is standard in the literature – would be more useful.

Achsani and Strohe summarise the results obtained for each method separately and come up with a large number of interdependencies between various stock markets. Their paper would benefit greatly, however, from extracting the common features of these results. What are the overall findings? How do the results in one analysis substantiate or thwart the findings in another? Can we make better use of the given methodology in order to clarify some of the results?

As an example, let me discuss below what the most interesting result is for me: the interdependence between the US and the Russian stock markets (as well as between the US and other stock markets) seems to be greatly reduced when comparing the time period before and after the Russian crisis in August 1998. This result is obtained by two methods: first, correlation coefficients show a decrease of co-variability; and second, the decomposition of forecast errors reveals a decrease of variation explained by the other market. But what about the other two methods? Bivariate Granger causality tests show that it is true in one direction, but not necessarily in the other. From table 6 it is not clear how the significance level changes from before the crisis to thereafter. As for the impulse response analysis, it is not distinguished between the period before and after the crisis, even though this would have been useful in clarifying the aforementioned finding. It would also be instructive to know if there is further support in the literature.

Irrespective of the analytical findings, the question arises as to how we can explain this decrease in interdependence between the US and the Russian (as well as other) stock markets. The effect of the US stock index on the Russian one may be explained by the influence of banks in Russia. The impact of the Russian stock exchange on the US stock market may be strong because of the dominant role of oil producers in the Russian stock index, but this should not have changed after the crisis. It would certainly be helpful to know more about the characteristics of the Russian stock index used in the analysis.

Overall, the work by Achsani and Strohe is a valuable first step in understanding interdependencies between the Russian and other stock exchanges. The analysis offers opportunities for discussing some very interesting results and provides an excellent basis for further investigations into the causal links between the Russian and other international stock markets.

References

ACHSANI, N. A., STROHE, H. G. (2002): "Dynamic Causal Links between the Russian Stock Exchange and Selected International Stock Markets", mimeo.

EUN, S. C., SHIM, S. (1989): "International Transmission of Stock Market Movements", *Journal of Financial and Quantitative Analysis* 24, 241-256.

SIMS, C. A. (1980): "Macroeconomics and Reality", *Econometrica* 48:1, 1-48.

D. Russia's Trade Relations: Structural Adjustment, Geographical Patterns and Terms of Trade

Olga Nosova

1. Introduction

The development of trade accelerates economic growth, provides stimulus to new forms of productivity, enhances specialization, and leads to a more rapid pace of job creation. The expansion of free trade promotes inflow of goods and services, the increase of competition in domestic markets, access to a new markets, as well as the dissemination of knowledge and technologies. The share of merchandise trade relative to value added is growing dramatically in the world, and is characterizing the integration of the global economy through trade.

The recent deceleration of global trade affects changes of the world trade structure of commodities and services. The recession of the world trade rate has resulted in a slowing down of development within high technology branches. The existence of trade impediments – including high tariffs, tariff escalation, tariff rate quotas, and trade practices – prevents countries from receiving trade benefits. The share of industrial commodities increases the whole volume of global trade. A World Bank survey forecasts optimistic future global prospects, the rise of world demand, the expansion of trade relations in the world, a growth in world savings, population, and the investment in education.

Russian integration into the international trade system is based on the reduction of restrictions on export products and services, continued liberalization, and the improvement of national production competitiveness. Trade liberalization provides lower restrictive barriers – especially in services markets –, the change of legal rules and norms, improvements in trade relations, and income growth. Countries that fully liberalize trade and investment in finance and telecommunications grow faster in comparison to closed economies. The analysis of basic trade policy concepts, the determination of economic prospects for the rise of Russian foreign trade, the geographical patterns and policy conclusions are considered in the paper. The question of Russia's future membership in the WTO is dependent upon the resolution of problems surrounding the adoption of international legal standards, the establishment of an international trade mechanism, combining country interests with those of the international community to ensure effective developmental outcomes, and finally WTO accession.

2. The Basic Economic Approaches in Modern Trade Theory

The question of the role of trade policy in a country's economic development is one of the fundamental scientific problems in Economics. Scientists attempt to establish optimal trade policy rules and predict future world trade perspectives. International trade has strong effects on the distribution of income, often producing losers as well winners (KRUGMAN/OBSTFELD, 2000). Economists argue that trade has very few differences to many other forms of economic change, which are normally regulated. Similar countries produce similar factor proportions, and this trade will not involve the income-distribution effects characteristic of more conventional trade. Some scientists explain the increasing divergence of per capita incomes as the result of an international division of labor and the long-term specialization of countries in trade.

Other researchers give more credence to the role of state policy in the trade performance. The welfare effects of trade and industrial policy under an oligopolistic system can be obtained if the government is able to set its policy in advance of firms' production decisions and if government policy commitments are credible. The assumption is that each firm fails to consider the effects of its own actions on the profits of other domestic competitors (EATON/GROSSMAN, 1986).

It is widely recognized by researches that scale economics play a crucial role in explaining the postwar growth in trade among industrial countries. Trade depends on the allocation of production resources in the country. A resource-abundant country can lose from international trade through decreasing returns on skills and can gain from trade through increasing returns on skills. Development paths of countries converge in the case of decreasing returns but may diverge under increasing returns (TROFIMOV, 2000). The traditional gains from increased specialization and exchange across countries, as well as trade in intermediate inputs bring efficiency gains that lead to an outward shift in the production frontier for final goods in each country. The decision of companies to spread production across countries results in an aggravation of the position of low-skilled workers (FEENSTRA, 1998). Additional gains from trade are determined from reductions in aggregate delivery costs resulting from to scale economies (CUKROWSKI/FISCHER, 1999).

Tariff and untariff methods are a significant aspect of the important instruments of international trade policy. The existence of untariff barriers provides for an arbitrary form of country behavior and creates uncertainty in trade relations.

Researchers point out that a country may have an incentive to use tariffs under imperfect competition when price exceeds marginal costs, so that a country which imports such goods pays a rent to the foreign firm (unless the firm happens to earn only normal profits). (BRANDER/SPENCER, 1981). Tariff peaks make damages to the economic development of poor countries. Fully one-third of exports of the poorest development countries face tariff peaks in at least one of the four major markets, the United States, Japan, Europe, or Canada (Global Economic Prospects, 2002).

The analysis of the above-mentioned approaches confirms the importance of the modern trade theory at present time. The result of the functioning Soviet planned economy was the predominance of trade relations among the former Soviet republics, small trade flows with the rest of world, and the development of specialization rather than diversification within the republics. Since the collapse of the Soviet Union, the Russian Federation has started pursuing an integration policy into the world trading system. Russia has country-specific advantages and is interested in reorienting its trade toward market economies to receive potential trade benefits. The elaboration of an effective trade policy provides gains from increased trade specialization and exchange of goods across countries transmit new growth to countries through robust demand. Gains from trade of intermediate inputs result in an outward shift in the production frontier for final goods in the countries and contribute economic growth.

3. Russian Foreign Trade Performance and Structure

The assessment of the results of world economic development demonstrates the improvement of the economic situation in Russia at the end of the 20th century. The expansion of consumer and investment demand and the rise of import goods deliveries stimulate the growth of GDP, industrial production, fixed capital formation, trade surplus, and the increase in real incomes of the population in the country. Economic growth is accompanied by a stabilizing ruble exchange rate and the fast increase of trade surplus. Leading economists and international forecasts foresee future economic growth in light of proceeding economic reforms in transitional countries and high world oil prices (Fig. D1).

Despite the marked positive tendencies in Russia, a World Bank study highlights the existence of the following basic economic problems: the domination of the large firms, mostly dealing with in raw materials; low productivity growth; and an absence of an effective mechanism of the implementation of economic reforms (The Economist, 2002).

The analysis of Russia's balance of payments data in 2000-2002 demonstrates current account surplus. Trade surplus expands to a record $60 billion or 25 % of GDP in 2000 (Tab. D1). A decline in income from the export of goods is compensated for by rising services export in 2001.

The financial account analysis depicts the reduction of capital flight from the country. Foreign direct investment (FDI) is the most acceptable instrument from the point of the stability of the balance of payments in Russia. FDI growth stimulates the development of machinery, the transport sector, and food services in Russia. The liabilities of the remaining investments are reduced in the balance of payments.

Fig. D1: Economic Outlook in NIS* (average, percent)

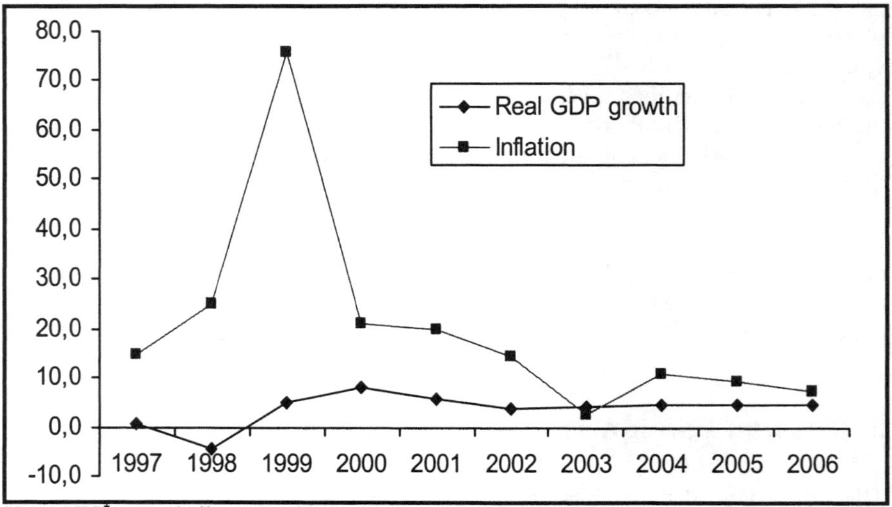

Note: NIS* - Azerbaijan, Kazakhstan, Russia and Ukraine.

Source: ECONOMIST INTELLIGENCE UNIT.

Tab. D1: Russia's Balance of Payments in 2000-2002 Q1, Billion US$

	1999	2000	2001	2002 Q1
Current account	24.7	46.4	34.6	7.2
Trade balance	36.1	60.7	47.8	9.5
Exports, f.o.b.	75.7	105.6	101.6	21.9
Import, c.i.f.	-39.5	-44.9	-53.8	-12.3
Services balance	-4.3	-7.6	-8.5	-1.8
Exports	9.1	10.0	10.9	2.6
Imports	-13.4	-17.6	-19.4	-4.4
Investment income	-7.7	-7.0	-4.1	-0.5
Received	3.9	4.3	6.2	2.2
Paid	-11.6	-11.3	-10.3	-2.8
Other items, net	0.6	0.3	-0.7	0.0
Capital and financial account	-15.9	-21.0	-17.2	-5.5
Capital Account	-0.3	11.0	-9.4	-0.1
Received	0.9	11.8	2.1	0.1
Paid	-1.2	-0.9	-11.5	-0.2
Financial account	-15.6	-32.0	-7.8	-5.4
Direct investment to Russia	3.3	2.7	2.5	0.5
Portfolio investment to Russia	-1.2	-10.3	-0.7	-0.2
Other items, net	-17.7	-24.4	-9.6	-5.7
Net errors and omissions	-7.0	-9.4	-9.2	-1.1
Change in reserves	-1.8	-16.0	-8.2	-0.5

Source: CENTRAL BANK OF RUSSIA (29 December, 2001, 28 June, 2002).

The empirical assessment OGUSTU (2001) of the supply export function and the demand function from FDI and other parameters demonstrate the statistical significance of these results, confirming the reintegration process of the former Soviet Union countries. FDI inflow influences trade diversification and promotes the development of bilateral economic relations among countries.

The model put forth by PANTELIDIS and KYRKILIS (1995) for predicting the potential effects of FDI is aimed at determining the necessary conditions for export-promoting FDI, import-substituting FDI, import-complementary FDI, and export-reducing FDI in Eastern European countries. The implication of the research illustrated that host country production should be internationally competitive in order to avoid any problems with the balance of payments.

The negative net errors and omissions demonstrate the improvement of unrecorded capital outflow. The recorded private capital net outflows and net errors and omissions amount to less than $3.5 billion or under 5 % of GDP (i.e. the average 2001 level). The rise in foreign currency and gold reserves in the second quarter 2002 (from $7 billion to $44 billion) further suggest a decrease in capital outflows (Economic Developments, 2002).

In accordance with Goskomstat data, foreign trade turnover in Russia exceeded $141 billion in 2001 and rose to 3.6 % in comparison to that of the previous year (Fig. D2). The deterioration in world competition and recession in developed countries lead to the reduction of world oil prices, decreasing production of petroleum products, as well as the production of metals, machines, and equipment. Russian economic performance has also been influenced by internal economic factors. These include the increasing costs of the real economic sector and the simultaneous rise in real wages, the quick increase of the price dynamics, and tariffs of national monopolies. The slow down in growth was caused by the correction of the restructuring programs aimed at providing entrance into new market segments in the country.

Fig. D2: The Export, Import and Current Account in Russia (Billion Euro)

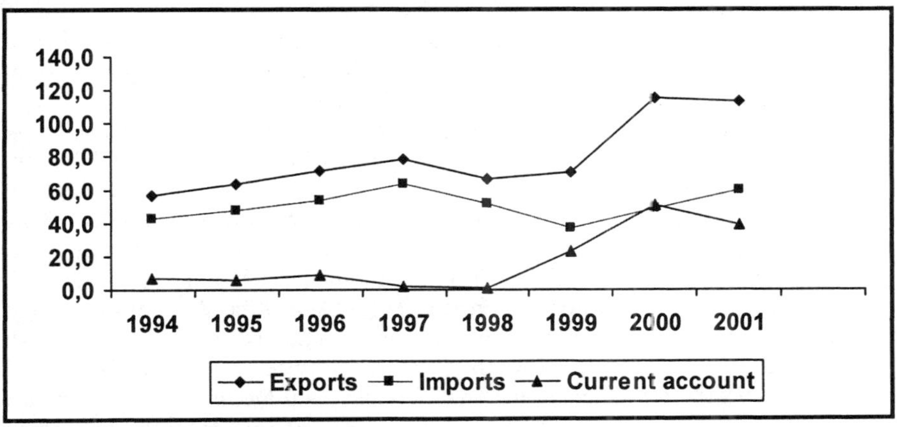

Source: GOSKOMSTAT OF RUSSIA.

The peculiarities of world competition and country development are reflected in the Russian export decrease to 2.3 % in 2001 (Tab. D2).

Tab. D2: Foreign Trade Indicators in Russia in 2001

	Foreign turnover	Export	Import	Trade balance
Total (billion US $)	141.9	100.7	41.2	59.5
Rate of increase (%)	3.6	-2.3	21.7	-
Non-CIS (billion US $)	116.3	86.2	30.1	56.1
Rate of increase (%)	4.3	-3.4	35.2	-
CIS (billion US $)	25.6	14.5	11.1	3.4
Rate of increase (%)	0.6	4.6	-4.3	-

Source: BULLETIN FOREIGN COMMERCIAL INFORMATION (2002), NO 37, 4 April, p. 2.

The value of Russian trade turnover saw its greatest increase in 2001 during the period spanning from 1992 to 2001. Russia's main trading partners are non-NIS countries. The share of these countries makes up 82 % in the overall trade turnover, including both exports (86 %) and imports (73 %) in 2001. The decline in oil prices, intermediate petroleum products, and non-ferrous metals are compensated through a rise in the volume of petroleum and power supply source deliveries. Machinery and equipment exports increased to 10 % and makes up 8.6 % of exports of non-NIS. The export of ferro-alloys decreased to 12 %, rolled iron by 23 %, copper to 13 %, nickel 5 %, and aluminum 4 %. The share of chemical production reached 6.8 % and that of mineral fertilizers increased to 6 %, while artificial rubber also rose to 6 %. The export of ammonia decreased to 5 % and methanol to 9 %. The export of timber and cellulose paper production shot up to 6 %, with its share comprising 5 % of non-NIS exports.

The Russian import of machines and equipment, food production and resources from non-NIS increased with its share making up 61 % in total imports. The share of machines and equipment equals 37.2 % in total import; food production and raw materials was 23.6 %.

Chemical production purchases increased to 30 %, including the decreasing of the share of imports from non-NIS to 19.9 %. The share of the rest goods is not significant and makes up only 1/5 of all imports from non-NIS countries.

Total foreign trade turnover made up $25.6 billion from NIS in 2001, including the increase of exports to $14.5 billion while imports decreased to $11.1 billion. The main export was fuel-power goods, albeit with a decreasing share in total export volume in 2001. The export of machines and equipment exceeded 23 %, export of chemical production rose to 17 %, including metal production at 31 %. Food deliveries and agricultural raw materials dominated NIS imports.

The share of fuel power goods increased to 1.2 %, and the share of timber and cellulose-paper products rose to 0.3 % in the commodity structure of Russian export (Fig. D3). The growth of Russian exports is caused by the stabilization of the exchange rate, strengthening national currency, and the unification of import duties. The export quota in 2001 increased for oil, petroleum products, certain kinds of timber production and mineral fertilizers, yet decreased for natural gas.

An analysis of the dynamics of Russian export points out that the basic trade indicators are drag behind average world indicators. The Russian export share in the world export of raw materials and intermediate products in 2000 is as follows: oil 8 %, copper 9 %, petroleum products 15 %, calcium phosphates 14 %, ferrous irons 15 %, molybdenum 15 %, mixed fertilizer 15 %, sulfur 17 %, diamonds for industrial purposes 19 %, platinum group metals (value assessment) 23 %, nickel 33 %, natural gas 33 %, and iron and concentrated products 52 %. The Russian share in the world export of military equipment equaled 30 % (Bulletin Foreign Commercial Information, 2002, NO 15).

Fig. D3: The Commodity Structure of Russian Export in 2001 (commodity groups, %)

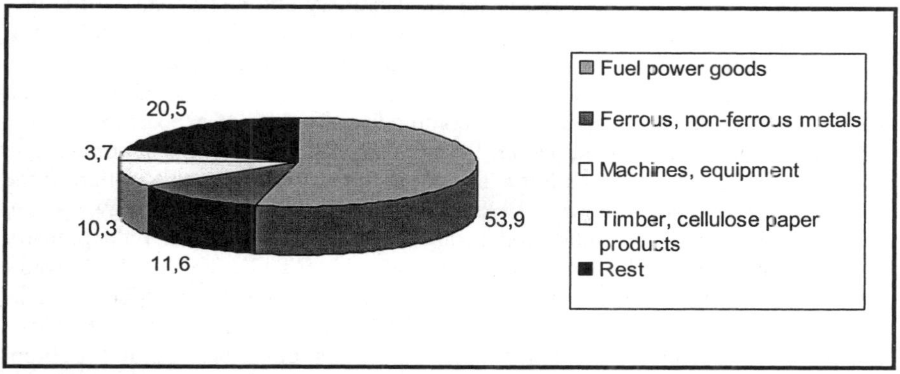

Source: BULLETIN FOREIGN COMMERCIAL INFORMATION (2002), NO 38, 6 April, p. 2.

The proportion of Russian machines, equipment and transport facilities did not exceed 0.4 % of the world export. In accordance with the estimations of scientists, the share of Russia's competitive production equaled 1/1000 of the world export. The export of Russian high technology products makes up 0.3 % in the total volume of world trade (SPARTAK, 2002). Russia has lagged behind developed countries in the growth rates on exports of finished products, especially know-how products. A comparison of basic foreign trade indicators demonstrates a reduction of the average increase of GDP per head, the total productivity growth in GDP, the rate of commodity export growth, the share in world export, and the commodity export share in GDP in Russia (Tab. D3). The existence of a long duration unbalanced economy, the deformation of the price mechanism, discrepancies in real sector needs as well as the volume of borrowing sources, the low rate of real capital accumulation, and an undeveloped financial-credit sphere all prevent the progress of market economy development in Russia. The distinguishing feature of Russian foreign trade is the high level of unorganized trade (shuttle trade), which makes up 21 % of imports and 1.5 % of exports and barter trade (KOSTUNINA, 2001).

Tab. D3: The Basic Foreign Trade Indicators in Russia

Indicators	1990	Estimated 2000
Average increase of GDP per head, number of times, 1990=1	6.20	4.00
Total productivity growth in GDP, number of times, 1990=1	5.40	3.80
Commodity export growth, number of times, 1990=1	11.92	6.92
Share in the world export, %	2.59	1
Commodity export share in GDP, %	7.80	35.70

Source: Constructed on data of BOLOTIN (2001).

The main causes for the small share of machinery and equipment in the total volume of exports are reductions in production, the low competitiveness of output, the backwardness of production base, and the infringement of cooperative ties throughout the former Soviet Union. The coefficient of export specialization shows the ratio of branch share in the commodity structure of exports to its share in the industrial production structure. When this coefficient exceeds 1, competitive advantages exist within the country. The coefficient of export specialization of the fuel industry in Russia between 1998 and 2000 equaled 2.6, metallurgy 1.4, the chemical industry 1.15, timber and cellulose paper industry 1.05, light industry 0.7, and machinery and metal processing 0.55 (SPARTAK, 2002). The light industry, machinery, and metal processing have low coefficients of export specialization. There are competitive branches of high technologies, including optic electronics, telecommunication equipment, new materials, optic devices, and program software.

The development of services (including telecommunication, finance, transport and etc.) influences the competitiveness of the country. Russia's export and import of services do not comprise a significant magnitude in the world trade of services. Russia takes 24th place in the world export of services and 21st place in the world import of services. The modern rise of internet trade affects its use in Russia. Growth of internet trade provides for an increase in the speed of transactions, the reduction of intermediate costs, and stimulates the creation of new distribute networks. The commodity structure of the national export is considered a barrier for the spread of the internet. The total value of concluded transactions exceeded $26.9 billion in 2000 (ZAHAROV, 2000). Export shares indexes to GDP demonstrate the interdependence of export and GDP values (Tab. D4).

Tab. D4: The Shares of Export Indexes to GDP in Russia (1995=100 %)

	1996	1997	1998	1999	2000	2001
Export	100.1	101.8	101.6	111.1	122.5	127.6
GDP	96.6	97.5	92.7	97.7	105.8	111.5

Source: BUSINESS FOREIGN COMMERCIAL INFORMATION (2002), NO 45, 23 April, p.2.

The adoption of a stimulating export program is a key item in the Russian foreign trade policy. The development of export specialization of competitive branches, trade diversification, and the acceleration of integration into the world trade system would provide for an expanded and strengthened foreign trade position in the world markets.

4. Geographical Patterns and Terms of Foreign Trade

The share of trade with European Union countries makes up 36.9 % of the total volume of Russian trade turnover. The NIS share equals 18 %, countries of the Pacific Economic Cooperation Group (PECG) 16.3 %, and Central and East European countries 13.7 %. The rate of Russian net export growth to the non-NIS exceeds the share of net export growth to the NIS. The main Russian trade partners in 2001 were non-NIS countries, whose share equaled 82 % of the total volume of trade turnover, including exports (86 %) and imports (73 %) (Fig. D4).

The Federal Republic of Germany is Russia's main trading partner. Germany's share in Russian trade turnover equals $14.9 billion, Italy -$9.1 billion, USA $7.3 billion, China $7.3 billion, the Netherlands $5.9 billion, Great Britain $5.3 billion, Poland $5.1 billion, Finland $4.4 billion, Turkey $3.8billion, France $3.7, and Japan $3.6 billion.

The shares of Belarus, Ukraine, and Kazakhstan are estimated to be the largest in Russian turnover within the NIS. The commodity structure is characterized by the dominance of petroleum and chemical products. The share of ferrous and non-ferrous metals has decreased.

Fig. D4: Net Export in Russia in 2001 (Mn US$)

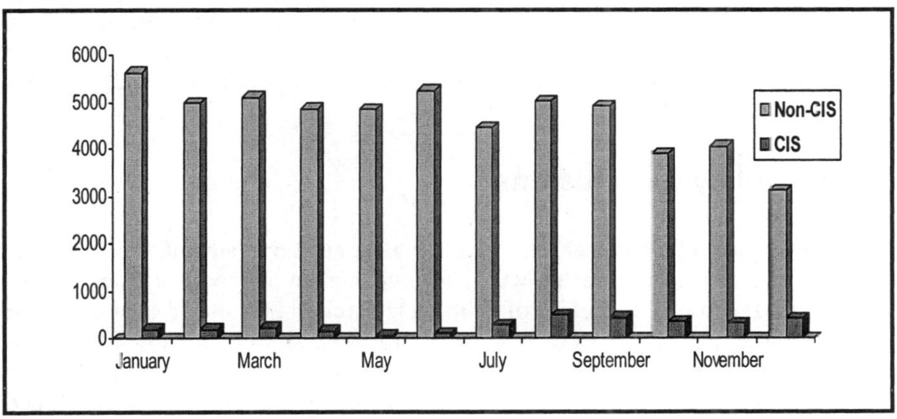

Source: BULLETIN FOREIGN COMMERCIAL INFORMATION (2002), NO 15, 14 February, p. 2.

Tariff regulation is considered one of most debated questions. Opponents argue that the abrupt rise of tariffs on natural monopolies could aggravate the perspectives of economic development. Moreover, tariffs can lead to a rise in the rate of inflation (SHARONOV, 2002). The general principal of tariff regulation should be the establishment of the different duties. Technology and equipment should have low duties; raw materials and half-finished products should have significant duties, and finished products the highest duties (MOVSESYAN, 2001). Petroleum and energy tariffs should be increased to the level of real economic costs (RUYBALKO, 2002). The Russian government has decided to place limits on price increases for natural gas, rail cargo, and electricity starting in 2003. This price regulation system was influenced by recent negotiations for WTO membership.

BOTCHIKOV (2002) compares the tariff domestic protection in Russia and in the Western Europe. The average Russian tariff was 16 % while that in the European Union was 27 %. The structure of tariff regulation is completely different in the Western Europe and is directed around a higher level of protection for the economy. The conditions for WTO accession should be the creation of the protection mechanism of the basic branches providing increased adaptation opportunities to Russian economy.

The convergence of national legislation and administrative rules of foreign trade regulation to international principals and norms are considered necessary conditions for Russia's future accession to the WTO. The main problems for Russia at the moment are the absence of a normative legal base, the lack of a highly educated staff, institutional infrastructure, and informational security. According to some estimates, Russia loses one to two billion dollars a year that could be earned if various Production Sharing Agreements contracts had been approved and made operational without delay (LAURILA, 2001). Russia's accession requires the maintenance of national production competitiveness; Russia should implement different customs duties in order to protect its domestic market. Russia's integration into the sphere of multinational regulation international trade should be based on the combination of branch development with competitive advantages and should be directed at protecting the development of vitally important branches.

5. The Policy Conclusions

This article has revealed that the existence of competitive advantages in Russia can generate substantial trade growth. The development of export-oriented sectors in the economy provides the rise of gains from foreign trade that should cover the budget deficit, the purchases of new kinds of goods, as well as know-how development. The high share of state debt, poor management organization, sluggish financial discipline, absence of legal enforcement mechanism, and undeveloped institutional infrastructure prevent the development of trade relations. Governmental policy should be directed at supporting and stimulating the development of export-oriented branches. The preparation of a special export-enhancing program should include the following policy-oriented measures:

1. The reorientation of export specialization and the increase of the share of finished products;

2. The development of trade diversification into wider product fields;
3. A restriction on the rise of tariffs for services and natural monopoly production, and the application of different tariffs for commodities;
4. The stimulation of investment growth in export-oriented branches;
5. The elaboration of a special customs duty mechanism aimed at protecting the development of high technology branches;
6. The adoption of a custom code, a law on technical regulations and laws on intellectual property in accordance with WTO legislation.

Appendix

Tab. D5: World Trade and GDP Growth (Percentage Change from Previous Year)

	Current Estimate		Current Forecasts	
	2000	2001	2002	2003
World trade (volume)	13.3	1.0	4.0	10.2
World GDP (growth)	3.8	1.3	1.6	3.9
High-income countries	3.4	0.9	1.1	3.5
United States	4.1	1.1	1.0	3.9
Japan	1.5	-0.8	0.1	2.4
Euro Area	3.5	1.5	1.3	3.6
Non-OECD countries	6.3	0.6	3.2	5.7
Developing countries	5.5	2.9	3.7	5.2
East Asia and Pacific	7.5	4.6	4.9	6.8
Europe and Central Asia (ECA)	6.3	2.1	3.0	4.2
Latin America & the Caribbean	3.8	0.9	2.5	4.5
Middle East and North Africa	3.9	3.4	2.9	3.6
South Asia	4.9	4.5	5.3	5.5
Sub-Saharan Africa	3.0	2.7	2.7	3.9

Source: WORLD BANK, Global Economic Prospects (2002).

Tab. D6: Foreign Trade of NIS, Baltic Republics and Russia in 2001 (per cent to 2000)

	Trade Turnover	Export	Import
Azerbaijan	77.6	96.1	59.0
Armenia	177.4	273.8	117.2
Byelorus	99.2	94.6	106.1
Georgia	118.6	137.0	108.4
Kazakhstan	105.8	121.0	90.2
Kirghizia	75.2	80.2	69.3
Moldova	109.3	113.9	106.3
Tadzhikistan	67.5	123.6	54.3
Turkmenia	29.6	107.5	8.2
Uzbekistan	105.3	148.3	87.5
Ukraine	104.8	104.9	104.6
Latvia	60.2	56.3	130.3
Lithuania	83.8	79.8	138.5
Estonia	100.6	100.2	106.0

Source: BULLETIN FOREIGN COMMERCIAL INFORMATION (2002), NO 22.

Tab. D7: Increases of Nominal Gas, Electricity and Rail Cargo Prices (%)

	2002		2003	2003-05
	Feb-March	July	preliminary limit	preliminary annual limit
Gas	20	15	20	25
Electricity	20	2.4	14-16	15-18
Rail cargo	16	6.8	12-14	9-12

Source: Russian Economy. The Month Review, BOFIT (2002), NO 6, p.2.

Tab. D8: Russia's Foreign Trade in 2001 (Bln. US Dollars)

	Total		Non-NIS		NIS	
	Export	Import	Export	Import	Export	Import
January	8196.7	2368.6	7165.1	1544.5	1031.6	824.1
February	8063.6	2896.9	6953.2	1979.4	1110.4	917.6
March	8734.1	3404.9	7468.5	2373.2	1265.6	1031.7
April	8492.5	3467.8	7288.6	2428.0	1204.0	1039.8
May	8578.8	3678.5	7421.2	2585.7	1157.5	1092.8
June	9113.6	3763.2	7695.7	2456.3	1417.9	1306.9
July	8106.8	3360.9	7038.2	2585.3	1068.5	775.6
August	8995,7	3485,6	7713,6	2694,4	1282.1	791.2
September	8400,6	3042,4	7259,1	2345,8	1141,5	696,5
October	7917,8	3656,8	6655,5	2759,6	1262,3	897,2
November	8280,5	3893.9	7073.4	3016.8	1207.1	877.1
December	7772.1	4217.5	6480.4	3352.1	1291.7	865.4

Source: BULLETIN FOREIGN COMMERCIAL INFORMATION (2002), NO 15.

Tab. D9: Export and Import of the Russian Federation to the Federal Land of Brandenburg

	Russian Export in 2001 in % to 2000	Russian Import in 2001 in % to 2000
Total	94.2	106.0
Resources	85.3	42.8
Half-finished products	155.7	85.2
Finished products	81.3	106.4
Food - stuffs	42.3	110.7

Source: BULLETIN FOREIGN COMMERCIAL INFORMATION (2002), NO 22

References

BOCHIKIV, S. (2002): Import Substitute Vector of Alternative Strategy of the National Economy, Russian Economic Journal, NO 3, p.3-10.

BOLOTIN, B. (2001): World Economy in Past Hundred Yeas, World Economics & International Relations, NO 9, 90-144.

BULLETIN FOREIGN COMMERCIAL INFORMATION (2002): About Foreign Trade in Russia in 2001, NO 37, 4 April, p. 2, NO 38, 6 April, p.2.

CUKROWSKI, J., FISCHER, M.M. (2000): Journal of Regional Science, Blackwell Publishers, Vol.40., NO 2, 311-322.

DYUMULEN, I. (2001): Russia on the Way to WTO, World Economics & International Relations, NO 9, 121-124.

EATON, J., GROSSMAN, G.M. (1986): Optimal Trade and Industrial Policy Under Oligopoly, The Quarterly Journal of Economics, John Wiley & Sons. Inc., May, 383 - 402.

ECONOMIC DEVELOPMENTS (2002): Russian Economy, The Month in Review, Bank of Finland, Institute for Economies in Transition, NO 6, p.1.

FEENSTRA, R.C. (1998): Integration of Trade and Disintegration of Production in the Global Economy, The Journal of Economic Perspectives, Vol. 12, NO 4, Fall, p.31-50.

GLOBAL ECONOMIC PROSPECTS (2002): World Bank.

KOSTUNINA, G. (2001): International Trade of Commodities and Goods, in: LEVINZEVA, N.: eds. International Economic Relations, Moscow, POCCPN, p.34-57.

KRUGMAN, P., OBSTFELD, M. (2000): International Economics, Addison Wesley Publishing Company.

LAURILA, J. (2001): FDI and the Russian Energy Sector: An Ill-Managed Partnership, Russian Economy. The Month in Review, BOFIT, 6 April P.4.

MOVSESYAN, A.G. (2001): The Transnationalization in the Wold Economy, Financial Academy to the Government of Russian Federation.

OGUSTU, M. (2001): Ukraine: "The Expected Miracle." The Problems and Reforms of the Investment Climate Improvement for Foreign Investors, in: VON KRAMON-TAUBADELAY, S., AKIMOVA, I.: eds, Fostering Sustainable Economic Growth in Ukraine: Kiev, Alfa-Print, p.205-214.

PANTELIDIS, P., Kyrkilis, D. (1995): Foreign Direct Investment and Trade Patterns of Eastern European Economies. Economia Internazionale, Vol. 48, NO 3, p.387-396.

RUSSIA'S ECONOMY. SCRATCH AND SNIFF (2002): The Economist, February 16, p.71.

RUYBALKO, T. (2002): Russian German Dialog of Economists, Economic Questions, NO 5, p.156-158.

SHARONOV, A. (2002): The tariff Regulation, Bulletin Foreign Commercial Information, NO 22, 2 March, p. 2-4.

SPARTAK, A.N. (2002): The Situation and Perspectives of Russian Export, Bulletin Foreign Commercial Information, NO 71-72, 29 June, p.1-4.

TROFIMOV, G. (2000): Economic Development and Gains from Trade, Moscow: EERC, 1-35.

ZAHAROV, A. (2000): The Development of Stock Exchange Market and the Economic Reforms Path, Izvestiya, 15 November, p.15.

Comments on: Russia's Trade Relations: Structural Adjustment, Geographical Patterns and Terms of Trade

Joachim Ahrens

Olga Nosova's paper essentially provides a descriptive stocktaking of the development of Russia's foreign trade, its commodity structure and its geographical direction during the first decade of systemic transformation. The author emphasizes the fundamental importance of opening up Russia's transition economy and the benefits that can be gained through increasing productivity, enhanced specialization, mass production, the import of knowledge and new technologies, access to new markets as well as enhanced competition in domestic markets.

It is argued that Russia has achieved significant progress in overcoming its legacy of the past, when 'artificial', politically-motivated and steered patterns of production and foreign trade dominated the 'socialist division of labor'. Especially since the 1998 financial crisis, Russia's export performance has considerably improved. Moreover, the current geographical pattern of exports and imports is essentially guided by comparative advantages and market forces. In addition, Nosova argues that foreign trade performance still lags behind that of other more successful transition economies in Central and Eastern Europe. Particularly, the dominance of energy products and raw materials in Russia's exports has made the domestic economy as well as fiscal policy making strongly dependent on (highly volatile) world market prices for these products. So far, the economy has not managed to sufficiently restructure and modernize domestic production and to strengthen its international competitiveness as a precondition to diversify Russia's exports. Key reasons for this failure include "the low rate of real capital accumulation, and an undeveloped financial-credit sphere (…,) reductions in production, the low competitiveness of output, the backwardness of the production base, and the infringement of cooperative ties throughout the former Soviet Union." Based on this stocktaking, the author concludes that "Russia should implement different customs duties in order to protect its domestic market." Furthermore, "policy should be directed at supporting and stimulating the development of export-oriented branches" through "a special export-enhancing program". Unfortunately, the paper is silent on how such a program should be exactly designed, whether or not the state apparatus has the capacity and capability to implement such a program, and how the desired policies could be enforced. Moreover, the need for domestic policy and institutional reform, which need to accompany and support further trade reform, is disregarded in the paper.

Furthermore, Nosova's contribution lacks a more systematic analysis of potential advantages that can be generated through an external opening up. These advantages essentially include the comparative-static benefits from foreign trade, the capability of high-productivity sectors to grow faster than domestic demand, dynamic welfare gains as well as disincentives to engage in corruption and other unproductive activities, i.e. phenomena frequently observed when trade barriers exist (MARTIN, 2000). It would have been useful to explore to what extent these advantages could actually be enjoyed by the Russian economy or why the theoretically expected positive outcomes have not materialized so far.

The following considerations highlight some aspects neglected in the paper, but which may help to explain why the recent positive developments in Russia's overall economic performance in general and in the foreign trade sector in particular may prove not to be sustainable. Although the Russian economy achieved remarkable overall growth rates over the last four years as well as substantial surpluses in its trade and current account, this success can be only partly attributed to progress in economic reform. Rather, it has been the outcome of a drastic depreciation of the ruble following the 1998 financial crisis. (Initially the ruble had lost about 80 % of its value vis-à-vis the US dollar.) This had a substantial impact on the Russian economy. First of all, import volumes substantially decreased and aggregate demand was redirected towards domestic products. Secondly, reductions in real wages helped to cut costs of domestic enterprises. Thirdly, world market prices for energy products increased significantly and boosted export revenues. Altogether, this induced a substantial rise in corporate profits and hence in domestic investment. These factors contributed to create some breathing space for the Russian economy, but there have already been signs of slower growth over the last two years. International energy prices have started to decrease, real wages have been growing again by about 20 %, and nominal wages even increased by more than 45 % in 2001. The additional purchasing power (in nominal terms) has contributed to more recent increases in imports, while export revenues even decreased due to the real appreciation of the ruble. These developments contributed to a considerable deterioration of Russia's foreign trade and current account as well as a massive reduction in corporate profits and investment growth. Furthermore, inflation is still too high. Given a relatively stable nominal exchange rate, this is particularly problematic, because the Russian export sector will have to bear the costs of a real appreciation of the ruble. Assuming relatively constant world market prices for Russian export goods, a further reduction of the foreign trade surplus can hardly be avoided. In sum, it has to be emphasized that the competitive advantage of the Russian economy on international markets, which was mainly caused by the strong nominal depreciation of the ruble after the financial crisis, has been steadily decreasing (SCHRETTL et al., 2002).

In addition, the transition towards an open, market-oriented economic system not only requires sustained reforms within the trade policy sphere such as the opening up of the system to other competitors, the development of indirect policy instruments and the elimination of distorted exchange rates. It also requires numerous interdependent policy and institutional changes in domestic policy making. Domestic reforms need to include the creation of secure private property rights, a coherent, market-oriented legal and regulatory framework, an effective and transparent tax system, a sound financial sector, consequent competition policies, and a debureaucratization of the economy.

While the Russian trade regime is not overly restrictive anymore, weaknesses in the functioning of basic market institutions have impeded an effective integration into the international trading system (MICHALOPOULOS, 1999). Although there are still some policy distortions relating to the foreign trade sector such as export tariffs, the main problems appear to concern domestic policy making. In this regard, Russia has remained a basket case after more than one decade of transition. While it had begun the systemic transformation with a seemingly shock therapy-like program in 1992, all subsequent reform efforts were of a piecemeal character. Until the end of the 1990s, virtually none of the many economic reform attempts materialized as expected (except for some temporarily limited successes in macroeconomic stabilization and more recently in institutional reform). Above all, political factors proved to be the most severe impediments to systemic transformation and economic progress. Initially, it was the vacuum of political powers in which the transition process was trapped. Subsequently, the government's reform policies were blocked by a parliament dominated by anti-reformist communist and nationalist forces. And more recently, the collusion between corrupt government officials and the new oligarchs have posed a serious threat to genuine market-oriented reforms including foreign trade reforms. In sum, a lack of effective governance seems to be the single most important cause for the continuing economic problems in Russia (AHRENS, 2002).

Important causes for the ongoing economic problems include a still insufficient institutional restructuring of the economic order, the lack of horizontal and vertical mechanisms of coordination and conflict resolution, and a state apparatus that has allowed massive rent seeking of old and new vested interests to take place. This increased the misallocation of resources and fueled inflation. Moreover, ill-conceived economic policies, an inconsistent assignment of political powers and administrative competences as well as political conflicts hindered sustained economic growth. In this context, factors such as the unstable banking and financial sector, deficits of the legal system that have not been in line with real market conditions, contradicting rules and regulations, and a substantial lack of rule enforcement have played an important role. Moreover, lasting conflicts between federal political institutions on the one hand and between Moscow and subordinated regional and local authorities on the other have proved to be considerable impediments to further economic reform. These conflicts have prevented the necessary consensus concerning the elaboration and implementation of a comprehensive and credible transformation strategy as well as the enforcement of agreed measures by the public administration.

At present, the most important measures to deal with persistent economic problems include:

- stabilizing the economy through tight fiscal and monetary policies;
- implementing an effective tax system, which would also help to reduce the need to finance the federal budget through tariff revenues and export taxes;
- continuing market-oriented institution building and enforcing institutions by an independent judiciary;
- introducing and enforcing private property rights;

- stabilizing and restructuring the banking and financial sectors;
- introducing hard budget constraints for state enterprises and enforcing the bankruptcy law;
- promoting competition by reducing public subsidies, thoroughly eliminating barriers to market entry (especially for foreign investors), and opening up the economy;
- implementing a social safety net for the inevitable losers from transformation; and
- streamlining and restructuring the economic bureaucracy at all levels of government.

Most of these measures, however, will only materialize in the medium or long run. And eventually, their success will strongly depend on the ability of policy makers to overcome the deeper roots of the economic muddling-through strategy, which mainly concern politico-institutional factors. The political system has to be stabilized, state institutions must be reinforced, an effective system of incentives and sanctions needs to be implemented, and responsibilities must be clearly assigned (AHRENS, 2002).

All of these domestic policy and institutional reforms and particularly fostering competition on the domestic market, the creation of secure private property rights, a transparent legal and regulatory framework, investment in the education system as well as accountable and predictable policy making are unalterable preconditions to improve the overall investment climate, to improve technological change and to foster productivity growth, to attract foreign direct investment, and to diversify the production structure and enhance the competitiveness of Russian products in international markets.

Finally, Western countries, particularly the European Union, could assist Russia in undertaking these reforms. First, they could offer technical assistance in order to support institutional reforms in the foreign-trade sector. This would help to reduce prevailing transaction costs and business risks. Second, Western trading partners could introduce a more open approach that allows for a better access of Russian goods (including manufactures) to their markets (HARE et al., 1996).

References

AHRENS, J. (2002): Governance and Economic Development: A Comparative Institutional Approach. Cheltenham, UK and Northampton, MA.

HARE, P., ESTRIN, S., LUGACHYOV, M., TAKLA, L. (1996): "Russia's Foreign Trade: New Directions and Western Policies", Centre for Economic Reform and Transformation, Heriot-Watt University, Edinburgh.

MARTIN, W. (2000): "Trade Policy Reform in the East Asian Transition Economies", World Bank Transition Economies Working Paper No. 2535; available on the Internet at http://econ.worldbank.org/files/1393_wps2535.pdf.

MICHALOPOULOS, C. (1999): "The Integration of Transition Economies into the World Trading System", World Bank Transition Economies Working Paper No. 2182; available on the Internet at http://econ.worldbank.org/docs/972.pdf.

SCHRETTL, W., DITTMANN, K., ENGERER, H., LODAHL, M., SCHROOTEN, M. (1999): "Russlands Wirtschaft auf riskantem Kurs", DIW-Wochenbericht 6/02.

E. The Internationalization of the Russian Gas Industry and its Export Potential

Christian von Hirschhausen

1. Introduction

The gas industry is a crucial element in Russia's strategy for economic development and international integration. It has often been stated that „what is good for Gazprom is good for Russia", and – even though it is debatable – this idea marks the thinking of the Russian elites still today. Russian gas also has an important external dimension: European gas import dependency upon Russia is expected to increase from its current level of 40 % to over two-thirds by 2030. The EU-Russia Energy dialogue is an outcome of this belief, as is the increased interest of Japan and even the United States in the future of Russian gas exports.

This chapter discusses the perspectives of the Russian gas industry and its export potential towards Central and Western Europe. Section 2 shows the role of energy, and in particular gas, for the Russian economy, whereas Section 3 analyzes the strategy of Gazprom towards internationalization. The potential future of Russian gas exports towards Europe is discussed in Section 4, with a conclusion in Section 5.[1]

2. The Role of Gas in the Russian Economy

2.1 The Role of Energy

Energy is by far the most important sector in the Russian economy, and a central pillar of its foreign trade. However, the country has been unable to pull the economy from its post-socialist slump. Rather, the structure of Russian economy resembles the dual structure of other resource-rich countries – such as Saudi-Arabia – which have been unable to turn resources into sustained economic growth. The energy industry provides almost one-third of industrial production, and more than a half of export revenues. Its contribution to the federal budget is

[1] This chapter draws on earlier work of the author and colleagues, mainly HIRSCHHAUSEN (2002), OPITZ/ENERGER/HIRSCHHAUSEN (2002), CHOLLET/MEINHART/HIRSCHHAUSEN/OPITZ (2001), and ENGERER (2003); the usual disclaimer applies.

said to be 20 %. Energy production and domestic consumption plummeted in the 1990s, by 27 % and 33 %, respectively, when compared with the 1988 record levels, and have only recently recovered (ENGERER, 2003, IEA, 2002). Tables E1 and E2 show the development of the oil and gas industry, respectively, and Table E3 shows the importance of energy exports for the Russian trade balance; Figure E1 shows the relevant export routes for Russian gas towards Central and Western Europe.

Declining domestic consumption reflects both the inability of industry and households to maintain consumption at increasing energy prices and, to a smaller extent, more efficient use of energy. The situation is undermined by the non-payment problem, which remains acute, though payment ratios have increased since 1999 (IEA, 2002). The situation is also affected by an increase in the internal market prices for energy resources which lags behind inflation, and the prices for domestic consumers of gas and electricity remaining state regulated. Administrative regulation also prevails for access to export pipelines and is often used by the government to carry out political goals. Curiously, primary energy consumption contracted less than aggregate economic output, leading to an increase of the energy intensity of official GDP, which already belonged to the highest in the world. The energy strategy of the Russian government has become more cautious recently, but it still predicts sharp increases of oil and gas production, from 323 mn. tons of oil to 360 mn. tons, and from 584 bcm of gas to 700 bcm (Russian Energy Strategy 2020, cited in GÖTZ, 2002, p. 40). Whether these objectives can be met is questionable (IEA, 2002).

Tab. E1: Russia's Mineral Oil Exports, 1995-2002

Region	1995	1996	1997	1998	1999	2000	2001	2002
				Crude oil (mn. t)				
CIS countries	26.1	20.6	17.1	19.2	18.8	16.9	22.5	18.0
Non-CIS countries	96.2	105.0	110.0	117.9	116.0	127.6	137.5	157.0
Total	122.3	125.6	127.1	137.1	134.8	144.5	160.0	175.0
				Oil products (mn. t)				
CIS countries	3.5	2.0	2.2	2.6	2.9	3.5	2.5	2.0
Non-CIS countries	44.0	55.0	58.4	51.2	47.8	58.4	68.5	73.0
				Total mineral oil (mn. t)				
Total	47.5	57.0	60.6	53.8	50.7	61.9	71.0	75.0
CIS countries	29.6	22.6	19.3	21.8	21.7	20.4	25.0	20.0
Non-CIS countries	140.2	160.0	168.4	169.1	163.8	186.0	206.0	230.0
Total	169.8	182.6	187.7	190.9	185.5	206.4	231.0	250.0

Source: ENGERER (2003), based on Goskomstat.

Tab. E2: Russia's Gas Balance (1996-2001)

	1996	1997	1998	1999	2000	2001
Production	601.0	570.0	551.3	551.0	545.0	542.4
Consumption	402.5	369.1	364.7	363.6	377.2	372.7
Exports	198.5	200.9	186.6	187.4	193.8	181.0
C.I.S	70.5	80.0	66.3	61.9	60.0	50.0
Non-C.I.S	128.0	120.9	120.3	125.5	133.8	131.0

Source: GOSKOMSTAT, BP.

Tab. E3: Russian Export Revenues from Oil and Gas Exports

	1994	1995	1996	1997	1998	1999	2000	2001	2002
bn USD or & Oil	14.6	18.3	23.4	21.1	14.5	19.6	36.2	34.0	39.2
of which: Crude oil	10.5	13.3	15.9	13.8	10.3	14.2	25.3	24.6	28.3
Oil products	4.1	5.0	7.5	7.3	4.3	5.4	10.9	9.4	10.9
Gas	10.6	12.1	14.7	16.4	13.4	11.4	16.7	17.8	15.9
Oil and gas	25.2	30.5	38.1	37.5	27.9	31.0	52.9	51.8	55.1
% of exports	37.4	37.0	42.5	43.1	37.5	41.0	50.3	51.0	51.9

Source: ENGERER (2003), based on Goskomstat.

Fig. E1: Western Russian Gas Export Routes

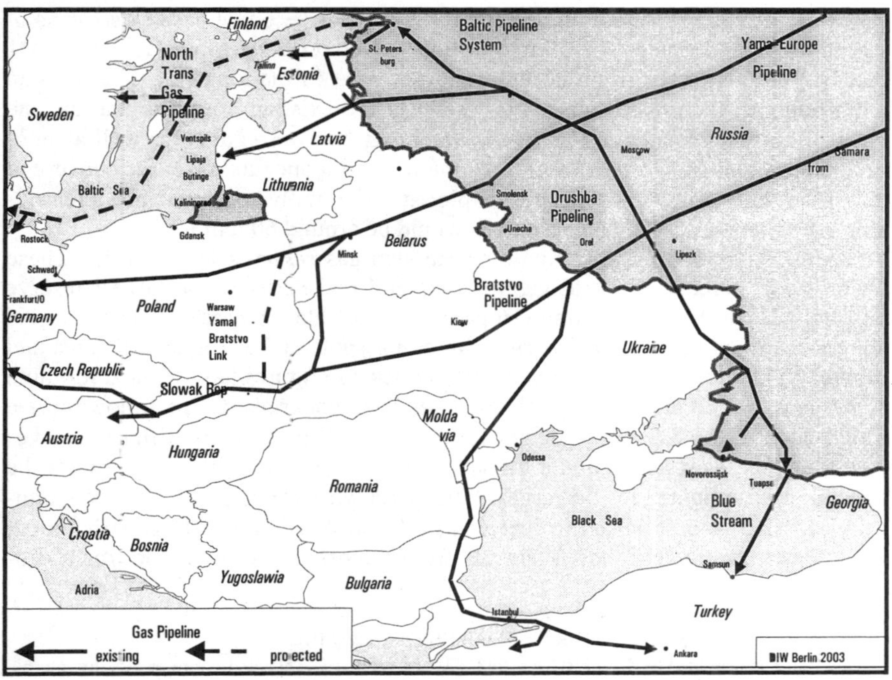

2.2 The Gas Sector: Resources and Reserves

The Russian natural gas sector has fared somewhat better than the rest of the energy sector, but it is in a difficult situation as well. Production fell as a consequence of sluggish domestic demand and constraints on exports, but also due to the gradual depletion of resources. Though the domestic price structure has been modified substantially since 1995, selling gas to Russian consumers is still by and large unprofitable (IEA, 2002). The payment discipline has not yet recovered sufficiently to warrant profitable domestic sales. It comes as no surprise, then, that exports to non-CIS-countries remains the only serious option. However, some doubts also exist on the long-term sustainability of this strategy: the reserve base, though still supposed to be the largest of the world, is shrinking; production has outstripped reserve additions since 1996.

Let's take a closer look at the resource and reserve positions of Russian gas:[2] GAZPROM (1998, 63) puts Russian gas *resources* at 226 tcm (total initial resources of 236.1 tcm minus cumulative production of 10.1 tcm). On the other hand, GRACE (1995) estimated the 'total Russian unproduced recoverable resource base' at only about 165 tcm. A closer look reveals that a large part of what is considered gas resources in Russia would hardly fit into the Western, market economy-oriented definition of resources, which requires that 'the existence of assessed volumes be scientifically supported and that the economic and technological prerequisites to their recovery do not demand conditions clearly over the horizon' (GRACE, 1995, 73). About 70 percent of the Russian resource base exists in as of yet undiscovered fields. The 39 tcm of undiscovered gas offshore (categories D1 and D2) are also unlikely to become relevant even in the long run. The Russian gas resources, then, realistically boil down to the existing 16 fields that are the basis of current production (Urengoy, Yamburg, Nadym regions) as well as non-producing fields in Western Siberia. If one were to reduce the resource concept to the Soviet categories A1-C2, that is, explored and initially appraised gas, a reasonable estimate for Russian gas resources would be around 60 tcm.

The most commonly used figure on Russian gas *reserves* is 47.3 tcm.[3] These make up 32 percent of world gas reserves and make Russia the largest reserve base in the world, ahead of Iran (16 percent) and Qatar (8 percent). The reserves are concentrated in Western Siberia, with minor spots in the Volga-Urals area and offshore. Doubts on the officially announced reserve figures have existed for quite some time, but no alternative evaluation has been undertaken. The following is a rough back-of-the-envelope attempt to check which part of the official reserves can be upheld as reserves under market-economy criteria. Table E4 contrasts the official reserve figures for the largest fields with what we consider to be economically justified reserve levels (called *adjusted* reserves, HIRSCHHAUSEN, 2002, 211). When subtracting those elements from the official reserves for which eco-

---

[2] The following section draws on HIRSCHHAUSEN (2002, 209 ff.).

[3] This figure is provided by GAZPROM (1998, 63) and regularly replicated, more or less, by international statistics, most notably the BP-Amoco Annual Statistical Review.

nomic feasibility is not clearly evident, the Russian gas reserve base shrinks to about 18–20 tcm. This is still a significant amount, but less than half of the internationally used figures.

Tab. E4: Russian Gas Reserves by Major Regions and Fields

	Official Reserve (bcm)	Adjusted Reserve (bcm)
Region/field and status	Figure	Estimate
Yamburg****	3900	2000-3000
Zapolyarnoye****	3000	3000
Urengoij***	3700	3000
Medvezhye***	640	600
others Nadymgazprom***	3000	1500-2000
Yamal**	10000	-
of which		
Bovanenko**	(4400)	-
Kharasevey**	(1300)	-
Kruzenstern*	(1000)	-
others Yamal*	(3300)	-
West Siberia**	10000	3000-4000
Orenburg (Ural-Volga)***	1000	1000
Surgut***	1000	1000
Severgazprom***	500	500
Tyum***	1000	1000
Astrakhan**	2100	1000
Stockman*	2200	-
Others	ca 5000	-
Sum	ca. 47000	ca. 18000-20000
of which		
Western Siberia	78 %	
Volga-Urals	10 %	
Eastern Siberia	2 %	
Far East	2 %	
Offshore	8 %	
By state of exploitation:		
**** in operation: plateau or rising		
*** in operation: tail (falling production)		
** under appraisal		
* undeveloped		

Source: HIRSCHHAUSEN (2002, 213).

Tab. E5: Russian Gas Output and Reserve Additions (1990–2000)

	1990	1991	1992	1993	1994	1995	1996	1997	1998	1999	2000
Production	613	618	620	601	581	570	575	571	591	592	584
Reserve Additions	2785	1741	1813	725	265	187	180	399	338	210	450
Ratio of Reserve Additions/ Production	4.54	2.82	2.92	1.21	0.46	0.33	0.31	0.70	0.22	0.35	0.77

Sources: GAZPROM (1998, 68), GAZPROM ANNUAL REPORTS (1997, 1998), IEA (2002).

3.3 Reserve Depletion and Additions: A Stylized Scenario

The depletion of existing fields is of concern to the Russian gas industry in the medium term, in particular to Gazprom which owns two-thirds of the reserves. Indirectly it also concerns European gas imports. Gas reserve additions in Russia have fallen significantly since the early 1990s. In the latter half of the 1980s, average annual reserve additions exceeded 2 tcm, which is about five times the consumption level. However, this ratio was not only inverted after 1994 but fell to a mere 0.22 in 1998 (see Table E4).

Most of the larger fields in operation have already passed their plateau rate and their yearly production is currently diminishing. This is the case most notable with the Orenburg field and in Siberia in Medvezhye and Nadym and Urengoy. Yamburg has nearly reached its plateau rate of 200 bcm and is likely to decline gradually. This leaves Zapolyarnoye as the only commissioned giant field where a significant production increase is to be expected. Figure E2 shows a depletion scenario for Russian gas reserves from producing fields.[4] We assume that about 75 percent of reserves are really recoverable. Furthermore, we assume a 'long-tail' for all fields, that is, gradually decreasing production after the plateau phase.

The scenario shows that production from existing fields will gradually decline in the first half of this decade; in 2005, production will still be above 500 bcm. However, the fundamentals are likely to change afterwards: with the expected phase-outs of major fields in Orenburg and Western Siberia, gas production from existing fields will fall more significantly in the second half of the decade. By the year 2015, only the giant Zapolyarnoye field will still contribute significantly to Russian gas output. This evidently raises the issue of replacement capacity from other fields, be they new giant fields, new large fields, or satellites; this issue is amply discussed both inside and outside of the Russian gas industry (GAZPROM, 1998, IEA, 2002).

---

4 'Other' fields include those commissioned before 1995 (Vyngapurskoye, Komsomolskoye) and those commissioned more recently (Tarkosalinskoye, Yubilyeynoye, Yamsovey); fields to be commissioned in 2001–05 are not included (these are mainly satellite fields of South Russkoye, Pestcovoye, Gubkinskoye).

Fig. E2: Depletion Scenario for Russian Gas Reserves from Existing Fields[5]

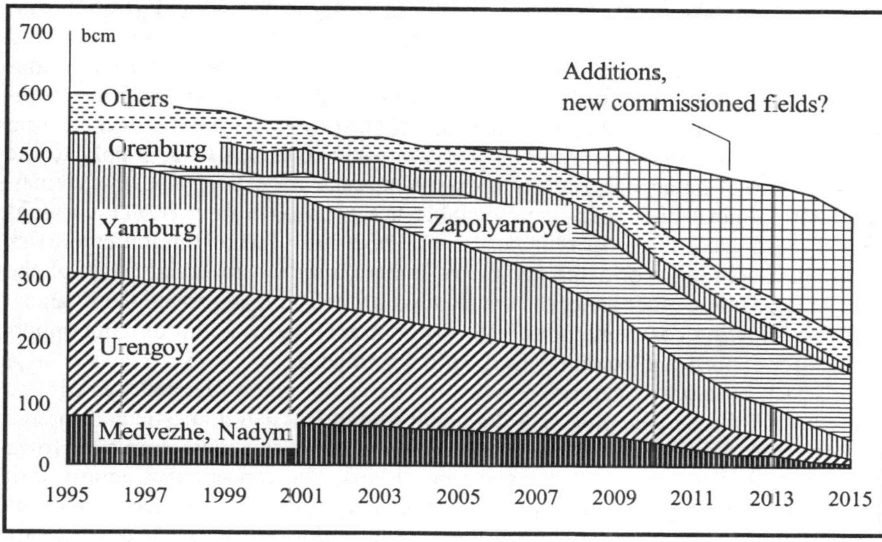

3. The Internationalization of Gazprom

Not only is there a need for more gas exports to maintain a comfortable position on foreign exchange earnings, but the corporate strategy of Gazprom also has to adapt to the new constellation, where the most important market is Western Europe (and perhaps Japan), and where downstream integration is deemed conducive to acquiring larger market shares on foreign markets. This section identifies some recent steps of Gazprom's internationalization strategy.

The internationalization (or: globalization) of energy companies is a worldwide phenomena and it is worthwhile to analyze the strategies of Gazprom within this international framework.[6] Globalization is supported by two main tendencies: first, internationalization focusing more *inwardly* on current business activities, acquiring resources, and building up new facilities in other places of the world, and second, orientation towards *outwardly* directed internationalization, focusing on diversification into business fields along the value added chain (refineries, filling stations, power plants, linked services), as well as on diversification into "neighboring" network led businesses (telecommunication, water supply, disposal of waste water, operation of airports, etc.).[7]

---

[5] Historical data (1995–98) is adjusted and may not fully correspond to real production of non-associated gas.

[6] This section draws on OPITZ, et al. (2002, 293 f., and 304 f.).

[7] In general, incentives to globalize result from the following reasons:

The institutional form for achieving these goals may vary widely. Mergers and takeovers may take place, as was the case especially in the oil and gas industry, with an increasing number of acquisitions and mergers during over the last several years. But this is not necessarily the sole opportunity. Resource deposits or concessions may simply be bought and downstream production and distribution facilities may be started from scratch. In the case of Gazprom, it was evident right from the beginning of economic reforms that, domestic revenues from supply to the Russian market being uncertain (non-payment, cash collection problems, remaining state control on prices, unpredictable tax policy), *hard currency* earnings from exports were the most reliable basis of cash flow and of foreign credit risk securing. Declining world market prices undermined the financial basis of the companies. On the other hand, the devaluation of the Ruble improved the financial situation allowing cost reductions in foreign currency terms and providing opportunities for exports and certain consolidation of finance.

In structural terms, Gazprom remains the vertically and horizontally integrated colossus of Russian gas, playing a dominant role in Russian domestic and foreign economics and politics; it is also the largest individual business employer (over 300,000 people, relatively unchanged since 1990). The conservative approach of maintaining post-Soviet enterprise structures within the gas sector can be contrasted with the proactive strategy of business *diversification* of downstream activity that Gazprom is pursuing both in Russia and abroad. Diversification is sought in five directions:

- development of an external resource base, mainly in the Arab Gulf region. For example, Gazprom is a major partner of the National Iranian Oil Company (NIOC) in the development of the gas resources in South Pars;
- gas-related activities, such as equipment, where Gazprom has been actively acquiring stakes or entire companies not only in Russia but also in Central Europe. Downstream diversification includes petrochemistry, such as the chemical complex in Novi Urengoi;
- energy-related activities: oil and electricity. With a production of about 10 mn t of condensates, Gazprom is already a considerable oil producer. The oil-only projects at Prirazlomnoye (Pechoara Sea) and Astrakhan (Caspian Sea) could make it a 'real' oil producer. Other oil/gas projects, such as Timan-Pechora, might be implemented in the long run;[8]

- Stagnation or slowly growing traditional markets where existing market shares and profit margins are coming under competitive pressure.
- Increasing costs of exploration and production of oil and gas reserves (development and application of new technologies) are faced with declining prices of final energy.
- The increasing pressure to increase shareholder value in a globalized capital market, where the aim to achieve a high market capitalization becomes an incentive for mergers or takeovers.

[8] In 1999, Gazprom took the leading role in a petrochemical holding structure, with activities ranging from condensate processing, petrochemistry, and retail business of fuel and gas. Gazprom has also expressed an interest in the power market, as a natural outlet for its gas. It has taken over the Pskov power plant at the Russian-Latvian boarder (swap of debt for 72 % equity of the company) and is

- other industrial activities add to the diversification and internationalization, e.g. telecommunication, where Gazprom is setting up a country-wide network. Minor activities include agriculture and tourism;
- finance and banking are the necessary activities of any post-Soviet company facing underdeveloped financial markets. Gazprom holds considerable shares of various well known and important Russian banks

The most spectacular case of internationalization is the *gas trading* business, where Gazprom has developed an extensive network of joint-venture companies all over Europe. The opening of the Interconnector between the United Kingdom and Western Europe, in which Gazprom has a stake, meant that the company is now able to compete on *all* European gas market segments itself. Table E6 shows the list of joint venture activities in Central and Western Europe. Over the last decade, Gazprom has indeed become a global gas group, and its importance as a supplier to the European gas markets must not be underestimated.

Tab. E6: Main Joint Venture Activities of RAO Gazprom in Central and Western Europe

Country	Joint-venture with ...	Company name
Austria	OMV	Gas und Warenhandels-gesellschaft
Bulgaria	Bulgargaz	JSC Top Energy
Finland	Neste	Gasum
France	Gaz de France	FRA Gaz
German	Wintershall	- Wingas
		- WIEH
	Daimler-Benz	Ditgas
Greece	DEPA	Prometheus Gas
Italy	SNAM	Promgas
	Edison	Volta
Poland	PGNiG	GasTrading
		JSC Europol Gaz
Romania	Romgaz	Wirom
Serbia		Progress Gaz Trading
Slovenia	Petrol	Tagdem
UK	British Gas et al.	Interconnector

Source: OPITZ, et al. (2002, 306).

4. Russian Gas Exports to Europe

In spite of the political, economic and social upheaval of the post-Soviet transformation crisis, the export of Russian gas to Central and Western Europe has conti-

engaging in projects in the Central and Western European markets as well (projects said to be in the pipeline in Western Ukraine, Poland, and Northern Germany).

nued, and even expanded, smoothly.[9] This trend is strengthened by the debate over the phasing out of nuclear energy in Europe, and the possible exhaustion of gas reserves in the North Sea. Russian gas exports to non-CIS countries have increased from 107 bcm (1994) to 137 bcm (2002) and the West European gas importers expect a further increase.

One major factor determining exports is the structure and development of *costs*. Some authors have expressed doubts as to whether Russian gas exports to Western Europe will be economically sustainable over the long term. The reasons for this are not only the capital replacement expenditures required for upgrading equipment, pipelines and compressors. They also include the fact that gas transport over long distances is expensive and most Russian gas is located along the Urals (South and North) and in Western Siberia, thousands of kilometers away from the centers of effective demand, mainly Central and Western Europe.[10] OME (2002) addresses the issue by estimating future European gas supply curves. They conclude that not Russian, but *Algerian* and *Norwegian* medium-cost fields would be able to supply the cheapest large additional quantities of gas to Europe: The future costs of gas supply to the EU-15 border are USD 1.34/MBTU for Algerian pipeline gas, and USD 2-2.20/MBTU for Norwegian pipeline gas; Russia is slightly more expensive than Norwegian gas, around USD 2.49/MBTU for the Ukrainian route.

Another issue is whether Russian gas exports can still increase significantly from current levels. Given capacity constraints on existing pipelines, increasing exports would require new infrastructure. For the time being, smaller export projects are carried out in the Balkan region.[11] Among the large projects, the first line of the Blue Stream project, connecting Russia with Turkey through the Black Sea, was finished in 2002, allowing an increase of Russian gas exports to Turkey. On the other hand, the Yamal project, under discussion for 15 years now, is not advancing on its critical issue, i.e. the development of the Yamal peninsula gas fields and the connection to the Northern Light pipeline at Uchta.

Russia's dominance in the European gas market has been and continues to be a critical issue studied both from an energy-economic and from a geopolitical perspective.[12] Political and economic instability in Russia and in the main transit

---

[9] We do not consider gas exports to CIS countries or the East (e.g. China, Japan, U.S. West coast) in this chapter.

[10] IEA (1994, Russian Energy Prices, Taxes and Costs, Paris, OECD) undertook an analysis of the hypothetical costs of gas delivery, assuming market economy cost accounting, including depreciation on capital. It concluded that under full-cost accounting, the Russian gas sector may not have been profitable in the early 1990s.

[11] An example is the Balkan expansion project, which is supposed to expand export capacity onshore through Ukraine, Romania, Bulgaria and down to Turkey. Transit capacity is to be increased by 14 bcm by the year 2002; the first stretch between Ghust (Ukraine) and Satu Mare (Romania) has already been started.

[12] The political and economic dependence of Western Europe upon gas imports from Russia has been dealt with in the literature from the beginning of the first long-term contracts in the late 1970s. The most extensive quantitative analysis of interdependence in European East-West gas trade was carried out by GRAIS/ZHENG (1996) showing that an improved reliability of gas supply from Russia is beneficial to the Russian gas exporting industry, to the gas transiting countries *and* to the West European gas importers.

country, Ukraine, have raised doubts about the reliability of supply, thus containing the market share of Russian gas on the West European market. Since the early 1990s, different options were discussed to contain the monopolistic power of Ukraine over gas transit to Western Europe. However, it took until the late 1990s for Russia, Belarus, and the West European gas importing industry to take concrete action in creating alternative transit capacity to meet additional demand on the West European market, and at the same time to weaken the monopoly power of Ukraine (see Figure E1):

- New capacities to transit large amounts of gas through Belarus and Poland were built within the framework of the "Yamal-Europe" pipeline. Initially conceived to transport gas from the Yamal peninsula to Western Europe, the Yamal-Europe pipeline is now used as a transit pipeline for gas from Western Siberia that transits through Belarus (Minsk - Nesvizh) and Poland (Kondratki - Wloclawek) to Germany (Frankfurt/Oder, Mallnow). The connection of the first 56" trunk was completed in November 1999, with a nominal capacity of 28 bcm, to which a second (and third) line could be added to carry the capacity to 56 bcm (84 bcm, respectively). This provides Russia with not only additional export capacity, but also with a strategic alternative to gas transit to Central and Western Europe that circumvents the politically unstable Ukraine;
- the next step to circumvent Ukraine is the project of the so-called Yamal-2 pipeline connecting Kondratki (Poland) to Velke Kapuzany (Slovakia), with a projected capacity of 60 bcm. This would allow the Western importers to use the Central corridor (with its high capacity and convenient connections to West European markets) while still not depending entirely upon Ukraine for transit. Yamal-2 has attracted significant interest from West European gas importers (e.g. Ruhrgas, Wingas, Gaz de France, Shell) who seem to consider the financing of this approximately 1 bn. USD project seriously.
- last but not least, there is now serious talk on the construction of a direct underwater link between Russia and Germany, the so-called NorthTransGas pipeline (IEA, 2002, 139, HUBERT/IKONNIKOVA, 2003). This would enable Russia to avoid dealing with transit countries; on the other hand, the high investment costs of this project, considered to be several bn. USD; have thus far prevented significant progress.

In essence, the former monolithic gas trade between Russia and Western Europe has become a multi-player game with significant effects on strategies and potential outcomes. CHOLLET ET AL. (2001) and HUBERT/IKONNIKOVA (2003) provide quantitative analyses of the different options Russia has to develop its exports. The scenarios indicate that rising market power of Russian gas in Western Europe is possible, but that it is uncertain whether the required investment will come about. The analysis also shows a tendency towards vertical integration between the producing countries (Russia, Turkmenistan) and the transiting countries (Ukraine, Belarus).

5. Conclusions

Russia has made significant progress with the internationalization of its gas industry, but the perspectives of gas exports are not as brilliant as the national energy strategy implies. Moreover, significant investments into gas pipeline infrastructure are required, and it is not clear who is willing and able to carry this burden. Thus, whereas the gas sector will remain an important source of employment, revenue, and foreign exchange, the Russian economy as a whole would be ill-advised to rely more heavily on the gas sector for its development.

References

CHOLLET, A., MEINHART, B., HIRSCHHAUSEN, C. V., OPITZ, P. (2001): Options for Transporting Russian Gas to Western Europe, DIW-Discussion Paper No. 261.

ENGERER, H. (2003): The Russian Energy Industry, DIW Berlin Weekly Bulletin (Wochenbericht 14/2003).

EUROPEAN COMMISSION (2001): Green Paper – Towards a European Strategy for the Security of Energy Supply, Luxembourg, Commission Document COM(2000)769 final.

GAZPROM (ed.) (1998): Strategic Development of the Russian Gas Industry, Moscow, Gazoil Press.

GÖTZ, R. (2002): Rußlands Erdgas und die Energiesicherheit der EU, Berlin, SWP-Studie S 12 (April).

GRACE, J. D. (1995): Russian Gas Resource Base Large, Overstated, Costly to Maintain, Oil and Gas Journal, Feb. 6, 73-74.

GRAIS, W., ZHENG, K. (1996): Strategic Interdependence in European East-West Gas Trade: A Hierarchical Stackelberg Game Approach, Energy Journal, Vol. 17, No. 3, 61-84.

HIRSCHHAUSEN, C. V. (2002): Modernizing Infrastructure in Transformation Economies – Paving the Way to European Enlargement, Edward Elgar, Cheltenham, UK and Northampton, MA, USA.

HUBERT, F., IKONNIKOVA, S. (2003): Strategic Investment and Bargaining Power in Supply Chains: A Shapley Value Analysis of the Eurasian Gas Market, Draft Paper.

INTERNATIONAL ENERGY AGENCY (2002): Russia Energy Survey 2002, Paris, OECD.

MINISTRY OF ENERGY OF THE RUSSIAN FEDERATION (2000): Energy Strategy for Russia until 2020 (in Russian), Moscow.

OBSERVATOIRE MEDITERRANEEN DE L'ENERGIE (OME) (2002): Assessment of Internal and External Gas Supply Options for the EU: Evaluation of the Supply Costs of New Natural Gas Supply Projects and Investigation of Related Financial Requirements, Executive Summary, Study for the European Commission.

OPITZ, P., HIRSCHHAUSEN, C. V. (2001): Ukraine as the Gas Bridge to Europe? Economic and Geopolitical Considerations, in: Hoffmann Lutz and Möllers, Felicitas (eds.), Ukraine on the Road to Europe, Heidelberg, New York, Springer.

OPITZ, P., ENGERER, H., HIRSCHHAUSEN, C. V. (2002): The Globalization of the Russian Energy Industry – A Way out of the Financial Crisis?, International Journal of Global Energy Issues, Vol. 14, 292-310.

F. Licence or Contract - What Kind of Petroleum Fiscal System is Required for Russia's Oil Industry?

Gert Ziener

1. Introduction

More than 10 years after Thane Gustafson (GUSTAFSON, 1989) characterised the condition of the Russian oil industry as 'crisis amid plenty', the situation has not changed for the better. Taking into account the huge resource potential, its performance is still far too weak. After a dramatic decline of oil output during the first five years of transition, production began to stagnate at a non-optimal level of about 300 mn tonnes per year. The main reason for this development was the absence of upstream investment due to an unstable institutional environment. Therefore, it seems to be necessary to implement new legal and tax instruments that provide incentives to make Russian oil projects more attractive for investors, mainly foreign oil companies.

2. Problems of the Oil Industry: Weak Production and Chronic Lack of Investment

Russia is known as one of the world's leading hydrocarbon producers. The country possesses 5 % of proven world oil reserves and as much as one-third of proven world gas reserves. The oil and gas sector generates roughly 45 % of the country's whole foreign exchange revenues. In 2000, revenues from oil exports alone exceeded $13 bn – money Russia urgently needs to finance imports and to settle external debts. Furthermore, some 13 % of Russian GDP comes from the oil and gas sector. Conditional upon further growth, the branch could be the driving force of Russia's economy in coming years.[1]

Despite these facts, the oil industry has undergone a serious crisis during the last ten years. After achieving its peak in 1988, oil production began to fall dramatically. During the first five years of transition (1991-1995), the drop was about 50 %. Since then, production has stagnated at a level of about 300 mn tonnes per year.[2] Considering the huge resource potential, such performance appears much too weak.

---

[1] For the statistical data see BP AMOCO, 2000, p. 4 and UNECE, 1998, p. 135.

[2] For the statistical data see BP AMOCO, 2000, p. 6 and Interfax-M&CN, 1999, p. 5.

The decline of oil production and oil export at the beginning of the transition process was mainly the immediate consequence of reduced government spending on the oil industry. Investment in exploration and production (E&P) fell sharply to just 35 % of the 1990 level by 1995. The investment gap has continued to widen until today, mainly due to inefficiencies in the internal structure of the industry and the lack of institutions, which foreign investors (oil companies) see as necessary provisions for investing their capital in long-term and risky E&P projects. According to the current Russian energy strategy, some $13 bn need to be invested every year in order to reach a production level of 360 mn tonnes per year in 2020 (ZVETKOV, 1999, p. 22).

3. Causes for the Problems

Various factors can be regarded as causes for the problems of the last decade, listed above. There are at least two main causes for the weak performance of Russia's upstream business: firstly, failures during the Soviet era and secondly, the circumstances of economic transition from a planned to a market economy.

The decline in crude output is mainly due to the deteriorating physical condition of established fields (e.g. Samotlor, Romashkinsk), which is a legacy of Soviet attempts to increase short-term production without regard for longer-term development possibilities. The pressure to fulfill production plans handed down by state authorities forced production units to allocate their funds primarily to production rather than exploration. Inefficient development of major oil fields combined with poor enlargement of the resource base and a growing shortage of modern oilfield equipment led to an investment and production crisis, which was heavily intensified during the transition process.

When transition started, the Russian oil industry was lacking capital. There were two clear options to reanimate it: rapid privatisation of the existing production units or external financing, mainly in the form of direct investment by foreign oil companies. However, the restructuring of existing enterprises and attraction of foreign investment were dependent on a stable institutional environment, which was hardly likely during the massive institutional change involved in systemic transition from a planned to a market economy.

Transition to a market economy has to be accompanied by the establishment of appropriate formal institutions. However, the implementation as well as the enforcement of laws, treaties, property rights etc. depend on their compatibility with the informal constraints of a society (WILLIAMSON, 2000, p. 597). If there is no such fit, the costs of running the system (ARROW, 1983 [1969], p. 48) will be too high. The institutional environment of a hybrid economic system fosters and permits pseudo-economic activities like barter, corruption, tax evasion etc., combined with massive uncertainties about future development. This is exactly the case in contemporary Russia. Numerous empirical studies have discovered that the degree of institutional uncertainty subjectively perceived by producing enterprises is higher in the transition economies of Central and Eastern Europe, and especially in the Commonwealth of Independent States (CIS), than in the rest of the world (BRUNETTI/KISUNKO/WEDER, 1998 pp. 353-348). Political risk, inadequate security of property rights, and unreliability of law and jurisdiction are highly negative for the extractive branch, especially for the oil sector. Due to the irreversible character of their E&P investment, oil companies react very sensitively to risks resulting from an insecure institutional environment. They will not invest their capital in countries with high political risk, where they would be vulnerable to expropriation or prohibition of profit repatriation. The relation between ownership risk, investment in the extractive branch and the intensity of natural resource use has been empirically shown by Bohn and Deacon (BOHN/DEACON, 2000, pp. 526-594). They found that resources such as oil, which can only be produced with a large input of capital, are exploited less intensively under high ownership risk.

Taking further important institutional factors (mentioned above) into consideration, it is possible to prove that the countries of the former Soviet Union use their oil reserves less intensively than oil producing regions with a stable institutional environment like North America (US, Canada) or Western Europe (UK, Norway). To demonstrate this point, it is useful to determine an index of institutional quality for various regions of the world.[3] This index (values from 1 to 6, the lower the better) is brought into relation with the ratio of oil production and proven oil reserves[4] (P/R Ratio) in those regions. Regions with poor institutional quality (higher indices), like Sub-Saharan Africa, Latin America and the CIS, show the lowest P/R ratio, which indicates that those countries make below-average use of their oil reserves (see Fig. F1).

This outcome demonstrates that the circumstances of economic transition have a major impact on growth of investment and production in the extracting branch of the countries of the former Soviet Union. Therefore, the decline in oil production in Russia can be at least partially explained by certain instabilities occurring in times of large institutional changes. The best examples are difficulties of creating a legal framework governing natural resource use as well as frequent and unexpected changes of important laws and tax regimes. Accordingly, foreign oil companies often criticise:

- inconsistent legislation (the law 'On production sharing agreements' partly contradicts to the law 'On subsoil');
- high tax pressure (mainly due to several excise taxes);
- low transparency of the tax regime (because of the vast number of different taxes, frequent changes of tax rates and tax bases);
- poor tax techniques (taxation is not adapted to the typical production cycle of E&P projects and their natural characteristics such as field size, on-shore or off-shore production, etc.).

---

[3] The index was determined by an evaluation of the results of the survey made by BRUNETTI, KISUNKO and WEDER, cited above.

[4] For the statistical data see BP AMOCO, 2000, pp. 4-6.

Fig. F1: Institutional Quality and Intensity of Oil Reserve Use

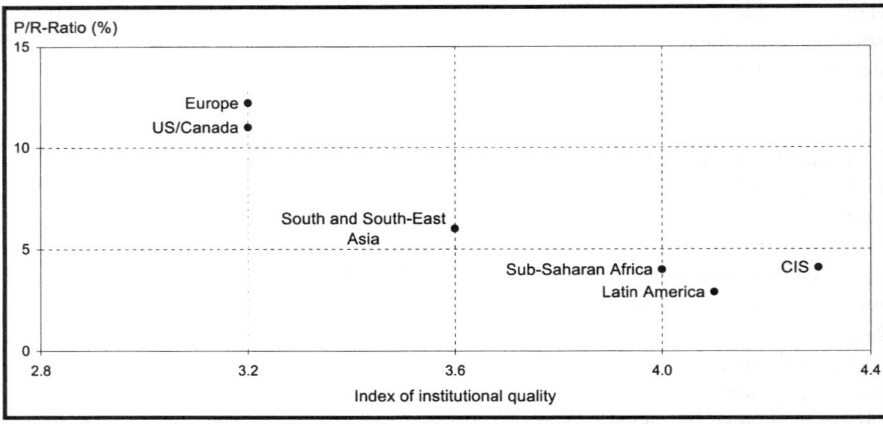

Source: Author's calculations based on data by BP AMOCO, 2000 (P/R-Ratio) and BRUNETTI, KISUNKO, and WEDER, 1998 (Index of institutional quality).

4. Improved Coordination of State and Private Interest is a Possible Way Out

Oil companies need a high degree of certainty about the future due to the long-term character of E&P projects. In developing countries or economies in transition, these are certainly often lacking. Special institutions that can protect investors from external risks arising in connection with unstable political and legal conditions have to be established. Simultaneously, such institutions have to coordinate private and state interests. Whereas the state wants to maximise the economic rent generated by the exploitation of its natural resources, investors want to obtain an appropriate share. In oil producing countries, it is usual to regulate state and private interest by so-called Petroleum Fiscal Systems. They represent all of the legislative, tax, contractual and fiscal aspects that govern petroleum operations within a sovereign nation/state and its provinces (JOHNSTON, 1994, p. 3) Thus, they serve as a framework for bilateral agreements, often called petroleum exploration and exploitation agreements, between a sovereign state (either the government or a national oil company acting on behalf of it) as resource owner and a private oil company that operates on the territory of the state. The first function of Petroleum Fiscal Systems is to govern the allocation of property rights of the extracted oil between the parties. At the same time, they represent the tax regime for the oil sector in an oil producing country. For such countries, it is very important to design a Petroleum Fiscal System acceptable to the investor as well as to the state itself. Obviously, this has failed in present-day Russia. Therefore, establishment of a legal framework that makes it possible to create a more favourable Petroleum Fiscal System could help attract more investment, giving way to a positive effect on production.

In the search for governance structures that provide strong incentives, the world oil industry has produced a wide spectrum of E&P agreements. However, all of them can be classified into two main categories: licence/concession-based systems (or tax/royalty agreements (TRAs)) and contractual systems such as production sharing contracts (PSCs) or service contracts.

In licence/concession-based agreements, the state as resource owner completely transfers its rights over the produced oil to the licensee (concessionaire) in exchange for the payment of a licence fee. Additionally, the investor has to pay a royalty for using the subsoil resources, which represents a certain percentage of the value of the produced oil (gross revenue). Furthermore, the investor has to pay taxes in accordance with the taxation system in force. Such systems are subject to constitutional (public) law, which means that the investor has no influence at all on the fiscal conditions; the state dictates them autonomously.

In contractual agreements, the state legally keeps its role as owner of the extracted oil, but transfers rights for a certain share of production to the oil company (in return for the work and services provided by the investor). The share of production taken by the state can be regarded as a tax paid by the investor in kind. PSCs are subject to civil law. That primarily means that the negotiated contractual terms can only be changed if both parties mutually agree on such change. Consequently, this system seems to provide more security for the foreign investor. This point will be analysed in detail in the following section.

5. What Kind of Fiscal System is Required for Russia's Oil Industry

The key question is what kind of E&P arrangements are appropriate for investors and the state based on the current political, legal and economic situation in Russia. By using a comparative institution approach, it is possible to conclude whether a contractual system (production sharing) or a licence/concession-based system is preferable. Six criteria are of special interest:

5.1 Contractual Efficiency

Cheung's (CHEUNG, 1969, pp. 1107-1122) findings about the efficiency of contractual arrangements in the agricultural sector can easily be applied to oil exploration and production. If high external risks occur, sharing the crop between the land owner and the tenant is superior to fixed-rent leases, because risk dispersion on both of the parties limits output uncertainties. For this reason, it would make sense to regulate oil and gas operations in high-risk countries (political and geological), such as Russia, through production sharing contracts between the state as resource owner and the private Oil Company rather than by fixed-rent lease-like tax/royalty agreements.

5.2 Immunisation Against Legal and Political Risks

Multinational oil companies concentrate their E&P activities primarily on oil-prospective countries/regions where laws and fiscal conditions are stable and property is safe. If – as in Russia – the institutional environment is unstable and future developments are full of uncertainty, a type of agreement is needed that can immunise oil companies from the political and legal risk threatening their operations.

With regard to TRAs (as used in Russia), all their terms are determined autonomously by the state. The investor therefore finds himself in a passive role and has no influence over the fiscal conditions to which he is subject. He would be affected by every single (discretionary) change of taxes and laws on subsoil use enforced by state authorities. Lack of continuity in taxation and permanent changes of tax rates or tax bases (as in Russia) makes it impossible for an oil company to calculate the long-term profitability of an E&P project. In the worst-case scenario, there would also be no protection against possible expropriation, e.g., if the whole transition process fails. Non-contractual systems are unable to immunise private investors against political or legal risks and cannot be recommended for oil-producing countries with a volatile institutional environment. Therefore, it is not surprising that TRAs are almost exclusively used by industrialised countries (e.g., US, Canada, UK, Norway or France) with long-term stable conditions in taxation and legislation.

Using contractual regimes (e.g., PSCs) that are subject to contract law as part of civil law would help reduce external risks, because the investor has much more influence ('voice') on the terms of the contract. The latter are negotiated bilaterally between the state and the investor. Furthermore, the negotiated fiscal (royalty, profit tax) and other contractual terms (cost recovery limit (percentage of net revenue the investor can use for compensating his expenses) and profit-oil split (sharing ratio of remaining revenues after costs are recovered)) are valid during the whole lifetime of an upstream project. If one party still wants to change certain terms ex-post, it is only possible if the other signatory agrees. Possible disputes are settled by arbitration (every PSC contains a special arbitration clause). PSCs can stabilise legal and fiscal conditions within an unstable institutional environment. Thus, PSCs are primarily used in petroleum-rich developing countries like Angola, Nigeria, India or Indonesia. Seen from this perspective, this is a more promising regulative instrument for Russian upstream business.

5.3 Adaptability

The degree of adaptability/flexibility of a Petroleum Fiscal System is determined by three factors:

- its adaptability to typical characteristics of the production cycle of an upstream project;
- its adaptability to the type of project (complete E&P projects can be distinguished from projects without exploration where only field development and production takes place and mere rehabilitation projects where idle wells are brought back into production);
- and its adaptability to characteristics of the oil field itself (field size, off-shore, on-shore, deep-water field, etc.).

The production cycle of an upstream project can be divided into four stages: early, mature, late and fading. Each of the stages is characterised by special features of production, revenues, costs and cash flow. A Petroleum Fiscal System should be adjusted to this cycle (KONOPLYANIK, 2001, p. 28). That requires sufficient flexibility of its components. The relevant terms of concession or licence-based systems have to be designed by the legislature. Since the fiscal conditions are non-negotiable (fixed-content systems), it lies in the hand of state authorities whether the system will be designed in accordance with the characteristics of the production cycle of a given project. The investor has no influence over this at all; he must accept the given terms or disengage (take it or leave it). TRAs tend to have sticky fiscal terms. Royalty rates, tax rates, special fees and tariffs are fixed and not graded in accordance with typical features of the production cycle. In this case, it seems doubtful that the investor will be able to generate an acceptable rate of return and that the state will be able to extract maximum economic rent from its oil business.

In contractual agreements, fiscal terms can be negotiated for each project individually. In this case, oil companies have much more influence over the fiscal design. The fine tuning of fiscal conditions in accordance with the production cycle and the nature of the project/oil field is possible. Sliding scales are often negotiated, which means that royalty and tax rates are graded in relation to production output, to the so-called R-factor (ratio of revenues and costs) or to the discounted cash flow generated in each period of the project. This ensures, for example, that the investor can enjoy lower tax rates or even tax holidays during the cost-intensive, unprofitable early stages of a project, whereas the tax burden will be higher in the high-profit stages of maturity. Furthermore, PSCs allow more scope for designing the system. Special 'adjusting screws' are used with the cost-recovery limit as well as with the profit-oil split, making it possible to further improve the adaptability of taxation to the type of project and the characteristics of the respective oil fields. For example, it is possible to set a higher cost recovery limit for cost-intensive exploration projects (e.g. the Sakhalin or Barents Sea projects in Russia) than for less costly rehabilitation projects (e.g. Western Siberia). The cost recovery limit can be aligned with the field size in the same way. A lower cost-recovery limit is needed if highly productive giant fields are exploited. Similar effects can be achieved by sharing profit oil between the state and the oil company in accordance with variables mentioned above or even according to the oil price.

Contractual systems (especially PSCs) also look superior based on the adaptability criterion. Because of the possibility of negotiating each component of the system with direct participation of the investor and better opportunities for designing the system, better adjustment of fiscal terms to the typical characteristics of upstream projects can be achieved. That enables more efficient taxation leading to higher profitability of E&P projects as well as increased tax revenues for the state.

5.4 Neutrality

In this case, the focus is on production efficiency in an intertemporal framework; this means that the rate of extraction, the timing of the development of known deposits, and the intensity of exploration for new deposits are effected by taxation in relation to a no-tax situation. In this setting, a tax is said to be neutral if it leaves the investor's profit maximising extraction plan unchanged from the no-tax situation (SUNNEVAG, 1997, p. 140). Smith (SMITH, 1997, pp. 5-23) has tested the neutrality of three alternative Fiscal Systems (the Russian licence, the Russian production sharing system and the US Federal licence) by applying them to the data of a typical West Siberian oil field using the criteria break-even oil price (see Fig. F2), break-even flow rate (see Fig. F3), and break-even development costs (see Fig. F4). The main findings are astonishing. To produce profitably (with an Internal Rate of Return of 15 %), the oil price has to be at least 22,65 USD/barrel if the Russian TRA is used. That is twice the no-tax situation. By using the Russian production sharing model, an oil price of only 16 USD/barrel is necessary for profitable production. Productivity must be on a level of 708 barrel per day if the Russian TRA is used, a level that is far from being realised. Only some giant oil fields produce at such levels. In the no-tax situation, only 41 barrels per day are required for profitable production. With 103 barrels per day, the Russian production sharing model seems good enough to develop the huge number of small- and medium-sized oil fields in Russia profitably. To extract the daily production from imaginary oil field development, costs of about 16.100 USD could be spent if no tax had to be paid. Using the Russian TRA, the cost restriction would be far lower – only 3.400 USD could be spent if the oil company wants to work profitably. That will not be sufficient to develop a typical West Siberian oil field. If the Russian production sharing model would be applied instead, the investor would be able to spend some 10.000 USD to extract daily production profitably. Taking those three criteria into consideration, the Russian licence system is far from neutral, whereas the production sharing model performs much better.

Fig. F2: Break-Even Oil Price

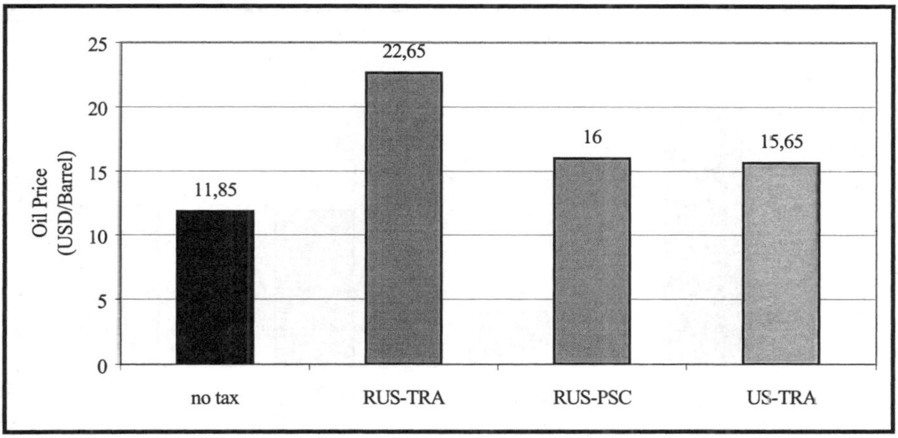

Source: SMITH, 1997, p. 10.

Fig. F3: Break-Even Flow Rate

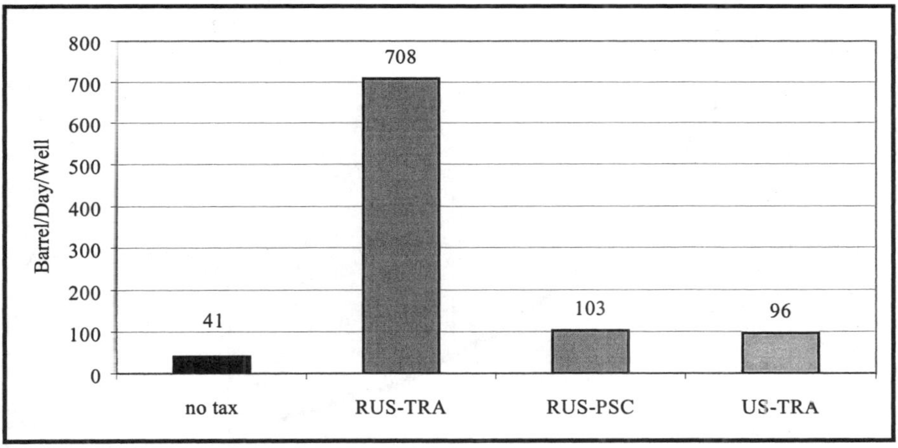

Source: SMITH, 1997, p. 11.

Fig. F4: Break-Even Development Costs

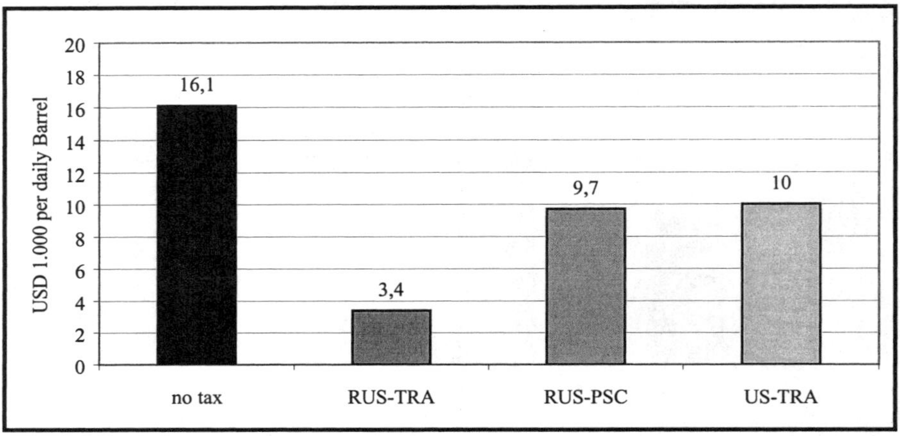

Source: SMITH, 1997, p. 12.

Fig. F5: Dependence Profitable Reserves (IRR = 20 %) – Oil Price

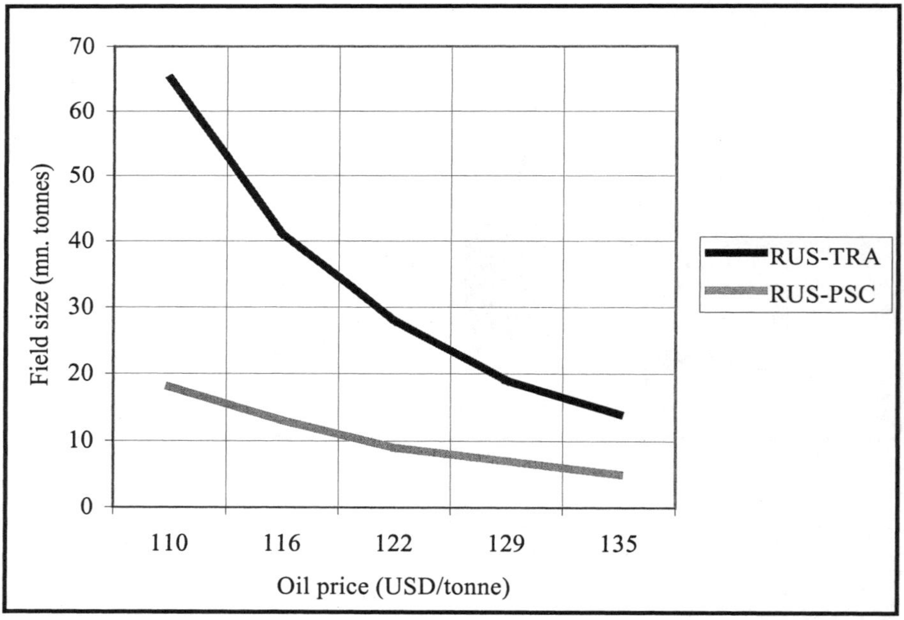

Source: TOKAREV, 1999, p. 21.

5.5 Resistance Against Falling Oil Prices

Tokarev's investigation (TOKAREV, 1999) deals with the relation between oil price and field size in front of the background of profitable production (Internal Rate of Return = 20 %) from a typical West Siberian oil field. If the TRA would be applied, small- and medium-sized fields (up to 30 mn tonnes of recoverable reserves) could only be exploited profitably, if the oil price exceeds 125 USD/tonne, whereas the Production Sharing model allows profitable production even from small (10 mn tonnes) fields under low-price scenarios (see Fig. F5).

5.6 Budgetary Effects

The primary interest of the state is focused on the appropriation of maximum economic rent from its natural (oil) resources. Seen from this perspective, it is interesting to find out which of the two systems generates higher budgetary effects. Several investigations by Konoplyanik (KONOPLYANIK, 1997) concluded that application of a production sharing regime in Russia would result in an expansion of oil output, tax base and tax revenues. It is estimated that recoverable reserves and cumulative production from a given deposit (over the lifetime of the project) would increase by five to eight times compared with that under the licence-based fiscal system currently in force. Consequently, the tax base and revenues are estimated to increase by roughly three times (see Tab. F1).

Tab. F1: Impacts of Production Sharing on Oil Output and Tax Revenues

	Current tax system	PSC	Ratio (PSC/current tax system)
Cumulative production (bn tonnes)	0.3	2.6	8.7
Costs ($ per tonne)	201	25.2	8.0
Total taxes ($ bn)	18.4	63.4	3.5
Tax per tonne ($ per tonne)	61.3	24.2	2.5

Source: UNECE (1998) p. 145.

The result of the comparative institutional approach shows that contractual E&P agreements such as PSCs are the superior regulative to co-ordinate state and private interest in the Russian oil sector. They are not only a favourable instrument to handle the external (political and legal) risks of investment in transition economies such as Russia; investors also have more influence on the conditions of the contract. That considerably contributes to the improved adjustment of fiscal terms to the characteristics of E&P projects. Last but not least, E&P agreements allow the Russian state to appropriate higher economic rents from its oil resources.

6. Russia's Oil Legislation: Rosy Prospects for Investors?

In order to explore, develop and exploit oil resources on the basis of contractual E&P arrangements, an appropriate law is needed. In the summer of 1995, a fairly favourable draft law on PSCs was drawn up by Russian and foreign experts. However, it was rejected by the Federation Council. Consequently, the final PSC law enacted by the President on December 30, 1995 contains many modifications and amendments contradicting general tax legislation and the law 'On subsoil' (YAKOVLEV, 1996, pp. 45-78). Due to the ambiguity of the PSC law, the relation between state and investor is not of a pure contractual nature. As such, the protection of the oil company from discretionary changes of legal and fiscal conditions is not essentially guaranteed, whereas the state obtains a 'loophole' to modify them in its own favour. Furthermore, the PSC law contains clauses whereby only a limited number of selected deposits and only 30 % of the country's oil reserves are allowed to be exploited under a production sharing regime.

Seen from the investor's perspective, it can be concluded that attempts to create a real alternative to the existing licence-based system have failed in Russia to date. Therefore, it is not astonishing that the latest legal developments are merely slight alterations of the existing tax/royalty regime (KONOPLYANIK, 2001, p. 28). In the summer of 2001, the Duma approved a package of laws, including an amendment to articles 26 and 27 of the Tax Code. Whereas article 26 envisages that import and export tariffs are no longer determined and enacted by presidential decree but by a special law, article 27 proposes the introduction of a new tax on the production of raw materials This new tax is designed to substitute the three kinds of taxes determining the tax/royalty system currently in force: royalties (6-16 % of gross revenue), mineral-resource taxes (10 % of gross revenue less the value of exploration expenses) and excise taxes (R55 per tonne of produced oil). The proposed new tax would be equal to 16.5 % of gross revenue from the sale of oil and gas. (Between 2002 and 2004, a temporary flat fee of R350 per tonne – deflated by an index reflecting oil price fluctuations – is planned for oil only).

It seems doubtful whether the new tax will stimulate investment and allow the state to appropriate higher rents. Firstly, the tax reduction is quite modest. Assuming that royalty rates of Russian upstream projects currently very rarely exceed 8 % of gross revenue and the mineral resource tax rate amounts to 10 %, reduction of direct taxes would only equal 1.5 percentage points (8 %+10 %–16.5 %). Secondly, the tax is related to gross revenue. For the investor, that means a higher tax burden in the early stages of production, where the project generates a negative net present value. Additional external financing would often be necessary, leading to higher capital costs and lower profits in later periods of the project. Thirdly, the royalty as the only (quasi) flexible component of the system in force is substituted by a sticky, non-negotiable duty, making it impossible to adjust it to the internal characteristics of E&P projects. To generate acceptable rates of return, investors will be forced to concentrate on exploitation of extremely rare but highly profitable giant and major fields, whereas development of a multitude of medium- and small-sized fields will be neglected. This will lead to further stagnation of production output and a decreasing tax base.

In view of the development we have outlined, the Russian oil sector does not yet seem to ready for (foreign) investment. Insufficient protection of investors and lack of flexibility of fiscal terms can still be identified as the main obstacles to reallocation of capital to Russian E&P projects by foreign companies.

References

ARROW, K. J. (1983 [1969]): The Organization of Economic Activity: Issues Pertinent to the Choice of Market versus Nonmarket Allocation, in Collected Papers of Kenneth J. Arrow, Vol. 2, Oxford: Oxford University Press, 133-155.

BOHN, H., DEACON, R. T. (2000): Ownership Risk, Investment, and the Use of Natural Resources, American Economic Review, Vol. 90, 526-549.

BP AMOCO (2000): Statistical review of world energy 2000.

BRUNETTI, A., KISUNKO, G., WEDER, B. (1998): Credibility of Rules and Economic Growth. Evidence from a World Wide Survey of the Private Sector. World Bank Economic Review, Vol. 12, 353-384.

GUSTAFSON, T. (1989): Crisis amid Plenty: The Politics of Soviet Energy under Brezhnev and Gorbachev, Princeton: Princeton University Press.

INTERFAX–M&CN (1999): Russian Oil Industry: Major Developments After August Crisis of 1998. March 28.

JOHNSTON, D. (1994): Petroleum Fiscal Systems And Production Sharing Contracts, Tulsa: PennWell Books.

KONOPLYANIK, A. A. (1997): Development of legislative and investment process in Russia under the Federal Law on Production Sharing Agreements. Paper presented at the 11th Annual APS Conference, Nicosia, 6-8 October.

KONOPLYANIK, A. A. (2001): Tax Code bill set to bolster investment, but requires redraft, The Russia Journal, June 22-28, 28.

SMITH, J. L. (1997): Taxation and Investment in Russian Oil, Journal of Energy Finance & Development, Vol. 2, 5-23.

SUNNEVAG, K. (1997): Investigation of the Neutrality of Petroleum Fiscal Regimes, Journal of Energy Finance & Development, Vol. 2, pp. 137-160.

TOKAREV, A. (1999): Comparative analysis of taxation schemes applicable for the development of Oil reserves of Western Siberia, unpublished working paper.

UNECE (1998): A Note on Production Sharing in Russia, in Economic Survey of Europe, No 3, 135-149.

WILLIAMSON, O. E. (2000): The New Institutional Economics: Taking Stock, Looking Ahead, Journal of Economic Literature, Vol. 38, 599-613.

YAKOVLEV, A. (1996): Production Sharing Agreements in the Russian Petroleum Sector. World Competition, Vol. 20, 45-78.

ZVETKOV, N. (1999): Na mirovoi rynok za investitsiyami, Neft Rossii, 5, 18-22.

G. Obstacles to Growth and Competition: The Political Economy of Corruption and Rent-seeking in Russia

Ralf Wiegert

1. Introduction

Since the meltdown of the financial sector and a short-lived dip downwards of overall production, which followed suit after the financial crisis in August 1998, the Russian economy has stabilized fairly well and achieved a remarkable high level of economic growth during at least three consecutive years by 2002. This surprisingly fast recovery was largely based on a surge in oil and gas prices on the world market and a sharp increase in international competitiveness of the Russian tradables sector after the large devaluation of the Ruble. Other factors like a more stable macroeconomic environment and major reform efforts may have played a crucial role as well. In 2000, economic growth in Russia was among the highest in the region, with an annual rate of 8.3 %; 1999 and 2001 saw growth rates of a-round 5 %; in 2002 growth slowed again to slightly more than 4 % (Tab. G1). These growth rates are encouraging, and one might conclude that only now, after almost a decade of recession, the Russian economy is bound to catch up with other more advanced transition countries like Poland and Hungary.

Tab. G1: Economic Growth in Selected Transition Countries, in %

	1993	1994	1995	1996	1997	1998	1999	2000	2001	2002	2001*
Russia	-8,7	-13	-4,1	-3,4	0,9	-4,9	5,4	8,3	4,9	4,1	64
Ukraine	-14,2	-22,9	-12,2	-10	-3	-1,9	-0,2	5,9	9,1	4,5	46
Poland	3,8	5,2	7	6	6,8	4,8	4,1	4	1	1	129
Hungary	-0,6	2,9	1,5	1,3	4,6	4,9	4,2	5,2	3,8	4	112

*Estimated level of GDP in 2001, 1989 = 100.

Source: EBRD (2002), Transition Report 2002, London.

Yet the question still remains whether this upturn will be sustainable for a longer period, even after the comfortable external circumstances – commodities prices and real depreciation – will almost have ceased to exist. By and large, the Russian economy is still hampered with many structural problems, of which each may impede future economic growth: a weak financial sector, which is far from the problems leading to the 1998 crisis, but which is very inefficient and, as regards the banking sector, not able to fulfill its role as a financial intermediary; infrastructure industries (energy, transport, telecommunications) awaiting coherent reform and efficient regulation; industrial enterprises relying on large implicit subsidies, most of which come in the form of cheap energy; and too large of a bureaucracy, which appears to be highly corrupt and therefore worsens the investment by extracting rents from companies and individuals' transactions.

The problems listed above may continue. Yet one may argue that other transition countries, e.g. those who managed to overcome the transition recession relatively fast (like Poland, where GDP in 2002 stands at 129 % compared with its estimated level of 1989 and where growth returned as soon as 1992/1993, Table 1), faced similar problems in the wake of the first economic upturn. There is, however, an interesting difference between macroeconomic indicators in countries like Poland or Hungary in the mid to late 1990s and Russia in 1999-2002: in the former countries the overall economic growth also led to higher investment/GDP ratios – during 1997-2000 the investment/GDP ratio in Hungary and Poland was always higher than 22 %, reaching even 30 % in Hungary in 2000. In Poland this ratio remained above the 26 %-level between 1999 and 2001 (Tab. G2). Another striking feature of the growth process in these countries was the comparatively high share of small and medium sized enterprises (SME) and of start-up enterprises in particular, which suggests an important role of start-ups and SME for the private sector and economic catching up (WORLD BANK, 2002).

Tab. G2: Investment Ratio in Selected Transition Countries*

	1993	1995	1997	1998	1999	2000	2001
Russia	20,4	20,9	19,1	17,5	16,1	17,8	19,6
Ukraine	24,3	23,3	19,8	19,3	na	na	Na
Hungary	18,9	20,0	22,2	23,2	27,8	30,1	26,6
Poland	14,9	18,7	23,6	25,3	26,4	26,3	26,0

*Investment rate in % of GDP.

Source: EBRD (2002), Transition Report 2002, London.

Russia has neither such an investment/GDP ratio – in 1999 and 2000 it remained far below 20 %, even with the backing of high economic growth, in 2001 it barely reached this mark – nor a private sector and a share of SME, respectively, comparable to the countries discussed above. Given the relationship between a viable private sector and economic growth, looking at the reasons for Russia's shortcomings in this respect should provide answers to the question of Russia's growth perspectives as well. Russia's enterprise sector desperately needs a boost of investment to modernize its capital stock and to get rid of its fairly outdated structure – the share of capital equipment not older than five years declined from 35.5% in 1980 to 9.7% in 1996 (as a percentage of total equipment) and the average duration of use of industrial equipment climbed from 9.5 to 14.1 years (LYNCH, 2002). As GÖTZ (2002) points out, the overall investment activities in 2002 are only able to cover the costs of maintaining the capital stock existing in the country but are not high enough to build additional capacities.

The increase of investment in Russia and the fact that this increase more than doubled the growth of GDP in 2001 lead STROUTCHENEVSKI (2002) to the conclusion, that investment-driven growth like e.g. in Poland during the 1990s is a serious possibility in Russia for the coming years. Whereas this view cannot be completely ruled out, several problems which are bound to impede such a relationship between investment and growth exist in Russia, some of which are associated with basic mechanisms of a market economy.

This paper, which draws largely on parts of my forthcoming Ph.D.-thesis (WIEGERT, 2003), wants to address this issue by looking on how the mechanisms of a market economy work in Russia; this looks first of all at the extent to which efficiency-enhancing competition has been introduced to the Russian enterprise sector during transition. One may show that there is a crucial lack of competition in Russia, not only as regards market structure and the behavior of dominant firms. Competition in Russia is supposed to be hampered by serious obstacles for all competitors and new firms in particular to invest. The role of the bureaucracy and corruption, the subsidization of old state firms and widespread crime pose barriers to investment and the expansion of firms. These barriers can be labeled as additional transaction costs for firms and individuals who want to use markets as a means to exchange goods and services. Higher transaction costs mean that firms either hide from these markets or simply do not trade and thus do not produce.

2. Transition, Competition and Efficiency

Economic transition from a centrally-planned socialist economy to a decentrally organized market economy was initiated because the latter was believed to further a more efficient allocation of resources and products and hence a higher national welfare. The allocation of resources and products, which was formerly done by bureaucrats, is taken over under market conditions by companies and individuals themselves whose transaction decisions in turn are guided by relative prices, indicating the scarcity of a product relative to another. If markets are the locations where supply and demand meet and transactions are made and prices provide the signals which guide them, then competition is the mechanism which ensures that

- companies are free to decide over production methods and resources according to their own plans,
- companies will do so with respect to maximum efficiency,
- individuals are free to choose between several alternative products and are able to decide according to their own preferences.

Thus, competition is necessary to bring about efficient use of resources and to satisfy demand; it is a crucial element in the system of incentives and control in market economies (HOPPMANN, 1977; HAYEK, 1968). Functioning competition among supply as well as demand results not only in efficient market outcomes in such a static sense described above, but also in a dynamic sense: A high level of competition forces companies to search for more efficient technologies and to implement available innovations in order to gain a lead position against competitors. For the society as a whole competition is crucial as well, because it provides a mechanism to restrict and control economic (and also political) power.

Introducing competition to a formerly socialist economy includes a broad range of problematic aspects which are, among others, associated with the structure of the socialist economy, relatively low-productive industries and the behavior of bureaucrats towards the evolution of new private firms. The main aspects of the introduction of competition during transition are shown in Figure G1. The figure connects the change of management behavior resulting from a higher level of competition with gains in static and dynamic efficiency and therefore with more widespread structural change and higher economic growth. The figure differentiates between tradable and non-tradable goods. As regards the former, competition may be enhanced by foreign firms when removing international trade barriers, but the start of new private enterprises and the privatization of state-owned enterprises play a crucial role as well. Of course, a functioning institutional framework (e.g. insolvency law) which poses a credible threat for market exit to unprofitable enterprises is also necessary and its enforcement is of primordial importance.

Fig. G1: Competition, Efficiency and the New Private Sector

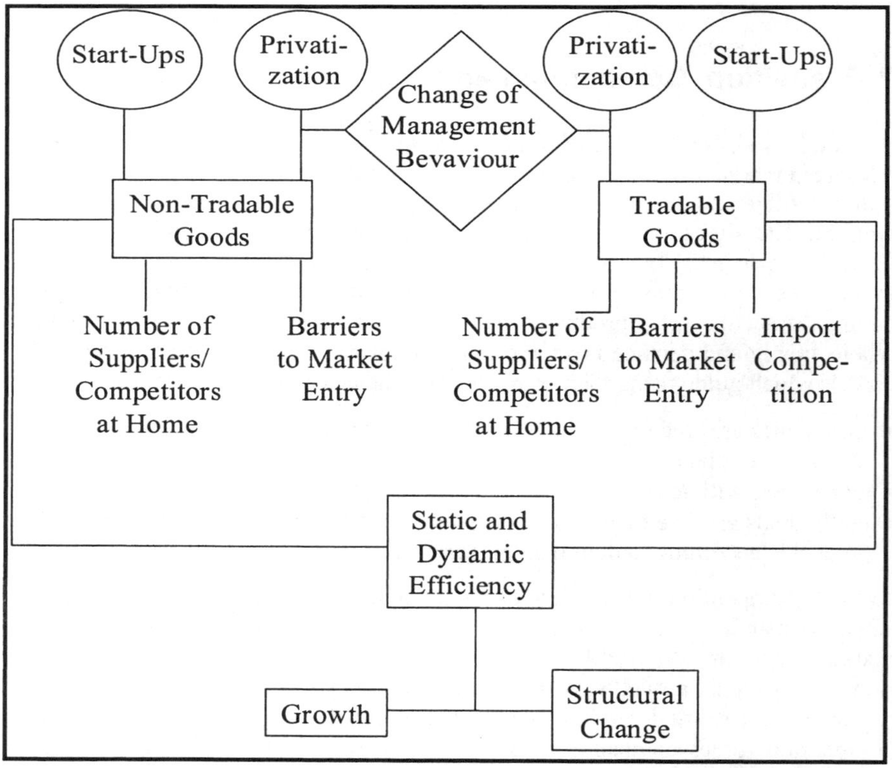

Introducing competition to the non-tradables sector is more complicated, since it requires the set up of new companies as competitors to the old established state-owned enterprises. A change of management behavior in the latter type of enterprises will be achieved only if market-type incentives and threats are implemented; usually they are associated with the removal of subsidies (either through direct payments or indirect subsidies of various sorts), with the privatization of the respective enterprise and other issues around the institutional framework mentioned above.

The achievement of change in management behavior and in corporate governance of state-owned enterprises is quite a complex issue which has drawn particular attention (EARLE/ESTRIN, 1998; BROWN/EARLE, 2000; EBRD, 1999), but this paper wants to focus on another – albeit related – aspect of competition in transition, which is supposed to be interconnected with the investment and growth-issue described in the introduction: A viable market-type competition always has two central aspects; first the removal of exit barriers as a means to enforce structural change on unprofitable enterprises, second – and of equal importance – the removal of entry barriers against new enterprises. High entry barriers result in low frequencies of market entry and thus in a low level of competition. This holds especially true for the non-tradables sector and is equally valid for the tradables sector if there remain high trade barriers during the transition process; high transport or communication costs resulting from an unproductive transport or communication system or the fragmentation of an economic area like in the Russian Federation impose rather high trade barriers which work like customs duties leading to remarkable price differences between regions (ELISSEEVA, 1999, 425f.; BERKOVITZ/DE JONG, 1999, 2001).

This kind of competition as a result from high barriers for market entry may be able to explain the investment behavior in Russia: Low frequencies in market entry lead to a small number of new private enterprises and usually a weak small and medium-sized enterprise sector, too, and thus lead to low investment rates by these enterprises. Less competition leaves old enterprises without any incentive for action as regards structural change, modernization and related investment. On the contrary, old enterprises are able to channel funds instead to other purposes including investment abroad. This relationship between competition, market entry and investment might explain why there is temporary high economic growth in Russia accompanied by an investment/GDP-ratio, which remains at a comparatively low level.

There is ample proof for a low overall level of competition in Russia, even if in some particular sectors competition seems to be quite high. Enterprise surveys show that competition pressure is felt to a much lower extent than in other transition countries, a differentiation between pressure from domestic and firms from abroad does not change the picture substantially (EBRD, 1999). BROADMAN (2000) has investigated the structural dominance of firms in single markets and claims an average value for the market share of the four biggest firms which usually does not exceed 60 % when considering Russia in total – a value common in the US as well. However, disaggregated figures for the regional level show that the respective market share is much higher – 95 % for the four biggest firms and 43 % for the biggest company alone. This must be considered before the background of a quite separated economic space in Russia which hinders substantial interregional economic activities to the extent that market concentration de facto is very high.

Corporate governance in Russia is dominated by the existence of large business groups, which emerged either as a group led by a bank (vertical integrated group) or an industry group, while the latter usually appears to be a looser alliance without a particular hierarchical control structure (JOHNSON, 1997; POPOVA, 1998; SCHRÖDER, 1999). The Russian government – arguing that creating internal capital markets within such business groups can overcome institutional shortcomings during transition and thus improve capital funding – for enterprise restructuring actively promoted the emergence of these business groups. However, politico-economic considerations were in fact at least equally valid for the choice of that strategy, e.g. receiving political support from private business groups during election campaigns in turn for handing over control of privatized firms as well as maintaining control of sectors by politicians even after state control was abolished. Financing within a business group is for most of Russia's firms the only way to get access to additional capital beyond retained earnings.

Business groups play an important role for economic development all over the world, in particular in developing countries, and such groups were common for most of the advanced OECD countries as well during industrialization and beyond. Yet with a higher sophisticated institutional framework and lower costs for securing property rights, the importance of business groups decreased and a more diversified business structure emerged.

The issue of whether internal capital allocation by business groups is more efficient than by external capital markets has been addressed empirically (SHIN/STULZ, 1998; RAJAN et al., 1998; STEIN, 1997). By and large, big diversified business conglomerates are regarded as less efficient due to agency conflicts between investors and managers and due to incentives for subsidizing low-performing divisions at the expense of the stronger parts of the group. PEROTTI/GELFER (2001, 1602), who analyze this issue with respect to Russian enterprises, state that these findings contrast with the importance of business groups in developing countries and the role such groups played during economic catching up in countries like Japan or South Korea. As regards the Russian case, they find evidence for higher redistribution of financial means in vertically-integrated and thus hierarchically structured business groups, which are mostly led by banks, in favor of high-yielding divisions. Yet they cannot rule out the problem that this redistribution happens basically for the private appropriation of value by controlling shareholders. Thus the question of the efficiency of business groups in Russia still remains; there is evidence for a tighter grip on members' investment decisions only in vertically-integrated groups.

The importance of business groups in Russia leads to the question of their influence not only on enterprise restructuring within their group, but also on competition and therefore enterprise restructuring in general and, to that end, on economic growth. KALI (2002) builds a model which tries to catch the relationship between a weak institutional framework, the emergence of business groups and economic development. In his model, business groups and informal contracting are particularly important in early stages of economic development when a functioning institutional framework has not materialized yet. Later on, as soon as more sophisticated mechanisms for transactions and capital allocation are needed, business groups should diminish again in favor of a more diversified business structure; probably outsourcing activities are of great importance. Otherwise, if the economy gets stuck in its concentrated business structure, growth rates will decrease and the country will eventually fall back again. If this holds true for Russia the current industry structure might be justified to some extent.

The next chapter will show that there are indeed serious shortcomings and obstacles for doing business in Russia, which together might argue for an internalization of transactions in a business group. But is Russia not different from countries like South Korea which needed large capital agglomerations to finance its entire industrialization? Despite a still concentrated structure, Russia is an industrialized country which is supposed to restructure its industry, not build it up. Therefore, a much more diversified industrial structure may be needed. This should only be achieved through a more competition-focused policy strategy. The role of business groups in Russia is further questioned by the low investment/GDP ratio and large capital flight. There might be a link between the introduction of competition and firms' will to invest.

3. Obstacles to Competition

During transition a large-scale structural change must take place: the old state sector shrinks whereas the private sector expands, taking over capital resources as well as parts of the labor force previously employed by state firms. Assuming that privatized, formerly socialist firms will lay off workers due to their relatively low labor productivity the foundation and expansion of new private firms and hence the openness of markets are crucial for reducing unemployment and for the success of the transition process itself. Consequently, one has to search for obstacles or barriers to market entry (and thus to the enhancement of competition) when asking about transitional failures like the one in Russia during the 1990s. As will be shown below, Russia built up or maintained large obstacles for market entry and doing business.

3.1 Corruption, Grabbing Hand and State Capture

In Russia corruption has got a long history. In his novel "The Dead Souls," Gogol describes quite nicely how in early 19th century-Russia a businessman has to bribe bureaucrats in a regional town's office to get the documents he needs. At the turn of the century, Russia ranks among the most corrupt countries in the world (EBRD, 1999; HELLMAN/JONES/KAUFMANN, 2000; TRANSPARENCY INTERNATIONAL, 2001). According to a study done by the Russian research institute INDEM (2002) bribes amount to an annual US-$ 36 bn. (around 12 % of GDP); about 10 % of each transaction's value has to be paid for bribes.

Various business surveys have shown that the behavior of state officials and corruption in particular obstructs business development in Russia seriously (RADAEV, 1999; EBRD, 1999; OECD, 2002). Dealing with state officials to get necessary documents or even to defend the company against officials who exploit their position in order to extract rents usually appears on the top of the list of the most serious obstacles for business development. Table G3 shows the results of a business survey among enterprises in the regions of Irkutsk, Tula, and Udmurtiia: Lobbying with the authorities together with defending the firm against officials exploiting their position is very difficult for roughly two-thirds of total respondents; the figures vary a bit when separating stable and unstable firms. In any case this task is perceived to be very difficult by a much higher percentage of firms than other problems like financial support, which one would expect to be cited as a prime obstacle for the development of business as well (given the poor state of the financial system in Russia).

Tab. G3: Barriers to Successful Development[1]

	Stable firms[2]	Unstable firms[2]	Total[3]
Lobbying your interests with the authorities	54,1	79,7	67,7
Defending yourself from officials' exploiting their position	63,7	69,2	66,7
Expanding the area of sales	41,0	61,1	51,4
Increasing of changing premises	48,2	53,8	51,2
The provision of necessary equipment	38,1	49,4	44,0
Access to bank credit	32,9	51,6	42,7
Receiving financial support from partners, other enterprises or entrepreneurs, and individuals	28,8	37,9	33,6
Ensuring the security of business	22,6	30,1	26,6
Obtaining licenses and certificates for production, goods or services	12,3	39,5	26,3
Hiring personnel with appropriate skills and qualifications	21,3	20,1	20,7
Receiving information and consultancy services when needed	9,4	10,9	10,2

[1] Respondents were asked "How difficult is it for your enterprise to solve the following tasks today?" Respondents could choose "very difficult", "not very difficult", "rather easy". The figures are the percentage of respondents who reported that the given task was very difficult.

[2] Respondents were separated in stable and unstable firms as regards their financial situation according to their own statements.

[3] Percentage of total number of respondents.

Source: OECD (2002), Economic Surveys: Russian Federation, Paris, 86.

One might say that corruption also exists in other countries which are in a similar situation like Russia – in systemic transition – that nevertheless perform much better. This poses the question on whether corruption in Russia has special properties and effects on economic development. In theory various reasons for bribing or receiving bribes are identified. According to ROSE-ACKERMANN (1999, 9-10), these can be separated into four categories: first surpassing regulations which may hinder business development and threaten efficient allocation as regards market transaction (bribes as speed money). This kind of bribing officials can still be efficiency-improving and therefore welfare-enhancing. A second reason is accepting bribes as a form of a payment in addition to the low level of the official salary; something which seems to be rather common in Russia. Third, paying bribes may also be reasonable for firms to reduce the tax bill or other monetary obligations against the public budget, and fourth, in case of illegal activities, such actors may want to protect themselves from prosecution by bribing officials, e.g. so that they turn a blind eye on their activities. Thus from an economic point of view, corruption can indeed lead to efficiency-improving effects. Theoretical analysis has shown that competition in the face of corruption is able to produce efficient market results (LIEN, 1986; BECK/MAHER, 1986).

Corruption may have various reasons, but many efforts in transition analysis have been devoted recently to the more far-reaching issue of rent-seeking (ASLUND, 1996; ZAOSTROVTSEV, 2000; PRITZL, 1997). These have brought considerable new insights into the effects of corruption as part of rent-seeking activities in Russia and in other countries. Two different views of rent-seeking have emerged, which focus on the behavior of state officials on the one hand and the activities of enterprises on the other hand.

State officials are regarded with respect to their behavior towards new enterprises as individuals who do not serve their original purpose as regards providing public goods like designing and enforcing laws, rather they exploit their position over firms that are not powerful enough to withstand these bureaucratic attacks. FRYE/SHLEIFER (1997) therefore divided the behavior of state authorities in different countries in three categories:

- state as invisible hand: government and other state authorities act according to the law and are subject to independent jurisdiction; they provide basic public goods and reduce regulations to the necessary minimum.
- state as helping hand: government and other state authorities act mostly above the law but use their power to promote commercial activities; state authorities redirect business decisions and impose a broad variety of regulations; corruption may exist in an organized form.
- state as grabbing hand: government and other state authorities act above the law and abuse their position for rent-seeking activities; they exploit their regulative power over individuals and companies in order to extract rents; a functioning jurisdictional system to control and impose sanctions on state authorities does not exist.

Such a division makes the problem that Russia faces clearer. Rather than having state authorities who at least in some way promote business development, concentrating on rent-seeking activities is quite common. ZAOSTROVTSEV (2000) remarked that rent-seeking behavior in Russia is not mere passive – e.g. officials who take bribes for licenses – rather they extort rents from enterprises. For example, the issue of regular inspections by various state officials is quite a commonly-known method for showing entrepreneurs that it might be necessary to pay some extra fee to an official himself.

Tab. G4: Spending of Entrepreneurs on Payments for Informal Business Services and the Number of External Inspections at their Enterprises*

Spending of enterprises on informal services	Share of total number of enterprises (%)	Number of inspections per month (%)					Average number of inspections
		<1	1	1,5-2	2,5-5	>5	
Significant	14,5	7	17	13	21	31	2,4
Insignificant	46,0	50	41,6	49	43	46	1,9
None	39,5	43	41,5	38	36	23	2,2
Total	100,0	100	100	100	100	100	2,1

*Survey by the Center for Political Studies, Moscow. Survey took place in November and December 1997.

Source: RADAEV (1999), 41.

ZAOSTROVTSEV (2000) explains this connection between inspections and the spending of enterprises on such "informal services" (see Tab. G4). The number of inspections is given by their number per month (varying from less than one to more than five). The second column gives an overview of the distribution of enterprises into the three classes of informal spending: Significant, insignificant and no spending at all. In the next column enterprises are redivided into groups according to the number of inspections per month, whereas each group is subdivided into the three classes of informal spending again. Table G4 shows that 14.5 % of all enterprises pay significant informal spending, 46 % have insignificant spending and 39.5 % do not spend anything in this respect. But with a growing number of inspections the share of firms which spend significant payments for informal services increases (from 7 % at one inspection to 31 % at more than 5 inspections); therefore the share of companies without any such spending declines. These results suggest that state officials in Russia behave rather like a grabbing hand and that enterprises are confronted with significant costs in order to lobby and defend themselves against state authorities.

As regards the activities of enterprises themselves, HELLMAN/JONES/KAUFMANN (2000) concluded from the results of the BEEPS-enterprise survey in transition countries done by the EBRD, that in Russia enterprises act as state captors. The capture phenomenon is quite common from regulation theory and describes enterprises that try to influence regulatory decisions or even initiate such measures by bribing or forcing state authorities to do so in order to gain advantage over competitors or to foster their market position (STIGLER, 1975). Almost the same incentives are relevant as regards the analysis of HELLMAN/JONES/KAUFMANN (2000); but in contrast to countries with a functioning institutional framework, there is an additional reason for state capture-activities of enterprises in Russia, that is their defense against extortionary state officials.

According to HELLMAN/JONES/KAUFMANN (2000), results from the BEEPS-Survey suggest that Russia can be labeled as a capture economy due to the fact that capture methods are quite common among companies. Companies "buy" regulations and implicit or explicit protection from authorities, whereas the latter usually provide such regulations as public goods. Above all SME and new private enterprises pay a considerable amount of resources and financial means to such activities. One may suggest that if they did not do that, they would not be able to start and go on with their business activities. Thus there are considerable additional costs for new enterprises from the very start.

Even more harmful to competition, established enterprises seek to buy state protection and regulation, too, and therefore impose insurmountable entry barriers for new firms. Such capture activities on behalf of established firms may especially occur in businesses where state authorities and the management of enterprises are well known to each other or are widely regarded to have a common historical background, like e.g. in the Russian banking sector.

3.2 Arrears, Tax Regime and Subsidies

Since the beginning of a tighter monetary policy in Russia, a phenomenon occurred which was not observed in other transition countries at this scale; this was a rather high stock of payment arrears, which persisted during the late 1990s and came down somewhat only during the recent economic upturn after the financial crisis of 1998. This stock of overdue payments was accompanied by the emergence of various forms of non-monetary payment which lead eventually to the notion of Russia's economic system as a barter economy (COMMANDER/MUMMSEN, 1999). Quite right, most of these forms of payments were regarded as a means for former socialist enterprises to adapt to the new economic environment and to continue production despite being illiquid. Many firms, which normally would have gone bankrupt, thus got the chance to stay on. One may argue that tolerating such developments for some time was necessary to avoid an industrial wasteland after transition began, but most of these forms of payments and habits remained quite common and even subsidies from public budgets and from cheap energy prices enhanced the level of assistance further, as will be shown below.

A high and further increasing level of subsidization, which persists over a longer period, reduces incentives for former socialist enterprises to restructure considerably and continues in some way the system of soft budget constraints, a property usually associated with the financial system for socialist enterprises (KORNAI, 1986). New firms will find it difficult to compete with established enterprises which get such public assistance; welfare gains which were expected by a more efficient use of inputs and innovations through the transition to a market system will therefore largely be forgiven.

As a result of an enterprise survey from November 1998, table G5 shows the importance of non-monetary forms for paying enterprises' tax bill. Only 6 % and 5 %, respectively, of the enterprises in the survey did not use barter or tax offsets, whereas 25 % and 31 % of the firms used such methods and for 12 % and 16 %, respectively, such methods were very important. The big majority of firms used barter and offsets as well, but told that these methods were not important for them.

Tab. G5: Importance of Non-monetary Methods in Minimizing Tax Bill (reply of respondents in %)

	Not important	Used, but not very important	Very important	Instrument is not used
Barter	68	13	12	6
Offsets	63	15	16	5
Veksels	47	8	9	36
Debt sales, Swaps	25	5	6	63

Source: PINTO/DREBENTSOV/MOROZOV (2000), 26.

Tab. G6: Public Budget Subsidies to the Russian Enterprise Sector, 1994-1998*

	1994	1995	1996	1997	1998
Explicit budget subsidies	10,2	8,6	7,9	8,6	5,9
Implicit budget subsidies[1]	0,7[2]	3,1[2]	7,6	7,4	10,4
Total budget subsidies	10,9[2]	11,7[2]	15,5	16,0	16,3

* in % of GDP.

[1]Does not include subsidies in form of ad hoc tax exemptions as well as net increase in overdue fines and penalties.

[2]Does not include subsidies imbedded in regional offsets.

Source: PINTO/DREBENTSOV/MOROZOV (2000), 12.

Table G6 confirms the results of the enterprise survey cited in Table G5. It shows the growing relative importance of implicit budget subsidies for the Russian enterprise sector from 1994 to 1998. While explicit budget subsidies declined from 10.2 % of GDP to 5.9 % of GDP, implicit budget subsidies experienced a remarkable rise from 0.7 % of GDP in 1994 to 10.4 % of GDP in 1998; the overall level of subsidies given by public budgets amounted to 16.3 % in 1998, which is already rather high.

However, the level of subsidies does not stop with the public budgets. Implicit subsidies to the enterprise sector through artificially low energy prices – mostly electricity and gas – are of almost equal importance. As regards the high stock of overdue payments, PINTO/DREBENTSOV/MOROZOV (2000) even call the Russian energy sector the "phenomenon's nucleus." For the period between 1993 and 1997, they quote an average level of subsidization by Gazprom alone of around 1.6 % of GDP; for the power sector the overall implicit subsidy varies between 1.6 % and 2.6 % of GDP (PINTO/DREBENTSOV/MOROZOV, 2000, 19, 21).

Tab. G7: Gas and Electricity Subsidies from RAO UES and Gazprom*

	1997	1998		1999	2000
	Sales Gazprom				
Value of sales[1]	91,9	103,4	167,0	250,9	
Actual sales[2]	69,0	68,2	68,0	97,2	
Effective sales[3]	30,3	34,7	40,9	103,3	(60,4)[4]
	Subsidies Gazprom				
Effective subsidy	61,7	68,7	126,1	147,6	(190,5)[6]
Effective subsidy as a percentage of actual sales	89,4	100,7	185,6	151,8	(196,0)[6]
Effective subsidy as a percentage of GDP	2,5	2,5	2,7	2,1	(2,7)[6]
	Sales RAO UES				
Value of sales[1]	172	196	315	482	
Actual sales[2]	154	144	152	217	
Effective sales[3]	78	95	118	285	(186)[4]
	Subsidies RAO UES				
Effective subsidy	94	101	197	197	(296)[6]
Effective subsidy as a percentage of actual sales	61	70	130	91	(136,4)[6]
Effective subsidy as a percentage of GDP	3,8	3,7	4,1	2,8	(4,2)[6]

*Rubles, bill. (unless otherwise stated).

1 Deliveries of gas and electricity on the domestic market evaluated at the 1996 relative price.

2 Deliveries of gas and electricity on the domestic market in current prices.

3 Cash and discounted non-monetary receipts for current and past domestic gas sales.

4 Current effective sales: cash and discounted non-monetary receipts for current domestic gas and electricity sales.

5 Value of sales[1] - effective sales[3].

6 Value of sales[1] - current effective sales[4].

Source: OECD (2002), Economic Survey: Russian Federation, Paris, 126.

Table G7 shows more recent data on implicit subsidies by energy suppliers (Gazprom and RAO UES). Subsidies are calculated as the difference between the total value of sales (to the prices of 1996) and the payments (monetary and non-monetary) actually received by Gazprom and RAO UES. Taken together, these implicit subsidies amounted to 6.3 % of GDP in 1997 and 6.2 % of GDP in 1998, which is somewhat higher than the figures given by PINTO/DREBENTSOV/ MOROZOV (2000). In 1999 effective subsidies climbed to nearly 7 % of GDP; in

2000 they seemed to go down, but this decline was partly due to the settlement of arrears accumulated during the years before. The value of current effective subsidies which takes heed of these effects shows an amount of subsidization for 2000 almost equal to the value of 1999 (a total of 6.9 % of GDP; 4.2 % from RAO UES and 2.7 % from Gazprom). To take the OECD-average for energy prices instead of the artificially low Russian price level illustrates the real scale of the subsidization of enterprises through energy inputs: the average OECD-prices for gas and electricity in 2000 would enhance the subsidization value close to 30 % of GDP (OECD, 2002, 127).

3.3 Rent-Seeking, Transaction Costs and Efficiency

The relationship between state authorities and enterprises in Russia is characterized by various forms of rent-seeking activities. To put it in fairly simple manner, the state acts as a grabbing hand, which extracts rents from firms by exploiting its regulatory power, and the enterprises try to protect themselves against such activities by paying bribes – by buying some form of protection against such state activities. In the end, firms capture parts of the entire legal framework usually provided as a kind of public good. This may protect them against grabbing hand-activities, but this also expands their costs and may pose a serious threat to other possible market entrants and other competitors who will not only have to deal with state authorities, but also with an established competitor who captured part of the rules of the business game.

One may identify three crucial aspects which are necessary to bring about structural change in the enterprise sector in transition: first high pressure from enhanced competition on old state-owned or privatized firms, second a critical minimum level of protection of property rights of investors and a business environment stable enough to estimate future profits, and third the overall amount of barriers for market entry and business expansion. It is obvious that these aspects are interconnected: With high barriers for market entry, there will be no pressure on established firms to restructure.

Payments for bribes or state capture-activities act as barriers for market entry; they are all the more severe barriers because they appear as sunk costs. These are costs which are in case of market exit not reversible again. Cars and computers may be sold and thus their costs can be partly reversed, but a firm cannot reverse bribes. As a consequence, sunk costs build up barriers for market entry as well as for market exit. Established firms with any such high risks like high sunk costs for state capture will be willing to stay in business longer and to defend their market position more vigorously.

Another kind of market exit barrier is continued soft budget constraints which enable unprofitable firms to stay afloat and in business. As was shown above the form of soft budget constraints in Russia has changed during the first transition decade, whereas at the turn of the century indirect subsidies through cheap energy inputs and various forms of reducing the tax bill are used. Soft budget constraints lead to an unnecessary prolonging of unprofitable firms activities who occupy market shares and resources otherwise taken over by new, possibly leaner and more profitable producers. As a consequence, soft budget constraints for unprofitable firms act as barriers for market entry as well.

Fig. G2: Rent-Seeking, Transaction Costs and Efficiency Problems

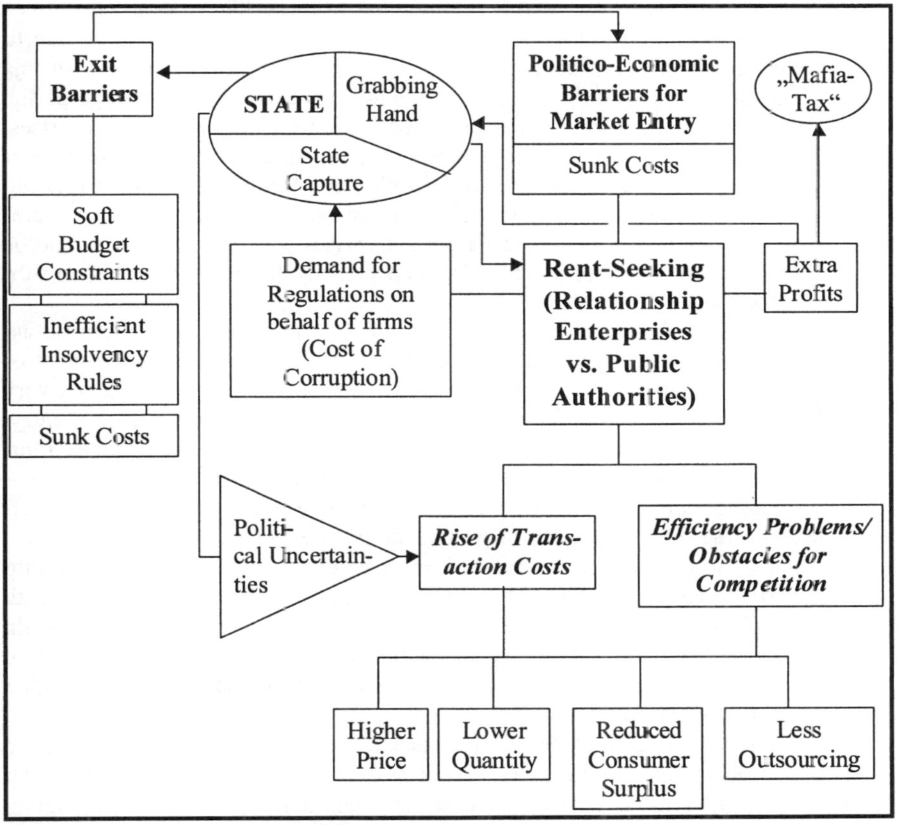

The connection between rent-seeking activities, soft budget constraints, market exit and entry barriers, efficiency problems and transaction costs is summarized in figure G2. It displays on the very left part barriers for market exit of unprofitable firms: soft budget constraints, inefficient insolvency rules and sunk costs – the last one in a purely business-related sense, meaning costs for marketing and other, non-reversible expenses. But exit barriers result from state activities as well: Politicians do not want to close big firms due to their important employer status or due to control reasons which facilitate rent extraction in an easy manner (see the model of SHLEIFER/VISHNY; 1994, for an explanation of how politicians interfere with large firms' operations). Further to the right, all these exit barriers are summed up to politico-economic barriers for market entry, whereas sunk costs resulting from rent-seeking activities are displayed separately below.

How do these exit barriers affect market entry or expansion for new firms? We have already seen that new firms have to act as state captors, resulting from their demand for regulations or the will to avoid interference of public authorities into their business operations. The problem of rent-seeking public authorities places a heavy burden on the business development of enterprises. This burden is aggravated still by inefficient firms unable or unwilling to cease. They occupy resources and, probably more important, they are able to sustain their market share due to uncompetitive advantages like e.g. implicit subsidies or political support. In this context outsourcing activities, which one should expect to happen as regards the wide range of products and services provided by former state-owned enterprises, do not take place in the face of these circumstances, because managers of former socialist enterprises as well as supporting politicians have an interest in running the full range of products and services to maintain the importance of the incumbent firm. If the exit barriers for inefficient enterprises were lower, there would be more frequent market entries due to better expectations for new firms to gain substantial market share.

The relationship between enterprises and public authorities, which can be assumed as guided by the rent-seeking considerations, is central to the problem of blocking the mechanisms of market competition in Russia: first due to its very existence as an extra burden for enterprises leading to a barrier for market entry, second as a means for enabling inefficient firms to stay on. Even worse, rent-seeking activities may create extra-profits on behalf of incumbent enterprises – due to e.g. a monopoly position by public authorities. Such extra profits, however, soon become the target not only of rent-seeking bureaucrats, but of criminal organizations as well (mafia tax), making it even harder for new firms to break into the established market structure. Thus, rent-seeking activities in combination with exit barriers basically have two effects: they lead – together with uncertainties on the political development – to higher transaction costs and, as long as competition does not take off, to efficiency problems with respect to market supply (higher prices, lower quantity and quality).

According to ARROW (1969, 48), transaction costs in a broad definition are costs which occur for running an economic system; this means costs for building up economic institutions as well as costs for maintaining and enforcing them. Individuals and enterprises, which usually profit from a functioning institutional framework, pay for that via the tax bill. In countries with a malfunctioning and inefficient institutional framework and additional transaction costs due to rent-seeking activities, using the official market system becomes more and more expensive for firms – using official markets means paying taxes as well as payments for grabbing hand- and state capture-strategies. Thus it is rational to turn to the unofficial system – the shadow economy – or to completely disregard investments in such an institutional environment and take the capital abroad.

High transactions costs create obstacles for outsourcing activities. Whereas socialist enterprises were to a high degree integrated vertically and also had a broad variety of activities apart from their core production, the outsourcing of many of those activities could bring about huge efficiency gains and create jobs in the emerging private sector. But a functioning official system of market institutions is without doubt a prerequisite for widespread outsourcing measures, because transactions, which have up to that point taken place within the enterprise, now have to be made by using official markets. Thus outsourcing activities, when confronted with high transaction costs, will be less frequent; it is even more rational to internalize business activities where possible or go on with the inherited, highly integrated structure.

The results of such an interconnection between rent-seeking activities, high-running transaction costs, low level of competition and low incentives for former socialist enterprises to restructure is obvious and can be seen in Russia in 2002. Although the country has experienced a period of high economic growth, only a slight increase of the investment/GDP-ratio can be recognized. Former socialist firms lack the incentive to invest and restructure their business activities and new private firms cannot or will not enter the official market and expand due to an uncertain institutional framework and high transaction costs, which are associated with official commercial activities.

Of course, these conclusions regarding low restructuring efforts somewhat exaggerate the real situation in Russia, since restructuring took place as a result of economic liberalization and opening up during the 1990s, a fact well documented (EBRD, 1999; BROWN/EARLE, 2000). But compared to countries more advanced in transition like Poland and Hungary, structural change in Russia still lacks considerable momentum, and pressure from market competition is lower (EBRD, 1999, 136). Given the widespread rent-seeking activities, high transaction costs, a low degree of competition, and in addition a comparatively small share of SME, one might indeed conclude that a competition blockade exists in Russia in 2002, impeding market mechanisms from taking place, mechanisms responsible for enforcing structural change and the efficient supply of goods and services.

4. Conclusions and Policy Options

The past considerations made clear that in the face of Russia's recognition as a market economy, basic mechanisms of such an economic system – competition and freedom of economic activity –, which ensure efficient supply of goods and welfare, have not yet taken root in the country's economy. Economic growth and catching up will depend on whether Russia will be able to fill its still large investment gap and overcome the capital flight problem. When compared to other transition countries, Russia faces an annual investment gap of around 5-10 % of its GDP.

This paper pointed out that much of the problem lies in malfunctioning markets and a heavy extra burden for new enterprises from rent-seeking activities in combination with exit barriers for inefficient firms. Hence a viable and flexible enterprise sector, in particular in its small and medium range segment which claims the larger part of the restructuring efforts in more successful transition countries, does not emerge. Thus economic convergence will happen only if rent-seeking and exit barriers are reduced substantially.

How can this be achieved? A broad variety of reforms have been enacted since 2000 but doubts remain whether these will be useful to tackle the competition blockade. Concerning the regulative power of state officials enabling them to extract rents from enterprises, the Russian government has abolished or curbed some of their instruments. But that seems to be far from enough; higher salaries and a better training for officials – including international cooperation – are also needed to improve public service in Russia.

A reform strategy which aims at the abolition of the competition blockade in Russia should include further crucial aspects:

- Redefining the role of the state in the economic system: The change of behavior of state officials from a grabbing hand to an invisible hand-model is probably the most difficult task. In a weak institutional environment like that in Russia, the import of rules can to some degree have a considerable impact on the reduction of the possible scope for authorities' decisions and arbitrariness and therefore reduce the opportunities for rent-seeking activities. In that sense EU accession countries have a remarkable advantage over countries like Russia, which are not required to adapt EU common law. But to some extent the rules which are given by the WTO may act in the same manner.

- Further opening-up of the country by reducing trade barriers and implementing reforms necessary for WTO-membership. WTO membership has to be accompanied by reform efforts in various sectors of the economy, e.g. the financial sector. It is noteworthy that economic gains from further integration into the world market can only be obtained by reducing the barriers for economic integration within Russia itself (out-dated transport infrastructure, high and persistent price differentials between regions and various regulations which impede the exchange of goods and services within Russia and lead therefore to an economic fragmentation of the country). Doubts remain in Russia whether WTO membership will lead to net gains for the country, because Russia's highly concentrated export structure cannot expect to gain much from liberalized trade – still worse, some argue, the reverse effect of liberalized trade and services – more competition from abroad – might lead to higher unemployment within Russia. But this view does not take into account that Russia today is a country with a one-sided integration into the world economy, leading to a high volatility in export earnings due to volatile oil prices, and with fairly outdated and uncompetitive industries in the remaining industrial sectors outside that of oil and gas. These problems can only be overcome by a higher degree of competition and thus stronger incentives to invest in restructuring efforts.

- Abolishing "bottlenecks" for enterprises, in particular in infrastructure services, and gradually reducing implicit subsidies through less state intervention as regards energy prices: This draws mainly on the reform and restructuring of the infrastructure sectors, which were, in particular the reform of electricity generation and distribution, discussed in Russia in 2002. Time is already running out for reforms in the electric power sector because lack of generation capacity might eventually lead to serious electricity shortages from 2003 onwards (OECD, 2002).

- Change of strategy in competition policy: Competition policy in Russia is characterized by overlapping duties and responsibilities on different federal levels and between certain ministries and other administrative units. Rather than having too few and too lax competition rules, competition policy often lacks the political will and power to enforce the law and decide according to the rules (BROADMAN, 2000). Decision power in competition policy should be streamlined and authorities better equipped with skilled personnel.
- Fiscal federalism – a case for more responsibilities and budget autonomy on the regional and local level: As a counteraction against increased accumulation of power on the regional level, Putin has pushed for a recentralization of state power since 2000, with respect to both responsibilities as well as revenue assignments. From the point of economic reform, in particular on the sub-federal level, this seems to be counterproductive, because reform-oriented regional and local governments might eventually be deprived of the fruits of their reform efforts. Rather than introducing a grand reform strategy from the federal level, the central government should focus on giving the lower level authorities more responsibilities and freer choice of raising revenues in order to let them pursue their own reform efforts. The OECD has made a case for a higher degree of regional and local autonomy (2002). Being able to implement reforms alongside their duties and reap the fruits in the form of e.g. higher tax revenues, which are not taken away by federal intervention, might indeed lead to more reform efforts on the sub-federal level, improving the business climate substantially.

The removal of competition blockades seems to be crucial for the future development of Russia's economy and for its chances to catch up. Once a rise in investment and the modernization of the industry take place in Russia, growth might be self-sustaining and no longer so dependent on external factors like oil price; an effect which will in itself bring much more economic stability to the country.

References

ARROW, K.J. (1969): The Organization of Economic Activity: Issues Pertinent to the Choice of Market Versus Nonmarket Allocation, in: The Analysis and Evaluation of Public Expenditures: The PBB-System, Joint Economic Committee, 91st Congress, 1st Session, Bd. 1, Washington D.C.

ASLUND, A. (1996): Rentoorientirovannoe povedenie v rossiiskoi ekonomike, in: Voprosy ekonomiki, Nr. 8/1996, 99-108.

BECK, P.J., MAHER, M.W. (1986): Comparison and Bribery in Thin Markets, in: Economic Letters, Vol. 20, 1-5.

BERKOVITZ, D., DEJONG, D.N. (1999): Russia's Internal Border, in: Regional Science and Urban Economics, Vol. 29, 633-649.

BERKOVITZ, D., DEJONG, D.N. (2001): The Evolution of Market Integration in Russia, in: Economics of Transition, Vol. 9, Nr. 1, 87-104.

BROADMAN, H.G. (2000): Reducing Structural Dominance and Entry Barriers in Russian Industry, World Bank Working Paper Nr. 2330, Washington D.C.

BROWN, J.D., EARLE, J.S. (2000): Competition and Firm Performance: Lessons from Russia, SITE Working Paper Nr. 154, Stockholm.

COMMANDER, S., MUMSSEN, C. (1999): Understanding Barter in Russia, EBRD Working Paper Nr. 37, London.

EARLE, J.S., ESTRIN, S. (1998): Privatization, Competition and Budget Constraints: Disciplining Enterprises in Russia, SITE Working Paper Nr. 128, Stockholm.

EBRD (1999): Transition Report 1999, London.

EBRD (2002): Transition Report 2002, London.

ELISSEEVA, I.I. (1999): Price Dynamics in the Russian Food Market, Heidelberg: Physica.

FRYE, T., SHLEIFER, A. (1997): The Invisible and the Grabbing Hand, in: The American Economic Review, Papers and Proceedings, Vol. 87, 354-358.

GÖTZ, R. (2002), Das russische Bruttoinlandsprodukt im internationalen Vergleich, in: Osteuropa Wirtschaft, Vol. 47, Nr. 4, 319-336.

HAYEK, F.A. von (1968): Wettbewerb als Entdeckungsverfahren, Tübingen.

HELLMAN, J.S., JONES, G., KAUFMANN, D. (2000): "Seize the State, Seize the Day". State Capture, Corruption and Influence in Transition, World Bank Policy Research Working Paper Nr. 2444, Washington D.C.

HOPPMANN, E. (1977): Marktmacht und Wettbewerb, Tübingen: Mohr.

INDEM (2002): Diagnostika rossijskoj korruptsii: Sotsiologicheskij analiz, Moskau.

JOHNSON, J. (1997), Russia's Emerging Financial-Industrial Groups, in: Post-Soviet Affairs, Vol. 13, Nr. 4, 333-365.

KALI, R. (2002), Contractual Governance, Business Groups and Transition, in: Economics of Transition, Vol. 10, Nr. 2, 255-272.

KORNAI, J. (1986): The Soft Budget Constraint, in: Kyklos, Vol. 39, Nr. 1, 3-30.

LIEN, D.H.D. (1986): A Note on Competitive Bribery Games, in: Economic Letters, Vol. 20, 337-341.

LYNCH, A. (2002): Roots of Russia's Economic Dilemmas: Liberal Economics and Illiberal Geography, in: Europe-Asia Studies, Vol. 54, Nr. 1, 31-49.

OECD (2002): Economic Survey: Russian Federation, Paris.

PEROTTI, E.C., GELFER, S. (2001), Red Barons or Robber Barons? Governance and Investment in Russian Financial Industrial Groups, in: European Economic Review, Vol. 45, 1601-1617.

PINTO, B., DREBENTSOV, V., MOROZOV, A. (2000): Dismantling Russia's Nonpayments System. Creating Conditions for Growth, World Bank Technical Paper Nr. 471, Washington D.C.

POPOVA, T. (1998), Financial-Industrial Groups (FIGs) and Their Roles in the Russian Economy, in: Review of Economies in Transition, 7/1998, 5-28.

PRITZL, R.F.J. (1997): Korruption und Rent Seeking in Lateinamerika. Zur Politischen Ökonomie autoritärer politischer Systeme, Baden-Baden: Nomos.

RADAEV, V. (1999): Wie in Russland Märkte entstehen: Vertragsdurchsetzung und Markteintritt, Berichte des BIOst Nr. 41, Köln.

RAJAN, R.G., SERVAES, H., ZINGALES, L. (1998), The Cost of Diversity: The Diversification Discount and Inefficient Investment, in: Journal of Finance, Vol. 55, Nr. 1, 35-46.

ROSE-ACKERMAN, S. (1999): Corruption and Government: Causes, Consequences and Reform, Cambridge: Cambridge UP.

SCHRÖDER, H.-H. (1999), El'tsin and the Oligarchs: The Role of Financial Industrial Groups in Russian Politics between 1993 and July 1998, in: Europe-Asia Studies, Vol. 51, Nr. 6, 957-988.

SHIN, H., STULZ, R. (1998), Are Internal Capital Markets Efficient? in: Quarterly Journal of Economics, Vol. 113, 531-552.

SHLEIFER, A., VISHNY, R.W. (1994): Politicians and Firms, in: Quarterly Journal of Economics, Vol. 108, 995-1025.

STEIN, J. (1997), Internal Capital Markets and the Competition for Corporate Ressources, in: Journal of Finance, Vol. 52, 111-134.

STIGLER, G.J. (1975): The Citizen and the State: Essays on Regulation, Chicago: Chicago University Press.

STROUTCHENEVSKI, A. (2002): The Performance of Savings and Investments in Russia, Russian Economic Trends – Quarterly Issue, Vol. 11, No. 2, 31-36.

TRANSPARENCY INTERNATIONAL (2001): 2001 Corruption Perceptions Index, Paris.

WIEGERT, R. (2003): Transformationskrise, Wachstumserfordernisse und Wettbewerbsblockade in Rußland, Heidelberg: Physica.

WORLD BANK (2002): Transition – the First Ten Years. Analysis and Lessons for Eastern Europe and the Former Soviet Union, Washington D.C.: The World Bank.

ZAOSTROVTSEV, A. (2000): Rent Extraction in a Rent Seeking Society, Spider Working Paper Series Nr. 10, St. Petersburg: Stockholm University, St. Petersburg State University.

Comments on: Obstacles to Growth and Competition: The Political Economy of Corruption and Rent-seeking in Russia

Some Results of the 1999 Business Environment and Enterprise Performance Survey (BEEPS)

Cathleen Faber

1. Design and Composition of the BEEPS

The 1999 Business Environment and Enterprise Performance Survey (BEEPS), building upon the World Bank's survey carried out for the World Development Report in 1997 and the ongoing World Business Environment Survey, was designed to assess the quality of governance across 20 countries of central and eastern Europe and the former Soviet Union from a firm-level perspective. The results presented here are based on the survey implemented during the period June to August 1999. From a statistical point of view, the BEEPS seemed to be highly representative and most of all comparable across countries. Results of the given survey presented a very realistic picture of the problematic situation of firms at the end of the last century.

The main questionnaire of the BEEPS contained over 70 questions. Governance-related questions discussed in this paper can be classified in two dimensions:

- macro-governance and
- micro-governance.

Macro-governance deals with a broad range of issues relating to the efficiency and efficacy of governmental institutions and policies. Firms were asked to rate the quality of public services across a number of dimensions including central government, parliament, the judiciary, utilities and the police, and to evaluate how serious various institutional obstacles are for their business, ranging across macro- and micro-economic policy, crime and corruption. Questions were asked about the legal system and its ability to protect property and contract rights and the predictability and transparency of policymaking.

The second set of questions to be discussed investigates the nature of direct interactions between firms and the state. This includes not only an analysis of the extent and type of state intervention in the operations of firms, but also the ways in which firms seek to influence the state. On corruption, firms were asked about the extent and frequency of bribery, the recipients of bribes and the nature of corrupt transactions.

The composition of the sample related to Russia, Ukraine, Poland and Hungary is given in Table g1. In general, 3,000 firms in 20 transition countries were asked.

Tab. g1: Composition of the Sample (Excerpt)

	Total number of firms	New private	Ex-state	State	Firms with FDI	Capital city	Other large cities	Smaller cities, towns and rural
Russia	552	283	230	25	37	87	232	233
Ukraine	247	147	73	25	30	37	88	122
Poland	246	160	53	25	40	38	83	125
Hungary	147	94	24	25	27	51	0	96

Source: HELLMAN/JONES/KAUFMANN/SCHANKERMAN (2000), 9.

2. Main Results of the Survey

To evaluate the quality of governance, the firms were asked to assess the extent to which different functions of the state posed an obstacle to their business in 1999. Ten key functions were rated by firms on a scale of 1 (no obstacle) to 4 (major obstacle):

- Policy instability
- Inflation
- Exchange rate
- Finance
- Taxes and regulations
- Infrastructure
- Functioning of the judiciary
- Corruption
- Street crime / theft / disorder
- Organized crime / mafia.

Figure g1 summarizes the rating of each dimension of governance in the form of star diagrams for each country. More than two-thirds of Russian firms answered that political instability, inflation, exchange rate, finance and tax regulations were moderate or major obstacles for their business. Corruption, organized and street crime were problematic for approximately one-half. Problems associated with physical infrastructure and with the strength of law and order were generally ranked as less serious obstacles. Firms regarded the functioning of the judiciary as one of the least significant obstacles for their business. In relation to other countries in eastern Europe there are differences, but the ranking of the major obstacles is essentially the same.

Fig. g1: Dimensions of Governance[1]

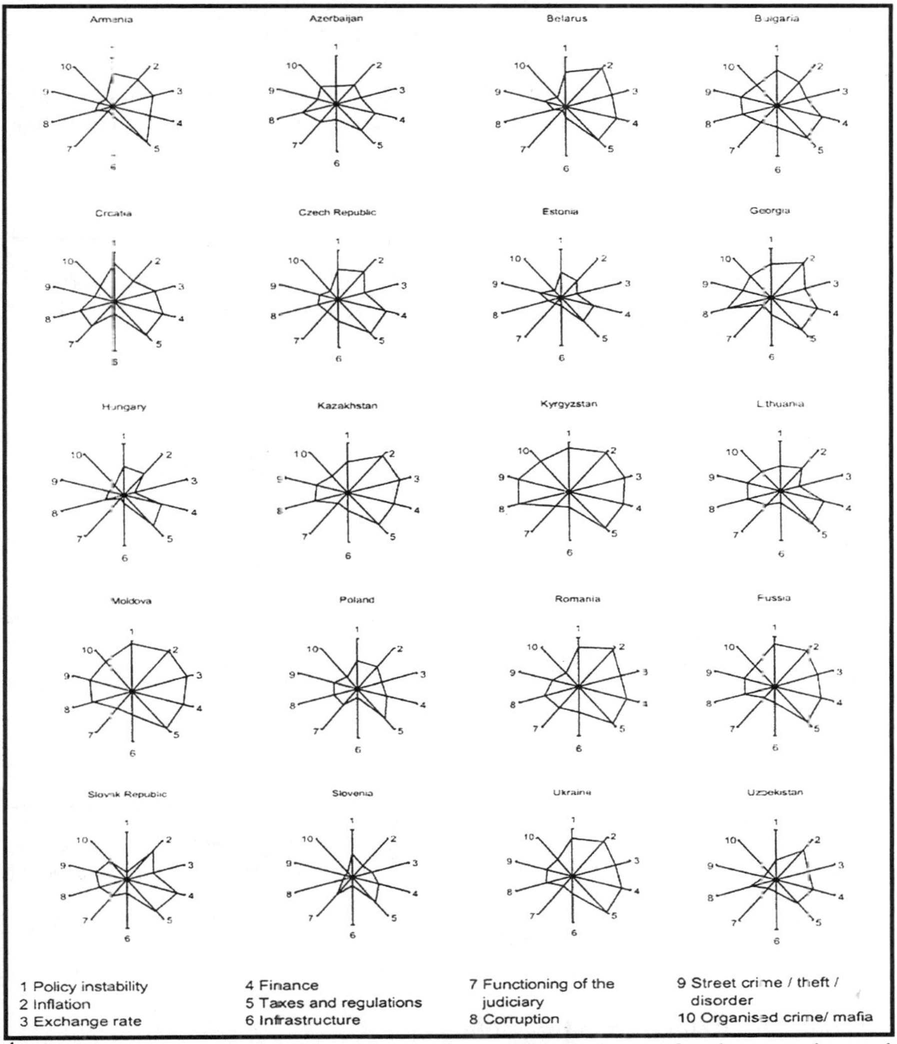

[1]Survey Question: „How problematic are these different factors for the operation and growth of your business?" Response categories: No obstacles, Minor obstacles, Moderate obstacle, and Major obstacles. Viewed is percentage of firms responding that the dimension of governance represented either a moderate or major obstacle.

Source: HELLMAN/SCHANKERMAN (2000), 6.

2.1 Policy Instability

For detailed information about politics, the respondents were asked to rate the overall quality and efficiency of outcomes delivered by public agencies and services (see Fig. g2). Compared to other countries Russian firms were more dissatisfied with central government institutions. Especially the quality and efficiency of central government and parliament were rated negative by nearly all Russian respondents. Services delivered by the Central Bank, the judiciary, police and armed forces were rated less problematic. Nevertheless, customs service got best performance with at least 50 % noticed desirable outcomes. There were high potentials for policymakers here compared to those results in Poland and Hungary.

Fig. g2: Quality of Public Institutions[1]

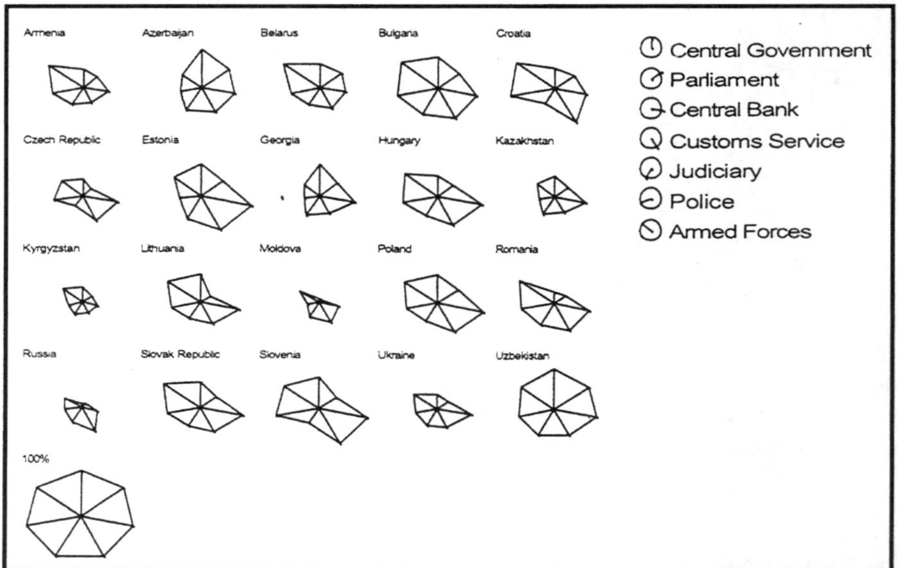

[1]Survey Question: „Could you please rate the overall quality and efficiency of services delivered by the public agencies or services?" Response categories: Very good, Good, Slightly good, Slightly bad, Bad, Very bad. Viewed is percentage of firms responding slightly good or better.

Source: HELLMAN/JONES/KAUFMANN/SCHANKERMAN (2000), 19.

2.2 Inflation, Exchange Rate, Finance

Results related to these three topics were strongly influenced by after-effects of the 1998 financial crises. Many of these problems have been under the process of being solved since 1999 when the survey was conducted. The Central Bank has stabilized the exchange rate and reduced inflation, despite the fact that the index of consumer prices continued to increase by nearly 20 per cent in 2000 and 2001.

2.3 Taxes and Regulations

Asked about firm's perspectives on the extent of regulatory burden for their business, problems related to tax regulations ranked as the most important obstacles for the operation and growth of Russian respondents in 1999 (see Fig. g3). Tax regulations were a moderate or major obstacle for more than 90 % of the firms.

Fig. g3: Regulatory Burden[1]

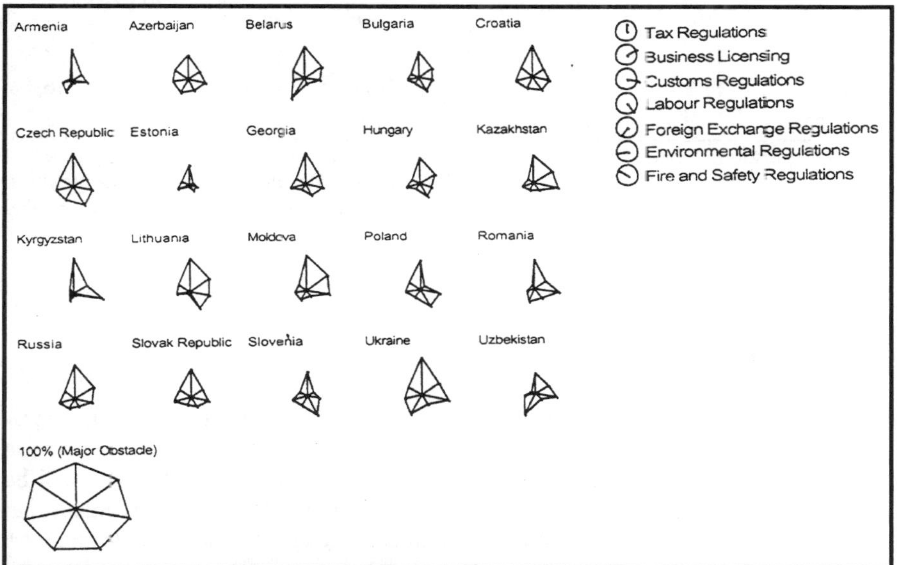

[1]Survey Question: „How problematic are the following for the operation and growth of your business?" Response categories: No obstacle, Minor obstacle, Moderate obstacle, and Major obstacle. Viewed is percentage of firms responding either a moderate or major obstacle.

Source: HELLMAN/JONES/KAUFMANN/SCHANKERMAN (2000), 34.

The tax reforms of 2000 and 2001 represented important steps towards the simplification and clarification of the Russian tax system. Nevertheless, problems remained in the Russian tax system. Although the explicit tax burden has been reduced somewhat, the combinations of formal and various informal taxes continues to impose a significant burden on many firms.[1]

The most direct form of regulation is intervention by the state in firm decisions. Firms were therefore asked how frequently the state directly intervenes. Table g2

---

[1] See OECD (2002), 46.

shows the proportion of firms in the survey that say they face significant state intervention in different areas of their operations. Surprisingly, the highest level of state intervention (average intervention index of 43.9) was reported in Hungary, one of the most advanced transition countries. State interventions were common on all types of operations in Hungary, but extremely high in wages. State intervention was less problematic in Russia. Mainly prices and sales were the subject of state intervention here. The average intervention index of Russia was relatively low compared to other transition economies.

Tab. g2: Type of State Intervention[1]

Country	Investment	Employment	Sales	Wages	Prices	Average Intervention Index
Russia	15,9	10,1	30,2	10,3	42,1	21,8
Ukraine	25,6	19,6	36,3	40,2	44,4	33,2
Poland	17,3	13,0	13,8	26,9	10,8	16,4
Hungary	37,9	38,2	40,0	59,6	44,0	43,9

[1]Survey question: "How often does the government intervene in the following types of decisions by your firm?" Response categories: Always, Usually, Frequently, Sometimes, Seldom, Never. Reported is the percentage of firms responding sometimes or more frequently.

Source: HELLMAN/SCHANKERMAN (2000), 15.

2.4 Judiciary

Functioning of the judiciary seemed to be a less important obstacle for the operation and growth of Russian firms. Normally the legal system is a crucial institution in a market economy. Firms and individuals need to know that contracts will be honored, their private property respected, and in the event of a disagreement that the courts are capable of deciding the matter in a fair and affordable manner. Firms were asked their perceptions of the legal system on a number of different dimensions; their responses are presented in Figure g4. Fifty per cent of respondents reported that the Russian legal system was affordable. Yet only a small number of firms regarded the legal system as fair and impartial, honest and uncorrupt, quick, consistent and reliable, and able to enforce its decisions.

Fig. g4: Perceptions of the Legal System[1]

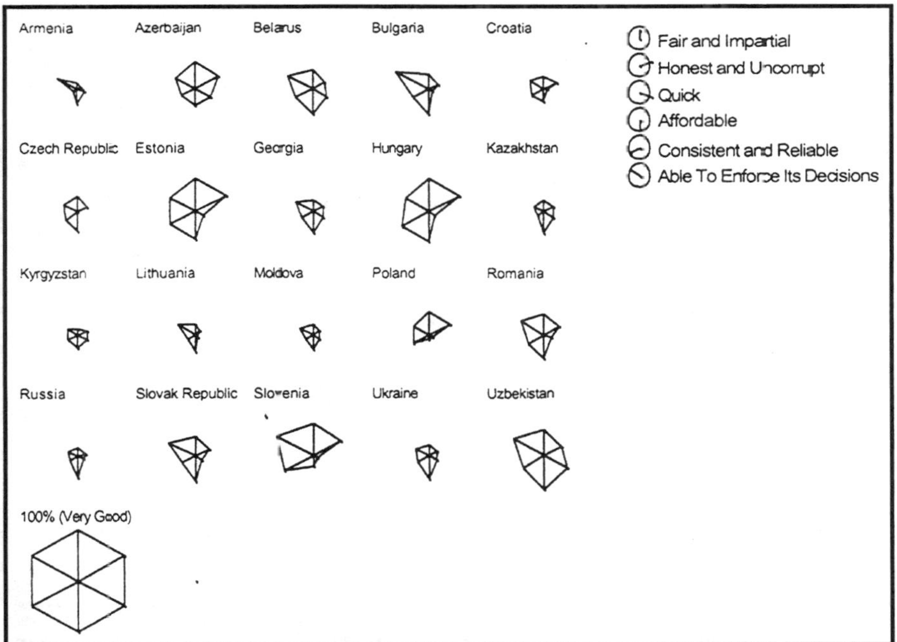

[1]Survey Question: „Thinking about your country's legal system, how often do you associate the following description with the court system in resolving business disputes?" Response categories: Always, Usually, Frequently, Sometimes, Seldom, Never. Viewed is percentage of firms responding frequently or more.

Source: HELLMAN/JONES/KAUFMANN/SCHANKERMAN (2000), 27.

2.5 Corruption and Crime

Approximately one-half of Russian firms pointed out that corruption was a moderate or major obstacle for business in 1999. To develop a measure of the impact of corruption and capture on the business environment, firms were asked to what extent the different forms of corruption (sales of parliamentary votes, sales of court decisions in criminal or arbitration cases, patronage, etc.) have had an impact on their business. Figure g5 shows that all eight forms of corruption were moderate or major obstacles for the operation and growth of nearly one-fourth of Russian firms. Figure g6 presents the firm's assessment of the degree of influence that they wield at different levels of government. In addition, firms in Russia were asked the same question about their local government. The results are remarkable in a negative sense. One-third of the Russian firms reported frequent influences in all areas of local government, while this figure was nearly one-sixth at the national level. Here legal regulations were needed as quickly as possible.

Fig. g5: Corruption[1]

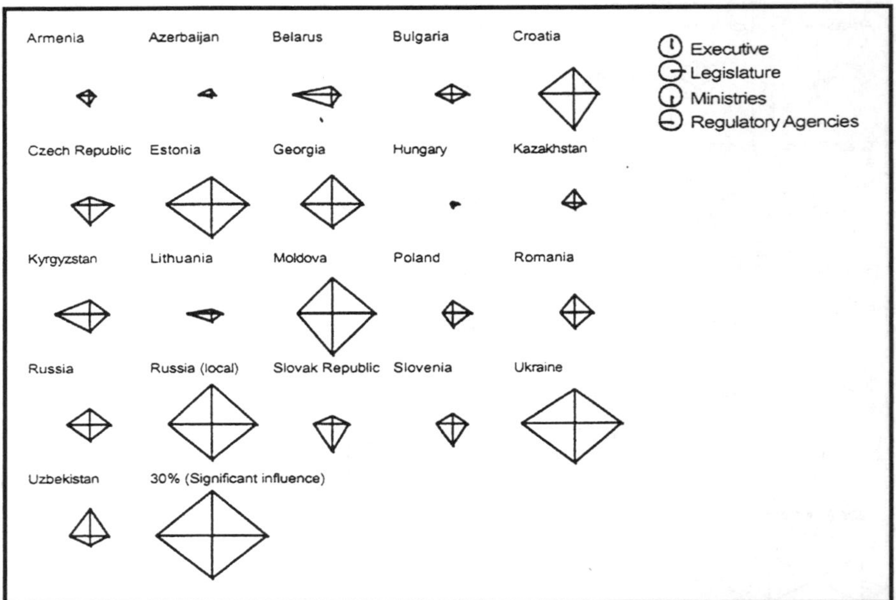

[1]Survey Question: „To what extent have the following forms of corruption had an impact on your business?" Response categories: No obstacle, Minor obstacle, Moderate obstacle, and Major obstacle. Viewed is percentage of firms responding either a moderate or major obstacle.

Source: HELLMAN/JONES/KAUFMANN/SCHANKERMAN (2000), 22.

Furthermore, state intervention imposes demands on the time of senior managers in enterprises. The first column in Table g3 presents estimates of the average proportion of senior management's time spent on dealing with government officials about the application and interpretation of laws and regulations. In Russia and the Ukraine, the "time tax" exceeded 13 percent of management time, while it is less than 10 percent in Poland and Hungary. In addition to time spent with government officials, firms were also asked about payments of direct private benefits to public officials in the form of bribes. Table 3 presents the percentage of firms bribing frequently or more and the amount of bribes in relation to revenues. Different "services" receiving bribes are presented in Table g4. The largest amount of bribes went to licensing (20 % of total bribes) and taxes (18 %) in Russia. Nevertheless, it was relatively low compared to that in the Ukraine (21 % licensing and 26 % taxes) and Hungary (44 % and 11 %, respectively).

Fig. g6: Influence over the State[1]

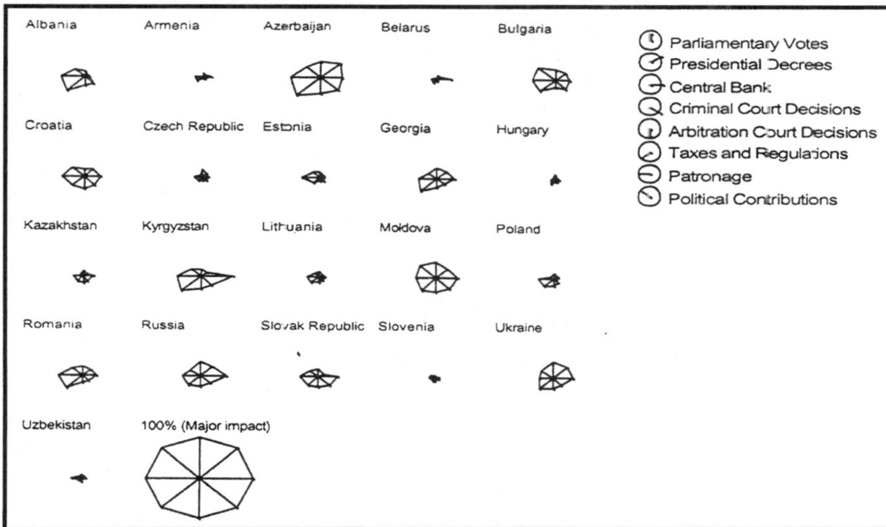

[1]Survey Question: „When a new law, rule, regulation, or decree is being discussed that could have a substantial impact on your business, how much influence does your firm typically have at the national level of government to try to influence the content of that law, rule, regulation or decree?" Response categories: Never, Seldom, Influential, Frequently, Very. Viewed is percentage of firms responding influential or more.

Source: HELLMAN/JONES/KAUFMANN/SCHANKERMAN (2000), 44.

Tab. g3: Time and Bribe Taxes

Country	Time tax[1]	% of firms bribing frequently[2]	Bribe tax (bribing firm)[3]	Bribe tax (all firms)
Russia	12,7	29,1	4,1	2,8
Ukraine	16,8	35,3	6,5	4,4
Poland	9,5	32,7	2,5	1,6
Hungary	7,2	31,3	3,5	1,7

[1]Survey question: "What percentage of senior management's time per year is spent in dealing with government officials about the application and interpretation of laws and regulations?" Response categories: Up to 1 %, 1 to 5 %, 6 to 10 %, 11 to 25 %, 26 to 50 %, more than 50 %. Categories were averaged.

[2]Survey question: "Thinking about officials, how frequently would you say the following statement is true: 'It is common for firms in my line of business to have to pay some irregular 'additional payments' to get the things done? '" Response categories: Always, Mostly, Frequently, Sometimes, Seldom, Never. Percentage of firms responding frequently or more is reported.

[3]Survey question: "On average, what percent of revenues do firms like yours typically pay per annum in unofficial payments to public officials?" Response categories: 0 %, less than 1 %, 1-1.99 %, 2-9.99 %, 10-12 %, 13-25 %, Over 25 %. Categories were averaged.

Source: HELLMAN/SCHANKERMAN (2000), 18/19.

Tab. g4: Bribes[1]

Country	Connection to public services	Licenses	Taxes	Government contracts	Customs	Courts	Health / Fire inspectors	Influence legislation	Other	Total
Russia	11,7	20,4	18,5	11,3	8,8	11,1	11,6	2,8	3,7	100
Ukraine	10,3	21,3	25,8	10,4	12,2	6,8	9,7	2,5	1,1	100
Poland	7,4	26,1	8,8	17,7	15,8	9,9	5,7	4,3	4,3	100
Hungary	7,3	43,6	10,9	11,1	14,2	3,1	3,3	1,4	4,9	100
Overall	10,6	22,0	19,4	14,6	12,2	7,9	7,8	2,6	2,9	100

[1]Average proportion of bribes spent on each "service".

Source: HELLMAN/JONES/KAUFMANN/SCHANKERMAN (2000), 41.

3. Policy Options

Results of the 1999 Business Environment and Enterprise Performance Survey showed several obstacles to economic growth and allowed for the comparison of the situation in Russia with 19 other transition countries in central and eastern Europe. From a Russian firm-level perspective there are still three major problems left: policy instability, tax regulation, and corruption.

Policymakers are asked

- to develop a more stabile framework for economic operations,
- to improve firm's trust in political decisions,
- to initiate a fair, quick, honest, consistent, reliable, and uncorrupt legal system,
- to manage a fair and clear tax system,
- to fight against corruption, and
- to limit one-sided influences of single firms on local and national government.

References

CARLIN, W., FRIES, S., SCHAFFER, M., SEABRIGHT, P. (2000): Barter and non-monetary transactions in transition economies - Evidence from a cross-country survey. EBRD Working Paper No. 50.

HELLMAN, J., JONES, G., KAUFMANN, D., SCHANKERMAN, M. (2000): Measuring governance and state capture: the role of bureaucrats and firms in shaping the business environment – Results of a firm-level study across 20 transition economies. EBRD Working Paper No. 51.

HELLMAN, J., SCHANKERMAN, M. (2000): Intervention, corruption and capture: the nexus between enterprises and the state. EBRD Working Paper No. 58.

OECD (2002): OECD Economic Surveys: Russian Federation. Volume 2002/5

H. Macroeconomic Situation in Russia: Growth, Investment and Capital Flows

Evgeny Gavrilenkov

1. Recent Trends

The Russian economy demonstrated relatively strong performance in 1999-2001 and is still doing well in 2002. At least macroeconomic indicators for 2002 look better than was thought likely in late 2001. Expected growth of about 4,0 % compares favorably with a limping Europe and US. After rising in the second quarter of 2002, oil prices remained high in mid 2002, and Russia was able to profit from a strong current account and continued windfall revenues. In the fall of 2001 and early in 2002 during the period of decreased oil prices and economic slow down in Russia, growth prospects were much more cautious.

Fig. H1: Growth in Industrial Output, 1994-2002

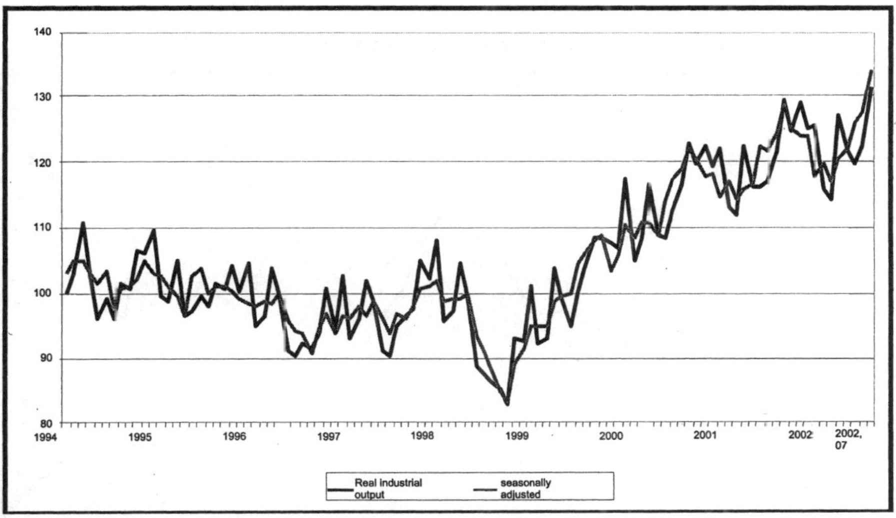

Following an increase in the price of oil, economic activity increased in Russia in the second quarter of 2002 and the recovery continued in the mid-year, so that industrial growth in January-September grew 4,0 % y-o-y, up from 2,6 % in the first quarter y-o-y (see Fig. H1). By the end of 2003, this growth figure should be even higher. The low growth in early 2002 was largely the result of a strong contraction in November-December 2001, brought on by decreased investment activity in the face of lower oil prices and gloomy prospects for the global economy. Conversely, mid-year acceleration in growth was stimulated by increased investment activity. At the same time, growing consumer demand stimulated domestic production, while appreciation in the euro kept imports at bay. A seasonal slowdown in economic activity is expected by the end of 2002, but this should not be as drastic as in 2001. This, however, will work out if oil prices remain at a level above $20 per bbl.

In spite of relatively high growth rates in the Russian economy in 1999-2000 (average annual GDP growth was about 6 %), the economy is operating at well below its potential and the current growth mechanism is not sustainable in the long run. This mechanism, which took root in the aftermath of the 1998 crisis and has developed considerably since 2000, depends largely on investment by exporters, in particular oil and gas companies. Investment affects industrial output significantly and therefore is, with a lag of around three months, reflected in real incomes and consumer demand, thus stimulating the rest of the economy. Russia is thus at a crossroads: if it can modify the existing growth mechanism, then higher and more sustainable growth rates are perfectly plausible in the long term. If not, then growth is likely to continue its decline. Lowering the entry barriers for businesses, cutting back the "red tape" and establishing a climate that will nurture their expansion are necessary preconditions for the emergence of this new growth mechanism. Reform of the financial sector is another key element. Those issues will be discussed below.

Fig. H2: Seasonally Adjusted Industrial Output and Investment, 1999-2002

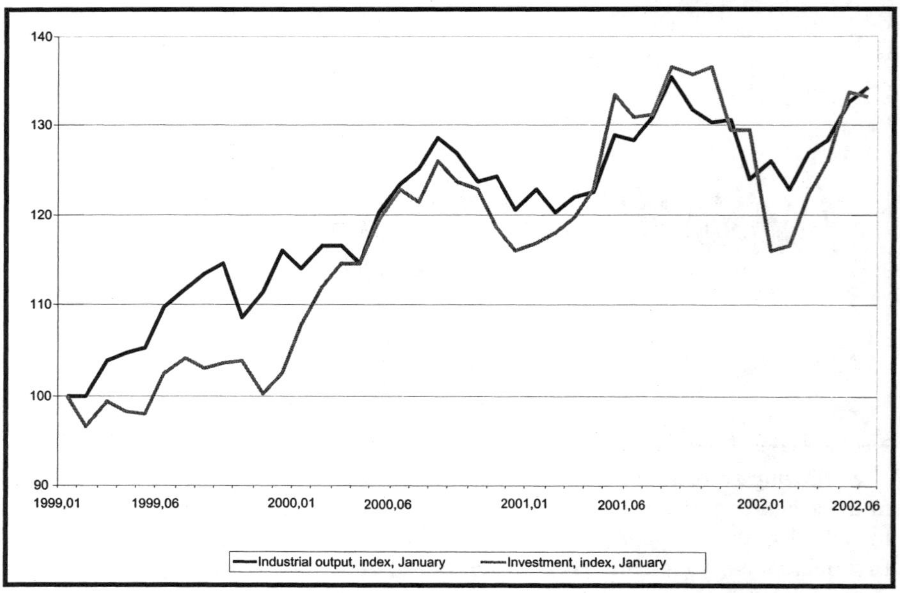

The Figure H2 shows that the growth mechanism that has developed in Russia over the past several years is still in place and output is largely driven by investment, mostly in the energy sector. Economic activity is thus driven by investment and tends to pick up mid-year. In fact, the graph below shows seasonally adjusted investment in fixed capital and industrial output for the period from 1999. From this graph it is clear that the relatively low output growth in early 2002 was largely the result of a contraction in output at end of 2001. From March, the economy once again began growing.

The graph points to a clear correlation between investment and industrial output growth. The shape of the growth curve would be essentially the same if some more aggregate output monthly indicators were taken, such as output in the five basic sectors (industry, agriculture, trade, transportation, construction). It is known that over 50 % of investment in Russia is within the energy and transport sectors. The latter is closely linked to the oil and gas industry since it includes pipelines. Therefore, overall industrial output is in fact determined by the investment plans of a limited number of exporters (other capital intensive export sectors, such as metallurgy and the chemical industry, also play an important role). This in turn affects GDP. The reason for this is that increased investment by exporters pulls up profits and wages in the manufacturing sectors which produce investment goods. Production and incomes in certain other related sectors also increase. With a lag of around three months, consumer demand goes up as well (aided also by increases in public sector salaries which likewise depend on profits from the energy sector, Russia's largest tax payer), thus stimulating production in a broader range of industries. Investment can thus be seen to be a catalyst for economic growth.

The rise in oil price between 1999 and 2000 contributed to higher profits for oil companies, which in turn translated into growing investment. Similarly, a fall in the oil price at end of 2001 resulted in a drop in investment and hence industrial output (see Fig. H3).

Fig. H3: Seasonally Adjusted Industrial Output and Oil Price

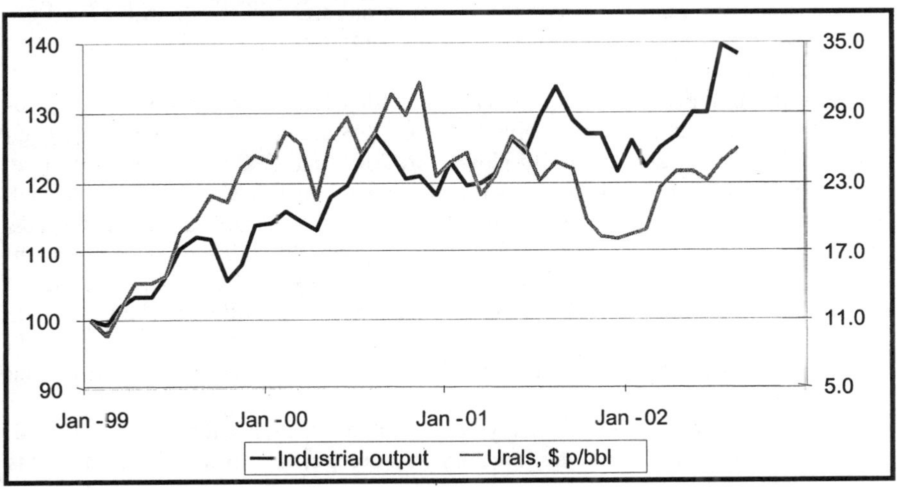

The Russian budget is also very much dependent upon oil price, which can be seen from Fig. H4 – the government was able to accumulate more budgetary revenues during the period marked by high oil prices.

Fig. H4: Oil Price and Budget Revenues, 1995-2002

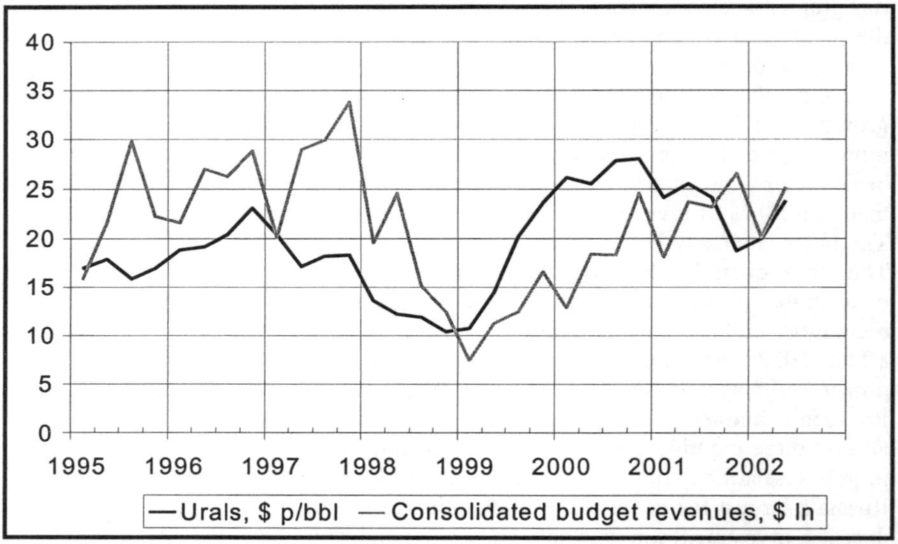

Fiscal performance will be discussed in the next section. Concluding this section we should acknowledge that in the short term, the government can do little to replace the existing growth mechanism. If oil prices stay at their current level, above $20 p/bbl, we can expect a further recovery in investment, a modest acceleration in growth mid-year and a slowdown each autumn, thus replicating the trend seen over the past few years. At the same time, it is quite clear that with respect to growth rates the Russian economy was (and still is) operating well below its potential, a problem compounded by continued capital flight, a topic also discussed below.

Since the initial potential for "cheap" growth from the low base and easy increase in capacity utilisation provided by the 1998 crisis had to some extent been exhausted, growth rates naturally slowed in 2001 and 2002. At the same time, slow progress on reforms failed to compensate for this shrinking growth potential. The government's most recent medium-term fiscal program therefore projects rather moderate growth rates for 2003-2005. In April 2002, the Russian president criticized the government for a lack of ambition, implying that it was assuming a continued dependence on oil prices and therefore essentially no change in the growth mechanism. This fresh call for an acceleration in structural reforms could have well been prompted by strengthening diplomatic relations between Russia and the West.

Reform has already begun in many key areas: tax, the natural monopolies, land, the labour market, pensions, the judiciary and deregulation of the economy. This process is still incomplete and hence the results may fail to impress. However, there have also been clear problems along the way. Certain regulations were found to be inconsistent, requiring a number of amendments to be passed, some of which (involving the Tax Code and Labor Code, for example) have had the effect of creating instability and hampering the business climate. The presence of an unreformed public administration has also impeded the general reform process. The government has been ordered to develop a concept for administrative reform by the end of 2002, but with the 2003 budget already formulated, actual restructuring is unlikely to start before 2004. As a result, progress on reforms through the end of 2002 and in 2003 is likely to be gradual and growth rates moderate.

2. Fiscal Performance

Government launched comprehensive tax reform in 2001 and 2002, a good time since oil prices remained high. The government reduced profit tax, personal income tax, social tax, and abolished some other minor taxes. As a result collection of the personal income tax increased and in fact fiscal performance was good in the past several years, allowing government to run surpluses and accumulate finance reserve against the background of foreign debt payments. At the same time, some problems originated from the reforms of corporate taxation. Low revenues in early 2002 raised concerns over the country's fiscal situation. In fact the drop was the result of a decline in profit tax collection and relatively low VAT collection, the former perhaps the reaction of businesses to the elimination of investment privilege and the latter due to the fact that the government started returning VAT to exporters (see Fig. H5 and H6).

Fig. H5: Federal Fiscal Balances in 2001-02, R Bln.

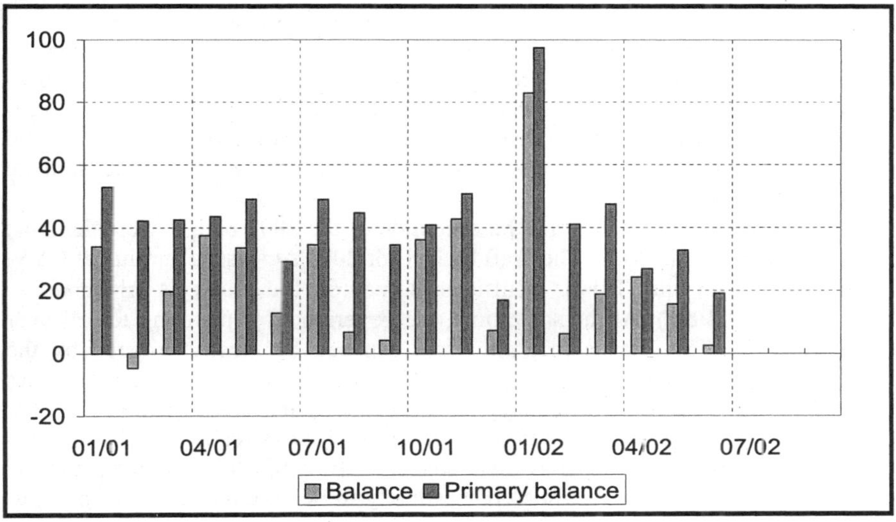

As often happens in Russia, businesses cashed in on the opportunity and applied for returns on "exports" that had actually never left the country. As a result, VAT returns to exporters in some regions were actually many times greater than their export revenues.

Above all, it is the lack of common honesty in Russia, in its narrowest and most ordinary sense, which astounds. This fatal flaw in character deprives the government of the opportunity to wield any reliable executive power, by robbing it of a necessary number of honest, faithful lower-ranking officials.

Historian and philosopher, Ivan Aksakov, penned these words in the mid 19th century. Little appears to have changed in Russia over the past 150 years.

Fig. H6: Cumulative Profit Tax and VAT as Percentage of Total Revenues, 2001-02

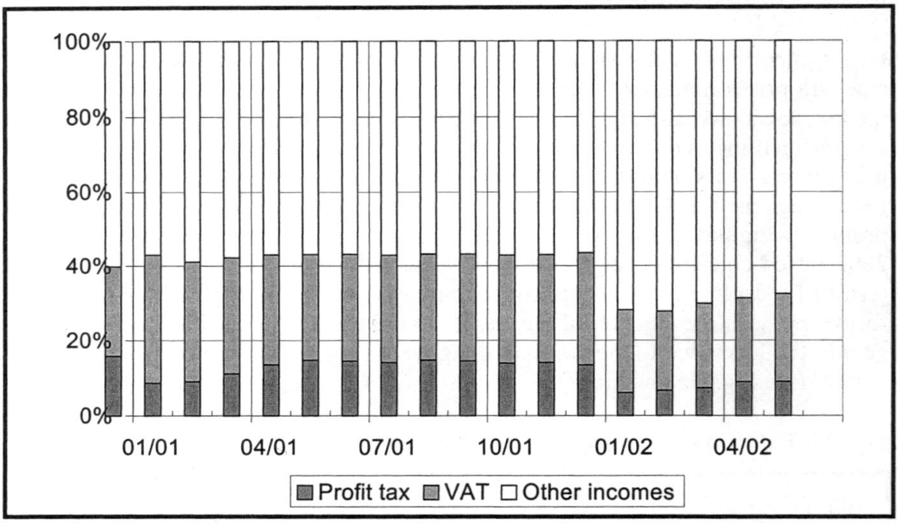

Nevertheless, following usual mid-year improvements in economic performance, fiscal performance recovered early in the second half of 2002 and tax collection increased substantially (also due to increased oil price), thus providing a solid start for the $6 bln financial reserve, which the government expects to accumulate by the end of 2002.

The draft budget for 2003 and the execution of the 2002 budget were the most debated issues in mid 2002. The draft budget for 2003 suggests a surplus of 0.5 % of GDP ($2.2-2.3 bln). This is insufficient to pay off the country's principal foreign debt ($10.8 bln). At the same time, the government is planning to roll over domestic debt. This means that the fiscal gap can be mostly covered by the planned $6 bln reserve. The rest ($3.0-3.1 bln) will come from domestic sources (such as borrowing, privatisation receipts and sale of state inventories).

In general, the government's fiscal plan for 2003 looks realistic, although growing non-interest spending does raise concerns. In 2003, this spending may be 40 % above the 1998 level, while GDP is likely to be up only 30 %. Such populism is understandable given that elections are coming up in late 2003 (Duma) and early 2004 (presidential). Once these are over, the government will hopefully make significant cuts in budget spending.

In addition to the foreign debt payments, there has been a clear upward trend in non-interest spending in 2002 and this has also contributed to the shrinking surplus, which is going to much lower in 2002 than a year ago. Growth in government spending is potentially more dangerous than planned debt payments and a cause for increasing concern. If there is any dramatic change in external conditions, then it will be extremely hard to backtrack and cut down on public spending. The situation is essentially the same for the consolidated budget.

As is well known, Russia's debt service payments are the highest in 2003, mostly due to a R10,8 bln hike in principal payments. These payments will actually require a surplus of about 2,9 % of GDP. If the government cannot achieve this, then it will need to make use of the financial reserve left over from 2002. Total foreign principal debt payments due in 2003 are R345,6 bln, which make the expected fiscal surplus look woefully inadequate. In fact, the financing gap can be covered by the reserve fund and domestic sources of R95,2 bln (of which R51 bln will come from privatization receipts and R20 bln from the sale of state inventories). The government has expressed a reluctance to borrow internationally and the Finance Ministry claims that foreign borrowing will not exceed $1,25 bln next year. While drafting the budget government appeared more likely to look for options closer to home, such as the Pension Fund, which is rapidly accumulating "excessive" resources. This will be non-market borrowing at low interest. Finance Minister Alexei Kudrin acknowledged that the fund has already acquired R10 bln of government non-tradable securities at relatively low interest in the first half of 2002.

The government considered, as usual, optimistic and pessimistic scenarios for 2003. The key difference between them is the assumed price of oil ($21,5 p/bbl and $18,5 p/bbl, respectively). Revenues are forecast on the basis of the optimistic scenario, while forecast spending is based on the more conservative scenario. Nominal GDP rises to R12,98 trln in the first case and the exchange rate is R33.7/$1. In the second case, GDP is R12.65 trln with an average exchange rate of R34/$1. According to government forecasts, GDP will therefore be somewhere between $372 bln and $385 bln.

The availability of Pension Fund monies could tempt the government to hike non-interest spending and this could be a source of macroeconomic instability. The graph below shows that after the 1998 crisis, non-interest spending contracted in real terms, but by 2000 had already grown back above the 1998 level. It accounted for 11.8 % of GDP in 1998 and, as the figure H7 shows, were above this level by 2001. The projected rapid growth in non-interest spending in 2002-03 is the result of a number of populist decisions made without any consideration for restructuring of the public sector. Public sector wages were increased substantially this year. In 2003, the government plans to raise them again, this time by 33 %.

Fig. H7: Non-Interest Expenditures and GDP in Real Terms (1998=100)

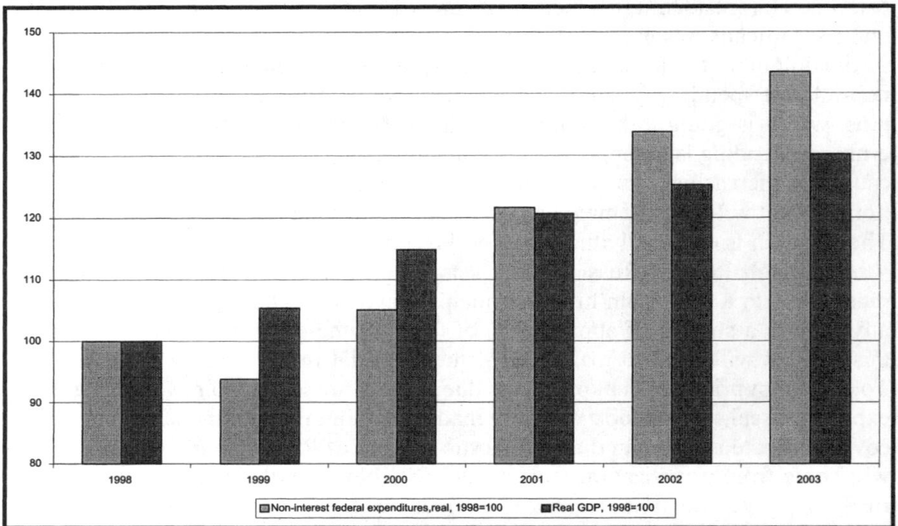

Note: Figures for 2002 and 2003 are from the budget and draft budget for those years (excluding social tax, effective since 2001). In fact, growth in non-interest spending in 2002 should be higher.

As was mentioned earlier, the period of "cheap" post-crisis growth, when output was growing largely due to higher capacity utilization, was coming to an end. To maintain sustainable, high growth rates, the economy requires modernization and investment. Since spare fixed capital capacities have been largely exhausted over the past few years, the economy required more labour to maintain growth in 2002. In fact, overall employment was up 2.8 % y-o-y in 1Q02 and 2.5 % y-o-y in 2Q02, the highest growth rate in several decades. At the same time, growth in efficiency on an aggregate level slowed relative to previous years.

The country's economic efficiency could actually suffer as wage increases in the public sector increase public sector employment at the expense of the private sector. Employment in such budget-financed sectors as "administration", "healthcare, sports facilities and social services", "culture and the arts" and "education" increased by 2.7 %, 2.2 %, 4.0 % and 1.5 % y-o-y respectively, while the number of people employed in production dropped 3 %. As a result, the number of people working in these sectors is now comparable with total numbers employed in production (around 22 % of the country's total employment figure). This industry produces around 30 % of GDP, while the four sectors above, the so-called "non-market services", generate just 10 %.

However, recent surveys indicate that now with spare fixed capital capacities exhausted, skilled labour (or rather the lack thereof) could itself become a limiting factor on growth. In recent years, the Russian population has been shrinking at the rate of 0.5 % a year and this trend is expected to accelerate. The table below shows the effect demographic trends are already having on macroeconomic indicators. From 1998-2002, annual average growth in GDP per capita was 0,5 %

higher than growth in GDP, and the cumulative effect should therefore mean considerably higher GDP per capita by the end of 2002.

In this respect, recent policies aimed at increasing public sector wages without first restructuring the sector, should be considered counterproductive. Such policies stir up forgotten paternalism and contribute to the misallocation of labour.

Tab. H1: GDP and Employment between 1995 and 2002

	1995	1996	1997	1998	1999	2000	2001	2002
GDP per capita	-3.8	-3.1	1.2	-4.4	5.9	9.6	5.6	4.3
GDP	-4.0	-3.4	0.9	-4.9	5.4	9.0	5.0	3.8
Employment	-3.0	-0.8	-2.0	0.1	-3.1	1.5	0.3	2.4

In 2001, the government was able to hike spending on the back of higher-than-expected tax receipts. This was done instead of building up the stabilization fund. Fiscal performance in 2002 is not as good as last year's. Thus it would be a good time to hit the brake on spending. Instead of this, the government has begun to borrow from the Pension Fund.

3. Growth Potential and Capital Flight

Calculations show that if the oil price stays above $20 p/bbl, investment will continue growing, thus stimulating the rest of the economy. As stated above, with respect to growth rates the Russian economy was (and still is) operating well below its potential, a problem compounded by continued capital flight. The figure H8 confirms that growth rates are very much dependent on oil prices and hence on the state of the balance of payments. Growth rates are roughly equal to the difference between the current account and capital flight (both measured as a percentage of GDP). In fact, the rate of growth is determined by that part of the export earnings that remains in the country. This rule for determining growth rates assumes that foreign direct investment (FDI) volumes are immaterial in net terms. This was certainly the case in Russia after the crisis, when net direct investment in the country was close to zero or even negative (i.e. Russia's own direct investments abroad were roughly equal to or exceeded FDI in Russia). Note: the 1997 positive growth rate was achieved, despite a weak current account and capital flight, due to record high capital inflows.

As the current account falls, the Russian economy is not only operating below potential, but that potential itself is shrinking. The decline in the current account is driven by real ruble appreciation and this trend is expected to continue. In order to achieve higher growth rates, there are therefore three theoretical options: (1) reduce capital flight while allowing real ruble appreciation, (2) increase capital inflows, or (3) devalue the ruble to increase the strength of the current account.

Fig. H8: Growth, Current Account and Capital Flight

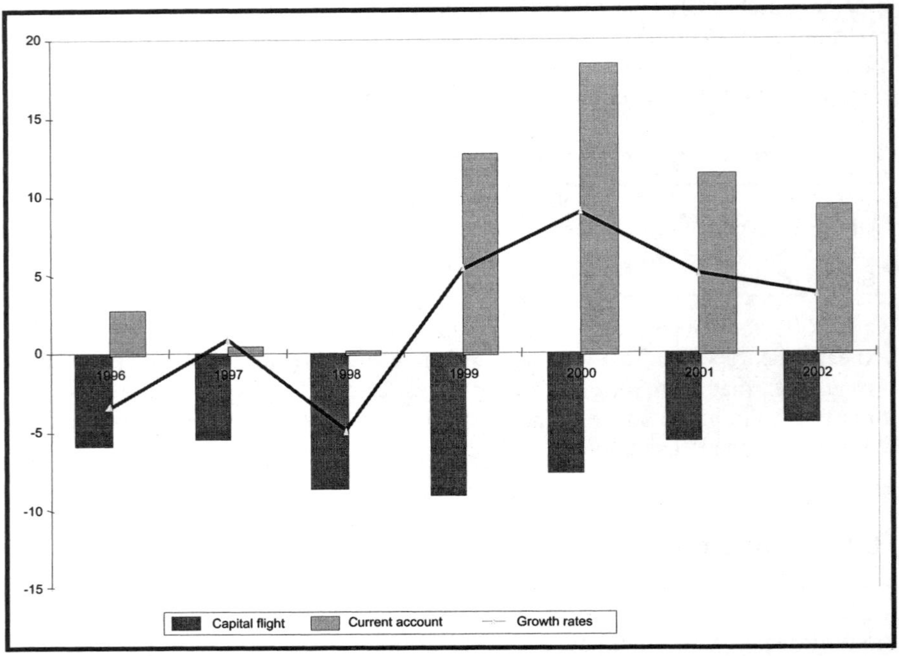

If the price of oil remains at or around its present level, then the ruble is unlikely to devalue. However, even if it does, option (1) is still a precondition for higher growth rates. Since high growth rates were achieved by increasing capacity utilization at existing enterprises in 1999-2000 and because this potential has now largely been exhausted, establishing a better business climate aimed at reducing capital flight and attracting foreign capital, thus rebuilding capital stock across the economy, therefore remains the most reasonable way of achieving higher growth rates. This should also contribute to a transformation in the sector structure of the economy.

4. Growth and the Chaebolization of the Russian Economy

Over the past few years, the Russian economy has delivered high rates of growth parallel to the emergence of increasingly stronger vertically-integrated conglomerates (for more details see GAVRILENKOV, 2002). A similar pattern was observed in the evolution of Asia's economic system. However, the benefits of these conglomerates on the Russian economy may be short-lived. One trait of such a system is a weak financial sector – in particular with respect to banks – and this is a major obstacle to growth. Another trait is high entry barriers for new businesses, which hold back the pace of new business development and reduce the potential for growth.

At the same time, the misallocation of investment in the absence of a strong financial sector contributes to the preservation of a sectoral structure to the economy and this, too, slows down growth rates, as greater resources pour into investment, while returns fall. Russia is again at a fork in the road. As was discussed above, one option is to reduce the entry barriers for business and develop the private financial sector. This could bring about a resumption of high, sustainable growth rates. The other is the road to a further strengthening of the "chaebols" as substitute intermediaries between savings and investments. This would build the foundation for a new crisis.

After a decade of contraction, the Russian economy badly needs high rates of growth in order to catch up with western economies. Russia also needs that growth to be sustainable. However, experience in many countries has shown that periods of high growth are often followed by stagnation or even contraction. This was true for the Asian economies, which grew fast in the 1960s to mid 1990s, but were severely hit by the crises in 1997-98. These were not financial or currency crises; their origins were much more fundamental and can be found in a number of serious macroeconomic imbalances resulting largely from poor institutions. This is a lesson that might serve Russia well.

Traditional growth theory assumes the existence of equilibrium or a balanced growth path, such that an economy tends to revert to its previous trajectory after a shock. Figure H9 is based on historical US figures (with investment-to-output ratios on the horizontal axis and GDP growth rates on the vertical axis). As can be seen, both variables have fluctuated within a relatively narrow range for several decades. This points to the fact that the economy has attained a kind of equilibrium, with 3 % growth against an average investment ratio of around 19 %.

Fig. H9: The US Economy

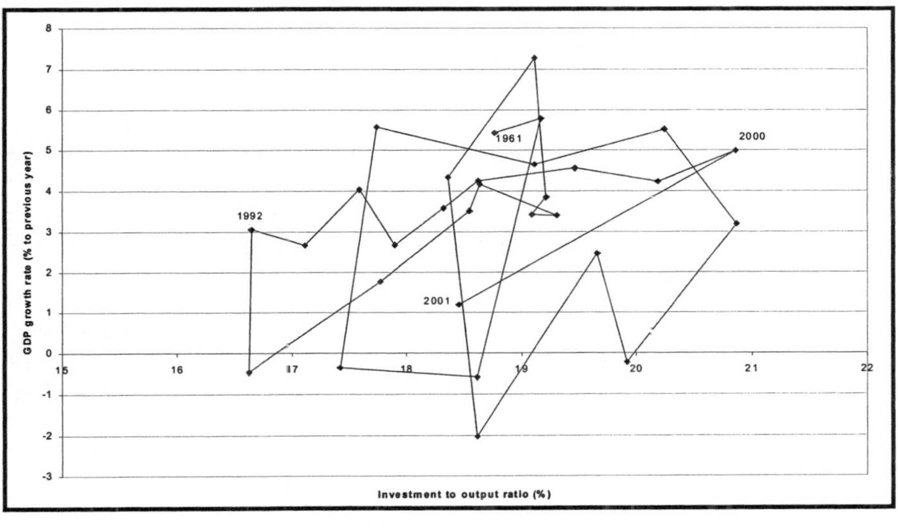

Similar graphs can be traced for other countries. In the case of developed economies, the results are similar to the graph above. Since investment ratios have remained relatively stable for decades, capital stock has been growing at roughly the same rate as output. At the same time, output has been growing faster than labour. This is important, as it means that in developed economies growth is largely driven by productivity rather than factor accumulation. Growing productivity contributes to higher incomes, which in turn stimulates production.

The figure H10 for Russia looks very different. Over the period from 1961 to the end of the 1980s, growth rates gradually slowed while the investment ratio doubled. As a result, capital stock grew eight times over the space of 30 years, while output only tripled. Faster growth in investment than output points to falling efficiency and misallocation of investment resources in the long run. Since the share of investment in GDP was steadily increasing in the absence of capital inflows, this means that consumption in Soviet Russia was growing at a slower pace than GDP, contributing to greater macroeconomic imbalances.

Fig. H10: Russia

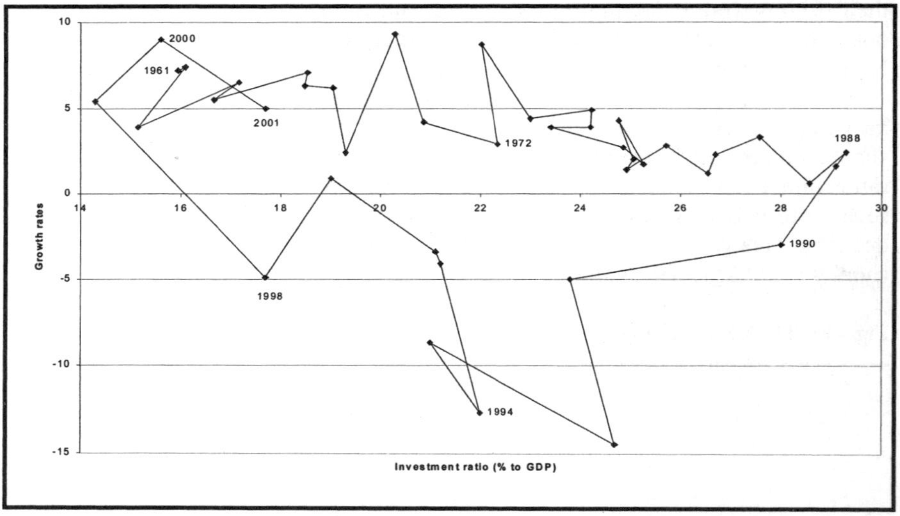

Partial liberalization at the end of 1980s resulted in a contraction in inefficient investment, which – although a step forward – also meant a decline in output. The start of Russia's transition crisis can therefore be attributed to the end of 1980s, a little earlier than the formal start of market transition in 1992.

The graph also shows that the period after the 1998 crisis happened to close a forty-year circle. As a result, the Russian economy was growing as fast in 1999-2001 as at the start of the 1960s, with the same investment ratio below 20 % of GDP. Unlike the US or other developed economies, Russia has never been close to finding equilibrium.

Fig. H11: Thailand

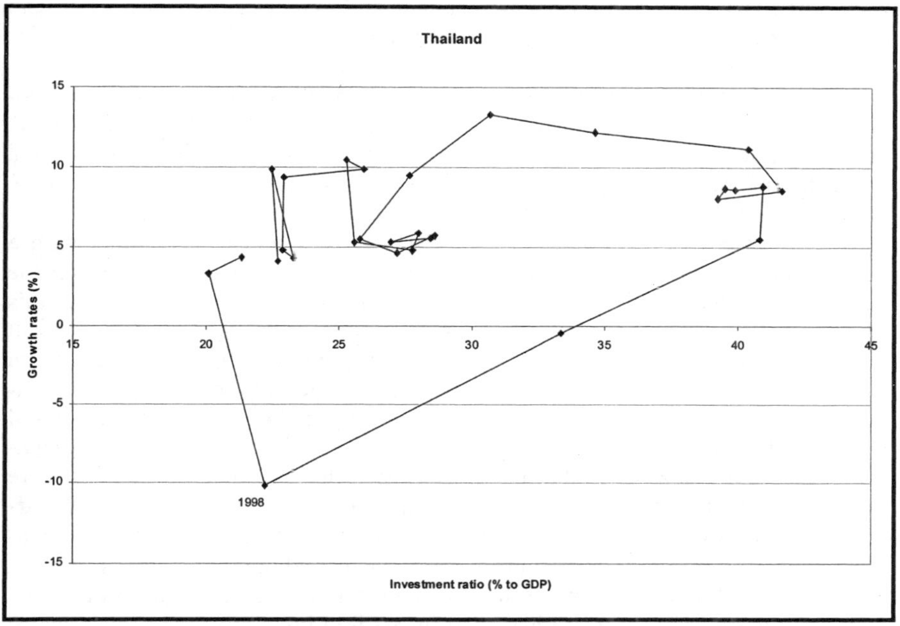

Fig. H12: Indonesia

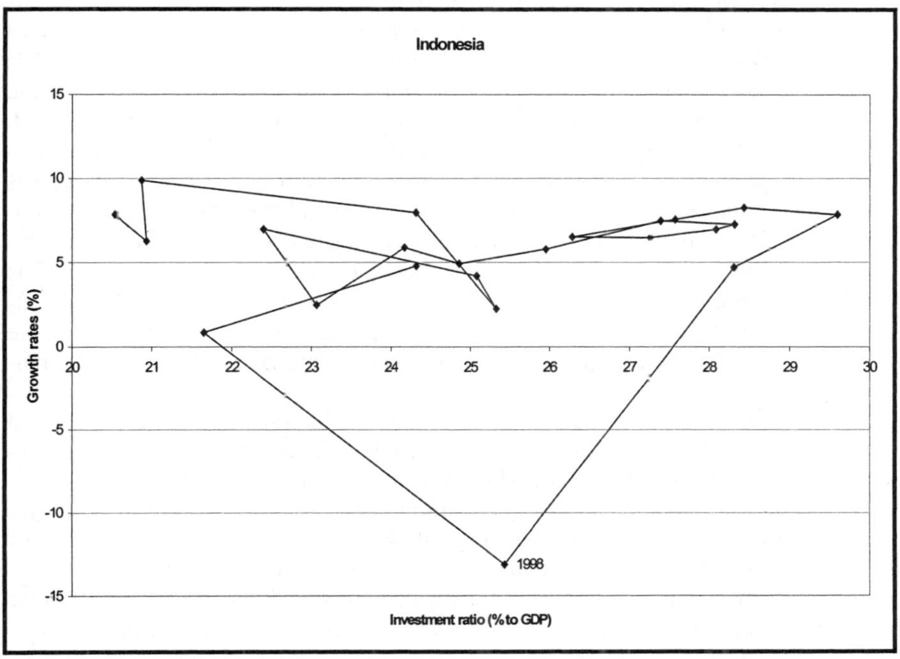

Similar cycles can be seen for other economies, such as those in South East Asia. The figures H11 and H12 show Thailand and Indonesia (similar patterns can be seen for Korea, Malaysia and other 'crisis countries'). Again, these economies have delivered unbalanced growth, with investment ratios increasing despite a lack of acceleration in output. The fact that growth has lagged behind capital accumulation again points to inefficient allocation of investments. Unlike in Russia, fast capital accumulation in the Asian economies occurred against a background of capital inflows, thus supporting growth in consumption. However, in the case of both Russia and Asia, a breaking point was certainly to be expected.

High growth rates in Russia in 1999-2002 were achieved in parallel with a strengthening in the vertically-integrated conglomerates, which emerged on the basis of metal, oil and gas exporters. Equally important is the fact that most of this growth was delivered by existing enterprises. New businesses, including small enterprises, were not growing as rapidly as they might. The economic system developing in Russia is therefore similar in many respects to those of Asian countries. There were indications that Gazprom had acquired a number of agricultural farms and food processing enterprises in Southern Russia. Meanwhile, oil companies were taking control of the manufacturing sector and metal producers were focused on acquisitions in the machine building sector, including car manufacturers and companies producing heavy machinery for road construction. In the autumn of 2001, the world's largest producer of nickel and other non-ferrous metals, Norilsk Nickel, announced plans to invest in agriculture and food processing. These exporters have therefore begun to invest in a broader range of companies across the economy. In the short and medium term, this may contribute to a substantial improvement in the country's macro indicators.

However, one of the major drawbacks of such a system is the development of very close ties between business and the government, be it federal or local. This means a lack of transparency in decision-making, less competition (both domestic and foreign), greater protectionism and more acute corruption. To some extent, this reflects the country's administrative system, in which the political and business elites have joint interests and tend to cooperate closely. A system such as this does not need a developed banking sector and financial markets, since the reallocation of financial resources can generally be arranged within the vertically-integrated conglomerates, or "chaebols". In the case of Russia, each chaebol is closely tied to one or several affiliated banks. Gazprom, which set up Gazprombank, is one such example. The result is a lack of transparency that explains the reluctance by Russia's corporate sector to accept international accounting standards.

A weak financial system is a common feature of the Asian economic model and the administratively driven system. A properly developed financial system should act as an intermediary between savings and investments and assume the risks of misallocation of capital. Therefore, transition crises are only natural in such systems and the crises experienced in Asia cannot be treated merely as banking or currency crises; their origins find themselves in poor institutions.

Aside from potential instability of growth, an underdeveloped financial sector may also contribute to other problems. Since an economic system dominated by a limited number of large conglomerates does not usually offer attractive financial instruments, it may be difficult to accumulate private savings and carry out the pension reform that was planned by the Russian government. International experience also shows that large vertically-integrated conglomerates suffer from relatively poor corporate governance, such as extensive use of cross-subsidization. In short, such a system may deliver rapid success, but it also gives rise to illusions among policy makers.

Russia is therefore now at a fork in the road. If it continues to evolve according to the Asian model, its economy will most likely follow a similar loop-type trajectory. After a period of growth, a new crisis will therefore be inevitable. However, if it can develop a more efficient financial system, there is a chance that high growth rates may be achieved against the backdrop of a relatively low investment ratio, probably not exceeding 22-23 % of GDP. A more efficient allocation of investment should also support sustainable growth.

Finland is a good example of a successful transformation. Since the Soviet Union was one of its major trade partners, the Finnish economy was to some extent affected by the same diseases as the Soviet economy. Finland developed capital-intensive industries focused on exports to the Soviet Union. Figure H13 shows that Finland's investment ratio used to be as high as in other crisis countries. The foreign trade shock which occurred in the early 1990s contributed to devaluation of the Finnish markka. This was accompanied by high unemployment, a contraction in output and a fall in investment activity. An adjustment period then brought about the emergence of a more efficient financial system. As a result, Finland was among the fastest growing European economies in the second half of the decade. New sectors of the economy, such as telecommunications, appeared in place of the previous capital-intensive industries.

Fig. H13: Finland

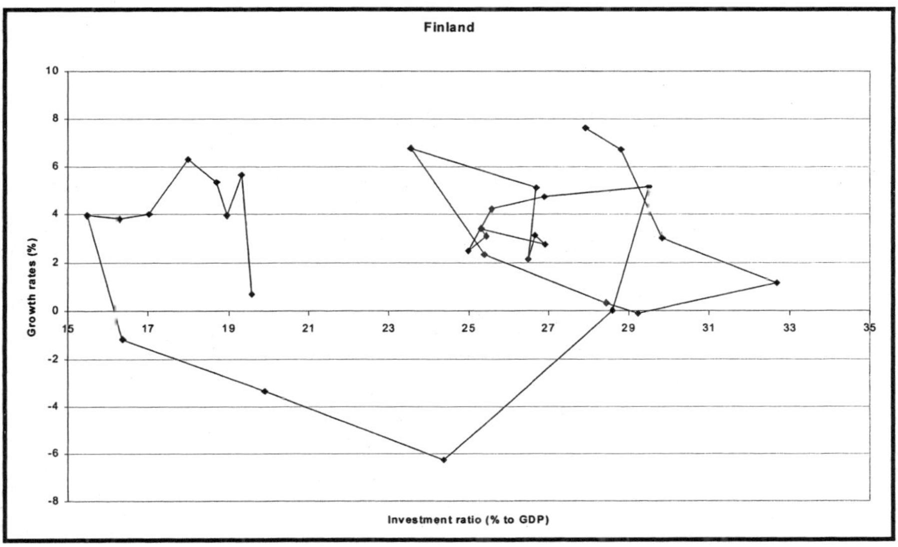

Russia's future therefore does not lie in the further exploitation of its natural resources, but in developing new export-oriented sectors. Reform of the financial sector is a necessary element of such a policy, as is the removal of "red tape". Ease of start-up for new enterprises and the expansion of successful businesses should also stimulate reform of the banking sector and the financial sector in general.

References

GAVRILENKOV, E. (2002): Economic Growth and Crises: Evidence From Russia and Some Other Hysteretic Economies, Carnegie Moscow Center, Working Paper No. 5.

Comments on: Macroeconomic Situation in Russia: Growth, Investment and Capital Flows

Rolf Jungnickel

Gavrilenko's paper gives a profound analysis of the growth record and determinants of the Russian economy and reasons why the growth potential is not fully exploited. Main impediments to structural change and thus to growth are seen in institutional deficiencies leading to inter-firm and inter-sectoral immobility of capital. Of the capital earned in the energy sector and invested in Russia, too little flows to other parts of the economy where it could yield higher returns. And it is not even efficiently invested in the energy sector which urgently needs upgrading of technical equipment. Furthermore, the capital available is not fully invested in Russia but taken overseas (Cyprus, Switzerland and the Netherlands are important examples). Capital flight is prevalent.[1] Obviously, the link between capital available and domestic investment and hence growth is impeded.

Gavrilenko establishes a rather stable relation of current account balance, capital flight and growth. Growth rates are roughly equal to the difference of current account surplus and net capital flight, both related to GDP. One gets the impression that Gavrilenko (on p.10) considers this a permanent and causal relationship. "In fact, the rate of growth is determined by that part of export earnings remaining in the country". This is where I would like to comment.

While it is obvious that net capital flight leads to growth losses, doubt comes up regarding the stable link of current account surplus and growth. There are at least two arguments to be brought forward here:

1. Growth performance cannot only be considered a result of net inflow or outflow of capital; of paramount importance is the formation and allocation of domestic capital never crossing Russian borders;

2. The growth effect differs according to the kind of capital transferred to Russia or from Russia to foreign countries.

The first argument is obvious. Higher growth rates could be achieved with less or even without any capital imports if Russia managed to improve conditions for the formation of capital and for its efficient allocation. Gavrilenko points to a number of institutional arrangements needing to be changed in this respect: less bureaucracy, predictability of legal and administrative decisions, de-"chaebolization", development of the financial sector, etc. These changes would

[1] Capital flight would not necessarily be a problem if this capital were repatriated to Russia and then invested there, taking advantage of a foreign status which could be preferentially treated, e.g. in terms of property rights and profit resp. interest remittance. These "re-investments" largely make up the dominating "other" component in total foreign direct investment in Russia. However, outward investment by Russian firms - including capital flight - clearly exceeds the inward flows. A significant share of flight capital thus seems to be invested abroad (NfA of 16.8.2002).

directly lead to a change in the hitherto parallel development of net international capital flows and growth rate. The fact that this relationship apparently was rather stable over the past years is not a causal necessity, but rather an indicator of persisting domestic impediments to growth.

The second argument, referring to the kind of capital flows from abroad, will be dealt with more extensively, since it is more related to the topic of this conference "Integration of Russia in the World Economy" - capital links obviously being a central element of integration. In view of the above-mentioned fact that there are net capital flows to Russia having been allocated inefficiently, the question arises whether other foreign sources of capital could be mobilised and more efficiently employed in the economy.

Inward-FDI Needed

In this respect, inward foreign direct investment (FDI) should receive more attention (FISCHER 2000). FDI has clear advantages over other capital flows. International experience shows that FDI flows are much more stable over time than e.g. portfolio investments (LIPSEY 2001). Once an FDI project is realised, there are sunk costs which make foreign investors less flexible regarding relocations. They can, therefore, bring in an element of stability into the economy and the foreign trade and payments situation.

Unlike Prof. Gavrilenko, I would not assess FDI in terms of financial capital only. Inflows of financial capital often are not even necessarily going along with the investment of foreign firms.[2] The main contribution of FDI to the host country is the transfer of technical, marketing, organisational or other know-how and the integration into international production and marketing networks. A number of studies have shown that foreign-owned firms mostly operate at a higher productivity, pay higher wages and lead to intensified integration into the international division of labour (OECD (1999); JUNGNICKEL (ed. 2002); PFAFFERMAYR/ BELLAK (2002); BORRMANN/JUNGNICKEL, KELLER (2003). This is important for both greenfield ventures as well as for acquisitions. Foreign investors develop and take their investment chances. They do not depend on a functioning financial system as much as Russian investors do, since they can put in their own resources. In fact, they could help to develop an efficient financial system. More FDI could, therefore, lead to increased average productivity of capital operating in the Russian economy and thus promote structural change and growth. In that case, Gavrilenko's hitherto stable relationship of growth rate and net capital transfer would increase.

Resulting questions are: What is the performance of Russia as a host of FDI and is there a potential of additional FDI? These questions can first be approached by comparing Russian inward-FDI with inward-FDI in other countries.

---

[2] For example, an investment project can be financed by local or international debt taken up by the subsidiary or an investment can be made by supplying know-how or by investment in kind.

Inward-FDI: High Potential, Poor Performance

Russia recorded a rather stable inflow of FDI with over 2 bn. USD annually since the mid-1990s (IMF 2002). The stock of inward-FDI quadrupled from 1995 to 2001. This compares with a growth of worldwide inward-FDI by the factor 2.4 (UNCTAD 2002). However, high FDI growth rates in Russia have to be seen against the background of a low base level, and the volume of inward-FDI depends, to a large extent, on the size of a country. Bigger countries will receive, ceteris paribus, more FDI than smaller ones. FDI values therefore have to be related to GDP if the FDI performance is to be compared internationally. According to this yardstick, Russia is way behind the international average and, in particular, behind the Central European Transition countries (Tab. h1) which have reached the average level of developed economies and are only slightly behind the EU(15).[3] This holds for FDI flows as well as for inward stocks (which are a more telling indicator than flows). Russia ranks only no. 104 out of 140 countries in a comparison of UNCTAD's FDI performance index.[4] Russia's FDI performance is clearly insufficient and far behind what is desirable.

Tab. h1: Inward-FDI in International Comparison (USD bn. and %)

Indicator		Host region				
		Russia	Poland	Hungary	China	EU(15)
FDI stock	2001, USD bn.	22	42	24	395	2649
	2001/1995, %	399	541	198	288	237
	% GDP, 2001	8	21	43	32	30
FDI flows	'99-'01, USD, bn.	9	25	6	128	1620
	'98-'00, % GFCF[a]	8	19	17	12	31
UNCTC FDI Performance Index, rank in 140 countries		104	38	49	47	44[b]

[a] Gross fixed Capital Formation; [b] average of Eucountries.

Source: UNCTAD (2002); own calculations.

To give an idea of the FDI potential in the various countries, UNCTAD (2002) has constructed an FDI potential index. This index is made up of the average of eight elements considered important determinants of FDI: Real GDP growth; GDP per capita; export quota; telephone mainlines per 1000 inhabitants; commercial energy use p. capita; R&D expenditure in % of GDP; students in tertiary education in % of population; general country risk.[5] The resulting FDI potential index is thus at large a composite of indicators of the level of economic development. Russia ranks no. 64 which is a much better position than in the performance index, although still clearly behind Western countries and the most progressed CEE coun-

3 High FDI performance of the EU is strongly influenced by the small average size of EU countries.

4 The FDI performance index relates the share of a country in worldwide FDI flows of the last three years to its share in worldwide GDP, see UNCTAD (2002), p.34.

5 The values of the various elements are normalised to a range between 0 and 1. For the scores of individual countries in the various fields making up the index, see UNCTAD (2002), Table A.II.2.

tries, such as Estonia, Hungary, Slovenia, Slovakia and the Czech Republic. The conclusion can be drawn from this that there is indeed room for more FDI. Russia did not fully take advantage of the potential of foreign investors. Gavrilenko's growth/net capital inflow relation could be increased by attracting more FDI.

Of course, general indicators such as the FDI potential index, are debatable. The selection of individual components as well as their weight can be criticised.[6] For example, it can be argued that the size of a country should be taken into account - large countries will normally attract more FDI, in absolute figures, than smaller ones. Furthermore, quantifying general "country risk" contains a lot of uncertainty and it may be argued that this factor is clearly underestimated with a weight of only one-eighth while the level of development receives much more weight since it is represented by three to five equally-weighted elements (income level, telephone lines, energy use as well as R&D expenditure and the students variable).

Fig. h1: UNCTAD's Inward-FDI Performance Index and Inward-FDI Potential Index for Selected CEE Countries 1992-94 and 1998-2000

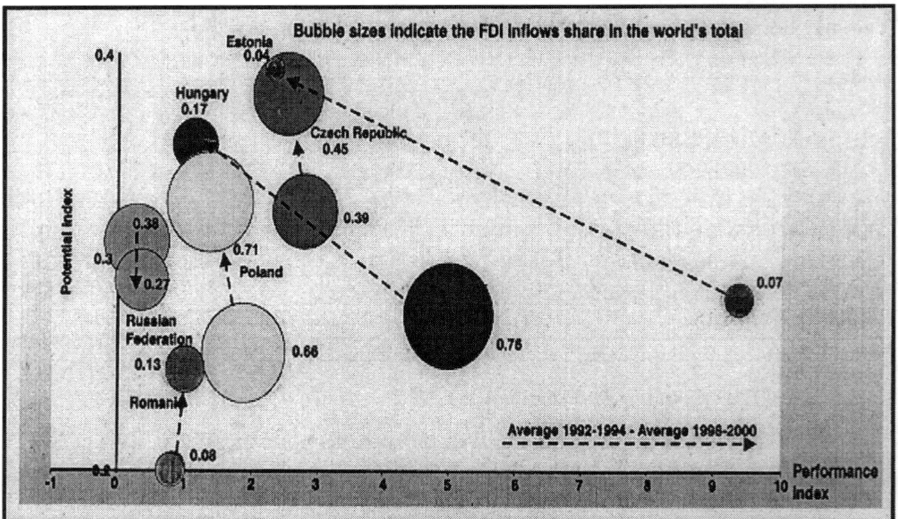

Note: In case that a CEE country did not exist before 1992, the period of the FDI Performance Index refers to 1992-1994.

Source: UNCTAD (2002), based on table II.1 and annex table B.1.

Nevertheless, structure and development of the index can give hints relevant to economic policy.

- First, it is interesting to note that Russia, contrary to other CEE countries (Hungary, Estonia, Slovenia) lost significant ground as a potential host to FDI during the 1990s. At the beginning of the decade, it ranked 37 and was among the

[6] The eight components enter with equal weight.

most attractive transition countries, although the FDI performance was poor at that time as well.

- The most obvious disadvantages of Russia as an investment location are in poor infrastructure and little openness to foreign trade.
- Special advantages of Russian locations can be seen in the high quality of human capital.[7] The share of students in tertiary education is rather high compared with most other transition economies and even compared with a number of highly developed countries. This can be considered an important factor in multinationals' investment decisions, in particular since it goes along with low income level.

Policy conclusions

The central question is: What can and what should be done in order to increase inward-FDI? Generally, experience from other countries, such as China and Mexico, shows that there is no worldwide capital shortage which could inhibit more FDI to a more attractive Russia. There rather is a lack of profitable investment opportunities in countries with low FDI.

International experience, in particular from CEE countries, further shows that FDI closely follows domestic economic development (fig. h2). It is strongly procyclical. A booming host economy is the most important attracting factor for inward-FDI - of course, given a minimum political and administrative stability. Recent disputes over allegedly illegally-privatised companies may more than compensate for positive location factors. The lawsuit about the Alstom-SEMS ownership is a case in point (HANDELSBLATT of 4.7.2001) that could deter further FDI. Foreign investors are "...confronted by the maze of contradictions and ambiguity still typical of Russian legislation and regulation" (HERTZFELD 2000). Efficient management is impeded by institutional deficiencies. "Life at the top (of a company, R.J.) is about hierarchy, connections, influence peddling and crisis management, not about organisation, forethought and planning" (THE ECONOMIST, 19.7.2001, p. S4). The EBRD (2001, p.23) has established a positive and significant correlation between progress in transition and inward-FDI. If potential high-tech investors feel their resources would not be fully protected against administrative or legal arbitrariness and if there would be uncertainty concerning the returns on investment, they may be reluctant to invest in Russia and to bring in all their competitive advantages. This would mean: Russia forgoes highly efficient investment.

---

[7] The component "country risk" was also rated relatively high for Russia. In view of numerous critical comments of investors with regard to legal certainty and administrative transparency and efficiency, this ranking seems a bit doubtful. For example, in a study on behalf of the Ost- und Mitteleuropa Verein, Russia is attributed much worse country risk (ifo 1999, p. 27).

Fig. h2: Inward FDI and Economic Growth in Central and Eastern European Countries, 1990-2001 (Billions of dollars and percentage)

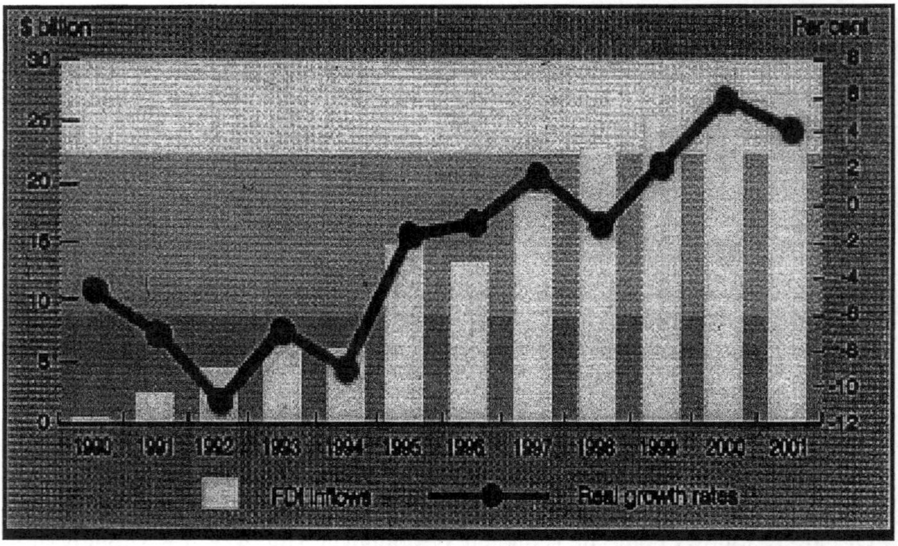

Source: UNCTAD (2002), based on FDI/TNC database.

A more open and reliable investment climate and a level playing field would thus open up chances to improve the sectoral structure of FDI. Traditionally, there is a bias of inward-FDI towards trade and natural resources industry (NZZ of 21.3.2002, HUNYA/STANKOVSKY 2002, see fig. h3). In particular, western retail chains are expanding rapidly (IHT of 11.8.2001 and HB of 27.12.2001). Modern investment in the financial sector and in high-tech manufacturing are rare. The combination of a highly qualified workforce available in Russia and modern technology brought in by western investors would probably yield the highest gains for the economy.

Fig. h3: Sectoral Distribution of Inward FDI and Total Investment in Russia (%)

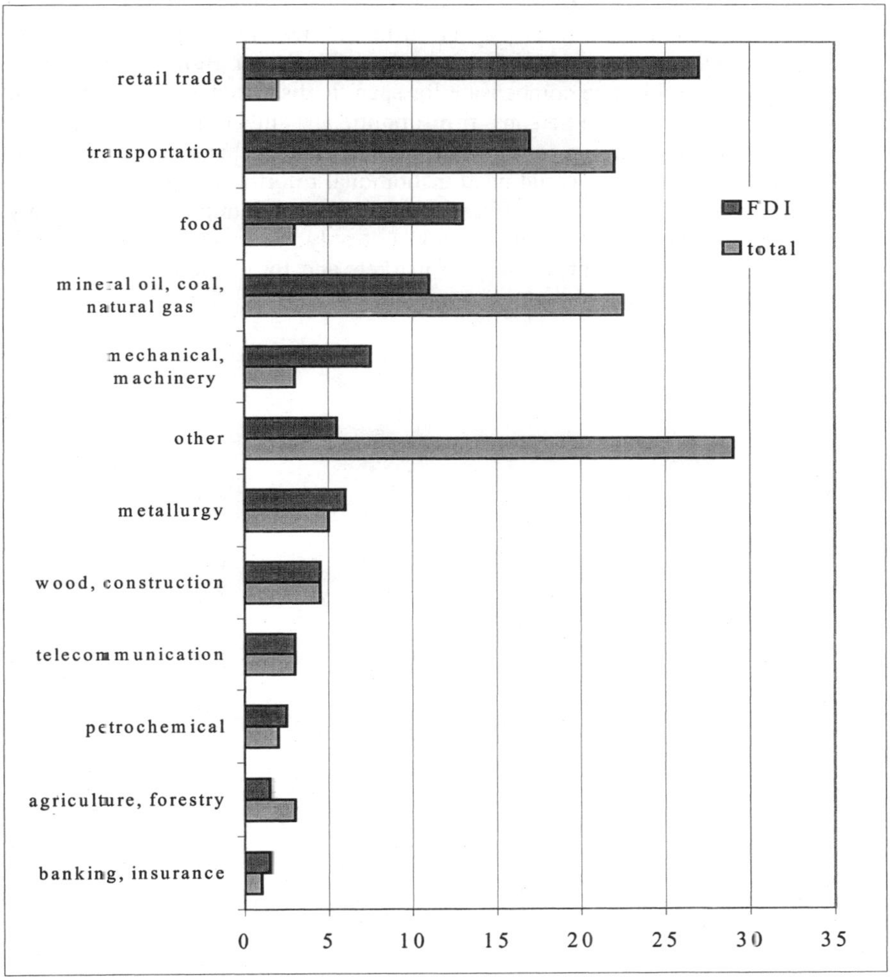

Source: GOSKOMSTAT, *as quoted in:* NZZ *of 21.3.2002.*

Since more inward-FDI is badly needed in Russia, the question comes up whether economic policy should use specific promotion measures to this end. Financial or other promotion would then mean a competitive advantage of foreign vs. domestic firms which can only be justified under certain conditions:

1. existence of positive external effects on domestic Russian firms;
2. compensation of specific disadvantages foreign investors are facing at Russian locations;
3. countervailing action against promotional measures of foreign countries.

The first condition can be taken as given, although the quantification of promotion costs and, above all, external effects will involve a great deal of uncertainty. Long run and short term effects may be different and they may depend on the functioning of labour, product and factor markets. The better argument for promotional activities would be to compensate for specific disadvantages resulting from networks of Russian private persons, firms, politicians and administration excluding or discriminating foreign investors. Compensation in this respect would not cost tax payers' money but would need institutional reforms as outlined in Gavrilenko's paper and many other publications. Legal and administrative certainty, transparency and non-discrimination would not only attract more FDI. It would also be essential for the contestability of markets and for economic development in general and thus be a desideratum independent of FDI.

References

BORRMANN, C., JUNGNICKEL, R., KELLER, D. (2003): Auslandskontrollierte Unternehmen - ein Gewinn für den deutschen Arbeitsmarkt? Baden-Baden, Nomos.

EBRD (2001):Transition Report 2001, London 2000.

THE ECONOMIST (2001): Good in Part, 21.07.2001.

FISCHER, P. (2000): Foreign Direct Investment in Russia. A Strategy for Industrial Recovery, Houndsmill, Palgrave MacMillan.

HB (HANDELSBLATT) (2001): Europas Handelskonzerne rollen Russland auf, 27.12. 2001.

HB (HANDELSBLATT) (2001): Verstaatlichung vertreibt Investoren., 04.07.2001.

HERTZFELD, J. M. (2000): Foreign Direct Investment in Russia: Battling Against the Odds, in: ICC and International Systems and Communications Ltd of London: The New Europe in the World Economy, London, (http://www.iccwbo.org/home/ conferences/reports/budapest/book_articles/hertzfeld.asp).

HUNYA, G., STANKOVSKY, J. (2002): WIIW-WIFO Database. Foreign Direct Investment in CEECs and the Former Soviet Union with Special Attention to Austrian FDI Activities, Vienna , July.

IHT (INTERNATIONAL HERALD TRIBUNE) (2001): Retail Push Gathers Pace In Moscow., 11.08.2001.

JUNGNICKEL, R. (ed.) (2002): Foreign-owned Firms - Are They Different?, Houndmills, Basingstoke, Palgrave Macmillan.

IFO (1999): Benchmarking der Markterschließungsstrategien wichtiger Wettbewerber Deutschlands auf den Märkten Ost- und Mitteleuropas, Ost- und Mitteleuropa Verein, Hamburg 1999.

IMF (2002): International Financial Statistics Yearbook 2002, Washington.

IMF (2001): Balance of Payments statistics Yearbook 2001, Washington.

LIPSEY, R. E. (2001): Foreign Direct Investors in Three Financial Crises, in: NBER Working Paper 8084, January.

NFA (NACHRICHTEN FÜR AUßENHANDEL) (2002): Fluchtkapital fließt in die Wirtschaft zurück., 16.08.2002.

NZZ (NEUE ZÜRCHER ZEITUNG) (2002): Russlands Wirtschaft finanziert sich selbst., 21.03.2002.

OECD (1999): Measuring Globalization. The Role of Multinationals in OECD Economies, Paris.

PFAFFERMAYR, M., BELLAK, C. (2002): Why Foreign-owned Firms are Different: A Conceptual Framework and Empirical Evidence for Austria, in: Jungnickel (ed. 2002), pp. 13-57.

UNCTAD (2002): World Investment Report 2002. Transnational Corporations and Export Competitiveness, New York, Geneva.

I. Problems of Russia with Financial Globalization

Grigori Feiguine and Tatjana Sedash

1. Introduction

Globalization is now one of the most important tendencies in the world economy. That is the "process of worldwide integration by international trade of goods and services, and by cross border transfers of capital an know-how. The main feature of economic globalization is the increase of these international transactions in relation to national transactions" (STIERLE, 1999, p. 3). The world economy has become more international and unified. The relations between national economies are becoming stronger and closer.

There are both quantitative indicators and qualitative dimensions of globalization. The qualitative dimensions of globalization include the following phenomena: internationalization of technical progress, development of industry and communication technologies, the opening of national markets in developing countries in the 80s and the disintegration of the word socialist system.

Figure 1 shows the quantitative indicators of globalization. There are exports, FDI (foreign direct investment) and international financial transactions (loans and derivatives).

Fig. I1: Indicators of Globalization, Index 1980 respectively 1988 = 100

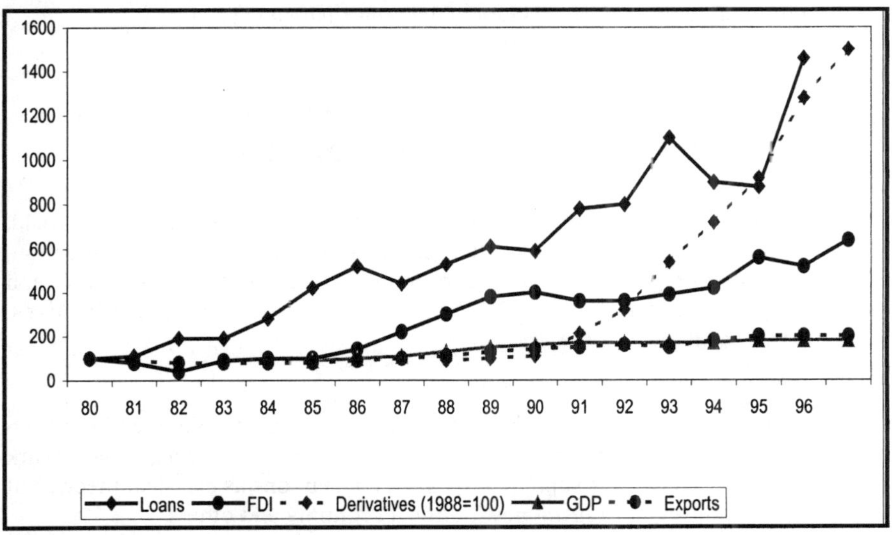

Source: STIERLE (1999).

The most important tendencies are as follows:

- exports increase more rapidly than GDP
- international direct investments increase more rapidly than exports
- international financial transactions increase more rapidly than international direct investments

Financial globalization is also a rapid trend. Financial liberalization and deregulation, the abolition of exchange controls, financial innovation, institutionalization and the growth of euro-markets are major elements of this process. But the benefits and negative effects of free capital mobility are objects of intense debate in contemporary economic literature.

Positive effects consist of the opportunity to direct capital to the most productive and profitable branches. The imports of capital allow for compensation in variations among incomes in various countries. Capital transfer is a good instrument for investment risk management. Incomes from capital investment are relatively independent from the situation in the national markets. The international capital inflows are the way for technology transfer in developing countries. In the end, the globalization of financial markets contributes to the creation of modern financial systems and has a positive effect on economic growth.

Yet the above-mentioned positive effects of financial globalization show itself only in certain conditions such as substitution and the addition of national savings by means of foreign capital inflows and the existence of human capital. The last factor is very important for the inculcation of new technologies. Some experts take note of financial crises in Asia (1997) and Russia (1998) and doubt the stability of world financial system under conditions of the globalization (BUCH/HEINRICH/PIERDZIOCH, 2001). The very idea that the financial systems of some countries are exposed to crises has become quite popular. Many scholars debate opportunities for eliminating these crises factors in national financial systems.

2. Globalization Scenarios – the Advantages and Deficits of Globalization in the Different Countries

The process of globalization is underway in nearly all countries of the world. However, different countries reach different levels in this process of globalization. Economic literature divides some countries into "won from globalization" and "lost from globalization" (NUNNENKAMP, 1998). Based on these perspectives, there are two scenarios of development:

scenario "win – win"

According to this scenario, globalization results in a profit obtained by all national economies. Thus, globalization brings forth welfare effects, which work universally. This scenario is supported by such conceptions as classical theories of international trade, evolutionism, new political economy and others.

scenario "win – lose"

This scenario is based on the estimation that globalization brings profit only to wealthy, well-developed countries. i.e. it amplifies the difference between developing and well-developed countries. Foreign economic policy oriented toward globalization is unsuitable for developing countries.

The first scenario is more likely if low levels of living standards in many developing countries is caused by such factors as civil regional wars, illiteracy, the lack of readiness to trade with other countries and the like, which have nothing to do with globalization. Countries in Latin America, Russia and former socialist nations, for example, were poorly integrated into the process of the international division of labor. Later on such economic policy was considered inexpedient (SIEBERT, 1997).

Despite the fact that the scenario "win – win" seems to be more advisable, the differences in the economic growth rate of the global-oriented countries are evident. In our opinion, this difference is determined by global benefits and deficits of the economy in different countries. Global deficits are regarded as a complexity of factors which do not allow the economy of one country to get immediate benefits from globalization. In connection with Russia, we would like to mention the following. As soon as market reforms started, Russia began pursuing a global-oriented foreign economic policy. With this underway, Russia has been suffering a downswing. The economic growth that can be observed since 1999 is mostly due to such factors as a favorable state of the world market and some growth of competitiveness of national enterprises as the result of ruble enrichment. Yet both these factors are nearly exhausted. On the one hand the ruble grew considerably in comparison to 1998, while on the other hand the landslide of oil prices is likely. As illustrated below, present economic growth cannot be considered stable. Unlike Russia, some countries of Eastern Europe have experienced stable and high enough rates of economic growth. (Table 1.)

Tab. I1: Economic Growth in Selected Eastern Europe Countries and Russia (%)

Countries	1992	1993	1994	1995	1996	1997	1998	1999	2000
Hungary	-1,3	-0,6	2,9	1,5	1,3	4,6	4,9	4,2	5,2
Poland	2,6	3,8	5,2	7,0	6.0	6,8	4,8	4,1	4,0
Slovenia	-	2,8	5,3	4,1	3,5	4,6	3,8	5,2	4,6
Slovak Republic	-	-	4,9	6,7	6,2	6.2	4.0	1,9	2,2
Czech Republic	-	-	2,6	5,9	4,3	-0,8	-1,2	-0,4	2,9
Russia	-14,5	-8,7	-12,7	-4,2	-3,4	0,9	-4,9	3.2	8,3

Source: WIIW (2001).

We think the Russian economy has experienced global effects which do not allow her to prosper with stable economic growth under existing conditions, despite a global-oriented policy. Russian global deficits become apparent in all the spheres characterizing quantitative variables of globalization (Figure 1). Table 2 shows the mechanisms of global deficit manifestation in Russia.

Tab. I2: Global Deficits of Russia (Kinds of Manifestation)

Indicators of globalization	Global deficits
Foreign commerce	Low competitiveness of Russian products results in export of raw material and import of consumer goods and equipment. Thus the structure of foreign trade is one-way. Under such conditions, domestic producers can sell their products only in the domestic market. With all that, they must consider international competition. The experts speak of a dual structure and the "Dutch Disease" of the Russian economy.
International direct investments	As a place for international direct investments, Russia has material shortcomings: insufficient legal insurance, shortcomings of tax system, unstable political situation, corruption at all levels. Foreign businessmen are not confident in the success of their long-term direct investments in Russia. Thus, positive effects from the implantation of foreign direct investments (technology transfer, management experience, staff motivation, "spill-over" effect) are not evident in Russia.
International financial markets	Russian financial sector has evident weaknesses: there is no actual mechanism of financial intermediary, insufficient level of crediting, insufficient resources of business banks, undeveloped competitiveness in the bank sector, weakly-developed market of shares. Under such conditions, the Russian financial market is unattractive for foreign investors. Besides, there is a constant threat of unpredictable cash withdrawals by foreign investors and a loss of customers by Russian banks (because major Russian corporations switch to the service of foreign banks). As such, the Russian financial system is exposed to crises under conditions of financial globalization.

The next sections will be devoted to an analysis of the problems in the Russian economy resulting from financial globalization.

3. Weaknesses of the Russian Financial Sector and their Influence on Financial Globalization

It is our belief that the future trends of any country in the process of globalization are defined by the operating efficiency of its domestic financial sector. As such, the problems of the Russian economy under financial globalization are caused by weaknesses in elements of its domestic financial sector. As is known, the financial sector of a country includes such elements as its bank system, equity market, money-market and market of derived financial instruments. The formation of the

Russian financial market started in the beginning of the 1990s, coming into being from the first three mentioned elements.

The current Russian bank system traces its roots back to the reform of USSR banking system started in the late 1980s. After taking first attempts to reform the Soviet Union bank system, the two-level bank system was introduced. This two-level system was formed after the acts "About State Bank" (11 December 1990) and "About Banks and Bank operations" (02 December 1990) were passed. The first act defines functions, strategies and objectives of the Central Bank of Russia. The second act defines the procedure of establishment and course of activities for business banks. Later, the former was passed as "About State Bank" (10 July 2002). The formation of business banks started in the beginning of the 1990s, whereby its proliferation was rapid through the end of 1994, declining however after 1995 (Figure 2).

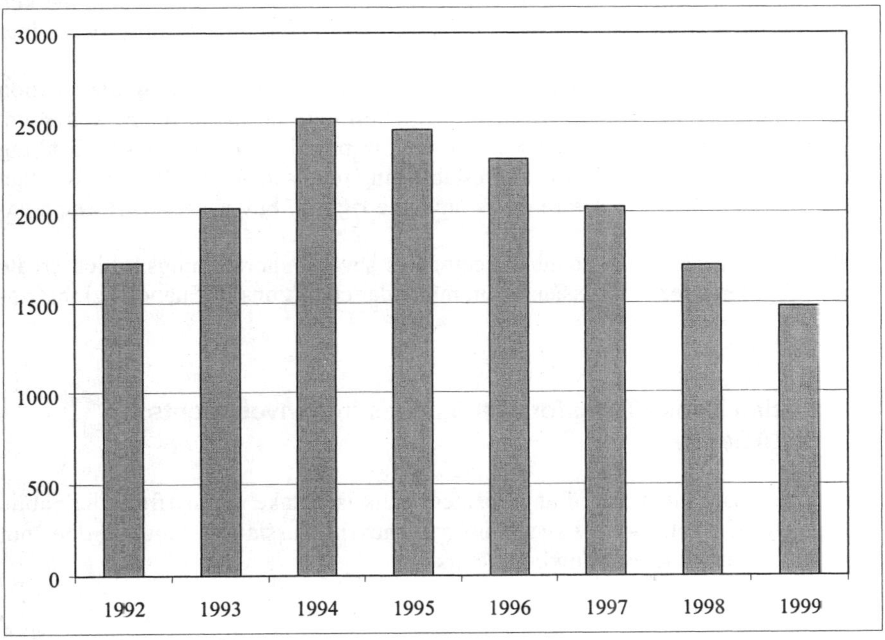

Fig. I2: Number of Commercial Banks in Russia from 1992 to 1999

Source: WIEGERT (1999).

The equity market began its development in Russia in the late 1980s. The process of development can be divided into several stages (DONDOKOVA, 1999). Safety stock first appeared in 1989, and the first Russian joint-stock companies came about in 1990-1991. The second stage of the development of Russian equity market started with voucher privatization, i.e. as state enterprises were transformed into public corporations. Each Russian was given the possibility to change his or her voucher for shares in an enterprise. Another important stage of development in the Russian equity market was the period when promissory notes were actively used (1993), as well as the issuing of state Treasury obligations (STO) and federal bonds (FB). These promissory notes were prevalent due to the phenomenon of non-payment. They were used as payments among enterprises. The development of the STO and FB markets is connected to the budget deficit; those kinds of securities were used for covering these deficits. The crisis of August 17, 1998 led to an extensive decline in the Russian security market, primarily due to the impossibility of the state to pay its liability. Since 1999, however, a kind of revival of the Russian security market connected to the capitalization of the Russian market of shares can be seen.

The Russian money market has developed since 1990. The act "About Foreign currency regulation and control," passed on 09 October 1992, played an important role in that process. It should be mentioned that the Russian money market is domestic, i.e. the Russian ruble is not convertible in the world exchange market. Thus, the Russian money market is not essential for the integration process into world financial markets. [1]

The formation of the Russian financial sector was accompanied by the creation of determinate conditions for Russian integration into the world financial system. The participation of foreign stock is possible in principal in the Russian banking system and there are possibilities for establishing representative offices by Russian banks abroad. Since 1997, foreigners have the right to buy shares of Russian enterprises and vice versa.

However, the Russian financial sector has several shortcomings which create serious problems for the Russian economy under conditions of financial globalization.

3.1 Russian Banks Transformed Savings into Investments Insufficiently

One of the basic functions of any business bank is to take money from the public and transform it into private-sector investments. In Russia this function does not work sufficiently due to following factors:

Low public savings

The low savings potential of the Russian people is defined by low income and distrust in banks (Table 3). In the beginning of the 1990s the depreciation took place, affecting most of Russians. Now only about 27% of Russians have savings (AKINDINOVA, 2000). Moreover, Russians do not want to take the risk of investing their savings into business banks.

---

[1] Passages A-F show the weaknesses in the Russian financial sector, which are related to the bank system and security market, as we are sure those two sectors define the problems of Russia during the integration process of financial globalization.

The following factors of distrust in the banking sector rose significantly after 1990: risk of unexpected loss of funds, distrust in private banks as well as the distrust in bank management and bank bureaucracy. As the result, only 50% of Russian savings have been invested in business banks, while this figure is often close to 100% in developed countries (VODYANOV/ SMIRNOV ,2001).

Tab. I3: Distrust to the Banking Sector (% of Population of Russia Consider to be Important)

Factors of distrust to bank sector	Before 1998	1998	1999	2000	2001
Distrust in state economic policy	73	98	94	84	85
Distrust in private banks	24	91	90	72	51
Distrust to state banks	83	12	32	43	44
Distrust in the state credit policy	60	99	95	83	73
Distrust in bank management and bank bureaucracy	20	70	64	52	53
Risk of lost funds unexpectedly	15	85	87	83	82
Risk of incorrect data handling	34	32	33	49	48
Criminality in bank sector	77	85	73	70	71

Source: SEREBYAKOV (2001).

Local financing in terms of financial and industrial groups

The financial and industrial groups (FIG) took on special significance in the first years of the 1990s. FIG is a unit of enterprises and credit institutions. Between 1992 and 1994, many banks were established within such groups. They were called "minor" banks, serving only enterprises within the FIG. They could not give loans to other enterprises in the private sector.

Thus, the mechanism of transforming public savings into investments is worked through poorly, i.e. enterprises lack a source for financing investment projects.

3.2 Insufficient Level of Crediting for Russian Industries

This phenomenon is apparent in the problem of transforming savings into investments. To be transformed into investments, savings must be given to enterprises in the form of loans. But the size of crediting by Russian business banks is very small. According to the experts, the sum of loans issued in the middle of 2001 within the Russian economy constituted 17 billions of dollars, or 8% of GDP. This about 10 times less than in developed industrial countries (WELFENS/WIEGERT, 2002). Thus, credit arrangement is a minor activity for Russian business banks. (Table 4). Short-term loans constitute the largest proportion of credits as long-term loans are considered risky.

Tab. I4: Credit Structure in Russia

	1992	1993	1994	1995	1996	1997	1999	2000	2001
Short-term credits Billion Rub.	4836	28982	79284	116751	196202,4	265935,3	137834	300235	348598
%	94,8	96,6	94,9	86,8	97,0	96,2	83,3	5,3	94,6
Long-term credits Billion Rub.	266	1037	4276,6	17757	6105	10374,8	27524	14753	19663
%	5,2	3,4	5,1	13,2	3,0	3,8	16,6	4,7	5,4

Source: Source: Goskomstat of the Russian Federation (2000). Russia in figures. p.16, Moscow ; Statistic of the Central Bank of Russian Federation in: www.cbr.ru , own calculations.

Only 5% of investments in capital assets is credited (GLAZEV, 2000). In like manner, economic growth after the crisis of August 17, 1998 was not financed by credits but by internal funds of enterprises. In 1999 and 2000, the volume of investments decreased. In the middle of 2000, the volume of accounts receivable of the private sector to business banks constituted 34% of the structure of their balance (compare, 1997 – 40% DIW, 2000). The level of crediting in some other Eastern European countries is higher in comparison to Russia (Table 5). The low volume of loans are the result of factors such as the general unstable economic situation in Russia, the low paying capacity of many Russian enterprises and non-transparency of their financial condition. The lack of qualified managers capable of evaluating the solvency of enterprises should also be mentioned. (BOFINGER, 1993).

Tab. I5: Private Crediting in Russia and in Some Eastern European Countries (% to GDP)

Countries	1993	1994	1995	1996	1997	1998	1999	2001
Poland	12,2	12,0	12,7	15,9	17,1	17,6	18,8	25,9
Hungary	20,7	21,4	18,6	18,7	20,4	20,0	20,6	31,8
Czech Republic	51,0	50,3	46,7	47,1	54,7	48,0	43,8	35,6
Slovak Republic	30,4	23,0	26,3	30,4	42,1	43,9	37,8	32.9
Slovenia	22,1	23,1	27,5	28,8	28,6	32,8	35,9	46,9
Russia	11,8	12,1	8,5	7,4	9,1	12,9	11,7	13,6

Sources: EBRD (2000), JP MORGAN CEE BANKING HANDBOOK (2002).

3.3 Under Liquidity of Russian Business Banks

The undercrediting of Russian enterprises is due to too little crediting resources for Russian business banks. In 2000 the total capital of Russian banks amounted to 6.2 billion dollars, which is comparable to that of one large foreign bank (GLAZEV, 2000). In addition, the possibilities of refinancing business banks are strictly limited. They can carry out such refinancing only via the Central Bank of Russia. Thus loans from business banks are not representative of the real crediting resources of Russia.

3.4 Hide State Effect on Capital Flow Distribution

The economic policies of developed countries are based on the rule of non-interference of the state in the process of capital flow distribution. But in the beginning of the 1990s, this was most certainly not the case in Russia. During the first years of market reforms, all enterprises could borrow enough resources to finance raising salaries and other expenses. At the beginning, all credits were distributed by Central Bank affiliates. In fact the state supported noncompetitive enterprises (potential bankruptcies) in this way. Despite the fact that such crediting ended later on, there were many incidences of direct or indirect influence of the state on state or business banks, forcing them to lend money to unprofitable enterprises. This policy resulted in the development of non-payments, unpaid wages and prevalent exchange.

3.5 Undercompetition in the Banking Sector

Since the beginning of market reforms, more than 2,500 banks have been established, but only some of them managed to find a solid position in the Russian market. One cannot help noticing the monopoly of the Savings Bank of Russia. Before the crisis of 1998, about 70% of total public savings was concentrated in the Savings Bank. After this crisis, its share increased to 90%. About 40% of all bank assets fall under the auspices of the Savings Bank (WIEGERT, 1999).

Lack of competition in the banking sector leads to negative phenomena such as high differentiation of interest rates, insufficient differentiation of business bank services and the absence of financial innovations. As a result, the financial needs of the Russian economy are not completely satisfied.

3.6 Underdevelopment of the Security Market

The Russian security market does not *de facto* carry out the function of financing domestic enterprises. Only about 1% of the financial assets of Russian enterprises are formed at the expense of share issues (TRETYAKOV, 2001). The Russian market is characterized by low capitalization (for instance comparable to some other Eastern European countries, Table 6), which does not defend Russian shares market from global speculative attacks.

Tab. I6: Market Capitalization in Russia and Some Eastern European Countries (% to GDP)

Countries	1993	1994	1995	1996	1997	1998	1999	2000
Poland	3,7	3,5	3,9	6,6	9,6	13,1	20,0	25,9
Hungary	2,3	4,2	5,8	12,4	35,2	30,0	35,7	31,8
Czech Republic	n.a	14,2	30,2	31,3	26,6	20,1	23,1	26,2
Slovak Republic	n.a	7,3	6,7	11,5	9,3	4,7	3,8	2,3
Slovenia	n.a	4,1	1,8	3,6	9,3	12,2	11,9	13,7
Russia	0	0,1	4,6	9,7	29,5	16,5	17,7	13,8

Source: EBRD (2000), CAIB EMERGING EUROPE (2002).

Investors do not consider the Russian shares market a source for long-term investing, but rather a source for financial profiteering. The reason for such low capitalization of the Russian shares market lies in the financial opacity of the Russian share issuer and in the lack of the legal defense of shareholders. The infrastructure of the Russian share market is not well-developed. Under such conditions, the shares of Russian enterprises are undervalued.

As such, the security market as well as an undeveloped banking system is a weak point of the Russian financial sector. In all, one could say that the Russian financial sector is not effective enough.

Taking into consideration the above-mentioned weaknesses in the Russian domestic financial sector, the globalization of world financial markets causes a number of additional problems:

- The weak financial sector is not attractive to foreign investors. The allowed market share for foreign capital has not yet been achieved. Therefore, the Russian financial sector cannot take profit from attracting foreign stock under terms of globalization.
- The weaknesses of the Russian financial sector are additional risk factors when considering direct foreign investments. For example, there is a risk of low crediting of an enterprise shares in foreign stock. An undeveloped security market leads to the lack of portfolio investments in Russia, as enterprises do not really get additional sources of financing at the expense of foreign portfolio investments under terms of globalization.

Thus the Russian financial system does not yield any real profit from globalization in world financial markets. But at the same time all negative aspects spelled out by experts are inseparably applicable to Russia. It should be noticed that these weaknesses of the Russian domestic financial sector make the integration of Russia within the world financial system rather problematic in the short run.

4. Strengthening the Financial Sector as a Means to Overcome the Globalization Deficit

Stable growth of the Russian financial market under conditions of world financial market globalization is possible only if its domestic financial sector strengthens. To achieve this, the following actions must be taken:

4.1 Bank System Reorganization

We shall now examine the main proposals for the reorganization of the banking system:

- Changes in the system of licensing business banks

The Expert Council to the State Duma of the Russian Federation proposed the following model for improving the system of licensing that only allows current operating business banks to be left in Russian market. General licenses can be obtained only by those banks owning equity capital totaling 1 trillion rubles in 2002, under the condition that those particular banks will be able to raise their owned capital to 2 trillion rubles in 2003 and 3 trillion rubles by the end of 2004. Those banks will be permitted to establish their regional representative offices, serve both corporate and private customers and cooperate with foreign banks. This actually means establishing a three layer system: the Central Bank, business banks with general license and business banks with limited license. (KIEVSKI, 2001)

- Further privatization of bank sector

The majority of Russian banks are private. However, some giant banks such as the Savings Bank and Vnesheconombank are still owned by the State. Further privatization of the banking sector is needed to increase the rivalry among Russian banks.[2] Experts are discussing possible models for privatization in the Russian banking sector. WELFENS and WIEGERT (2002) insist that the major part of credit be given to private banks in Russia as a result of privatization. They recommend that the Savings Bank of Russia be divided, with follow-up privatization of its parts. But at the same time, this partial privatization of the Savings Bank should not suggest principal changes in the system of insurance arrangements for existing bank deposits. Later on, these systems must be differentiated from particular fiscal institutions singled out after partial privatization of the Savings Bank. This is also necessary to attract world institutions such as the European Bank of Reconstruction and Development and the World Bank to the process of privatizing Russian banks.

Representatives of rating agency Fitch Ratings offer a proposal by which the Russian government must have limited involvement in the capital of leading Rus-

---

2 Presently, competition is only being developed at the regional level under due to the monopoly of the Russian Savings Bank. MATOVNIKOV points out that the positive effect of bank competition lies in increasing the total amount of loans issued (MATOVNIKOV, 2001).

sian banks, while the Central Bank must pull itself out from the capital of Vneshtorgbank and from the capital of its foreign affiliates or subsidiaries (Eurobank in France, Moscow Narodny Bank in Great Britain, Donau Bank in Austria, and Ost-West Handelsbank in Germany); the Government of Russia should also leave the capital of all Russian banks (approximately 400 in all) where they have their share undisturbed (PAGE/LONGSDON/GILES/CLAPP, 2002).

- Carrying out of bankruptcy procedures and license cancellation for insolvent banks

The banking sector will have operating ability and be stable only if all potential bankruptcies among business banks are called "bankruptcies *de jure*," meaning that their licenses will be revoked. Currently, this so-called bankruptcy procedure is being carried out very confusingly. Among five operating banks in Russia, for example, three are operating with cancelled licenses; among 1322 existing operative banks, 750 whose procedure liquidation was not yet finished are still operating on cancelled licenses. By the end of 2000, banks with cancelled licenses comprise an alternative bank system that was actually left unregulated. It takes about 9-10 months to reach a decision on bank liquidation (MATOVNIKOV, 2002). To provide a consecutive process of insolvent bank liquidation, there must be such measures with definite criteria for insolvency identification and clear legal regulations for bankruptcy procedure.

- Increasing foreign participation in the banking sector

During the 1990s, foreign participation in the Russian banking sector was limited. It was not supposed to be more than 12% of the whole amount of constituted bank capital. This quota is planned to increase to 25% (EPISHEVA, 2001); it is admitted that foreign capital can contribute to the development of new bank services within the Russian market. It is worth mentioning that the experience of some Eastern European countries whose foreign share in the banking system constitutes 30-60% (EPISHEVA, 2001).

- Establishment of independent bank supervision

Political influence on many bank transactions is still common in Russia, decreasing the efficiency of the banking system as a whole. So, it is essential that an independent body for supervising bank operations be established. For this established body to work effectively, clear criteria for licensing and license cancellation must be established. Additionally, it is necessary to improve the regulations of legally approved inadvisability for risk transactions.

4.2 Establishment of Legal Foundation for Mortgage Development

One of the major factors illustrating the backwardness of the Russian financial sector is a poorly-developed system of issuing loans when mortgage is a guarantee. Giving loans is a highly risky business in Russia. Scholars estimate that the default rate on bank loans is much higher in Russia than in developed countries.[3] For example, illegal income makes it difficult to evaluate the creditworthiness of a particular borrower. Moreover, unstable financial situations could lead to the loss of a borrower's income. Therefore, the development of mortgage as a guarantee for issuing loans is an essential prerequisite for developments in the credit market. Mortgages can be considered one of the main forms of crediting for small businesses (KALAMBET, 1999; AGANBEGYAN, 2002). The "Land Code of the Russian Federation", dated 28 September 2001 allows for having title to land, and the addition of the regulation "About Mortgage" from 11 February 2002 are important steps in the development of the mortgage market in Russia.

4.3 Increased Capitalization in the Russian Shares Market

The Russian shares market has a lower capitalization in comparison to those of western countries, and it is not considered a place for long-term investments by foreign investors. According to the opinion of some experts, a rise of capitalization in the Russian shares market in 2000-2002 is not stable enough. Thus portfolio investments in the Russian economy are of a short-term, speculative nature (MAYOROV, 2002). To make the Russian shares market a more reliable financial market for businesses, share issuance must become more transparent and understandable for foreign investors. Kept accountancy and statistics records according to western standards would allow foreign investors to adequately evaluate the financial state of business, possibly leading thereby to the greater attractiveness of Russian shares.

The fulfillment of these above-mentioned suggestions will help make the Russian financial market stronger and further its integration in the world economy. A strengthening of the financial sector will lessen the risk of the unpredictable removal of investments and also minimize customers' losses in Russian business banks. In this way, foreign investment within Russia would not be as risky as it is now.

[3] There is no official data for this in Russia. One of the reasons is the insufficient development of the mortgage market (IVANOV, 2001).

References

ACT OF THE USSR [SAKON SSSR] (1990): About State Bank (O Gosudarstvennom Banke), 11.12.1990.

AGANBEGYAN, A. (2002): Transformation, Marktreformen und Wettbewerbspolitik in Russland, in: DUWENDAG, D. (ed.): Reformen in Russland und deutsch - russische Wirtschaftsbeziehungen, Baden-Baden, pp. 23-33.

AKINDINOVA, N. (2000): The Inclinations of the Citizens of Russia to Saving: Tendency of the 90th (Sklonnost naselenia Rossii k sbereshenjam: tendenzii 90-ch godov), Economic Problems (Voprosi ekonomiki), Vol. 10, pp. 80-96.

BOFINGER, P. (1993): Erfahrungen mit Geldpolitik bei Existenz starker mikroökonomischer Verzerrungen, in: HERR, H., WESTPHAL, A. (ed.): Transformation in Mittel- und Osteuropa. Makroökonomische Konzepte und Fallstudien, Frankfurt/Main, New York, pp. 172-201.

CAIB (2002): Emerging Europe Monthly, October.

CENTRAL BANK OF RUSSIAN FEDERATION (2002): Bulletin of Banking Statistics, in: www.cbr.ru, various issues, Moscow.

DONDOKOVAA, E. (1999): The Securities Market in Russia: Development and Foundation Peculiarities (Rinok zennikh bumag v Rossii: osobennosti stanovlenia i rasvitia), The St. Petersburg State University, St. Petersburg.

DIW (2000): Deutsches Institut für Wirtschaftsforschung. Wochenbericht, N15, Berlin.

EBRD (2000): Transition Report -Employment, Skills and Transition, London.

EPISHEVA, I. (2001): Transnational Banks: New Possibilities for Business in Russia (Transnatsionalnie banki; novii vosmoshnosti dlja biznesa v Rossii), Banking (Bankovskoe delo), Vol.7, pp. 27-31.

GLAZEV, S. (2000): The Ways to Overcome Investment Crisis, Economic Problems, Vol. 11, pp. 13-26.

GOSKOMSTAT OF THE RUSSIAN FEDERATION, (2000): Russian Statistical Annual-Book (Goskomstat Rossii. Rossiiskii statistitcheskii eshegodnik), Moscow, p. 509.

IVANOV, V. (2001): Mortgage Lending (Ipotechnoe kreditovanie), Moscow.

JP MORGAN (2002): Cee Banking Handbook, October.

KALAMBET, A. (1999): Small Business Investments via Mortgage Lending (Investirovanie malogo bisnesa tcheres ipotechnoe kreditovanie), Investments in Russia (Investizii v Rossii), Vol. 9, pp. 8-40.

KIEVSKI, V. (2001): Proposals of the Bank System Reform (Predloshenia po reformirovanij bankovskoi sistemi), Banking (Bankovskoe delo), Vol. 9, pp. 18-19.

MATOVNIKOV, M. (2001): Benefits of the Bank's Competition (O polse bankovskoi konkurenzii), Banking (Bankovskoe delo), Vol. 3, pp. 2-38.

MATOVNIKOV, M., OVTSHAROVA, A. (2002): Russian Banks: Long Life after Death (Rossiiskie banki: dolgai shisnj posle smerti), Securities market rinok zennich bumag), Vol. 6, pp. 37-39.

MAYOROV, D. (2002): The Fall-Winter Optimism (Osenne-zimnii optimism), Securities market (Rinok zennich bumag), Vol.5, pp. 28-30.

NUNNENKAMP, P. (1998): Verlierer oder Gewinner? Entwicklungsländer im Zeitalter der Globalisierung, Kiel.

PAGE, N., LONGSDON, J., GILES, A., CLAPP, L. (2002): Bank Reform in Russia, Securities market, Vol. 1, pp. 22-27.

SEREBRYAKOV, S. (2001): Bank System - Will it be a New Crisis? (Bankovskai sistema -budet li novii krisis?), Banking (Bankovskoe delo), Vol. 8, pp. 7-10.

SIEBERT, H. (1997): Weltwirtschaft, Stuttgart.

Statistic of the Central Bank of Russian Federation www.cbr.ru → statistica→ statstica po bankowskoj sisteme→ dannie ob objemach predostawlennich kreditow 1999-2003.

STIERLE, V. (1999): Globalisierung und Globalität: Schrittmacher, Merkmale, Reversibilität, INFER, Berlin.

THE FEDERAL ACT OF THE RUSSIAN FEDERATION [FEDERALNII SAKON ROSSIISKOI FEDERAZII] (1990): About Banks and Bank Operations (O bankach i bankovskoi dejatelnosti), 02.12.1990, new edition 24.06.1992.

THE FEDERAL ACT OF THE RUSSIAN FEDERATION [FEDERALNII SAKON ROSSIISKOI FEDERAZII] (1998): About Mortgage (Ob ipoteke zaloge nedvisimosti), 16.07.1998, new edition 11.02.2002.

THE FEDERAL ACT OF THE RUSSIAN FEDERATION [FEDERALNII SAKON ROSSIISKOI FEDERAZII] (2002): About State Bank (O tsentralnom banke Rossiiskoi Federazii), 10.07.2002.

THE FEDERAL ACT OF THE RUSSIAN FEDERATION [FEDERALNII SAKON ROSSIISKOI FEDERAZII] (1992): Foreign Currency Regulation and Control (O valutnom regulirovanii i valutnom kointrole), 09.10.1992, new edition 18.04.2001.

THE FEDERAL ACT OF THE RUSSIAN FEDERATION [FEDERALNII SAKON ROSSIISKOI FEDERAZII] (2001): Land Code of the Russian Federation (Zemelnii Kodeks Rossiiskoi Federazii, 28.09.2001.

TRETYAKOV, V. (2001): Stock Market in the Year 2000: Tendencies and Perspectives (Fondovii rinok v 2000 godu: tendenzii i perspektivi), Banking (Bankovskoe delo), Vol. 1, pp. 5-9.

VODYANOV, A., SMIRNOV, A. (2001): Investment Policy - What Methods of the State Regulation are More Preferable? (Investizionnai politika - kakim metodam gosudarstvennogo regulirovanii otdat predpochtenie?), The Russian Economic Journal (Rossiiskii ekonomicheskii zhurnal), Vol.12, pp. 10-32.

BUCH, C., HEINRICH, R., PIERDZIOCH, C. (2001): Globalisierung der Finanzmärkte: Freier Kapitalverkehr oder Tobin-Steuer?, in: Kieler Diskussionsbeiträge, Institut für Weltwirtschaft, Kiel.

WELFENS, P., WIEGERT, R. (2002): Reform des Bankensektors und Stabilität in Russland, in: DUWENDAG, D. (ed.): Reformen in Russland und die deutsch - russischen Wirtschaftsbeziehungen, Baden-Baden, pp. 211-228.

WIEGERT, R. (1999): Der russische Bankensektor im Prozess der Systemtransformation, Potsdam.

WIIW (2001): HANBOOK OF STATISTICS, Vienna.

Comments on: Problems of Russia with Financial Globalization

Michael Vogelsang

The paper from Grigori Feiguine and Tatjana Sedash addresses the linkages between financial globalization, financial liberalization and transformation in Russia. The authors emphasize the international welfare effects of financial globalization and the risks of a weak domestic banking sector in Russia. They present a pessimistic view of Russia's economic future and consider its economy to be unstable.

In the macroeconomic part of the paper, the authors point out the "global deficits" of the Russian economy which may cause an unstable economic development in Russia. These are low competitiveness of the industrial sector, mono-structure of trade, the political and legal shortcomings and the weak financial sector. The fact that Russia had mostly suffered small or negative growth rates during the 90s in contrast to the other east European transformation countries is judged as evidence that Russia's economic future might be gloomy as well. But the crucial question should be whether the crises of 1998 also caused long term positive effects due to the subsequent legal and tax reforms and the sharp devaluation of the rouble? The most recent macroeconomic data show a GDP growth of 4.3 % in 2002[1] and a strong positive current account which temporarily contradict the pessimistic view of the authors. A more detailed analysis of the consequences of the crises should assess the trade-off between

- the new comparative advantage of the raw material sector as a stabilizing element for the current account and
- the attraction of foreign direct investments causing further agglomeration and growth effects on the one hand and
- on the other hand, the dependency on the varying international oil markets, which means an import of instability and also a cause for delay of necessary adjustments in the industrial and political sector in the case of relatively high oil prices.

In the second part, the authors analyse the Russian banking system and mention these indicators for its weakness: Insufficient transformation of savings into investments, low public savings because of distrust, risks and criminality, insufficient level of crediting of Russian industry, short-term structure of credits, under-liquidity of banks, under-competition in the bank sector, insufficient differentiation of services, and underdevelopment of the security market. According to the authors, the result of these weaknesses is that the Russian economy sustains the disadvantages of financial globalization without being able to benefit from the advantages.

---

[1] Estimation of Goskomstat according to WORLD BANK, see Russian Economic Report, WORLD BANK, March 2003.

In Part 3, the authors therefore recommend the strengthening of the financial sector and a reorganization of the banking system. The proposed set of measures are: further privatization, expulsion of insolvent banks, increasing foreign participation, establishing independent bank supervision, creating a legal base for mortgages and raising up capitalization of the share market.

In summary, the paper addresses a crucial topic of developing economics from a Russian point of view. The idea and the structure of the paper are fine and give a good impression of the "delay" of Russia's economy in the transformation process in the banking sector. But it would be desirable that the authors more clearly show the interdependencies between globalization and financial weakness. Which effects of globalization are aggravating, which are softening the problems? Indeed the relationship between globalization and economic health in the financial sector is ambiguous: domestic competition of foreign banks helps in terms of efficiency, and initiates foreign direct investments and knowledge spill-overs. On the other hand, the dollarization of the Russian economy and the huge amounts of dollars in the bank balances are clearly a risk for economic stability caused by globalization. Even the IWF researchers point out (Prasad, Rogoff, Wei, Kose 2003) that the total effect of financial globalization is not clear and that it depends for instance on the degree of corruption. The significance and consequences of corruption and rent seeking in the Russian banking sector should therefore be worked out in more detail. Furthermore the paper should take into account that the '98 crises may require a more differentiated macroeconomic evaluation because the patterns of trade and capital flows with the rest of world dramatically changed after the crises. A more detailed description of the positive and negative effects of globalization would be desirable. Last but not least, the monetary regime and the role of the central bank are crucial for the results of financial globalization. Therefore the problematic combination of central bank and supervision authority in Russia should be emphasized and the currency dilemma of the Russian central bank should be pointed out: Allow a depreciation of the rouble against the US$ and endanger bank balances, or accept a real appreciation which is detrimental to international competitiveness of industrial production in Russia? The most recent depreciation of the US$ against the Euro makes it easier for the Central Bank to stabilize the rouble against US$, but the question of long-run sustainability of this exchange rate policy will remain on the political agenda.

From the microeconomic point of view, it should be noted that in the Russian economy, large differences exist in terms of efficiency and competitiveness. Consequently the specific sectors have individual requirements for their banking purposes so that a detailed analysis of the consequences of a weak banking system should also consider the industrial structure. Furthermore one would expect the authors to address some basic questions which are discussed in the literature on transformation and developing countries. Thus there are reasonable arguments that adjustment crises in the transformation and globalization process must be accepted, similar to business cycles in more developed market economies. From this point of view, the Russian experience is very important for the guidelines of international economic policies in the future and suitably Grigori Feiguine and Tatjana

Sedash present some valuable arguments and details on the Russian banking sector in their paper.

References

PRASAD, E., ROGOFF, K., WEI, S.-J., KOSE, M. A. (2003): "Effects of Financial Globalization on Developing Countries: Some Empirical Evidence", IWF Paper, March 2003.

RUSSIAN ECONOMIC REPORT (2003): The World Bank, Russia Country Department, March 2003.

J. Russia on the Threshold of the WTO: Some Problems and Options

Ruslan Grinberg

Russia is engaged in negotiations on WTO accession since the second half of the 1990s. Certain progress was made through numerous meetings of the Working Party and bilateral negotiations between Russia and interested WTO members. It is considered possible for this country to accede to the influential international organization by 2004, though some serious problems, including technical ones, still exist.

This date was set as a follow-up to the two following considerations. First, existing problems can be solved in the Working Party and in the process of bilateral negotiations. Secondly, according to the resolutions of the Doha Ministerial Conference, the next round of reforms in the global trade system is to be accomplished by 2005, which could bring Russia under the necessity of starting another round of WTO negotiations. The Russian authorities hold that Russia's WTO membership is not only in line with economic reforms but also can improve the country's image as a market economy.

In the era of globalization it is impossible to overcome a protracted crisis, to carry out economic modernization and achieve sustainable growth without active participation in world trade and other forms of international economic relations.

For this reason, Russia has no other alternative but to accede to the WTO. The benefits of this step for this country are evident. First, it joins in the game according to civilized international rules, which are sure to help overcome the semi-anarchy of the 1990s that has consolidated almost institutionally ("route's inertia"). It is now extremely important to mobilize the society to achieve the transparency of Russian corporations, first of all in the so-called natural monopolies. On this matter one cannot but agree with the WTO requirements. It is especially necessary as the Government is not able to effectively control these monopolies in general and their costs in particular, even though the executive vertical was restored in the past years. Almost arbitrary pricing for goods and services they produce leads to the speeding-up of inflation and therefore impedes economic recovery that started three years ago.

Secondly, the country gets an additional opportunity to struggle with antidumping measures widely taken against Russia. The Government has every reason to hope that if Russia becomes a WTO member with the officially recognized status of having a market economy, consumers' claims will be laid on corresponding firms but not on the state (as is the case now), which will somewhat relieve the pressure it is subject to: according to the Russian Minister for Economic Development and Trade, in connection with these claims the country loses up to 3.5 billion dollars annually. It is hard to tell to which extent these losses will decrease after Russia accedes to the WTO. What is more important for the country is that it will be officially recognized as a market economy. Finally, it is necessary to accede to the WTO because WTO member countries account for 96 % of world trade, and it is impossible to participate effectively in the international division of labour and to influence the course of events not being a member of this organization.

One of the characteristic features of Russia's attempts to accede to the WTO is that this process is dominated by a small number of officials sticking to the Government's directives and to the President's course for Russia's integration into the global economy. Unfortunately, for a long time Russian citizens and firms were not engaged in discussing the arising problems, having no opportunity to fully express their points of view and defend their interests. The situation changed radically only in 2002, when it suddenly became clear that the negotiations had come to the deadlock. Tough requirements of WTO negotiators, first of all of the EU and the USA, made it necessary for Russia to choose between three options:

1. *Compromise in order to fulfill the set task as for the date of WTO accession.* Adherence to this course would make Russia a party to the asymmetrical system of economic relations. The 'cost' of compromise is extremely high: 'To accede to the WTO now, Russia has to meet the requirements of the EU and the USA to fully liberalize foreign access to the banking sector in exchange for their acknowledging of Russia's right to conserve low prices for energy resources'[1]. In my view, this option is absolutely unacceptable.

2. *Admit that it is impossible for Russia to accede to the WTO until the end of the current decade.* This idea is based on a widespread conviction that it is not expedient to accede to the WTO before reforms are completed and the phase of sustainable growth is achieved. Forcing the accession process is very dangerous in the context of forming a new structure in post-Soviet territory. No doubt, the full use of the potential of vast territory with rich natural resources, developed transport infrastructure, significant unemployed capacities, and qualified labor is in the interests of Russia, as well as of almost all other former Soviet republics. Today the CIS with its vast area (more than 20 mln sq. km) and 5 % of the world's population accounts for only 3 % of world GDP, 2 % of world export and 3 % of world investment.[2] As for Russia, respective figures for this country are: 2.5 % of the world population, 2.4 % of GDP, and 1.3 % of export.[3]

The Institute for International Economic and Political Studies, Russian Academy of Sciences, is engaged in studying the influence of the size of economic structures (countries, regional and sub-regional groups, currency unions, etc.) on the efficiency and sustainability of economic growth in the process of liberalizing and opening to foreign markets. This analysis shows that economic structures are optimal according to the global criteria when their internal market capacity is about 300 million consumers. At present the USA, the EU, China, India, NAFTA, Mercosur, and ACEAN represent such structures (the Soviet Union used to be

1 IZVESTIYA, 20.02.03

2 BULLETIN OF THE INTER-PARLIAMENT ASSEMBLY OF THE CIS, 1999, No 5, p.125; EKONOMIKA I ZHIZN, July 2001, No 26, p.6.

3 WORLD ECONOMIC OUTLOOK, April 2000. IMF, Washington, p.99.

among them, too). These formations are able to evolve efficiently using mostly their own resources, maintaining sufficient sustainability while remaining open to foreign markets and global influences.[4]

Concerning Russia, one can state that only within such an economic structure, organized as the Free Trade Zone or the Eurasian Economic Community (EurAsEC), or the Common Economic Area (the Presidents of Russia, Belarus, Ukraine, and Kazakhstan announced recently their intention to create it), it can get a chance to fully realize its potential in the sphere of production, technology, and innovation, and to strengthen its positions in interaction with other regional groups.

Unfortunately, most of the post-Soviet countries have not yet solved this vital problem: they have chosen the least effective variant of acceding to the WTO on the individual basis, and the resolutions they have adopted on the coordination of their actions in this sphere are still unimplemented. Russia and Kazakhstan agreed to synchronize their actions concerning their accession to the WTO. Russia and the Ukraine would have an opportunity to coordinate their positions in the framework of the 'union of four', though in the course of individual negotiations Ukraine has already signed several protocols seriously contradicting Russia's positions.[5] An opinion is expressed that the accession of the CIS members to the WTO will hamper integration in the post-Soviet territory, because the rules of the WTO contradict certain agreements within the CIS, which is bound to cause numerous inquiries at the International Arbitration Court.[6]

This can explain one of the specific characteristics of Russia's position in the accession negotiations; that is, its will to preserve the system of preferential trade relations with post-Soviet states, economic activities there being regarded by Russia as a priority direction of its foreign economic policy.

The effect Russia's accession to the WTO might have on its relations CIS members will be considered below.

3. Since the business elite split up into two groups according to their attitude on the advisability of the WTO accession in general and the date of accession in particular, the importance of political factors increases considerably. The emerging interest of the society, in which one can also see some signs of cleavage, furthers the development of this trend. The cleavage manifests itself in the fact that on the one hand Russian consumers cannot but welcome new relatively cheap imported goods of high quality that may appear on the home market after Russia accedes to the WTO, but on the other hand millions of industrial and office workers in food, furniture, pharmaceutical, metallurgical, chemical, automobile, and aircraft industries suffer from a loss of jobs and a decrease in income levels as a result of Russia's WTO accession.[7]

---

4 For more information please see Issues of Globalization and Regionalization on the Territory of the Former USSR. IIEPS/RAS, Moscow, 2002 (in Russian).

5 IZVESTIYA, 25.02.2003.

6 IZVESTIYA, 14.03.2003. The author of this study wrote about the possibility of this unfavorable scenario. See Bankovskoye obozreniye, No 9, 2002, p.17-18.

7 Unfavorable consequences of Russia's WTO accession for the said branches are revealed by the study 'The Consequences of Russia's Accession to the WTO for This Country's Economy', carried out by THE RUSSIAN ACADEMY OF SCIENCES AND THE NATIONAL INVESTMENT

In an extremely difficult situation when there is a conflict of interest between business circles and the society is split into two parts – those who may win and those who are most likely to lose as a result of accession –, it is evident that *the decisions on the expediency of accession and its date, as well as on possible compromises in the course of negotiations will be taken on the top political level.* In this connection it is essential not to allow for an excessive misbalance of lobbying groups in order to avoid serious economic and social damage.

Having assessed the consequences of realizing these said options, one can conclude that, taking into account the country's interests, objective necessity for the formation of the post-Soviet economic area, and technical problems (the establishment of customs control on the borders with the CIS countries, some alterations of the trade regime within the CIS, etc.), Russian negotiators, as well as their EurAsEC partners, should avoid forcing negotiations or maybe even make a pause in the negotiation process.

This position is based on the fact that Russian firms are not ready, either objectively or psychologically, to suddenly face heavyweight rivals on the international arena. Opinion polls show that only 25 % of Russian firms consider themselves ready to compete against foreign producers on the domestic market, 18 % on CIS markets, and 9 % in western markets. Only 10 % report they are ready for Russia's WTO accession.[8]

In my opinion, within the period of 8-10 years Russia's unbalanced economy will be able to smooth over the most critical disproportions, a free trade zone will be created in the post-Soviet territory, and progress will be made in the process of regional integration.

During the preparatory stage and in the process of negotiations the consequences of Russia's accession to the WTO were assessed with the view of the three most important issues.

1. *The role of the tariff and customs policy in protection of the home market, especially during the transitory period.* The response of the Russian economy to WTO accession at the macroeconomic, sectoral and regional levels is estimated in a number of studies, first of all in the above-mentioned joint study of the Russian Academy of Sciences and National Investment Council. The researchers have come to the following conclusion: 'Changing the system of import duties to meet the requirements of the WTO will have little negative effect on macroeconomic dynamics. Any of the said scenarios will not decrease the GDP dynamics more than by 1 percentage point.' Moreover, if Russian negotiators manage to defend the level of import duties they propose to their partners, the GDP is expected to grow at the initial stage after accession by 0.6 %

COUNCIL (Moscow, 2002, p.8). In the report of the International Labor Organization it is mentioned that the light industry with its 3 million employees will suffer most seriously. Over five years in textile, footwear and furniture industries the production will fall by 16-27 %, employment –by 1.5-7.3 %. Production in food industry will decrease by 4.6-4.8 %, in other industries – by 14-37 %. 8 million farmers are also likely to face serious problems. See Izvestiya, 26.02.03.

[8] Impact of Russia's Accession to the WTO on its National Economy. RUSSIAN ACADEMY OF SCIENCES AND NATIONAL INVESTMENT COUNCIL, Moscow, 2002, p.10 (in Russian).

due to the reduction of imports by 2.7 %.[9] As for the sectoral and regional levels, the dynamics there are expected to be similar, though in some sectors and regions the negative consequences may be more serious, as was mentioned above.

Under these conditions the government is right to struggle with all its force to preserve a transitory period for so-called sensitive branches: metallurgy, agriculture, service sector and some other branches. It is necessary to note that its behavior is rather flexible. For example, its position as to insurance business is not very protectionist, and the authorities have good reasons for that. What the government proceeds from is that, first, less than one-third of legally-approved quota for the foreign capital in the total capital of insurance companies is taken up. Secondly, the wide spreading of reinsurance schemes objectively increases foreign influence, so one should not be opposed to the liberal measures the WTO insists on.

The metallurgy issue is more or less clear. As for agriculture, the situation here nonplusses WTO negotiators; current-day Russia is simply unable to subsidize this sector. The WTO is against any subsidies in principle, including those in the agrarian sector. In view of the extreme deficiency of material and financial resources required to support and protect its economy, Russia lays down an 'exotic' but rather reasonable condition. Now only 1.5 billion dollars a year are devoted to agriculture. Russian negotiators suggest that in the long run this figure will grow to between 17 and 20 billion, and only after that will the system of subsidizing be phased out, complying with the principles of the WTO. But for WTO negotiators it sounds very strange, since acceding countries usually struggle to preserve the existing subsidies or protectionist measures, pledging to cut down these measures gradually. Russia acts the other way round: not subsidizing its agriculture now for lack of resources, it reserves the right to support this sector in the future.[10] This is also the case with the Russian aircraft industry. Such an approach seems reasonable, taking into account both the present level of the Russian national economy and its enormous disproportions.

Supporters of the WTO accession believe that the expected negative consequences cannot prevent Russia from joining this organization, especially in the event the RF Government succeeds in coming to mutually-acceptable agreements concerning the above problems. However this view is far from common in this country. Those in doubts, as well as those opposing the WTO accession, insist that no quantitative evaluations are enough to comprehend the complicated situation, especially as 'the devil sits in details'. According to them, the main thing is that the *systemic* consequences of accession (such as migration, tariff and non-tariff

---

[9] IBID., p.8. Two main scenarios were considered. According to the first one, import duties are reduced gradually from 10.92 % to the negotiated bound tariff rate. The second (optimistic) scenario implies the possibility to considerably raise the average bound tariff rate up to 19.18 % when acceding to the WTO and then to reduce it to 12.82 % by the end of the transitory period. For the data on bound tariff rates see www.wto.ru/documents.asp?stats1&1+16.

[10] However even in this very sensitive sector of national economy Russian negotiators are flexible and inclined to compromise. At the meeting of the Working Party (April 2003) they agreed to reduce both the size of annual agricultural subsidies (to USD 13.1 billion) and the size of agricultural export subsidies (to USD 300 million) and to limit agricultural imports by several trading groups only.

regulation of raw material export and regulation of home tariffs on electric energy and transport services) remain unclear. Actually, these issues are those that determine the outcome of negotiations. The methods and scale of the state's involvement in the solution of the said problems, government support for high technologies, government procurements, a huge gap between fuel and energy prices on the home and foreign markets, and the need to change the legislative system so that it complies with the rules of the WTO prior to acceding to this organization – all these issues also belong to systemic conditions. Meeting such requirements may result in conservation of the deadlock situation in the Russian economy and make it inadmissibly susceptible to external influences.

Among the systemic issues, the two-level system of fuel and energy prices and the methods of their regulation are of special importance. WTO negotiators, first of all the EU and the USA, have taken a tough position, claiming that low prices on the home market are a latent form of subsidizing exports and production in general. By declaring low home prices for fuel and energy illegitimate, the WTO negotiators try to deprive Russia of its right to avail itself of its natural competitive advantages. Demanding to decrease the price gap, they refer to the Agreement on Application of Article VI of the GATT and the Stature of the Price for Home Consumers.[11] However, they do not take into consideration the structure of the Russian economy known for its extremely high energy consumption, severe natural conditions, the difficulty of access to oil and gas fields, extraordinarily high share of transportation in the total production costs, especially in case of exports, etc.

It seems that the EU's main concern is to keep Russia a stable supplier of energy resources and raw materials – thereby not allowing its transformation into a strong competitor – rather than to regulate Russian home prices. (The European countries pay almost equal prices for imported fuel and raw materials from different countries, and Russian gas is even the cheapest.) An abrupt elimination of the disparity in home and export prices would inevitably result in an economic collapse and deep social crisis. Nevertheless, it is worth emphasized that that fuel and energy prices for both firms and citizens in Russia are gradually being raised.

If a compromise is not found, the date and the expediency of Russia's WTO accession will be difficult to forecast. In my opinion, the proposal of the Russian Union of Industrialists and Businessmen is worth considering. This Union suggests that in exchange for the EU's acceptance of the two-level fuel and energy price system (with its step-by-step transformation into a one-level system) Russia could agree to liberalize some financial services.[12]

2. *The assessment of systemic consequences of the WTO accession* comprises the second component of preparation in the negotiating process. In this context, what can we reproach the Government with? Only with its indifference towards structural priorities, which actually makes Russia's position in negotiations with the WTO unclear. There is a saying, "If you don't know where to sail,

[11] THE WORLD TRADE ORGANIZATION: Documents and Comments. Moscow, NP, 2001, p.48 (in Russian).

[12] COMMERSANT, 25.10.02.

> there will never be a favorable wind for you". In my opinion, this illustrates the absence of Russian structural policy quite well. If you have *neither industrial nor structural priorities*, it is actually not important how long the negotiations with the WTO might be. Maybe it is an extreme appraisal, since some sensitive sectors can be regarded as priority spheres requiring protection. However, separate parts do not secure integrity.

The government did publish the priorities of the WTO accession, but the question is: do they reflect current public interests? As I mentioned above, negotiators depend to a great extent on directions of the Prime Minister and the President. At the same time without a set of priorities to proceed from one may end up defending the clan interests. And the point is not that the authors of the said directions are always under numerous influences, which they are not always able to resist. Rather the mechanism for decision-making is not based on the approved development strategy, either for the economy as a whole or for its priority sectors, thereby requiring government protection at both national and international levels.

Lacking such a strategy, one may accede to the WTO straight away. They say, Queen Victoria taught her daughter before the girl's first marital night, "Just close your eyes tight and think of England". Sometimes it seems that Russian negotiators approach the dialogue with the WTO only with the thoughts of Russia, no matter how irrational they might be. In any case, a possibility still remains to apply the principles of regressive protectionism. It means that while protecting selected sectors of economy, it is necessary to take measures preventing them from getting used to depending on government assistance.

It is clear that sooner or later Russia will agree to reduce and even cancel many duties – gradually in some branches, as a one-stroke action in others. It is also clear that it should be reflected in a corresponding program, determining conditions and stages of this process. And it is evident that such a normative document does not exist so far. Consider the dispute on the protection of the Russian automobile industry. In my opinion, it now makes no sense to introduce additional barriers simply for the sake of it. At the same time, it is the case that the said regressive protectionism can be applied to ensure a socially safe transition to controlling positions of the foreign capital in this industry.

It is also important to clear up the situation in the country's banking system. First of all one should note that the Russian banks feel rather healthy despite default (1998), having regained and even exceeded some pre-default indices (in particular, assets and personal deposits). One can see a new tradition being established in Russia: banks go bankrupt, bankers win. This should be kept in mind while listening to the bankers claiming that the foreign capital can by no means be allowed to enter this sphere. They allege that otherwise money of their compatriots deposited in foreign banks will not serve the Russian economy. These threats are emotional, but do they have any real basis? First of all, the fact is that there is no foreign capital expansion in the Russian economy in general and in its banking sphere in particular. According to law, the foreign bank capital cannot exceed 12 % of the total bank capital in Russia. It is not much, and even this quota is not taken up. Neither do we see foreign banks queuing for licenses to operate in Russia.

It is not that their presence is undesired; an unattractive investment climate is to blame. Theoretically, providing this improves and foreign capital is more widely seen in Russia, the home investors' money will be able to somehow participate in the development of the western economy. But first, is this worse than the demonetization of the Russian economy during many years and massive dollarization of the national money circulation? Secondly, a significant fact is that while residents deposit two billion dollars annually in domestic banks, up to 20 billion dollars leave Russia every year – legally and illegally. One has to accept the fact that the internationalization of the domestic banking system is inevitable. The task is not to impede in this process but to learn how to control it.

To alleviate the negative consequences of the WTO accession, it is important to speed up the process of bringing Russian legislation in line with both the achieved level of the country's economic transformation and international trade norms, while at the same time rejecting ungrounded requirements to accomplish this process before accession.

3. A number of problems are to be solved in connection with the necessary coordination of the two processes – acceding to the WTO and *organizing the CIS economic area*. Due to its size, rich natural resources, economic, technological, financial and human potential, Russia might strengthen its positions in the region by acceding to the WTO. However the situation is not that simple. Several members of the Commonwealth have already become WTO members. Consider the Kyrgyz Republic, which acceded to the WTO in 1998. It is an example of an almost completely open economy, which is connected with the fact that this country is small and its economy is of a relatively simple structure. That is why the government does not worry about the protection of its internal market. Taking into account a very narrow range of production in Kyrgyzstan, it was accepted into the WTO on conditions that are rather favorable (for WTO members mostly). For the same reasons Georgia and Moldova have acceded to the WTO earlier than Russia (in 2000 and 2001, correspondingly).

I have already referred to the data on the level of home market protection in Russia at the initial and final stages of tariff binding. There is a sharp distinction between the accession conditions of the first three CIS countries and those proposed for Russia, which will undoubtedly hamper the process of integration in post-Soviet states.

Tab. J1: Compromises and Commitments of the First Group of CIS Countries in the Process of WTO Accession (Depending on the Year of Accession)

Country	Year of accession	Per capita GDP (USD)	Tariff compromise on agricultural products	Tariff compromise on other products	Participation in sectoral initiatives	Aggregate support for agriculture	Export subsidies for agriculture
The Kyrgyz Republic	1998	300	11.7 % (mostly 5-20 %) without transitory period (exception is made for wool – 5 years). No SPM.[13]	6.7 % (mostly less than 10 %), transitory period – 7 years.	Most of 'zero' initiatives, chemical harmonization, ITP[14]	5 % of GNP in agriculture	zero
Georgia	2000	620	12.1 % (mostly 12-20 %), transitory period – 5 years. No SPM.	5.8 % (mostly 0-12 %), transitory period – 5 years.	All 'zero' initiatives, except for spirits, chemical harmonization, ITP	10 % of GNP in agriculture	zero
Moldova	2001	370	Mostly 10-15 %, maximum 40 %, transitory period – 4 years. No SPM.	Mostly 10-20 %, maximum 40 %, transitory period – 4 years.	All 'zero' initiatives, except for spirits and furniture, chemical harmonization, ITP	Reduction by 16 % during 4 years	zero

Source: WT/ACC/7; WTO Secretariat; World Bank Review, 1999; UNCTAD (www.wto.ru/documents. asp?f=stats3&1).

In the event transformation is not completed, unconditionally surrendering positions for foreign access to banking and financial spheres of these countries implies the creation of grave problems for all forms of integration within CIS territory, especially for the EurAsEC. Import duties on agricultural products, the level of aggregate support for agriculture, and 'zero' sectoral initiatives also differ to a great extent from country to country.

This situation is fraught with dual consequences for Russia. First of all, import privileges the Kyrgyz Republic grants to other WTO members allow Russia to use this country, being within the Free Trade Zone of the CIS, as a "sluice" to obtain access to more capacious markets of other CIS members. Secondly, in the course of WTO accession negotiations, which are held not with this organization's execu-

[13] SPM – special protective measures in agriculture.

[14] ITP (Ministerial Declaration on Trade in Information Technology Products) implies zero import duties and no other tariff trade barriers for Information Technology Products. According to Kazakh experts, Kyrgyzstan made commitments on 13 non-binding initiatives advanced by some WTO members concerning several groups of goods. 'Zero' initiative is a commitment to reduce import duties on certain goods to zero.

tive bodies but with interested WTO members, some of the latter might seek benefits for themselves in exchange for backing Russia's WTO accession.

So, while carrying on economic and political dialogue with Kyrgyzstan, Moldova and Georgia as WTO members, Russia has to counter their attempts to obtain maximum favorable conditions in bilateral relations in exchange for their support in WTO accession negotiations. The same problem can be generated by Ukraine, in case it does not adhere to the four Presidents' agreement to coordinate conditions of accession to the WTO.

The sudden accession of Kyrgyzstan to the WTO, not coordinated with other CIS members, produced the greatest negative impact on the Customs Union, which was transformed into the EurAsEC (Russia, Belarus, Kazakhstan, Kyrgyzstan, and Tajikistan) in 2000. From the point of view of the WTO, the existence of the Customs Union, allowing its members considerably differing trade regimes, is illegitimate. The intention of the four countries to create a common economic and customs area along with the already existing EurAsEC looks like an attempt to overcome the 'Kyrgyz syndrome' in order to resume the integration process. This does not mean, however, that the Kyrgyz Republic will stay clear of the common tendency. One of the possible ways for Kyrgyzstan to rejoin the process of integration is to use the procedures allowing for the reconsideration of WTO accession conditions in connection with the country's joining the regional group, the EurAsEC. Recently Kyrgyzstan declared its intention to do so. In March 2003 the President, L. Kuchma, charged the Ukrainian Government with clearing up the extent to which agreements that Ukraine had signed with the WTO were in this country's interests. According to the data available, 'all Kuchma's initiatives relating to the revision of the WTO resolutions are connected with the creation of the "union of four".[15]

In my opinion, if Kyrgyzstan and Ukraine realize the declared intentions, this will, first, increase the degree of coordination between the CIS countries as to the conditions of their WTO accession, thus promoting mutual trade and giving a new boost to the free trade zone, and secondly, give hope that integration processes in post-Soviet territory will speed up.

Russia will accede to the WTO on the condition that it promotes the modernization of its national economy and the completion of the reform process. In order to carry negotiations through successfully, Russia has to take some urgent measures. Most important among them are:

- develop and approve Russia's industrial policy to form a basis for the selective protection of manufacturers and stimulation of competition on the domestic market, and to lay down the guidelines for WTO accession negotiations;
- introduce the government system of information on foreign trade and legislation (prices, terms of trade, mechanisms for settlement of trade disputes, etc.) open to domestic firms and business circles – otherwise they will not be able to take full advantage of the opportunities that accession to the WTO offers in international markets;

---

[15] VEDOMOSTY, 27.03.03.

- start training staff specialized in WTO issues for businesses and government structures;
- promote dialogue between the Government Commission for WTO accession, Russian delegation and advisory business structures;
- carry on regular consultations on WTO issues with the CIS countries;
- monitor not only discriminating measures taken by our foreign trade counteragents but also all trade barriers created by their policies and publish the results of this monitoring regularly.

K. Russia and the WTO: What is at Stake?

Ognian N. Hishow

1. Introduction

After several years of merely sluggish progress following Russia's application for WTO-accession in the first half of 1999, President Putin put the issue at the top of his reform agenda and preparations remarkably sped up. In addition, debate inside and outside Russia regarding the pros and cons of the membership in the club accelerated too. Questions are being asked about the general and specific costs and benefits. The overall conclusion is that despite a possible sectoral and regional drawback in the short run, a considerable advantage for the Russian economy will follow in the long run. But even immediately after the accession, Moscow will reap the first fruits by getting a leverage to defend its interests before an established dispute-settlement body and thus to counter arbitrary anti-dumping and other discriminatory measures against Russian exports.

As for the West, it encourages Moscow to accede to the organization to reduce political risks and uncertainties in bilateral trade and cooperation. However, at least in the next few years, there will be no huge economic gain for the West, since the trade volume with Russia will remain low by international standards. Also Western direct investment and acquisitions cannot surge as long as Russia boasts large current account surpluses, whereas a poor investment environment causes an ongoing capital export.

2. Russia's Worries: Totally Altered GDP-Breakdown by Sectors?

Pending membership in the WTO can be seen as the other important challenge Russia's economy has to deal with following its transition from a planned to market economy ten years ago. President Putin is determined to complete this step soon, so alongside the preparation for the accession the discussion of the oncoming changes to the economy and society has gained momentum as well. Russia's case is also being heatedly debated abroad, which is a bit unusual. After all, out of roughly 190 sovereign nations the overwhelming majority of them, currently 144 countries, are members of the club. Even former Soviet republics like Kirgyzstan, Georgia and Moldova quietly acceded to the WTO.

The case of China occupied the headlines in a similar way. Is then the size of an economy the most important reason for the partners to worry about its trade policies? The answer is: perhaps, yes. Although Russia's GDP is in current dollars just a fraction of the size of the US- and EU-economies, the approaching WTO accession raises questions, fears and expectations whose intensity could be attributed to a much bigger candidate. But they are justified, because sooner or later Russia will rank among the most advanced nations, at least in Europe.

To become an equal part of the modern world, Russia must obtain membership in any important international club. In strictly an economical sense, a country expects growth and welfare effects from international trade. If every country participated in a complex system of free international trade the benefits would have been even greater. Though the economic impact of far reaching agreements about trade liberalization is difficult to estimate, some sources (OECD) suggest a gain to the world economy of more than $ 200 billion annually once the Uruguay Round agreements are fully in force. Thus the question is: since the Russian Federation submitted her application for WTO accession almost 9 years ago, why did it take so long to enter the final stage of the application procedure?

On the asset side, Russia will immediately save as much as several billion dollars of reduced cost for her steel and metal exports now encountering various tariff and non-tariff obstacles. But on the liability side, critics say, the economy is facing a negative "accession dividend" in the form of output decline up to several percent of the annual GDP (COTTRELL, 2002, p. 4). This fear pertains to the broadly spread conviction among economists and academics that the collapse of the economy in the early nineties was a result of the sudden exposure to international competitors.

Advocacy for trade derives from proven macroeconomic long term advantages but one should mind the cost-benefit effects on the affected persons. In Russia, as well as in every other country, the cost will be felt by specific, often well-organized groups. At the same time, much of the benefits will accrue to broad, diffuse populations. For instance, progress on bank and financial services will hurt the small but influential class of bankers and nouveau riches, offset by far larger but less visible consumer gains. The former are expected to resist. Yet General Equilibrium Models (GEM) suggest that membership may translate into output gains of up to 3,2 % in the medium run and an impressive 25 % in the long run (YUDAEVA, 2002, p. 3-4). Thus the government must surmount the opposition of various lobby groups torpedoing liberalization.

From the viewpoint of the trade theory after trade barriers have been removed, income redistribution between abundant and scarce resources will take place. Owners of abundant factors will benefit from this opening, since those factors will be used more intensively. Owners of scarce factors will be hurt by the opening of trade, for instance the import-competing industry. Recently exactly this happened: After 1992, industries rich in natural resources and raw materials grew rapidly ensuring a rising Russian share in word oil, gas and metal supply. Other sectors like manufacturing, where advanced technology and effective capital per worker were at the time of the opening scarce relative to Western competitors, suffered or even went bankrupt.

With a further opening, approaching lobbyists and conservatives call for protection of the import-competing sector and for a nationally-determined industry policy. Such a protection rests traditionally on a system of import tarrifs and quotas to encourage domestic producers to control the national market. The weak point of this policy is that import tariffs not only halt imports but they discourage exports as well. The advantage of keeping foreign competitors off the domestic market is mostly by weakening their own export opportunities. In the case of export subsidies, the reverse occurs. It is the economics that causes this paradox (in a special form known as Metzler paradox): A shift in the terms of trade takes place which either hurts the producers of export goods or the import competing sector. For instance, exporters suffer a lower relative price of their goods. As a result, more producers give up export activities and switch to the production of the protected goods distorting even more the "natural" division of labor between sectors and countries. Moreover, the initial idea of the authorities to help build up a strong export industry fails. The macroeconomic price of such a policy is even higher: to keep the subsidized industries alive, more taxes must be levied on the healthy sectors and thus medium and long term growth will be endangered. Just this was the case in many developing countries during the 6os and 70s, which appear to have lost pace instead of speeding up the output growth. A protection itself does not create a comparative advantage, especially in manufacturing and in advanced services like telecommunications or banking. There are often fundamental reasons for failure to withstand foreign competition other than a simple lack of experience with producing given goods or services. If a country lacks skilled labor in that special sector, serious entrepreneurs, managerial competence, and has problems of administrative organization, or the rule of law, these problems cannot be solved by trade policy alone. High rates of protectionism have allowed industries in many Latin American countries to exist, though their cost of production is much higher than the price of imports they are intended to replace. Protectionism also tends to promote production at an inefficient small scale, precisely in the auto industry. Further questions beyond growth rates arise too: Selected protectionism causes income inequality to rise, while nations with relatively liberal trade policies had increased their welfare across all social groups since the 60s and 70s (BHAGWATI/SRINIVASAN, 1979, p. 62-81). Russia must carefully contemplate what is worthwhile to protect. Thus the conclusion of who is to blame for the overall decline of the economy in the 90s is not straightforward. Studies suggest that the output crisis alone cannot be attributed to the opening up to the outside world. The overall disorder following the break up of the Soviet Union struck the sectors harder than the redistribution of trade itself.

Meanwhile, an adjustment process across the <u>industrial sector</u> has taken place and therefore a further after-accession shock is likely to be insignificant. Yet it is likely that, mostly in the short run, opening up will involve adverse social consequences. Industries that lack resources to position themselves on the market (either producer of import competing or export goods) may encounter output decline and lay-offs. Unfortunately, a good deal of the labor force in the former Soviet industry was employed at plants producing military equipment, and some of them have managed to survive the "big-bang" Prime Minister Gaydar launched in 1992. These remaining dinosaurs are likely to become the first victims of the WTO accession, since it will enforce more realistic prices and sales revenues that are out of rich of an industry used to relying on subsidies. Model-based projections suggest that in the first year following an import surge output will drop in (apart from food processing industry) machine-building and steel production. But many industries would register growth already in the second year after the increase in imports, mainly because competitiveness of the domestic producers is likely to rise thanks to Western know-how more easily penetrating Russia's economy (CEFIR, 2002, p. 7). Considering the costs of not joining now, it may turn out that the postponed hard choice will entail even greater deindustrialization later. A further removal of customs duties will have minor effects on the competitiveness of the exposed industries since they provide little protection at this time. The average tariff rate applied to a number of industries range from 7 to 15 %, which is modest by international standards. Worse yet, almost half of imports evade customs duties, so the effective rate remains low. Liberalization of the trade with goods will thus have only a minor effect, because a major opening-up has taken already place and further tariff reduction is rather unlikely.

Questions remain, however. While tariffs are not regarded as a crucial obstacle to accession, trade partners insist that Russia must remove any hidden subsidies. Especially the notoriously low energy prices domestic producers enjoy deliver arguments to raise anti-dumping measures against Russian competitors on the world market, for instance aluminum companies.

The auto industry enjoyed years of protection but failed to grow out of the stage of an "infant industry," which translates into a political call for preserving the current tariff and longer grace periods. As foreign automobile makers want to enter the Russian auto industry, they face a protection rate of 25 percent and Russian consumers therefore lose out. For prestigious reasons, this situation can last almost indefinitely although the international companies will sooner or later assert an ever growing chunk over the market. But provided the government decides quickly against the auto lobby, macroeconomic gains can be expected.

Major effects are expected to come within the service sector. This sector scored great success in the nineties by replacing industry from the leading position in the economy. Only after the commencement of the economic transition, market-oriented bank and financial services, wireless telecom, IT-based services, etc. emerged as entirely new industries in Russia. But by international standards the new services industries are weak and Russian negotiators notoriously fear that the entire sector is not competitive, i.e. the western banks, insurance companies and travel agencies will enter the market and suppress it. The main concern is that, on the one hand, various services and tourism are not yet developed, thus they will be dominated by foreign competitors alone. On the other hand, the relatively prospering sector of public and private education services might collapse. But WTO-advocates claim that foreign consulting companies will help to promote industrial activities, and regional banks will only benefit from the accession (RUSSIA ON THE WAY TO THE WTO, 2002). For instance, Russian commercial banks are small and the variety of services they provide is still narrow. Russia's banking sector boasts combined assets of roughly 97 billion dollars, or less than one-tenth of any of the largest international banks. Distrust of (commercial) banks is broadly spread among the private household sector, and the large shadow economy also avoids banks. In the nineties, small and inexperienced private banks mushroomed, but soon failed. Large amounts of deposits were siphoned out of the country, whereas dubious financial schemes benefited the new bankers at the expense of the depositors. The result is that a good deal of private savings is deposited in gherkin jars and mattresses at home. Confronted with a lack of deposits, the (private) banks prefer to extend short-term credits, creating an overburden on the short-term liabilities of their balance sheets. Moreover, the sheer size of the huge state-owned savings bank (Sberbank) may sometimes restrain competition (Tab. K1).

Tab. K1: The Biggest State-Owned and Private Bank Compared, $ Billion, as of January 1, 2002

Indicator	Saving- (Sber-)bank	Alfa-Bank-Group
Assets	25,6	2,7
Deposits, of which	20,7	2,7
Share in country's total	64,2 %	4,4 %
Share in private deposits	71,6 %	2,1 %
Credit extended, of which	12,6	1,4
Share in country's total	25,2	2,8
Branches	1,216	84
Employees	200,000	7,071
Net profit	0,84	0,09

Source: NEUE ZÜRCHER ZEITUNG, October 10,2002, p. 10.

Despite the promise the new chairman of the Central bank made to pursue more transparency in the banking system, there has still been no formal pressure on banks to be more open. Only the Sberbank has part of its shares publicly quoted. Although most large banks apply international accounting standards, small banks still resist. Moreover, the final introduction of international accounting standards in 2004 at the latest should not be just a formal act, but needs to be accompanied by measures envisaging proper bank supervision. In 1998, for example, all large banks that failed had published neat IAS figures. But they still struggle to improve the legal status of the lender who is less protected by the law than the borrower. In Russia, the issue of collateral requires serious improvement. Insiders point out that the preconditions of bank lending extend even to the reform of Russian courts (SALONEN, 2002, p. 1).

Not surprisingly, bankers – especially in the regions and remote places where conditions for competition are poor – feel uncomfortable. They do not see WTO membership as offering any sort of positive opportunity. As for the public, there is a widespread lack of understanding of what WTO accession might mean, accompanied by suspicions of unwelcome foreign interference in the Russian monetary sector. Not only private banks clearly feel unready to meet foreign competition: the President of Sberbank has argued for restrictions on the activities of foreign banks in Russia for at least ten years after accession. Other bankers have supported this view (HARE, 2002, p. 14).

Obviously, unless the overall conditions for banking improve, foreign banks will have little incentives for making much headway in their engagement. But without competition from international players and lacking technology and know-how transfer, the Russian banking industry will encounter less pressure to modernize and adapt. Rather a "muddling trough"-mentality will dominate and once gotten used to block foreign competitors, the bank lobby will fiercely defend any further attempt to open. It is still not too late to rethink hitherto policies like not allowing foreign bank branches. As foreign credit institutions are perceived by the population to be much more reliable than the fledged domestic banks households, firms will prefer to deposit their savings there and so help to develop an up-to-date banking system. For macroeconomic reasons this is welcomed: Only a full developed and working banking system allows the money supply to match the demand for money and thus to provide the economy with the cash it needs for growth. In addition and for the same purpose, the 12 percent-ceiling on foreign share in total bank capital must be lifted soon. Moreover, the authorities must remove obstacles to international banks for making major acquisitions of Russian banks in the next couple of years, mainly to gain local retail banking capacity.

Some senior Duma representatives have urged Russia to accept substantial liberalization in the fledgling insurance market, while the companies themselves feel unready and WTO negotiators representing the EU in particular press for greater openness.

Telecommunications must undergo modernization whereas transportation companies must reduce costs and account agencies must be up-to-date with the international standards of account. Not surprisingly, lobby groups behind those sectors demand extensive protection by using the "infant industry" argument. They insist on limiting foreign presence in a number of service sectors and even on keeping the state monopoly in others. In the banking sector, they call for limits on the combined foreign equity share as well as on the restriction on the method by which foreign banks operate (no branches, no lending). In the insurance sector, foreign bidders must be prohibited from participating in the compulsory insurance schemes, which are vital to their Russian engagement (YUDAEVA, 2002, p. 3). In the telecom industry, the incumbent monopoly Rostelecom is supposed to keep its monopoly on long-distance and international calls until 2010. Moreover, foreign operators are expected to limit their equity share to prevent a take-over or dawn raids on Russian companies.

In agriculture, the picture is even more confusing. Agriculture is the most regulated sector across the developed world where market principles work least. If cost-related allocation of resources applied, the land-abundant US would have completely supplied Western Europe and Japan with agricultural products. Actually for political reasons, this sector is heavily protected even in the most competitive countries, and this is in accordance with the WTO rules. Yet after joining the WTO, nations are supposed to reduce agriculture subsidies. The deepest cuts, up to 20 %, are made by the Western countries and some moderate reductions, about 13 %, occur in emerging markets (USTENKO, 2001, p. 9). In Russia, where subsidies are modest by international standards, cuts will barely take place. The opposite is true: WTO rules set ceilings on annual subsidies, currently $16 billion for Russia (CEFIR, 2002, p. 8). That is even more than the economy can bear in the years to come. Thus, because of low and poorly-enforced tariffs, one can consider Russia's agriculture unprotected.

Nevertheless, foreign competitors pose a threat to Russian farms, which employ 8 % of the labor. Hence in preparation of the accession, Russia should negotiate higher tariffs and improve customs collection. But the current proposal is likely to fail, since it envisages an initial rise in tariff levels and a subsequent decrease after up to seven years (YUDAEVA/BESSONOVA/KOZLOV, 2002, p. 1).

Tab. K2: Actual, and Proposed Initial and Final Rates of Import Tariffs*

Item	Effective import tariff rate in 2001, %	Proposed initial rate, %	Proposed final rate, %
Agricultural goods	14,70	34,71	25,11
Industrial goods	9,73	14,32	9,84
All traded goods	10,92	19,18	12,82

* Weighted averages.

Source: http://www.wto.ru/documents.asp?f=stats1&t=16.

Thinking that trading partners are prepared to accept such an unfavorable offer (Tab. K2) is unrealistic; thus, the Russian side has to move away from this position. However, it is supported even by liberal Russian economists, making it a die-hard idea: on the one hand advocates of Russian interests admit that for WTO partners, it sounds strange to demand an increase in tariffs. Usually acceding countries struggle to preserve the existing subsidies or protectionist measures, pledging to cut down these measures gradually. On the other hand, they argue that not subsidizing the agriculture now for lack of resources bears the right to support this sector in future. They claim such an approach is reasonable (GRINBERG, 2002, p. 3). But in the long run, only improved management and overall modernization may raise the productivity and thus the competitiveness of Russia's agriculture.

3. The Interests of the (EU-) Partners

Western partners also expect benefits that materialize in the form of more goods and services sold to Russian companies. They insist on ceasing any unfair trade practices by Moscow like price dumping or market access quotas. However, the accession will not entail an immediate overall turnover hike and hence a considerable reshuffling of the existing trade pattern cannot be expected. Although Russia's trade turnover has risen fast since the ruble devaluation in 1998, the importance of the Russian market to the EU and Germany remains limited. Some Central European emerging markets reach higher trade turnover with Germany than Russia and so do most of the other EU-partners (Tab. K3).

Tab. K3: Germany's Major Trade Destinations (Goods) in 2001, Billion Euros

No	Country	Turnover	Percent
1	France	122,34	10,3 %
2	United States	112,75	9,5 %
3	United Kingdom	91,47	7,7 %
4	Netherlands	85,58	7,2 %
5	Italy	83,18	7,0 %
6	Belgium	59,82	5,0 %
7	Austria	53,34	4,5 %
8	China	31,80	2,7 %
9	Czech Republic	29,40	2,5 %
10	Poland	28,70	2,4 %
11	Russia	24,70	2,1 %
12	Other 218 partners	464,52	39,1 %
	All countries	1187,6	100,0 %

Source: FEDERAL STATISTICAL OFFICE, Foreign trade data, in: www.destatis.de/download/aussh/aussh_d/rang2001.pdf.

Will this change dramatically soon? Since big economies tend to be less open than small countries, one can expect that in the long run the share of the exports and imports in the Russian GDP will even decrease. Thus, in the long run, trade turnover will, at best, grow alongside the overall GDP growth; say, at an annual rate of 4 % (when a fairly respectable sustained GDP growth is considered). This means that trade turnover may grow from a current level of $150 billion to about $200 billion in 2010 (by using the compound interest formula). This is below the current trade turnover volume of other comparable economies like Canada ($510 bn), China ($429 bn), or Mexico ($344 bn) but more than Brazil ($110 bn in 2002). So the expected trade growth will not be enough for a significant higher rank on the list. This partly explains the lesser attention West Europeans pay to the WTO case of Russia than Russia itself does.

If the trading of goods and services[1] will not expand massively, where does ant further Western interest in Moscow's WTO accession lie? In a broader context, trade constitutes not only of exchange of goods but also of capital. In a globalized world, capital flows outperform traditional trade flows and an important part takes the form of foreign direct investment. Unlike other East European emerging markets, Russia has attracted little foreign capital in the nineties; Poland, Hungary and the Czech Republic boast a much larger cumulative FDI stock than Russia[2], which translates into even bigger per capita values. From a macroeconomic viewpoint FDI is the mirror picture of current account deficits when the foreign reserves stock is considered almost constant. In the nineties, Russia always exported more than was imported but because of huge debt service expenditures, the capital account closed negatively. Unfortunately, the gap between demand for and supply of foreign exchange could not be closed by an inflow of funds in the form of FDI. (Also in the nineties, the exchange reserves fluctuated but on balance did not change significantly.) By contrast, Hungary, which faced huge current account deficits during that time, easily financed them by FDI. While the investment climate here improved, it remained notoriously bad in Russia. A good deal of the problem results from excessive bureaucracy with complicated and contradictory regulations. Estimations suggest that the actual number of licensing requirements is closer to 2,500, roughly 40 times more than the comparable number in the West (RAUTAVA, 2001, p. 4). The ensuing dead weight losses are estimated to prove an additional burden on the companies of up to 45 % of the corporate tax. This partially explains why the FDI amount even decreased in 2001 and 2002.

After the accession to the WTO, things may improve considerably on the regulation and bureaucracy front. This does not mean, however, that FDI inflows will immediately swell. The reason is the still huge Russian current account surplus, which translates on the one hand into rising foreign exchange reserves. On the other hand, it causes the capital account to close negatively, i.e. Russia must export more capital than it imports. Fortunately, the current account tended to diminish after 2000, but with an expected 8-9 % of the GDP in 2002, it will continue to act as a natural barrier to more FDI (which is capital import). Thus, at least soon

---

[1] Trade with services is as a rule smaller than trade with goods, and its growth rate in the long run follows that of the former.

[2] $28, 21, 20 and 18 billion, respectively. Sources: ECONOMIC COMMISSION OF EUROPE, GOSKOMSTAT.

after the accession, a capital flow- and FDI-boom appears unlikely, causing foreigners not to feel too engaged with Russia's WTO issue.

4. Paperwork versus Economics (Rules or Exchange Rate?)

Although the decision to join the club is a political one, it will have economic consequences as well. But as in many other East European emerging markets that recently acceded to the WTO, only a limited initial demand and supply shock is expected to hit Russia. First, the government is currently about to consider a proper protection of the most exposed sectors like banking or agriculture by sufficiently high tariff rates or longer lasting grace periods. Secondly, Russian businessmen and managers are used to circumventing regulations and until the enforcement of the customs legislation has improved, the gain will need more time to adapt. But the most efficient tool for keeping foreign competitors out of Russia remains the exchange rate.

After the ruble collapse in 1998, a dollar-price hike took place and suddenly made most of the Western goods imported for cheap dollars unaffordable. Russian manufacturers utilized this competition advantage and regained position on the food, textile and other less-protected markets. In the years following this development, the combination between an almost fixed nominal exchange rate and a high rate of inflation caused the ruble to appreciate in real terms, although the current level is still far off the initial one (Fig. K1). Thus in the years to come, all things being equal, there is much more "air to breathe" for Russia's businesses, gaining time to raise competitiveness and rearrange sectors as well goods structures to withstand foreign pressure.

But how much time is actually left? Considering a sustained annual growth of 4 percent in Russia and 2 percent in the West in the next few years, the income gap between both trade partners will continue to exist for a while. Actually, due to a peculiar statistical effect, this gap will initially even grow. The result is a much lower overall price level in Russia than in the West; thus a market-set nominal exchange rate will make Western imports "too expensive" for ordinary Russians for quite some time. (Assuming the Central bank is determined to cut inflation rates, we can expect real appreciation to slow, which is a precondition for the exchange rate barrier to work). The conclusion is that Russia should speed up the accession process, as the partners currently feel the ruble is undervalued in real terms. Studies suggest that there is a correlation between antidumping filings and macroeconomic factors, especially the real exchange rate. Inspection of the application of the antidumping law by major users in the 1980s and 1990s delivers evidence that real appreciation of the domestic currency increases filings as well as a fall in the output does (KNETTER/PRISA, 2002, p. 1). A daunting previous experience therefore delivers a strong pro-WTO argument; dozens of limitation measures are in place worldwide (HARE, 2002, p. 11). Because of grim growth prospect in many countries, anti-dumping lobbying may increase again. Accession to the WTO will allow Russia to improve status for its exports, thus reducing the costs of anti-dumping suits and increasing business opportunities for those firms that are not currently exporting.

Fig. K1: Real and Nominal Exchange Rate Index, Ruble per Dollar on Quarter-to-Quarter Basis

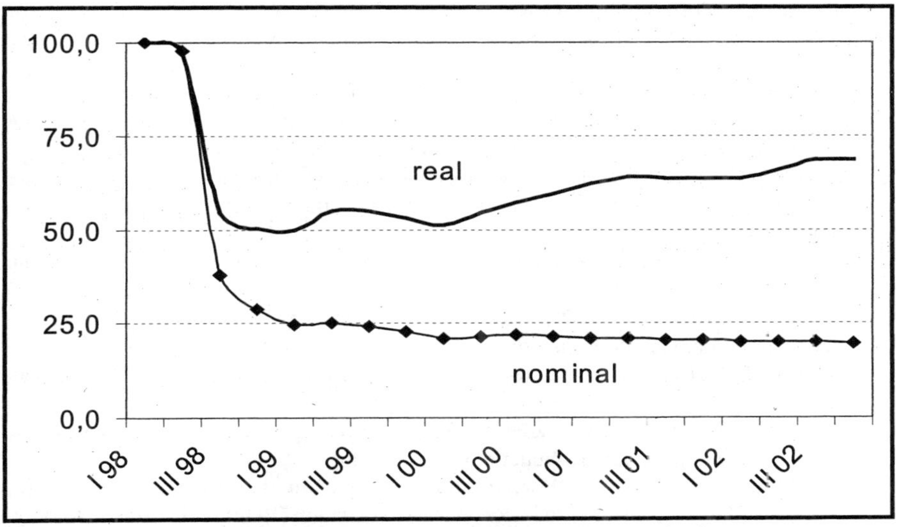

Note: Deflated by CPI; CPI and exchange rate 2002 government projection.

Source: GOSKOMSTAT.

As for the Western interests, the current Western export volume will not increase significantly after the accession. The main reason is the still low per capita income in Russia that is expected to grow for decades until Russia has caught up with the EU (HISHOW, 2002, p. 5-20). Rather the opposite may happen; due to improvements in the Russian customs law enforcement, the effective rate may even rise. Nevertheless, new sectors are developing in Russia, which are starving for fresh Western capital and know-how, especially in the financial services and telecom sector. So an opening-up of the economy in accordance with WTO rules offers far more chances than the current situation.

To integrate Russia into the world economy, capital flows are of crucial importance. Now the main barrier to more FDI is the gap between a high saving rate (roughly 25 % of the GDP) and a low investment rate (currently 16 % of the GDP). It is thus the sore investment climate causing a massive capital flight to safe havens abroad. Continuing reforms and overall improvements in compliance with the WTO requirements may encourage more Russian investors and businessmen to start investment projects. The result will be an increasing demand for Western capital goods and a reversal of the current account from now positive to then negative. This will pave the way for FDI and seal Russia's liberalization.

References

BHAGWATI, J., SRINIVASAN, T. (1979): Trade Policy and Development, in DORNBUSCH, R., FRENKEL, J., eds.: International Economic Policy: Theory and Evidence, Baltimore.

CEFIR (Center for Economic and Financial Research) (2002): Russia in the WTO: Myths and Reality, Moscow, http://www.cefir.ru.

COTTRELL, R. (2002): Russia assesses costs of joining WTO, in: Financial Times, 07/18/02.

GRINBERG, R. (2002): Russia on the Threshold of the WTO: Some Problems and Options. Paper prepared for the Workshop "Economic Growth and Economic Opening up in Russia" on 20-22.9.02, Potsdam, Germany.

HARE, P. (2002): Russia and the World Trade Organization, in: Russian-European Center for Economic Policy Working Paper Series, July 2002, http://www.recep.org/rp/harewtoe.pdf.

HISHOW, O. (2002): Russische Wirtschaft: Langer Marsch zum Wohlstand, SWP-Studie S31, Berlin.

KNETTER, M., PRISA, T. (2002): Macroeconomic Factors and Antidumping Filing: Evidence from Four Countries, in http://papers.nbr.org/papers/W8010.

RAUTAVA, J. (2001): Faster progress through liberalization, in BOFIT, The Russian Economy, 5/2001, www.bof.fi/bofit.

RUSSIA ON THE WAY TO THE WTO (2002): Brief outlines of the newsletter, http://www.wto.ru/ru/content/bulletin/bullJulAug.doc

SALONEN, I. (2002): The role of foreign direct investment in the Russian banking sector, in Bank of Finland, Institute for Economies in Transition (BOFIT): Russian Economy, The Month in Review, 12 July 2002.

USTENKO, O. (2001): Vstuplenie Rossii v WTO: cemu nas ucit opit drugigh stran?, CEFIR, www.cefir.ru.

YUDAEVA, K. (2002): Russia's WTO accession: current state of negotiations, and forecasts of the effects, in: Center for Economic and Financial Research, Moscow, http://www.cefir.ru.

YUDAEVA, K., BESSONOVA, E., KOZLOV, K. (2002): Russian Industry and the WTO Accession: Death Knell or New Beginning?, in: SITE/Worldbank Working Paper 33, May-June 2002.

L. The Role of Russian Regions in Economic Modernization and Opening up: Evidence from St. Petersburg and other Regions

Nina Oding

1. Introduction

Globalization is accompanied by another worldwide process: that of the regionalization of social, political and economic life. Russia is no exception. In a federation as large and diverse as Russia, however, the policies of the regional and local governments play a crucial role in determining outcomes. On one hand, the focus of the inter-budget relations reform is shifted to regions, while on the other hand, regions compete for investments that require investor-friendly environments.

The aim of this paper is to describe major common regional development challenges and address the development problems and trends in St. Petersburg in more detail.

Over the last three years, the Russian economy has improved its performance and enjoyed strong growth. Oil and gas exports and the effect of the Government's macro-policy have helped to support growth and favor domestic investment to meet domestic demand. In addition to this macroeconomic achievement, progress with institutional reform has created more transparency and equal treatment throughout the economy.

The crucial question on the agenda now is Russia's competitiveness and its opening up to the world economy. Negotiations on accession to the WTO raise many important questions about the ability of the Russian economy to cope with world competition, its development from a raw materials exporter towards value-added products, how the Russian economy can modernize for handling the challenge of the knowledge economy, and how its economy can become attractive for FDI and achieve major advances in efficiency. In a word, the point is to understand how Russia's opening up could benefit its citizens and firms.

In the last decade of the 20th century, the economic development of a number of Central and Eastern European nations was critically influenced by a global event, i.e. the crash of the socialist economic system. This centrally-planned construct was totally dominated by the interests of the communist bureaucracy that alone decided what should be produced, how, and for whom, regardless of the actual internal demand. The priority was production for the sake of production, with producers enjoying soft budget constraints. The result was bogus economic growth serving as a facade for a deficit-ridden economy with commodity shortages, a low quality of goods and services, and a catastrophic over-consumption of resources per end-product unit. Within such a system of interests, external trade was often used as a political instrument; it did not reflect the comparative advantages of different countries and totally ignored economic, cultural or geographic factors.

Thus, the marketwise transition from a planned/distributive economy required an extensive structural refurbishment of the economic system that led inevitably to a transitional slump. Given the important cleansing role of this slump, it should not be assessed along the same lines as any downward movement in a well-established market economy (ZAOSTROVTSEV, 2001, p. 13). For market forces had begun economic restructuring, shedding those production capacities that turned out low-demand goods.

2. Investment in Russian Regions

Investment process studies should be one of the key elements of any review of Russia's economic situation and development prospects. In connection to this, one should bear in mind the following points:

Firstly, Russia is very much a heterogeneous country; Russian regions have always developed erratically, and the uneven development, prosperity and investment activity levels have been one of the major challenges for the country throughout its history. Of the many Russian regions' typologies existing to date, the CEPRA project typology appears to be the most trustworthy (BOOTS/DROBYSHEVSKY/MALGINOV, 2002). It was built by conducting a quality analysis and superposing the results of a multi-dimensional classification of Russian regions based on economic potential, living standards, and investment activity indices. The investment activity typology shows investment prospects by different region categories. It also reveals the fact that the investment climate in a given region depends not only on the taxes/preferences interplay, but also on the quality of the judicial system and on the degree of regional power bodies' interference in the financial and economic matters of local enterprises.

Secondly, the current status of inter-budget relations in the Russian Federation is a serious hurdle to economic reform (OECD, 2002, pp.160-161). It provides no incentive for responsible budgeting and economic policies by regional and local bodies, resulting in a relatively unfavorable economic climate, high market entry costs, and administrative barriers. If one wants to substantially change this situation, one has to change the conditions under which regional and local bodies operate. As to the current system of inter-budget relations, it suffers from a seemingly overwhelming federal control over sub-national budgets assigning expenditure responsibilities to lower budgets without any guarantee of autonomy in the determination and execution of their expenditures. Regional and local budgets have been extraordinarily burdened by the accumulation of numerous unfounded federal expenditure mandates throughout the 1990s. (LAVROV/LITWACK/SUTHERLAND, 2001, p.12). However, in practice, sub-national authorities enjoy a substantial degree of informal autonomy, and this results in a lopsided competition environment and rent-oriented behavior. This includes direct participation in the capital of financial institutions, "indirect" participation through affiliated companies, control of utilities, various inspections, closed ties with the courts and federal anti-trust or tax bodies and police.

Thirdly, the focus on the significance of FDI may change at different stages of economic transformation. As Bellak C. (BELLAK, 1998) shows, the initial transformation phase sees FDI exert a stabilizing influence by updating existing capital assets. Later on, in contrast, these concentrate on restructuring within growing industries.

It should be noted at this point that the problem of reliable FDI statistics in Russia has not yet been effectively solved. This is something that may be attributed in part to the fact that the country's statistical system is undergoing transformation itself, and in part to the unsolved technical and methodological problems with FDI assessment. As Dohrn R.(DOHRN, 2000, p.129-130) notes, by applying a generally accepted method to measure potential inconsistencies in FDI assessment by comparing incoming investment figures with external investment data existing in donor countries, one can observe a huge discrepancy between the two. At the receiving end, there is a tendency to overstate the actual amounts of investment lured. The by-sector distribution of FDI is even less clear. For example, the EBRD (1999) indicates that FDI is predominantly concentrated in the primary sector, while Russian state statistics also report that the FDI by-industry structure is dominated by the fuel industry. In 2000, most foreign companies operated in income-inelastic spheres, e.g. in food processing, the tobacco industry and beverage production. Using the approach mentioned above, Dohrn R (DOHRN, 2000) indicates that despite a long history of capital imports into Russia, most FDI still is used for the stabilizing of traditional industries (the fuel and power production complex). This does not mean, however, that investments are channeled into the "wrong" industries - the former pride of the soviet economy (mechanical engineering, machine-tool building, power engineering, electronics, and aircraft construction). Rather, they simply go to the industries with guaranteed highest returns. The geographical distribution of investments is even more demonstrative: Moscow garners over 40 % of all FDI in Russia. The geographical distribution of foreign investment sources led by Cyprus, Luxembourg, and Switzerland showed that they rather represented re-exports of Russian capital. The 2000 foreign investments in Russian non-financial sectors (led by the U.S.A., Germany, France and the UK) amounted to over USD10 billion, of which only 40 % represented investments in business development, while the rest were accounted for by international organizations' loans to the government. Data on the per capita FDI distribution in the west and east of the country (SAVIN, 2001) are also of interest (Tab. L1).

The uneven distribution of investment across Russia confirms the opinion that geographical distances are a hurdle to FDI (DOHRN, 2000).

However, the most important factors determining investment activity in the regions are those of resources (mainly natural) and the structure of the regional economy (AVERKIN/ASTAPOVICH/AFONTSEV, 2001, p.479). On the one hand, the diversified structure of the economy attracts investments, while on the other, it provides for comparatively high purchasing power of the population, something that is also an incentive to investors (JUMPPONEN, TIUSANEN, 2001, p. 15). Many foreign companies in Russia therefore, function in income-inelastic spheres, e.g. in food processing, tobacco and beverage production. There are also some coattail cases: packaging for local demand, hotels and restaurant activities are also branches with a foreign flavor.

Tab. L1: FDI by Region, 2001 First Quarter

Region	FDI (USD '000)	Permanent residents at 01/01/01 ('000 residents)	FDI per capita of permanent population	Area '000 sq. km	FDI per sq. km. USD/sq. km.
Russia total	2,717,737	144,819.1	18.8	17,075.4	15.9
Western regions	2,121,427	104,472.4	20.3	3,955.8	536.0
Eastern regions	596,310	40,376.7	14.8	13,119.6	45.0

It should be pointed out that the rate of savings in the Russian economy has always remained within the 15-24 % GDP bracket, a level that conforms to that shown for Western economies. However, the savings do not transform into investments because infrastructure and investing institutions are lacking while the population distrusts banks, especially after the 1998 meltdown. In turn, the country's finance and crediting sector can only grow after the ownership-rights situation on the corporate securities market is normalized, and the existing system's risks reduced.

The main source of data on investments in Russian regions is the State Statistics Committee. However, its information on foreign investments is not always accurate. The existing forms of statistics do not provide for clear separation of foreign investments in fixed assets.

3. Role and Development of St.Petersburg

St. Petersburg is traditionally among the most attractive targets for foreign investment in Russia: in 1998, with 3.5 % of all foreign investments in the country, it was only behind Moscow (49.8 %), Moscow Oblast (6.0 %), Tatarstan (5.8 %), and Omsk Oblast (3.8 %).

The St. Petersburg Statistics Committee keeps a separate register of foreign investments in the section "External Economic Activities", where it applies the international classification of investments into direct investments, portfolio investments, etc. This system differs radically from that used for registering domestic investments, making it difficult to compare the two types of investments. (Tab. L2).

Foreign investors penetrate the Russian market via SPb. The reason for the influx of foreign investments was the belief that the vast country being so behind in consumer satisfaction would generate substantial profits. In the case of SPb the draw is not only the logistic position of the city with its port and the proximity to the West. It is also its large population and the high level of technical education and experience. In 2000, the hard currency direct investments amounted to USD134.9 million only, while total foreign investments were USD 1,147.5 million. The bulk of foreign investments go to manufacturing industries, in particular to the food industry, mechanical engineering, and metalworking. These are followed by telecommunications, trade, and public catering, something which reflects foreign investors' priorities as they opt for goods and services with guaranteed local market demand. At this stage, foreigners tend to invest only in facilities with short repayment periods (that produce goods in high demand on the domestic market), in the renovation and expansion of separate manufacturing units, as well as in raw-materials industries and industries producing goods with a low degree of processing that are in demand on international markets. The countries that lead by the volume of investments in St. Petersburg are the USA, the Netherlands, Finland and Germany. In 1998, the top ten-investor countries included Cyprus (the well-known offshore zone), the Netherlands, and Luxembourg. As numerous surveys have shown, St. Petersburg businesses believe that, given certain conditions, the volume of investments in the city could be much greater. This has become especially evident in recent years, with the more attractive investment climate of the neighboring regions (Novgorod, Leningrad, and Vologda Oblasts) becoming a factor behind their rapid economic growth.

Tab. L2: Foreign Investments Received, USD Million

	1995	1996	1997	1998	1999	2000	2001
St. Petersburg	157.5	175.3	234.0	413.3	698.5	1,147.5	1,171.3
St. Petersburg's share in Russia, percent	5.3	2.5	1.9	3.5	6.7	11.0	13.0

Source: RF GOSCOMSTAT 1998 p. 750, RF GOSCOMSTAT 1999, PETERBURG-COMSTAT 1999 & 2001b.

Like all other Russian regions, St. Petersburg is in the middle of a tumultuous period in which it is basically impossible to come up with a reliable long-term forecast, to say nothing of a long-term development concept or priorities, given the high degree of both political and economic uncertainty. Even an attempt to measure the past structural changes and identify the economic prospects for the nearest future faces significant methodological and technical hurdles because of the difficulty in obtaining reliable data.

If the slump is to be overcome and sustainable economic growth provided for, St. Petersburg needs wide-scale investments. At this stage, there is a need to find answers to the questions concerning the peculiar features of the current investment process in the city, and the opportunities and constraints lurking around the spatial development of St. Petersburg.

For many years, the city has suffered from a lack of funds not only for development, but also for maintaining its residential stock and infrastructure in an operable condition. St. Petersburg has been chronically plagued by a host of municipal-economy challenges that include a catastrophic state of the water supply and engineering networks, the sewerage and sewage treatment system, as well as the municipal transport, roads, and electricity supply to downtown districts. Up to 40 % of the city's heat-, and water-supply networks require replacement, while 15 million square meters of residential space are in need of capital repairs. To this end, the city spends up to 25 % of its budget each year, a level that equals or even exceeds the average relevant municipal expenditure rates in European cities.

The aggregate 2001 domestic investment from all sources amounted to R50.97 billion (about USD 1.5 billion). The aggregate investments are dominated by extra-budget funds (70 - 80 %), with almost two-thirds provided by mixed-ownership enterprises of the manufacturing, transport and construction industries themselves (Tab. L3).

Tab. L3: Investments in Fixed Assets by Source of Investment, as % of the Total

	1995		1996		1997		1998		1999		2000		2001
	RF	SPb	RF	SPb	RF	SPb	RF	SPb	RF	SPb	RF	SPb	SPb
Budget funds, including from:	20.4	25.1	20.1	29.8	20.7	18.8	18.7	14.0	17.0	17.0	21.6	21.0	29.0
The federal budget	10.1	12.8	9.9	13.1	10.2	11.6	6.5	4.0	6.4	3.0	5.8	6.0	18.0
regional and local budgets	10.3	12.3	10.2	16.7	10.5	7.2	12.2	10.0	10.6	14.0	14.8	15.0	11.0
Extra-budgetary funds	78.2	74.8	79.9	70.2	79.3	81.2	81.3	86.0	83.0	83.0	79.4	79.0	71.0

Source: RF GOSKOMSTAT 1998 p. 735, RF GOSKOMSTAT 1999, PETERBURG-KOMSTAT 1999 & 2001b.

One of the specific features of the investment process in St. Petersburg is share of budget funds in the total volume of investments that is above the Russian average. However, in 1998 the share taken by the federal budget fell from 11.6 % to 4 %. By 2000, the situation had returned to normal, with the local budget's share growing as well. Thus, the overall share of the funds from all budgets (29 %) spent on the city's development reached its 1996 levels. Another source for city infrastructure development funding is the Territorial Road Fund (R 3,398.1 million in 2000). However, the opportunities for a substantial reallocation of budget expenditures for investment purposes are also limited, as the city's capital expenditures have already reached their ceiling. Annual allocations for the city's development amount to USD300 million from various budgets and budget funds. We believe that this circumstance somewhat slackens the drive to search for new funding sources; but a necessity to select the most lucrative and efficient ways to utilize capital investment remains. However, to achieve this goal, one has to change the existing framework by which infrastructure, housing and utility facilities are regulated.

At the same time, the city's economic growth is hindered by a number of its internal peculiarities and controversies. On one hand, to be able to use its investment potential to its full extent, St. Petersburg needs a structural overhaul of its economy; on the other, this structural overhaul is impeded by the presence of manufacturing capacities that depend on centralized funding within defense orders. In addition, the recent series of redistributions of financial responsibilities between regional budgets and the federal center has increased the burden on municipal budget expenditures. This narrows the local authorities' room to maneuver, creates budget uncertainty and undermines the city's creditworthiness. These events are taking place against the background of increasing competition between Russian cities and territories where the luring of new businesses is concerned, and this brings into sharp relief another urgent task – that of improving the city's investment climate.

A modern market economy is an economy of services and non-material products. The share of St. Petersburg's GRP taken by services has consistently exceeded 50 % since 1994 (Tab. L4).

Tab. L4: Gross Regional Product Structure (in Current Prices, as % of the Total)

	1994	1995	1996	1997	1998	1999	2000
GRP in market prices, including:	100.0	100.0	100.0	100.0	100.0	100.0	100.0
Commodity production	36.4	33.9	32.5	28.7	33.0	35.3	33.1
Services, including:	54.7	57.1	62.3	65.0	60.6	54.4	58.7
Market services	45.4	47.6	50.0	56.2	53.3	48.9	51.6
Non-market services	9.3	12.3	8.8	8.8	7.3	5.5	7.1
Net commodity taxes	8.9	9.0	5.2	6.3	6.4	10.3	8.2

Source: PETERBURGKOMSTAT, 2001a, p. 10, PETERBURGKOMSTAT, 2002b, p. 10.

The actual share of market services must be even higher, because this sector is especially notorious for its shadowy operations. This evolution shows that, due to significantly smaller market-entry barriers, the services sector is much more flexible with respect to market demand. In the structure of the GRP by industry (Fig. L1), market-wise transformations are reflected in the first place as a surge in the share taken by trade and public catering. It should be noted that the diminished share of transport and telecommunications does not reflect their actual growth figures: most of their tariffs are regulated and artificially contained by the state, thereby equating with the indirect subsidizing of manufacturing industries.

Both in St. Petersburg and Russia-wide, excessive or non-competitive types of products or production were washed out of the market. Beginning in 1995, manufacturing ceded its leading position in the city's economy to transport and telecommunications. At the same time, the downturn in manufacturing industries was uneven in character, something that drastically changed the share taken by different industries in total manufacturing output. In the first place, the slump sapped the mainstay of St. Petersburg manufacturing; its defense enterprises lost state funding. Instead, transport, telecommunications, power production, power engineering, the food industry, natural monopolies, shipbuilding, and instrument making surged ahead. Manufacturing output grew in 2000, with the best results being shown by mechanical engineering and metalworking, the food industry, the construction materials industry, and metallurgy.

Fig. L1: By-Industry Structure of Gross Added Value (in Current Prices, as % of the Total)

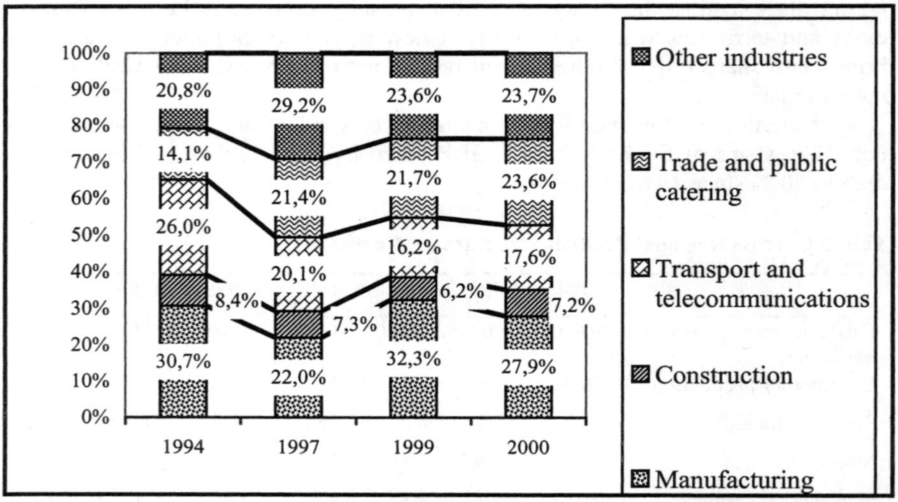

Source: PETERBURGKOMSTAT, 2001a, p. 28, PETERBURGKOMSTAT, 2002b, p. 28.

Fig. L2: Manufacturing Output Evolution (1991 as 100 %)

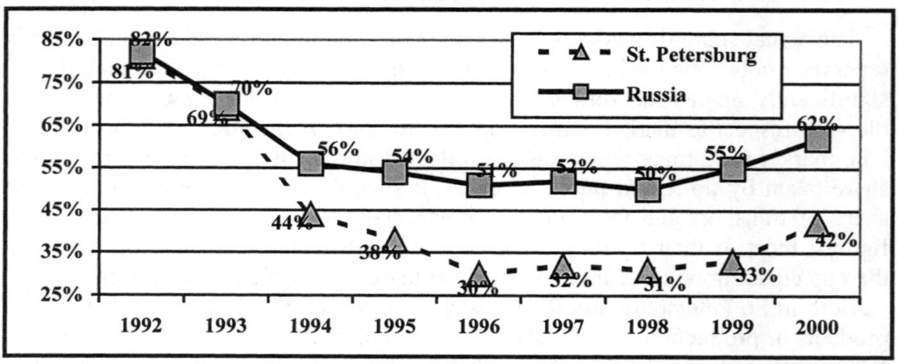

Sources: BANK OF FINLAND, 2001, PETERSBURGKOMSTAT, 2000 p. 115, PETERSBURGKOMSTAT, 2001c, p. 49.

External trade is of constantly increasing importance to the St. Petersburg economy. In 2001, the city's external trade turnover amounted to USD5 872 million (third position among Russian regions after Moscow and Tymen Oblast (Fig. L3).

Fig. L3: Evolution of St. Petersburg's External Trade in 1997-2000 (USD Million)

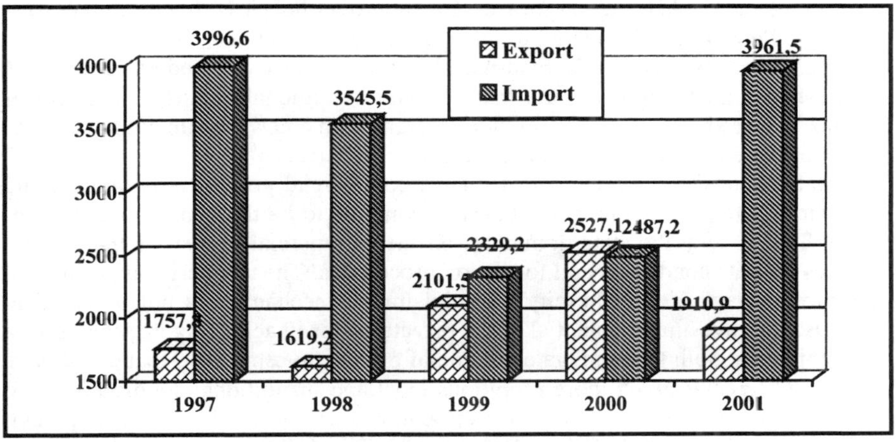

Sources: FOND FEDERAL'NYKH I REGIONAL'NYKH PROGRAM PRI PRAVITEL'STVE SANKT-PETERBURGA 2001, PETERSBURGKOMSTAT 2001b, p.158.

Since the devaluation of the ruble in autumn of 1998, the city's external trade balance gradually bottomed out, from (-) USD227.7 million in 1999 to (+) USD39.9 million in 2000. However, the external trade balance was negative again in 2001. It should be remembered that unlike many other Russian regions, St. Petersburg does not sell raw materials but rather products with a high degree of value added by processing (chiefly, machines and equipment). Machines, equipment, ferrous and non-ferrous metals, and metalwork comprised almost 75 % of the city's exports, with 47 % of all exports being in the form of mechanical engineering products. Raw materials, food, machines, equipment, and petrochemical products dominate imports.

4. Outlook and Conclusions

In the nearest future, objective macroeconomic reasons rule out a significant inflow of foreign investments in the city. The funds that may arrive will be destined for the support and development of already existing production capacities (mostly in food, telecommunications, trade and public catering enterprises). The city may provide additional incentives for business/investment activities through the application of local laws already adopted and through the developing of new regulations and procedures. However, it is important to note that the set of problems to be solved if the investment climate in the city is to be improved has remained the same for many of years. Naturally, these include the "federal constituent", such as federal civil laws, tax and customs policies, etc., as well as the countrywide business regulations, contract enforcement, and implementation of court decisions. Nevertheless, the distribution of investments by region shows that regional policies are also very important in attracting foreign investments.

Regions have taken radical measures to improve their investment climate surround St. Petersburg. Compared to other northwestern regions, St. Petersburg has too high sales, property, and road-users' taxes. In 2001, the federal authorities established a new profit tax rate that permits the regional-budget constituent of this tax to be reduced, and thus provides regions with a new instrument to compete for investments by improving their investment climate.

The St. Petersburg market for profitable commercial properties is limited, and both the federal and municipal authorities continue to be the main property managers. That is why the state dominates on the commercial-properties market and dictates both its conditions and formation procedures. The most critical problem at the current stage is that the city's administrative mechanism is not prepared to fully use the investment potential of the private sector in achieving citywide goals. This applies to both the aggregate volume of private investments – that could have been much greater given more propitious legal and institutional conditions – and to the results of the investment process (the territorial distribution of development, and the overall state of the urban environment). The city is in acute need for a new urban planning strategy with a system of clearly-stated targets and goals.

In terms of geopolitical opportunities, St. Petersburg focuses on a worldwide integration that considers integration in the Baltic Sea Region as the first strategic step. Certain features evidence the strengthening in the role of St. Petersburg as the Russian "window on the west".

It is important to understand the need for the orientation of St. Petersburg's main industries to be extended towards foreign markets, as well as for a favorable business climate to be established. Investors are faced with enormous compliance costs and delays, as well as onerous permits and licensing. The business climate must stimulate economic growth and become the main factor in attracting resources and investments to St. Petersburg.

References

AVERKIN, A., ASTAPOVICH, A., AFONTSEV, S. (2001): Politika privlecheniya pryamykh inostrannykh investitsiy v rossiyskuy, Biuro ekonomicheskogo analiza, TEIS, Moscow.

BANK OF FINLAND. INSTITUTE FOR ECONOMIES IN TRANSITION (2001): Russian Economy, Month in Review, N 7-8 (see also http://www.bof.fi/bofit/).

BELLAK, C., (1998): Lessons from Austria's Postwar Pattern of Inward FDI for CEECs, WIIW-report, Vienna, 251.

BOOTS, B., DROBYSHEVSKY, S., MALGINOV, G. (2002): Typology of Russian Regions, Consortium for Economic Policy Research and Advise. Moscow.

DOHRN, R. (2000): Foreign Direct Investment in Russia: An Engine of Structural Adjustment? in WELFENS, P., GAVRILENKOV, Ev., eds: Restructuring, Stabilizing and Modernizing the New Russia. Economic and Institutional Issues. Springer.

EBRD (ed.) (1999): Transition Report, London.

FINANCIAL COMMITTEE OF ST. PETERSBURG ADMINISTRATION AND ICSER LEONTIEF CENTRE (2001): Saint-Petersburg 2000-2001, St. Petersburg.

FOND FEDERAL'NYKH I REGIONAL'NYKH PROGRAM PRI PRAVITEL'STVE SANKT-PETERBURGA (2001): Spravochnik investora "Sankt-Peterburg-2001".

ICSER LEONTIEF CENTRE AND ADMINISTRATION OF ST. PETERSBURG (1998): The Strategic Plan for St. Petersburg, St. Petersburg.

JUMPPONEN, J., TIUSANEN, T. (2001): The Investment Climate in Russia. Part 1 - General Features. Lappeeranta University of Technology, Studies in Industrial Engineering and Management.

LAVROV, A., LITWACK, J., SURTHERLAND, D. (2001): Fiscal Federalist Relations in Russia: A Case for Subnational Autonomy, OECD.

OECD (2002): Economic Surveys: The Russian Federation, Moscow, Ves' Mir.

PETERSBURGKOMSTAT (1999, 2001,2002): Sotsial'no-ekonomicheskaya situatsiya v Sankt-Peterburge i Leningradsky oblasti, St. Petersburg.

PETERSBURGKOMSTAT (2000): Sankt-Peterburg i Leningradskaya Oblast' v 1999 godu, St. Petersburg.

PETERSBURGKOMSTAT (2001): Sankt-Peterburg 2000. Kratkiy Statisticheskiy Sbornik, St. Petersburg.

PETERSBURGKOMSTAT (2002): Valovyi regional'nyi produkt Sankt-Peterburga i Leningradskoi oblasti v 1994-2000 godakh. Statisticheskiy Sbornik, St. Petersburg.

RF GOSKOMSTAT (State Statistical Committee of the Russian Federation): Rossiiskiy Statisticheskii Eizhegocnik 2000, 2001, Moscow.

RF GOSKOMSTAT (1998): Regiony Rossii, Vol. 2, Moscow.

RF GOSKOMSTAT [State Statistical Committee of the Russian Federation] (1999): Sotsial'no-ekonomicheskaya situatsiya v Rossiiskoi Federatsii, Moscow.

SAVIN, V. (2001): Inostrannye investitsii v raspredelenii po subectam Rossiiskoy Federatsii v 1 kvartale 2001 goda, Investitsii v Rossii, №10, p.18-21.

ZAOSTROVTSEV, A. (2001): Structurnye izmeneniya in: VASIL'EV, S.,ed., Desyatiletie ekonomicheskikh reform v Sankt-Peterburge, ICSER "Leontief Centre", St Petersburg, 11-27.

Comments on: The Role of Russian Regions in Economic Modernization and Opening up: Evidence from St. Petersburg and other Regions

Markus Ksoll

Nina Oding presents a well-written and sound exploration of conditions and barriers to economic growth in Russia, with a special focus on St. Petersburg. It draws from the author's rich knowledge of the local economy. Oding's contribution is structured in four main sections: introduction, conditions and basic structure of investment in Russian regions, the role and development of St. Petersburg, conclusions and outlook. The following comments, given along this line, are predominately from a regional economics perspective.

1. Introduction

The introduction places regional development in Russia in the context of globalisation, the challenges of opening up the Russian economy, and the transition from planned to market-driven allocation. Oding stresses the strong need for competition and restructuring. Although not explicitly giving an overview of the paper's plan, Oding defines the aim of the paper as explaining the role of regional conditions and policies in regional competition for private economic activity and investment. This question is indeed at the heart of regional policy debate in general and is highly relevant to transition studies.

2. Investment in Russian Regions

To understand basic conditions for investment in Russian regions, Oding reviews some of the recent empirical literature and identifies as major features:

- the heterogeneity between Russian regions with respect to economic potential, income as well as regional authorities' behaviour,
- the unfavourable status of Russian inter-budget relations, i.e. in particular the lack of regional budget-responsibility, as well as a gap between formal and perceived regional control,
- and the changing role of FDI in economic transition.

The later aspect is further explored in a description of FDI's sectoral and geographic structure in Russia, and its dynamics. This section is very informative.

It would have gained, however, from at least some reference to the characteristics of FDI established in the literature on international factor movements, according to e.g. Dunning. Similarly, taking account of general location factors would have further structured the analysis. An extra explanation and distinct analysis of capital re-imports via Cyprus versus FDI carried out by Western enterprises with respect to its sectoral purpose would be additionally worthwhile. The particular importance of FDI for the current situation in Russia is identified at the end of the section, i.e. the malfunctioning of the national banking sector and its inability to transform private savings into measurable investment activity.

3. Role and Development of St. Petersburg

The core of the paper is an in-depth description of the role and development of St. Petersburg. Other regions are not subject of the analysis, so the title is slightly misleading in this respect. The choice of St. Petersburg as a case study, however, is well motivated by its position as an outstanding target for foreign investment. After a brief look at structural characteristics of regional investment, Oding turns to the determinants for St. Petersburg's increasing share in foreign capital inflows, which are in line with classical location factors: geographical proximity, accessibility from abroad, comparatively high education standards, and large market potential. Oding's hypothesis is that given the above-mentioned favourable conditions, foreign investment in St. Petersburg could be much higher than it is today. The city's potential is not exploited for constraints which are then neatly elaborated. They consist of:

- A lack of regional funds for sustainably maintaining and improving vital infrastructure networks, namely water supply, electricity and transport. Although their share in St. Petersburg's public expenditures is similar to that of Western cities, its level is far from allowing a catching up.
- Impediments to structural change placed by the regional industry's strong dependence on the defence sector, which seems to be tragic in two ways. Firstly, St. Petersburg's industrial base is especially sensitive to erratic cuts in the defence budget. Secondly, these industries are especially far from market orientation. This explains the decline of St. Petersburg's manufacturing output in total and in Russian comparison as illustrated by fig. 2.
- Lacking reliability of municipal budgets following the redistribution of fiscal responsibilities between regional and federal authorities. According to Oding, this highlights the strong need to improve the city's investment climate.

Putting the latter aspect against the background of competition between regions – as is done in the paper – would need some explanation of why it is relevant to St. Petersburg more than to other Russian regions. The roles of St. Petersburg's service sector evolution as well as that of its external trade balance are insufficiently integrated in this section, notwithstanding the careful line of reasoning otherwise. It should be noted that from an export base theory point of view narrowed to St. Petersburg, there need not be a distinction between extra-regional and international trade.

4. Outlook and Conclusion

Oding concludes by stating that the above-mentioned problems have remained fairly stable for many years and addresses three more impediments to investment activities in St. Petersburg, i.e.

- a publicly-dominated property market,
- unfavourable fiscal conditions compared to surrounding regions, and
- business laws and regulations (licences, permits) causing delays.

It is these points that the emphasis for policy recommendations is placed on. To achieve the necessary improvement in the regional business climate, Oding asks for new regulations, tax cuts, regional policy measures and a new urban planning strategy with clearly defined goals. Unfortunately, the contribution is cutting a bit short in this respect, as it does not specify such measures and a viable regional strategy for St. Petersburg or other Russian regions. Therefore, the main value of Oding's contribution lies in sorting out the structural barriers for further development in St Petersburg as an important basis for turning abundant regional visions, such as becoming a "hub of international trade" and a "gateway for information and investment", into reality.

One general question remains: Is regional policy in Russia embedded in a general strategy, or is it driven by individual beggar-thy-neighbour approaches? Yet the classical goal of co-ordinated regional policy, i.e. to achieve equal living conditions across an entire nation, is rather hard to achieve in an economy as large and diverse as Russia. From a broader (federal) point-of-view, the policy recommendation would be ambiguous between equity considerations – implying that St. Petersburg would not need extra promotion – and a growth pole type of strategy – implying a focus on St. Petersburg and a number of similarly promising places in Russia. Accepting the concept of growth poles, in implicit accordance with Oding's contribution, it should be stressed that this idea is based on the promotion of self-induced innovative activities. The key then lies in the efficient provision and improvement of an infrastructural framework for private economic engagement.

List of Figures

List of Tables

List of Contributors

Noer A. Achsani,
University of Potsdam, Germany

Joachim Ahrens,
University of Göttingen, Germany

Frank Bohn,
University of Essex, United Kingdom

Cathleen Faber,
University of Potsdam, Germany

Grigori Feiguine,
St. Petersburg State University of Economics and Finance, Russia

Evgeny Gavrilenkov,
Bureau of Economic Analysis, Troika Dialog, Moscow, Russia

Ruslan Grinberg,
Russian Academy of Sciences, Moscow, Russia

Christian von Hirschhausen,
DIW German Institute for Economic Research, Technical University Berlin, Germany

Ognian Hishow,
Stiftung Wissenschaft und Politik Berlin, Germany

Andre Jungmittag,
European Institute for International Economic Relations (EIIW), University of Wuppertal, Germany

Rolf Jungnickel,
Hamburg Institute of International Economics, Germany

Albrecht Kauffmann,
European Institute for International Economic Relations (EIIW), University of Potsdam, Germany

Markus Ksoll,
University of Potsdam, Germany

Markus Neimke,
Ruhr University Bochum, Germany

Olga Nosova,
National Technical University Kharkov, Ukraine

Nina Oding,
Leontief Centre St. Petersburg, Russia

Tatjana Sedash,
St. Petersburg State University of Economics and Finance, Russia

Hans G. Strohe,
University of Potsdam, Germany

Michael Vogelsang,
Stock-TV, Düsseldorf, Germany

Paul J.J. Welfens,
European Institute for International Economic Relations (EIIW), University of Wuppertal, Germany

Natalja von Westernhagen,
Deutsche Bundesbank, Frankfurt/M., Germany

Ralf Wiegert,
European Institute for International Economic Relations (EIIW), University of Potsdam, Germany

Gert Ziener,
Technical University of Mining and
Technology, Freiberg/Saxony,
Germany

Further Publications by *Paul J. J. Welfens*

P. J. J. Welfens
Market-oriented Systemic Transformations in Eastern Europe
Problems, Theoretical Issues, and Policy Options
1992. XII, 261 Pages. 20 Figs., 29 Tab., Hardcover, ISBN 3-540-55793-8

M. W. Klein, P. J. J. Welfens (Eds.)
Multinationals in the New Europe and Global Trade
1992. XV, 281 Pages. 24 Figs., 75 Tab., Hardcover, ISBN 3-540-54634-0

P. J. J. Welfens (Ed.)
Economic Aspects of German Unification
Expectations, Transition Dynamics and International Perspectives
1992. XV, 527 Pages. 34 Figs., 110 Tab., Hardcover, ISBN 3-540-60261-5

R. Tilly, P. J. J. Welfens (Eds.)
European Economic Integration as a Challenge to Industry and Government
Contemporary and Historical Perspectives on International Economic Dynamics
1996. X, 558 Pages. 43 Figs., Hardcover, ISBN 3-540-60431-6

P. J. J. Welfens (Ed.)
Economic Aspects of German Unification
Expectations, Transition Dynamics and International Perspectives
2nd revised and enlarged edition
1996. XV, 527 Pages. 34 Figs., 110 Tab., Hardcover, ISBN 3-540-60261-5

P. J. J. Welfens
European Monetary Integration
EMS Developments and International Post-Maastricht Perspectives
3rd revised and enlarged edition
1996. XVIII, 384 Pages. 14 Figs., 26 Tab., Hardcover, ISBN 3-540-60260-7

P. J. J. Welfens (Ed.)
European Monetary Union
Transition, International Impact and Policy Options
1997. X, 467 Pages. 50 Figs., 31 Tab., Hardcover, ISBN 3-540-63305-7

P. J. J. Welfens, G. Yarrow (Eds.)
Telecommunications and Energy in Systemic Transformation
International Dynamics, Deregulation and Adjustment in Network Industries
1997. XII, 501 Pages. 39 Figs., Hardcover, ISBN 3-540-61586-5

P. J. J. Welfens, H. C. Wolf (Eds.)
Banking, International Capital Flows and Growth in Europe
Financial Markets, Savings and Monetary Integration in a World with Uncertain Convergence
1997. XIV, 458 Pages. 22 Figs., 63 Tab., Hardcover, ISBN 3-540-63192-5

P. J. J. Welfens, D. Audretsch, J. T. Addison, H. Grupp
Technological Competition, Employment and Innovation Policies in OECD Countries
1998. VI, 231 Pages. 16 Figs., 20 Tab., Hardcover, ISBN 3-540-63439-8

P. J. J. Welfens, G. Yarrow, R. Grinberg, C. Graack (Eds.)
Towards Competition in Network Industries
Telecommunications, Energy and Transportation in Europe and Russia
1999. XXII, 570 Pages, 63 Figs., 63 Tab., Hardcover, ISBN 3-540-65859-9

P. J. J. Welfens
EU Eastern Enlargement and the Russian Transformation Crisis
1999. X, 151 Pages. 12 Figs., 25 Tab., Hardcover, ISBN 3-540-65862-9

P. J. J. Welfens
Globalization of the Economy, Unemployment and Innovation
1999. VI, 255 Pages. 11 Figs., 31 Tab., Hardcover, ISBN 3-540-65250-7

P. J. J. Welfens, J. T. Addison, D. B. Audretsch, T. Gries, H. Grupp
Globalization, Economic Growth and Innovation Dynamics
1999. X, 160 Pages. 15 Figs., 15 Tab., Hardcover, ISBN 3-540-65858-0

R. Tilly, P. J. J. Welfens (Eds.)
Economic Globalization, International Organizations and Crisis Management
Contemporary and Historical Perspectives on Growth, Impact and Evolution of Major Organizations in an Interdependent World
2000. XII, 408 Pages. 11 Figs., 20 Tab., Hardcover, ISBN 3-540-65863-7

P. J. J. Welfens, E. Gavrilenkov (Eds.)
Restructuring, Stabilizing and Modernizing the New Russia
Economic and Institutional Issues
2000. XIV, 516 Pages. 82 Figs., 70 Tab., Hardcover, ISBN 3-540-67429-2

P. J. J. Welfens
European Monetary Union and Exchange Rate Dynamics
New Approaches and Applications to the Euro
2001. X, 159 Pages. 26 Figs., 12 Tab., Hardcover, ISBN 3-540-67914-6

P. J. J. Welfens
Stabilizing and Integrating the Balkans
Economic Analysis of the Stability Pact, EU Reforms and International Organizations
2001. XII, 171 Pages. 6 Figs., 18 Tab., Hardcover, ISBN 3-540-41775-3

P. J. J. Welfens, B. Meyer, W. Pfaffenberger, P. Jasinski, A. Jungmittag
Energy Policies in the European Union Germany's Ecological Tax Reform
2001. VII, 143 Pages. 21 Figs., 41 Tab., Hardcover, ISBN 3-540-41652-8

P. J. J. Welfens (Ed.)
Internationalization of the Economy and Environmental Policy Options
2001. XIV, 442 Pages. 57 Figs., 61 Tab., Hardcover, ISBN 3-540-42174-2

P. J. J. Welfens
Interneteconomics.net
Macroeconomics, Deregulation, and Innovation
2002. VIII, 215 Pages. 34 Figs., 30 Tab., Hardcover, ISBN 3-540-43337-6

D. B. Audretsch, P. J. J. Welfens (Eds.)
The New Economy and Economic Growth in Europe and the USA
2002. XII, 350 Pages. 28 Figs., 59 Tab., Hardcover, ISBN 3-540-43179-9

C. E. Barfield, G. Heiduk, P. J. J. Welfens (Eds.)
Internet, Economic Growth and Globalization
Perspectives on the Digital Economy in Europe, Japan and the U.S.
2003. XII, 388 Pages. 34 Figs., 67 Tab., Hardcover, ISBN 3-540-00286-3

J. T. Addison, P. J. J. Welfens (Eds.)
Labor Markets and Social Security
Issues and Policy Options in the U.S. and Europe, 2nd edn.
2003. X, 402 Pages. 56 Figs., 52 Tab., Hardcover, ISBN 3-540-44004-6

T. Lane, N. Oding, P. J. J. Welfens (Eds.)
Real and Financial Economic Dynamics in Russia and Eastern Europe
2003. XII, 293 Pages. 50 Figs., 63 Tab., Hardcover, ISBN 3-540-00910-8